Science for Policy

ECOLOGICAL ECONOMICS AND HUMAN WELL-BEING

Series Editors:

Joan Martínez-Alier, Professor of Economics and Economic History at Universitat Autonoma de Barcelona. He is also the founding member and former President, International Society for Ecological Economics (ISEE).

Pushpam Kumar, Environmental Economist, Institute for Sustainable Water, Integrated Management and Ecosystem Research (SWIMMER), and Department of Geography, University of Liverpool, UK.

Technical Editor: Virginia Hooper

This Series offers the best and most recent works in the transdisciplinary field of Ecological Economics, whose focus is the study of the conflicts between economic growth and environmental sustainability.

Books in the Series:

Deliberative Ecological Economics
Edited by Christos Zografos and Richard B. Howarth

Corporate Accountability and Sustainable Development
Edited by Peter Utting and Jennifer Clapp

Water, Agriculture, and Sustainable Well-being
Edited by Amita Shah, Unai Pascual, and Jayanta Bandyopadhyay

Environmental History and Ecological Economics
Edited by John McNeill, Mahesh Rangarajan, and José Augusto Pádua

Payment of Ecosystem Services
Edited by Pushpam Kumar and Roldan Muradian

Indicators and Scenarios for Sustainable Development
Edited by Joachim Spangenberg and Nilanjan Ghosh

Science for Policy
New Challenges, New Opportunities

edited by
Ângela Guimarães Pereira
and
Silvio Funtowicz

OXFORD
UNIVERSITY PRESS

OXFORD
UNIVERSITY PRESS

YMCA Library Building, Jai Singh Road, New Delhi 110 001

Oxford University Press is a department of the University of Oxford.
It furthers the University's objective of excellence in research, scholarship,
and education by publishing worldwide in

Oxford   New York
Auckland   Cape Town   Dar es Salaam   Hong Kong   Karachi
Kuala Lumpur   Madrid   Melbourne   Mexico City   Nairobi
New Delhi   Shanghai   Taipei   Toronto

With offices in
Argentina Austria Brazil Chile Czech Republic France Greece
Guatemala Hungary Italy Japan Poland Portugal Singapore
South Korea Switzerland Thailand Turkey Ukraine Vietnam

Oxford is a registered trademark of Oxford University Press
in the UK and in certain other countries.

Published in India
by Oxford University Press, New Delhi

© Oxford University Press 2009

ISBN-13: 978-0-19-569849-7
ISBN-10: 0-19-569849-5

Typeset in AGaramond 11/12.5
by Eleven Arts, Keshav Puram, Delhi 110 035
Printed in India by Parangat Offset, New Delhi 110 020
Published by Oxford University Press
YMCA Library Building, Jai Singh Road, New Delhi 110 001

Contents

Tables, Figures, and Boxes

Boxes

Foreword

In ecological economics, we distinguish trends from surprises. Trends are the slow movements in environmental, demographic, social, and economic variables. Thus, we may look at longitudinal changes in the intensity of energy usage in the economy or point to the links between rates of economic growth and different forms of pollution. This is one way to seek an understanding of the changing world, but it is not the only one. We must also focus on unexpected surprises. In 2002, the European Environment Agency published a monograph called *Late Lessons from Early Warnings*. This was a collection of studies on the delayed administrative and public reaction to the initial alarms regarding some, now well understood, sources of ecological damage. These included damage from asbestos, low level radiation, DDT, and ten other examples of failure to apply, for many decades, what is now called 'the precautionary principle'.

We can usefully discuss two sorts of science. The 'mainstream' may be broadly classified as being reductionist in style. It has been useful to help prove the links between, for example, the use of tobacco and some forms of cancer, or the obvious link between coal burning, sulphur dioxide emissions, and acid rain.

But environmental and health issues often need to be confronted before there is enough research to prove an indubitable point. These issues are often very complex. In such cases, one has to rely on the 'post-normal' approach. The post-normal approach, explained in 1987 by Silvio Funtowicz and Jerome Ravetz, depends on public debate, and allows an essential role for the 'extended peer community' to adjudge the value of an argument. It recognizes the influence of social values on all research, up to and including basic statistical tests of significance. It is an appropriate approach when either systems-uncertainty or decision stakes are high; or under other conditions when the puzzle-solving approach of normal science is not appropriate. Thus, post-normal science (as explained in this book) is not only a welcome extension of democratic deliberation, but also a necessary outcome of uncertainty and complexity, and addresses the urgency to take decisions in areas in which time is increasingly a luxury we cannot afford. The development of ecological economics since the late 1980s was intimately linked to the growth of the post-normal science.

The preface by Sheila Jasanoff, and several other chapters acknowledge that it is often impossible to remove or reduce uncertainty to quantifiable, insurable risk in the application of new technologies. When problems first arise, the issue is uncertainty or ignorance surrounding degree of risk, as was the case for a long time regarding excessive emissions of carbon dioxide. Several topics inhabiting such ambiguated territory are discussed in this volume. One chapter deals with climate change, challenging the simplifications of the Stern report. Other chapters focus on chemical risks, and especially on the debates (so relevant to India) on transgenic crops and water management. Another kind of subject matter dealt with in this volume has a methodological character, explaining how the 'extended peer review' required by post-normal science is carried out in practice. We also discuss nuclear energy—and the inability to translate uncertain future costs to present economic value. The nuclear industry, we know, operates everywhere without a full fledged system of insurance. This is indeed a topic of current interest in India.

The present volume has authors from India, Europe, Mexico, South East Asia, Australia, and the United States. It stands on its own as a contribution to science and technology studies, applied to the conflicts between economy and environment. It is also serves as a useful complement to the books in this series on *Corporate Accountability* and *Deliberative Ecological Economics*.

March 2009

Joan Martinez Alier
Pushpam Kumar

Preface
Border Crossings: Social Sciences and Public Policy

SHEILA JASANOFF

NEW AGE ANXIETIES

Former US Vice President Al Gore, who won the popular vote in the 2000 presidential election in November, only to lose the White House to a divided Supreme Court in December, re-entered the political fray five years later, first with a documentary film that won an Oscar award, and then with a book that took impassioned aim against the administration of President George W. Bush, the man who beat him to the presidency. The film, *An Inconvenient Truth*, displayed Gore as science communicator *par excellence*, in posture somewhere between professor and carnival showman, enthusiastically embracing the scientific consensus on climate change and warning viewers of the terrifying consequences of not acting in time. His book, *The Assault on Reason* (Gore 2007), excoriated the Bush administration for lying to the American people and instilling in them a fear that overwhelms their capacity to reason. Between the covers, Gore laid out a wide-ranging analysis of defects in the current workings of American democracy, including findings from social psychology establishing, in his view, that people are incapable of reasoning in the face of fear.

Coming from a prominent politician on the eve of an American election year, Gore's book was bound to raise partisan hackles; and so it did (Brooks 2007). More important for our purposes, and for the future of democracy, are two themes animating both of the former vice president's forays into the mass media: that science matters for policy; and how politicians and the public deal with claims about the world matters for democratic government. Although these issues are not on the public agenda for the first time, attitudes toward them are markedly different from the techno-optimism of the American Progressive era at the turn of the twentieth century, or the technophilia that drove many mid-century development projects, from the Green Revolution to an orgy of dam building to address the world's irrigation and energy problems. The mood today is more sceptical, more divisive, and less assured—not only about the benefits to be expected from innovations in science and technology but, as importantly, about the human capacity to make wise use of them.

Many reasons can be cited for the concerns of the moment. In part, with the advent of new information and communication technologies, the forms of human accommodation with technoscience have changed, so that—both metaphorically and in practice—today's technological visions involve more distributed, fluid, and unpredictable regimes of use and governance. The concreteness of the nuclear power plant (Winner 1986) has been supplanted, or at the least supplemented, by the virtuality of the internet. In part as well, public expectations about the assessment and management of science and technology have evolved, so that older discourses of the republic of pure science and of market-driven technological innovation no longer satisfy public demands for transparency and accountability (Jasanoff 2003). In part, science, technology, and governance have all spilled beyond the borders of the nation-state, raising new questions about who is in charge. Against their will and often in complete ignorance of the lurking others, governments, corporate boards, and law-abiding citizens today share information, and thereby also power, with hackers, cybercriminals, digital data miners, satellite cameras, DNA data banks, and terror networks. Not for nothing has the sociologist Ulrich Beck (1999:1) characterized this new 'second modernity' as a time of 'organized irresponsibility'.

Curiously, a prime casualty of this new age of information and informatics appears to be public confidence in the power of reason. Gore's book title represents reason as under attack, which sounds bad enough, but inside the book darker fears prevail. The author quotes a scientist at Stony Brook University, Charles Taber, as saying, 'The Enlightenment model of dispassionate reason as the duty of citizenship is empirically bankrupt'. That statement echoes many that I myself heard during the years of the Bush presidency, from academic colleagues who see the achievements of the Enlightenment challenged by an array of irrational fringe groups that seem on the ascendant: intelligent design adherents who block the teaching of evolution; new age crystal gazers who influence high-ranking politicians; proponents of alternative medicine who reject vaccines; disbelievers in the viral theory of AIDS; climate sceptics; opponents of stem cell research; protesters against genetically modified crops; and advocates of quack remedies for mental illness.

Not perhaps since Immanuel Kant's famous essay 'What Is Enlightenment?' (Kant 1784) has the term 'Enlightenment' figured so often, or so anxiously, in the discourse of public intellectuals. That essay, as Michel Foucault observed some 200 years later (Rabinow 1984), was written at a time when periodicals posed questions that had not previously been answered, in order to encourage debate in the nascent public sphere. Kant's answer was an exhortation to individual men (he had a low opinion of women's ability in this regard) to shake off their self-imposed bondage to intellectual superiors, to dare to know, and to make use of their own informed reason, especially when speaking to the public at large.

Today, questions about the Enlightenment seem to arise rather out of a sense of despair in the very possibility of reason. The social sciences are contributing to that assessment through their study of individual and group behaviour. Under the heading of 'biases and heuristics', behavioural economists have sought to establish that human choices deviate in predictable ways from the dictates of rationality (Kahneman et al. 1982). More recently, economics and psychology have joined forces with the new neurosciences to identify and characterize cognitive deficiencies in human thought processes. Coupled with the power of imaging technologies to localize thought within the brain (Dumit 2003), these findings, as Gore's book illustrates, are entering into political discourse in novel and influential ways. Images of the mind appear to confirm that centres of emotion, such as fear, dominate over centres of logic and reason. Science in this way unsettles the assumption of 'dispassionate reason' that has been a cornerstone of democratic political thought, rendering it empirically bankrupt in Taber's extreme formulation. Such pessimism, needless to say, does not bode well for the future of democracy.

Against this epochal unrest, when society's dependence on science and its anxiety about science's cultural and political authority both seem pitched too high for comfort, how should ecological economists or other social scientists approach the topic of science and public policy? What has been learned about this relationship through more than half a century of policy-making for and with science, and what specific light does experience shed on current concerns about genetically modified organisms (GMOs), climate change, and nuclear power? Once the most venal assaults on reason are set aside—those prompted solely by partisan interest or desire for personal gain— have we made any progress in dealing with a human predicament that includes both the benefits of greater knowledge and the costs of not being omniscient? What lessons can we draw, in particular, that are relevant to the role of the social sciences in policy making? Some of the most salient answers are grouped below under three headings: preferences; uncertainty; and reflexivity. These observations do not add up to a formula for perfect problem-solving, but they do suggest that, with respect to linking knowledge and action, the long march of the Enlightenment is leading us, if not straight, then interestingly ahead nevertheless.

PREFERENCES

Controversies over nuclear power, leading to a *de facto* moratorium in the United States and parts of Europe, widespread mobilization against dams in developing countries, and debates over GMOs and climate change at the turn of the twenty-first century have revealed a growing problem for science and technology policy. The public, it turned out, was not always willing to accept technological developments deemed beneficial by governments, international organizations, and multinational corporations; nor, in the case of climate change, did they necessarily accept the direst of expert predictions. Why should this be so? After all, if assessments of risk and benefit are grounded in sound science and logical reasoning, there should be widespread agreement on all of these issues. If the experts are right, and their rightness was originally taken almost as an article of faith, then the public's contrary dispositions need to be understood and set straight. The social sciences geared up to help policy makers deal with the problem of public distrust.

One line of inquiry, centred in the field of decision theory, sought to explain the split between lay and expert perceptions of risk. The expert position—that is, the position corresponding most closely to an accurate estimate of likely harm—was held to be the only rational basis for policy development. Lay opposition then became, by definition, deviant. It could be set aside as not meriting the decision maker's respect, although it still called for explanation. Decision theorists used various means to get at why the public (that is, non-experts) seemed systematically to attach greater probabilities of harm to some sorts of technologies than others, even though accident statistics proved these perceptions to be in error. For example, in surveys conducted during the 1970s, college students, environmentalists, and politically active women all evaluated risks from cycling and even automobile driving as lower than those from nuclear power, although records of accidents and deaths showed these lay judgements to be plainly false. A potent picture of the public grew up around these demonstrations: as a body swayed by emotion and fear, tending to overestimate risks from unfamiliar, dreaded, and distant events, but unconcerned about the lethal dimensions of mundane experience. Money spent to assuage such fears was considered to be money poorly spent (Breyer 1993).

The literature on public perceptions of technological risks drew strength from buttressing studies in the emerging field of biases and heuristics. Bringing together economics and psychology, and focusing on individual behaviour in games involving economic decisions, these experiments demonstrated that people are influenced by allegedly irrational concerns, particularly in situations involving prospective loss rather than gain; they attach too much weight to personal experience, recent events, and other irrelevant or 'distorting' factors to permit a mathematically rational weighing of probabilities. Both, decision theory and behavioural economics thus displayed human cognitive capacity as flawed, and central to that dismal assessment was the finding that experimental subjects value mathematically equivalent things as not equal. Such behaviour violates a widely accepted and normatively compelling axiom of reasoning: that likes should be treated as like, and unlikes as unlike. Failure to respect this basic constraint suggests that people do not understand their own preferences well enough to function as fully rational actors.

While the experimental and quantitative social sciences cast the public as the problem, a radically different account of preference, choice, and rationality emerged from areas of the interpretive social sciences. This mode of analysis is not concerned with establishing the conditions under which people deviate from a preordained standard of rationality (for example, valuing like outcomes of economic loss or gain alike); rather, it seeks to ascertain the reasons that people themselves offer for making choices that seem irrational when judged by mathematical probabilities alone. The latter way of framing the key analytic question avoids what social scientists term the sociology of error—that is, reserving explanations only for positions that are deemed to be wrong, whereas no explanations are sought for positions that are considered correct. Instead, many sociologists of knowledge embrace the so-called symmetry principle (Bloor 1991:3–23), which holds that the sociological inquirer should look impartially at justifications for both right and wrong claims. Only in this way can the analyst gain access to certain meta considerations of knowledge-making, such as, why people hold on to supposedly wrong beliefs, which kinds of arguments they consider persuasive and which ones not, and how the criteria of public credibility relate to other features of social and cultural context.

The symmetrical approach to querying rationality leads to a more complex understanding of individual and group preferences than studies of perceptions, biases, and heuristics. Instead of dismissing some preferences as irrational from the start, interpretive methods help illuminate why a given set of choices can elicit a multiplicity of justifiable responses. With regard to GMOs, for example, evidence has mounted that Europe's widespread rejection of genetically modified crops was associated with cultural preferences for *ex ante* assurances and empirical demonstrations of manageability that were not satisfied by conventional risk assessments. In particular, whereas US biotech companies convinced regulators that no new risks attached to the technique of genetic modification, the European public saw sharp enough breaks from earlier agricultural practices to demand explicit legislative authorization and tougher attitudes toward risk (Jasanoff 2005). Primed by historical encounters with the life sciences and technologies—from Germany's unspeakable experiences in the Nazi years to Britain's economic and social disaster with 'mad cow disease'—the European public preferred not to take on faith the safety and security assertions offered by governmental experts (Marris et al. 2001). The European Union's (EU's) growing commitment to the precautionary principle, a policy mandate written into several of the EU's constitutive legal documents, formalized the preference for ensuring that new technologies do not open up frontiers of ungovernability. By contrast, US policy seemed content to deal with the cost of accidents in *ad hoc*, unsystematic ways after things went wrong in agricultural biotechnology, as in the notorious StarLink and Prodigene cases (Winickoff et al. 2005).[1]

---

[1]In the StarLink case, a genetically modified corn species approved for growing only as animal feed found its way into a wide variety of corn-based foods for people. In the Prodigene case, failure to root out one year's growth of an antibiotic

These reactions to biotechnology provide evidence of a quite general conclusion from social studies of science and technology. Complex technological systems, such as agricultural biotechnology, do not simply improve productivity in one or another specific particular: increasing crop yield, adding new characteristics, cutting down energy or fertilizer inputs, or reducing labour. Technologies that succeed in the world operate far more as complex forms of life. They remake the ways in which people imagine and conduct their day-to-day existence, think about themselves, and shape their relations with one another. By favouring one way of doing things over another, technologies are necessarily distributive, and they may affect prior social practices in ways that profoundly destabilize tradition and experience. Monsanto's plan to develop the so-called Terminator technology, a form of gene modification that would have rendered seeds sterile, encountered steep opposition from farmers worldwide because it would have 'terminated' not only a plant's reproductive capacity but the age-long farming practice of storing and replanting seed from one season to another. In this case there was not even a promise of compensatory benefits to farmers. Against such social and political intrusion, more calculable risks (for example, lower productivity, increased energy needs, possible crop failure) paled into insignificance.

When weighing up the costs and benefits of technologies, then, quantitative estimates of physical or environmental harm do not begin to register the complexity and intensity of people's preferences. At stake in innovation are not simply determinate benefits that can be compared with equally determinate costs. Preferences that may be affected include commitments to ways of ordering the very rhythms of existence, including expectations of privacy and autonomy, security and intimacy, social status and stability, certainty about what lies ahead, and the desirable pace of change. Given the incommensurability of these values, the evidence from risk perception studies, biases and heuristics experiments, and cognitive neuroscience cannot simply be taken as proof of irrationality. Such studies can perhaps more usefully be read as offering added insights into what people need and want—to retain in their present and to risk in their future.

---

producing plant contaminated crops grown on the site a year later. Both cases caused hundreds of thousands of dollars in losses, and the costs were shouldered partly by the US government and partly by the private sector.

UNCERTAINTY

The human race arguably knows more about its condition at this moment than at any time since its appearance on the earth. Yet the consequence of that knowledge has not been greater certainty about what will happen or what should be done. With an uncannily sensitive finger on the pulse of the contemporary condition, Ulrich Beck (1992) called this the state of—'reflexive modernity'. It is a state in which the proliferation of knowledge has increased many individuals' capacity to intervene in the world, and hence, for such privileged actors, both a real and a felt sense of personal agency. With increased knowledge comes the ability to question, and along with that a waning of trust in the established, structured, institutionalized order of things. Put aphoristically, the more we know, the more we know we do not know. Knowledge, in other words, undermines both certainty and trust by engaging in a dialectic with its counterpart: ignorance.

In some policy circles, the phrase—'unknown unknowns' has been invoked, only half-humorously, as part of the unavoidable context of decision making. Donald Rumsfeld, architect of America's 2003 invasion of Iraq, famously said at a 2002 Defence Department briefing, 'As we know, there are known knowns. There are things we know we know. We also know there are known unknowns; that is to say we know there are some things we do not know. But there are also unknown unknowns—the ones we don't know we don't know'. Ignorance, whether known or unknown, produces its own 'tragic choices' (Calabresi and Bobbitt 1978), for just as economic resources are never adequate to serve all of society's needs, so informational resources, too, are in chronically short supply, and decisions have to be taken without knowing all the consequences they will lead to. Non-knowledge, moreover, is a structural phenomenon. As Rumsfeld, by no means a professional social theorist, intuitively appreciated, knowing that there are gaps in information does not mean that the gaps can necessarily be filled; and for gaps that cannot even be seen, no remediation is possible. Accordingly, just as a great deal of institutional work is aimed at keeping tragic economic choices out of the glare of publicity, so much of the work of risk governance is directed toward reassuring the public that unknown unknowns will not affect their material comfort, security, or well-being.

How is such reassurance achieved? Purpose-built for the task are the burgeoning technologies through which uncertainty is bounded, characterized, and at the limit rendered seemingly tractable. No modern state could survive without an exhaustive stock of such instruments in its administrative armamentarium, and the sciences of prediction, measurement, and assessment—economics foremost among them—have all developed to keep pace with the growing appetites of the state. Models are created to break a larger reality into its functional, manipulable components. Heuristics are devised to reduce complex problems into simpler, more tractable units. Scenarios are constructed to mimic, and thereby render navigable, the discrete pathways by which events can be expected to unfold, including the worst cases imaginable. Techniques of valuation are invented to permit comparisons among actions and consequences that would otherwise be wholly incommensurable. And indicators are devised to provide early warning signs of trouble, as well as to measure progress on fronts for which governments have assumed responsibility, and are, therefore, accountable.

In spite of all these efforts, surprises happen, and these are sometimes costly. A near meltdown at the Three Mile Island nuclear power plant in Pennsylvania put the US nuclear industry indefinitely on hold. The practice of feeding meat and bone meal to cattle in Britain caused an epidemic disease that, against all prediction, leapt the species barrier and killed dozens of people. Despite energetic efforts at border control, infected cows were found in Germany and Canada, entailing massive slaughter of herds and costly slumps in meat exports. Industrialization brought greater mobility, health, and prosperity, but growth-enabling fossil fuels were found to be endangering planetary health and the livelihoods of increasing numbers of people.

Curiously, though, developments such as these have done little to undermine the administrative state's fundamental premises, or promises, of calculation and control. Indeed, one sees in the rise of new fields of environmental analysis—addressing climate, vulnerability, and sustainability, for example—a continuation of paradigms of governance that push formality, objectification, and quantification into yet more complicated territories, and in the process fail to acknowledge the ungovernability of the unknown. The production of these analytic tools, moreover, has largely escaped the supervisory authority of the nation-state, gaining footholds in international agencies and private think-tanks that operate outside the discipline of democratic scrutiny and control.

For a world bent on calculation, yet continually taken aback by shocks and surprises, it is well to pay attention to the devices by which non-knowledge comes to be seen as insignificant—or, more accurately, as not worth acting on. For it is out of those areas of not knowing that the painful surprises most often emerge. Some common strategies of backgrounding ignorance have been identified by the social sciences of interpretation and explanation (Porter 1995). They include the processes of boundary drawing, by which some aspects of knowledge are characterized as facts, and hence as potentially amenable to scientific inquiry, whereas other are relegated to values, which may be fit subjects for moral or political deliberation but are not the preserves of science.

Possibly the most powerful of these techniques, however, is the bifurcation of narratives of success and failure, assigning to them different and asymmetrical causes, as in the sociology of error described above. When a planned project succeeds, it is because the experts who designed it got it right (the atom bomb, the moon landing, the test-tube baby); if it fails, it is because the consequences could not have been foreseen and were unintended (thalidomide, Chernobyl, 'mad cow'). Built into this discourse is an avoidance of responsibility for catastrophic loss or damage arising from ignorance. Morally, people cannot fairly be held accountable for harms they did not intend. Epistemologically, the frame of unintended consequences creates a divide between beneficial consequences, which are always known and intended, and harmful ones that are unintended and unknown. Since no rational decision maker could possibly intend harm, planners are absolved of the need to probe too deeply the unknowns that lie outside the limits of their intent and imagination. Those unknowns typically include matters relating to the context in which an innovation is taken up and put to use, that is, factors bearing on its uptake into environment and society. As a very broad generalization, the knowns lie more often in the traditional physical, biological, and engineering sciences; the unknowns belong to the social sciences and to transdisciplinarity.

From a discursive move that frees planners and designers of responsibility for unintended consequences, it is but a short step to blaming those further downstream in the production system. A story about the early emergence of resistance to Monsanto's extremely popular and successful herbicide Roundup illustrates how responsibility subtly shifts to the user. Roundup's virtual domination of the US herbicide market is largely the result of its pairing with another Monsanto invention, genetically modified crops that are resistant to the herbicide. The popular technological package of crop plus herbicide created ideal environmental conditions for the development of resistant strains. But whose lack of foresight gave rise to this ecological niche? Not that of the corporate planners who, in the eyes of one viewer, had known exactly what they meant to promote: 'The Monsanto scientists understand the possibility of resistance', said Joseph Di Tomaso, a weed specialist at the University of California at Davis. 'The real problem is the farmers. It's just so darn easy for them to control their weeds with Roundup' (Pollack 2003). Knowledge, then, has many fathers, and in the social sciences even uncertainty can claim its guardians; only ignorance, like failure, remains a scientific orphan, the property of untutored farmers and other lay publics.

REFLEXIVITY

The social sciences of the twentieth century, including most notably economics, have wrestled long and hard with both preferences and uncertainties, finding sophisticated ways to represent and measure them so as to render them tractable. In that process of disciplining, as we have seen, both concepts are reduced in complexity and meaning. What enters the decision maker's world perforce is what the methods of the relevant sciences, natural and social, are capable of putting on the table. Yet the resulting partial image continually gets taken for the whole because, individually and institutionally, our tendency is to naturalize what we know, take for granted that what we see is how it really is, and block out contrary evidence until it becomes too powerful to ignore. This, in effect, was the thesis of Thomas Kuhn's (1962) seminal work on scientific revolutions. Normal science, Kuhn argued, takes place within a paradigm whose constraints scientists for the most part do not bother to question. Revolutions only happen when the weight of the contrary signals and unanswered questions becomes so great as to force a wholesale re-examination of the foundational paradigm, and perhaps to overthrow it.

Ecological economics, along with most transdisciplinary sciences of recent decades, operates closer to the domain that Silvio Funtowicz and Jerome Ravetz (1990, 1992) termed post-normal science. These are fields of inquiry in which the rules by which science ought to be done, including conventions for determining what the objects of investigation are and how one should approach their study, are more indeterminate than in canonical normal science. In these comparatively grey zones, choices abound, and the boundary between subjectivity and objectivity is correspondingly blurred. How to draw the line between what counts as science and what will be seen as guesswork, unsupported speculation, or sheer politics becomes contested and often fiercely fought. Much of the work of modern expert advice can be seen as an answer to this problem. Such bodies, when they function with integrity, offer reassurance that the available facts have been thoroughly canvassed, opposing views and values taken on board, and judgment exercised in the public's best interest (Jasanoff 1990).

Expert advisory bodies, like other close-knit scientific communities, are considered reliable because they provide a socially desirable form of reflexivity—the practice of looking inward at and critiquing the body's own forms of reasoning. The diversity of viewpoints comprising such bodies is a source of strength. The internalized, cross-disciplinary capacity for self-reflection and self-criticism is what makes the judgements of a global assessment body such as the Intergovernmental Panel on Climate Change (IPCC) more trustworthy than the opinions of individual, discipline-bound, and possibly interest-driven climate sceptics. But even the best institutionalized and most honestly exerted critical capacity is never sufficient to guarantee that an expert body will deliver the best available knowledge, let alone have access to an ultimate reality. Deliberations within such groups are always constrained by organizational factors, the state of disciplinary knowledges, limitations of time and money, contingencies of membership, sensitivity to external circumstances, and cultural biases, or civic epistemologies (Jasanoff 2005), that predispose even the most self-aware observers to leave some features of the context unexamined.

In the world of the Enlightenment, the terms reason and science—and their correlate, objectivity—operate as doorstops against reflexivity. To label a claim as scientific or rational is to set it outside contingency, in a domain where context no longer matters. It then becomes *prima facie* unreasonable to question the claim on the basis of contextual factors. It may be a matter of considerable historical interest that a young American geneticist named James Watson joined forces with a slightly older British scientist, Francis Crick, in 1953 in a laboratory at the University of Cambridge to solve the mystery of the structure of DNA. But for the world at large, those facts do not in any obvious way speak of the reality of the chemical composition of the famous double helix, nor to what can be done with that knowledge.

The presumed correspondence between scientific facts and natural reality, however, is hard to achieve and always provisional.

Sometimes, human attempts to mould the natural world provide reassuring confirmation of scientific hypotheses; at other times, unexpected corroboration comes from unlooked for events or observations in other areas of inquiry. Outside the carefully structured and rule-bound turf of normal science, however, the reliability of scientific claims rests more on the processes by which people argued their way to those conclusions than on faithful adherence to theoretical principles or agreed-upon methodologies. Indeed, it is often only after people have resolved their disagreements about how to find the facts that one can convincingly say closure has occurred with respect to theory or method. The IPCC's successive reports illustrate this gradual process of consensus-building. It is not through blinding flashes of insight nor the application of pristine theory that such a body gains legitimacy, but through painstaking gathering of evidence from disparate sources, multiple rounds of critical review, often cutting across disciplinary boundaries, and repeated revisiting (and sometimes correcting) of earlier conclusions in the light of new knowledge.

Most robust social institutions have practices that promote reflexivity, for without some capacity for inward-looking critique and learning they would rapidly be overwhelmed by error and ignorance. Democracies send voters to the polls every few years to correct earlier bad choices. The sciences and, to some degree, science-based regulation (Jasanoff 1990), conduct peer review to weed out gross errors. Technologies are refined in the light of operational glitches. Markets respond to consumer signals, as corporate executives do to quarterly balance sheets and financial forecasts. The law uses litigation, discovery, and cross-examination to question orthodoxies. But institutions that wish to survive also have stopping points, places beyond which they will not allow questioning of their own epistemological or social foundations. Unbounded scepticism, as philosophers have argued for centuries, is no platform for a humanity that wishes to act on the basis of its own knowledge.

Without entering into arcane debates about the limits of scepticism, however, we can see the merit of periodically revisiting institutional stopping points to see whether they hold up in the light of changing knowledge. For example, evolving understandings of human nature rendered unacceptable the rules that once kept women and non-white minorities from going to the polls in Western societies. The old exclusionary rules were based on biological representations that eventually became untenable. Similar vigilance is required when institutions today ground their barriers against reflexivity on the claim that they are relying on 'science'. If one conclusion emerges forcefully from three decades of scholarship on science for policy, it is that the knowledge on which we would rest our most significant decisions is always underdetermined. It is possible to draw from almost any available set of claims disparate conclusions that look equally well justified. It becomes essential then, at a minimum, to look beneath the competing claims and conclusions and evaluate the solidity of the basis for those claims on moral as well as epistemological grounds. For powerful institutions, this obligation translates into allowing more second looks by those inside and outside their walls. Pragmatically, institutions may feel the need to foreclose reflexivity beyond a point; philosophically, the door should always be held open a crack to let new light shine in.

TOWARDS MORE REFLEXIVE SOCIAL SCIENCES

Let us return then to the role of the social sciences in public policy. The social sciences have long been partners in the exercise of political power. Indeed, Michel Foucault and other historians of the social sciences attributed the very rise of these fields to the needs of the modern state to characterize its publics and their problems, and so to enable and justify governance. That mutual dependence—of states on science and the sciences on the state—has, if anything, intensified since the mid-twentieth century, in the period of reflexive modernization. Yet, as the sciences seek to serve the state, the multivalency of people's preferences and the inevitability of ignorance are just two phenomena that substantially strain their capacity to provide reliable bases for reasoned public action. New knowledge begets new uncertainties, which in turn foster the search for additional knowledge, in an unending spiral of attempted rationalization by experts and distrust from citizens. To label lay responses as irrationally fearful, as some policy leaders have done, is to miss the point that doubt and uncertainty are to some extent the legacies of a wider diffusion of knowledge.

To cope with the demand for knowledge that can be acted on, a frequent response within the social sciences has been to simplify the complexities of individual and group behaviour, and to background ignorance about society, nature, and their interaction. This strategy has the merit of producing models and quantifiable results that emulate the natural sciences, but it does so at the risk of oversimplification

and potentially nasty surprises. Interdisciplinary conversations, such
as those between ecology and economics undertaken in this volume,
can do much to open up the blind spots that the sciences tend to
develop on their own, in short, to promote more radical reflexivity
than disciplinary communities can muster within themselves. Such
dialogue will be most welcome if it leads the social sciences to a deeper
appreciation of the contexts as well as the forms of human cognition
and behaviour. In time, that second enlightenment may even help
to assuage the anxieties of today's uneasily reflexive moment.

REFERENCES

Beck, Ulrich, (1992), *Risk Society: Towards a New Modernity*, London: Sage.
_____, (1999), *World Risk Society*, Cambridge: Polity.
Bloor, David, (1991), *Knowledge and Social Imagery*, Chicago: University
of Chicago Press.
Breyer, Stephen, (1993), *Breaking the Vicious Circle: Toward Effective Risk
Regulation*, Cambridge, MA: Harvard University Press.
Brooks, David, (2007), 'The Vulcan Utopia', *New York Times*, New York,
29 May 2007.
Calabresi, Guido and Philip Bobbitt, (1978), *Tragic Choices*, New York:
W.W. Norton.
Dumit, Joseph, (2003), *Picturing Personhood: Brain Scans and Biomedical
Identity*, Princeton: Princeton University Press.
Foucault, Michel, (1984), 'What Is Enlightenment?' ('Qu'est ce que c'est
les Lumiëres?'), in Paul Rabinow (ed.), *The Foucalt Reader*, New York:
Pantheon, pp. 32–50.
Funtowicz, Silvio and Jerome R. Ravetz, (1990), *Uncertainty and Quality
in Science for Policy*, Kluwer: Dordrecht.
_____, (1992), 'Three Types of Risk Assessment and the Emergence of
Post Normal Science', in Sheldon Krimsky and Dominic Golding (eds),
Social Theories of Risk, London: Praeger, pp. 251–73.
Gore, Al, (2007), *The Assault on Reason*, New York: Penguin.
Jasanoff, Sheila, (1990), *The Fifth Branch: Science Advisers as Policymakers*,
Cambridge, MA: Harvard University Press.
_____, (2003), 'Technologies of Humility: Citizen Participation in Governing
Science', *Minerva*, Vol. 41, pp. 223–44.
_____, (2005), *Designs on Nature: Science and Democracy in Europe and the
United States*, Princeton: Princeton University Press.
Kahneman, Daniel, Paul Slovic, and Amos Tversky (eds), (1982), *Judgment
under Uncertainty: Heuristics and Biases*, Cambridge: Cambridge
University Press.
Kant, Immanuel, (1784), 'Was Ist Aufklärung?', *Berlinische Monatsschrift*,
pp. 481–494.

Kuhn, Thomas, (1962), *The Structure of Scientific Revolutions*, Chicago: Chicago University Press.

Marris, Claire, Brian Wynne, Peter Simmons, and Sue Weldon, (2001), *Public Perceptions of Agricultural Biotechnologies in Europe (PABE Final Report)*, FAIR CT98–3844 (DG12—SSMI), *European Commission Report*, Brussels: European Commission.

Pollack, Andrew, (2003), 'Widely Used Crop Herbicide is Losing Weed Resistance', New York, *New York Times*, 14 January 2003.

Porter, Theodore M., (1995), *Trust in Numbers: The Pursuit of Objectivity in Science and Public Life*, Princeton: Princeton University Press.

Rabinow, Paul (ed.), (1984), *The Foucault Reader*, New York: Pantheo.

Slovic, Paul (ed.), (2001), *The Perception of Risk*, London: Earthscan.

Winickoff, David, Sheila Jasanoff, Lawrence Busch, Robin Grove-White, and Brian Wynne, (2005), 'Adjudicating the GM Food Wars: Science, Risk, and Democracy in World Trade Law', *Yale Journal of International Law*, Vol. 30, pp. 81–123.

Winner, Langdon, (1986), *The Whale and the Reactor*, Chicago: University of Chicago Press.

Abbreviations

ACIA	Arctic Climate Impact Assessment
AHDR	Arctic Human Development Report
AIA	Advance informed agreement
AMAP	Arctic Monitoring and Assessment Programme
AFSSA	French Food Safety Agency
AIDS	Acquired Immune Deficiency Syndrome
AR4	Fourth Assessment Report
BASF	Badische Amilin und Soda Fabrik
BGH	Bovine Growth Hormone
BST	Bovine Somatropin
BLGMO	Biosafety Law for Genetically Modified Organisms
BSE	Bovine Spongiform Encephalopathy
CAG	Comptroller and Auditor General
CAP	Common Agricultural Policy
CBA	Cost–Benefit Analysis
CBD	Convention on Biological Diversity
CC	Climate Change
CEC	Council of the European Communities
CO_2	Carbon dioxide
CONABIO	National Commission for Biodiversity
CNDA	National Centre for Beekeeping Development
CST	Scientific and Technical Committee for the Multifactor Study of the Honeybees Colonies Decline
CTD	Centre for Technology and Development
C3ED	Research Centre on Economics and Ethics for Environment and Development
DA&C	Department of Agriculture and Co-operation
DAE	Department of Atomic Energy
DG	Directorate General
DGAL	Direction Générale de l' Alimentation
DNA	Deoxyribonucleic acid

DST	Department of Science and Technology
EC	European Commission
EEA	European Environment Agency
EFSA	European Food Safety Authority
EIA	Environmental Impact Assessment
EPA	Environmental Protection Agency
EU	European Union
FAR	First Assessment Report
FBTR	Fast Breeder Test Reactor
FPR	Farmer Participatory Research
FSA	Food Standards Agency
GDP	Gross Domestic Product
GHE	Greenhouse Effect
GHG	Greenhouse gas
GM	Genetically modified
GMO	Genetically Modified Organism
GWP	Gross World Product
HEIA	High External Input Agriculture
HWR	Heavy Water Reactor
IA	Impact Assessment
IAD	Institutional Analysis and Development
IAM	Integrated Assessment Models
IFOAM	International Federation of Organic Agriculture Movements
IISc	Indian Institute of Science
ILO	International Labour Organization
IPCC	Intergovernmental Panel for Climate Change
IPM	Integrated Pest Management
ICAR	Indian Council of Agricultural Research
KARP	Kalpakkam Reprocessing Plant
kerDST	Kerbabel™ Deliberation Matrix
KIK	Ker Babal™ Indicator Kiosk
KQA	Knowledge Quality Assessment
LA	Lead Authors
LEIA	Low External Input Agriculture
LGEEPA	Federal Law on Ecological Equilibrium and Environmental Protection
LOSU	Level of Scientific Understanding
LMO	Living modified organism
LNT	Linear no-threshold hypothesis
MEA	Multilateral Environmental Agreements

MNP	Milien en Natuur Planbureon
MS	Member States
MW	Megawatt Assessment Agency
NGO	Non-governmental Organization
NPA	Natural Protected Areas
NPP	Nuclear Power Plant
NUSAP	Numerical, Unit, Spread, Assessment, and Pedigree
OECD	Organisation for Economic Cooperation and Development
OIE	World Organisation for Animal Health
O&M	Operations and Maintenance
PFBR	Prototype Fast Breeder Reactor
PDF	Probability Density Function
PET	Pedigree Exploring Tool
PHWR	Pressurized Heavy Water Reactor
POP	Persistent Organic Pollutant
PISA	Programme for Integrating Social Aspects in Nuclear Research
PSA	Probabilistic Safety Assessment
PTD	Participatory Technology Department
QA	Quality Assurance
QAAT	Quality Assurance Assistant Tool
RIPWiG	Rural Innovation Policy Working Group
RTPS	Raichur Thermal Power Station
RVs	Reference Values
SAR	Second Assessment Report
SAU	State Agricultural University
SCK-CEN	Belgian Nuclear Research Centre
SPS	Sanitary and Phytosanitary Agreement
S&T	Science and Technology
SR	Stern Review
STARD	Science and Technology Applications for Rural Development
STS	Science and Technology Studies
TAR	Third Assessment Report
TIDE	Technology Informatics Design Endeavour
UCIL	Uranium Corporation of India Limited
UK	United Kingdom
UN	United Nations
UNAF	National Union of French Beekeepers
UNEP	United Nations Environmental Programme

UNFCCC	United Nations Framework Convention on Climate Change
US/USA	United States/United States of America
USDOE	US Department of Energy
WG	Working Group
WMO	World Meteorological Organization
WTO	World Trade Organization
WWF	World Wildlife Fund
WFD	Water Framework Directive

1

Introduction
Science for Policy: Opportunities and Challenges

ÂNGELA GUIMARÃES PEREIRA AND SILVIO FUNTOWICZ[1]

A: What is the relation between knowledge, governance and policy?
S: One of the key features of our Western civilisation is the strong relation between knowledge and action. In particular to what we call modernity, this relation was established between science as a privileged form of knowledge and action. I call it action but this can be more concretely defined as policy, as regulation, as law or as governance. In order to understand concepts like knowledge economy or ideas of the influence of science in society today, we have to understand first this relation between science and governance...[2]

This chapter provides an overview and begins with a brief introduction of five conceptual models of the relation between science and policy, first published in Guimarães Pereira et al. (2006). The models trace the co-evolution of science and policy through a deepening appreciation of the process of the use of science in policy.

The chapter then reflects on each of the fields this volume addresses—Genetically Modified Organisms (GMOs), Climate Change, Energy, and Sustainable Development—in the light of the framework of relations between the science used in each case and the policies that it has underpinned. Last but not least, this chapter summarizes the main message of the book that may inspire the

[1]These are the opinions of the authors and cannot be taken as that of the European Commission.
[2]In Podcast: material of the course e-kam school, available at: *http://193.145.107.234/vl4s_new/Talks/Science per cent20& per cent20Governance.html*

necessary operational changes in the relations between science and policy in the light of the post-normal framework.

The perspective of this volume is that of narrating policy-related stories from a scientific perspective; these stories are also about real people facing real challenges. They are reflexive stories, having in common the emergence of a new awareness, the increasingly recognized need for changing the ways in which knowledge is produced and deployed; especially scientific-based knowledge that is used to foster, support, or legitimate public policy-making processes.

FIVE MODELS OF SCIENCE AND POLICY: FROM EXPERT DEMONSTRATION TO POST-NORMAL SCIENCE

Our modern (so-called 'Western') civilization is based on science in several ways. Science is the basis of the material culture that has transformed the world so much; and within the institutional framework of modern states, it is also a primary source of legitimization for policy arguments. This does not imply that extra-scientific concerns have no place in policy—on the contrary—they might then be charged with being exactly extra-scientific and accordingly susceptible to criticism for being irrational, emotional, or unknowledgeable.

There is a vast literature belonging to social and political theory and the political sciences that addresses the complexities involved in understanding modernity and the modern state, from Max Weber to contemporary theorists on what perhaps innocently may be called late modernity. Hence, we are not in doubt of the usefulness of, for example, Ulrich Beck's analysis in terms of second modernity and reflexive modernization, by which society becomes aware of and reacts to the fact that the production of 'goods', in the most general sense of benefits and welfare, entails processes by which hazards and problems are produced and distributed (Beck called them 'risks'). Indeed, our contribution may be seen as an instance of reflexive modernization. Likewise, our perspective is highly sympathetic to Bruno Latour's claim that 'We have never been modern', that modernity always involved a deep paradox insofar as it had to produce a secular ideology of clean separations between nature and culture; science and politics; and most deeply, between things and signs, in order to achieve an unprecedented level of interaction, intervention, and a mixture of them in the production of what Latour calls hybrids. Accordingly, there is hardly any place left in nature on Earth with a state unaffected by culture, or hardly any aspect of human life and culture which is not exposed to naturalization by scientific explanation, etc. With Latour, an attempt can be made to understand how the present state of affairs, with the urgent problems of natural resources, the environment, and technology, were inscribed at an early stage into the development of the modern state.

Nevertheless, the perspective of this book is a different and a narrower one, attending more to the practical challenges of operationalizing the task of reflexive modernization than describing or explaining it. In that sense, the 'theory' developed below has a different status: it aims at providing a pragmatic guide to highly contemporary processes and trends within the management and governance of environmental and technological problems in modern states. Our 'models of policy', accordingly, are to be taken for their heuristic value, the 'modern model' (Funtowicz 2006) being an attempt to distil the essential characteristics of the normative conception of the relation between science and policy in knowledge-intensive fields of policy, as seen from within, from an actor perspective. Hence, the modern model is one of perfection and perfectibility, one that presupposes that the scientific facts are unproblematic, that they can provide rigorous demonstrations of the truth, and hence that can also provide the correct 'good' policy. As such, the modern model is not an empirical description of reality at a direct level, but an experience-based empirical description of a normative conception, an ideal that we believe to be held both by many scientists and policy makers, but also an explication of what we believe to be a constitutive norm implicitly written into modern institutions.

Funtowicz (2006) identified several conceptual models of the relation between science and decision-making in policy processes. The empirical point here is that reflexive modernization currently appears to have come to a stage in which policy-makers and institutions increasingly recognize that the modern model is in crisis. This recognition follows a deepening appreciation of the process of the use of science in policy. Hence, in the myriad of policy processes and institutional and regulatory developments, one may identify the emergence of a handful of new norms that Funtowicz (2006) described as new 'models', or rather deviations from the modern model. These are briefly described below:

- The 'modern' model (perfection/perfectibility): Scientific facts (unproblematic), employed in rigorous demonstrations, would determine correct policy. According to this model, there are no limits to the progress of man's control over his environment, and no limits to the material and moral progress of mankind. This is the classic 'technocratic' vision.

- Precautionary model (uncertain and inconclusive information): In real policy processes, it is discovered that scientific facts are neither fully certain in themselves, nor conclusive for policy. Progress cannot be assumed to be automatic, and control over the environment can fail. Because of this imperfection in the science, there is an extra, normative element in policy decisions, that is, precaution, which both protects and legitimizes decisions. The precautionary principle is introduced as a means of 'protecting' the value of science on shaping policy.

- Framing (arbitrariness of choice and possible misuse): In the absence of conclusive facts, scientific information becomes one among many inputs to a policy process, functioning as evidence in the arguments. Debate is known to be necessary, as different stakeholders have their own perspectives and values shaping their arguments. The framing of the relevant scientific problem to be investigated and even the choice of the scientific discipline to which it belongs, becomes a prior policy decision, forming part of the debate among those affected by the relevant issue. Different scientific disciplines become competing stakeholders; whoever 'owns' the research problem will make the greatest contribution to policy and will enjoy the greatest benefit. When such a political process of the framing of the issue produces a wrong policy result, this amounts to a misuse of science.

- Demarcation (possibility of abuse of science): The scientific information and advice used in the policy process is created by people working in institutions with their own agendas. Experience shows that this context can affect the contents of what is offered, through the selection and shaping of data and conclusions. Although they are expressed in scientific terms, the information and advice cannot be guaranteed to be objective and neutral. The advicers are assumed to act with professional integrity, but they may actually be motivated by self-interest. In this sense, science can be abused when used as evidence in the policy process. A clear demarcation between the institutions (and individuals) that provide scientific information, and those where it is used is advocated as a means of protecting science from political interference that would threaten its integrity. It also ensures that political accountability rests with policy makers and is not shifted, inappropriately, to the scientists.

- Extended participation: Given these acknowledged imperfections in the deployment of science in the policy process, it becomes ever more difficult to defend a monopoly of accredited expertise for the provision of scientific information and advice. 'Science' (understood as the activity of technical experts) is included as one part of the 'relevant knowledge' to be brought in as evidence to a process. The ideal of rigorous scientific demonstration is replaced by that of open public dialogue. Citizens become both critics and creators in the knowledge production process as part of an extended peer community. When policy-relevant science is recognized as uncertain, complex, and contextual, new approaches for knowledge production are necessary:

The insight leading to Post-normal Science is that in the sorts of issue-driven science relating to...[*complex societal issues*], typically facts are uncertain, values in dispute, stakes high, and decisions urgent.... In post-normal conditions, such products the goal of achievement of truth or at least of factual knowledge may be a luxury, indeed an irrelevance. Here, the guiding principle is a more robust one, that of quality. (Funtowicz and Ravetz 1990)

THEMES COVERED IN THE VOLUME

The contributors to this volume are scholars and practitioners operating at the interface between science and the policy sphere. They describe cases of contemporary policy issues to illustrate the processes, challenges, and promises of using policy relevant science in governance. The themes they tell reflect major crises in the relationships between producers and appliers of science for policy. For instance, if science cannot produce truth with the time horizon of a decision, then new decision-making styles are necessary. These will incorporate the management of uncertainty, and acknowledge the value-ladenness of science as well as the instrumental and sometimes manipulative use of scientific arguments. In one way or the other, the themes fit within the models described earlier.

Jasanoff introduces the subject of this book along the lines of a changing society and changing science. She suggests new perspectives, in controversial locations of this *problematique* such as GMOs, climate change, and nuclear energy.

Genetically Modified Organisms

The themes regarding GMOs are looked at from several perspectives and they provide a rich panorama of the motivations and implications of the introduction of GMOs in the food chain.

Chapter 6, 'Mexico's Biosafety Policy Regime: A Critical Analysis' by Alejandro Nadal, and Chapter 8, 'Critical Issues in the Regulation of Genetically Modified Organisms' by Lim Li Ching and Lim Li Lin, focus on how scientific uncertainties in the of introduction of GMOs have led to precautionary regulation, which is in line with the second model of science and policy relationship: the precautionary model. They examine the scope, limitations, and challenges of the wide implementation of the Cartagena Protocol on biosafety. Nadal's statement that 'if there is a science policy imperative to provide additional support to the development of molecular biotechnology, this can and must be addressed through formal science and technology policy instruments, and not through a regulatory law' recalls the facts/values distinction of the Demarcation model. Li Ching and Li Lin make the case that at least a precautionary model of science and policy is a fundamental policy making in this case.

Chapter 9, 'Role of Scientific Information in Food Policy Making: The Case of GMOs' by Samarthia Thankappan, reflects on how the controversial introduction of genetically modified (GM) foods into the European Union (EU) became a focus for a wider debate over the regulatory role of science, in particular, for food science. It is interesting to note how the mandate of the recently created European Food Safety Authority (EFSA) is requiring 'objective and reliable scientific advice' to policy makers. Thankappan describes the actual policy-making developments that recall the arbitrariness of choice and possible misuse of science of the Framing model.

In Chapter 5, 'The Future of Agriculture: GMOs and the Agonizing Paradigm of Industrial Agriculture', Mario Giampietro claims that current GMO policies are framed by a 'wrong narrative'. He describes technical progress in agriculture as being locked-in in a 'Concorde syndrome', that is, innovations have the goal of doing more of the same, in spite of the fact that nobody is happy with what is happening now. We are in a situation similar to the third model of science and policy relationship: Framing (arbitrariness of choice and possible misuse).

Chapter 7, 'Spain and the European Debate on GM Moratoria vs Coexistence' by Rosa Binimelis and Roger Strand, offers a perspective

of the European debate on coexistence of GM crops with organic/
conventional farming. Stakeholders of Catalonia (Northeast Spain),
where GM maize has been grown since 1998 side by side with organic
and conventional agriculture, express different perspectives on
coexistence, GM 'contamination', damage, and liability, and argue
that neither the local socio-political dimension nor concerns of
scientific uncertainty is accounted for by EC recommendations. This
is a typical situation where we would argue that the extended
participation model of science and policy should be adopted.

Climate Change

Chapter 10, 'Is Climate Change Cost-Benefit Analysis Defensible?': A
Critique of the Stern Report' by Paul Baer and Clive L. Spash,
critically examines the Stern Report (2006) where normal economic
(cost–benefit) analysis is applied to the accepted estimates of the
global costs and benefits of greenhouse gas (GHG) control showing
the need for immediate action on economic efficiency grounds. The
authors demonstrate how climate change policy definition is ill-
suited for that type of analysis. The case presented by these authors
recall the Framing model.

In Chapter 11, 'Uncertainty Communication: The IPCC Reports',
Tiago De Sousa Pedrosa looks at how the communication of
uncertainty in climate change reporting by IPCC has effected policy
during the last decades. It then looks at the ways in which organized
civil society appropriates scientific uncertainty in their public
communications. Hence, it discusses how uncertainties are exploited
according to the policy context. It is proposed that pedigree assessment
methodologies (described in Chapters 3 and 15) could be used by
IPCC to communicate uncertainties in a more systematic way. The
theme described in Chapter 11 may easily recall arbitrariness of choice
of the Framing model.

Chapter 12, 'Ecology and Economy in the Arctic: Uncertainly,
Knowledge, and Precaution' by Julic Aslaksen, Solveig Glomsrød,
and Anne Ingeborg Mhyr, looks at the specific case of climate
change and the uncertainties of other issues and how they affect
the Arctic region and the people living there. They claim that
conceptual and empirical challenges of evaluating sustainability
and developing precautionary approaches require processes for
stakeholder participation, recognition of ethical values, and use
of traditional ecological knowledge. This contribution makes

the case for an extended participation model of science and policy relationship.

Energy

In Chapter 13, 'Radioactivity Within Without', Martin O'Connor maintains that the class of 'nuclear waste' is an icon, a symbol of the great adventure (and the uncertain destiny) of our technological civilization. The chapter develops proposals for conducting multi-criteria, multi-stakeholder evaluation as an aid to governance of our long-term participation in the radioactivity life cycle. He develops a list of six principles of quality, performance, and responsibility for multi-criteria, multi-stakeholder stewardship option evaluation, which provides a framework for extended assessments that the extended model of science and policy precludes.

In Chapter 14, 'Ignoring the Costs: Energy Planning and the Dismal Economics of Nuclear Power in India', M.V. Ramana and J.Y. Suchitra maintain that nuclear power has been a focus of India's energy policy, completely uninfluenced by economic science, and how India's Department of Atomic Energy (DAE) has sold nuclear power as a cheap and viable electricity generation option with little basis in fact. In their chapter, the authors carry out a detailed estimate of the cost of producing plutonium to fuel breeder reactors and show that the cost of electricity from breeders will be high. This is a case of poor quality of science informing policy—perhaps a good example of Funtowicz's Demarcation (possibility of abuse of science) model.

In Chapter 15, 'Re-negotiating the Rate of External Cost Calculations in the Belgian Nuclear and Sustainable Energy Debate', Matthieu Craye, Eric Laes, and Jeroen van der Sluijs describe the application of pedigree assessment to the calculation of external costs of nuclear energy. Value-laden assumptions made in the calculation chain were collectively discussed and qualified in a structured way by policy-makers, stakeholders, and experts. The chapter analyses the possible contribution of pedigree assessment to the functioning of the science–policy interface, in line with the Funtowicz's Extended Participation model of science–policy.

Sustainable Development

Chapter 16, 'Impact Assessment and Quantitative Modelling in European Policy Development' by Andreas Thiel, uncovers the institutions that guide the selection of quantitative *ex-ante* policy assessment tools in the European Commission's Impact Assessment (IA) practices. A conceptual framework and a methodology are devised to these ends. He concludes that the choices of desk officers are informed by their procedural motivation to produce successful policy proposals. His theme recalls the Demarcation model described earlier in this chapter.

In Chapter 17, 'Innovation for Eco-friendly Development: Towards Institutional Reform in Scientific Research and Policy Making', Rajeshwan S. Raina addresses the major and hitherto uncontested assumption that new environment-friendly technologies enable ecologically sustainable development. She analyses the rules and institutions that govern science and technology (S&T) research policy making within the government, explaining how these institutions enable or constrain the utilization of knowledge for development. Her case recalls the Framing model of science and policy.

In Chapter 18, 'Quality Tales in Sustainable Water Governance Cases', Ângela Guimarães Pereira takes cases of water governance in Europe to explore how quality of knowledge is seen as a lesser preoccupation by those who take decisions based upon consultancy and academic studies. These are actually just instrumental to decisions decided much earlier. Her case is clearly described by the Framing model's arbitrariness of choice.

A Post-normal Momentum

> Congress should do everything possible to hear from scientists. (…)
> But Congress and scientists need to stop pretending that science alone can determine policy decisions (Goldson 2007).

Since Mike Hulme's article in *The Guardian*[3] about climate change falling in the post-normal framework, the momentum is set for deepening a reflection of current policy making and the science production process that grounds it.

This volume provides, through the salient topics it discusses, the evidence that the current understanding of the relation between science and policy is no longer functional, and that it has to be changed to a science-policy model based on quality. Hence, it provides insight in different ways of reflecting upon and developing science that fits the extended model of science policy relationship.

[3] *http://environment.guardian.co.uk/climatechange/story/0,2032821,00.html.*

The themes discussed in this volume illustrate the importance of 'post-normal' concepts for governance in order to ensure that knowledge is relevant and it is produced and deployed with integrity. There is a need to embrace a different science-policy model when facts are uncertain, values are in dispute, stakes are high, and decisions urgent. These last features define a post-normal science situation. This acknowledgement has several implications for governance, for those who produce science and for those who deploy it, which have to be comprehended. The methodological section of the book deals with the implementation of the extended participation model, looking at how uncertainty, ambiguity, and quality of science for policy making can be managed through participatory action.

Chapter 2, 'Uncertainty Assessment in a Deliberative Perspective' by Jean Marc Douguet, Martin O'Connor, and Jeroen van der Slujis, proposes a selection of tools to assess the nature and the extent of uncertainty linked to knowledge production and use, in order to integrate uncertainty in processes of environmental evaluation. The tool catalogue to assess uncertainty has been developed to take into account three types of concerns, including the identification and analysis of the various forms of uncertainty that stakeholders and decision makers have to face, the quality of knowledge and its evaluation by the scientific community and/or an extended community of peers, and also the pertinence of knowledge in expressing uncertainty. The challenge addressed is to work with a permanent exchange, argumentation, and sometimes compromise between different principles of choice, hence a challenge for the implementation of 'extended participation' model of science and policy.

Chapter 3, 'A Quality Assurance Framework for Policy Making: Proposing a Quality Assurance Assistance Tool (QAAT)' by Serafin Corral Quintana, proposes a framework through which the quality of knowledge that informs a policy process can be explored and communicated to all social actors involved in the policy process because he claims that, in [environmental] public policy-making the assessment of the quality of policy-making procedures should be considered as an essential element of the policy process itself. The chapter offers a methodological example of how the 'extended participation' model could work in practice.

Chapter 4, 'Multi-causal Relationships in their Socio-political Context' by Laura Maxim and Jeroen van der Sluijs, offers a reflection on multi-causality. In its socio-political context, multi-causality can be used as an argument in discursive strategies meant to downplay the responsibility of one major anthropogenic cause of an environmental problem. Based on the case study of the risk to honeybees of the insecticide Gaucho® in France, the purpose of the present work is to show the correlation between the way of framing (multi-)causality in expertise of environmental risks, the conflicting relationships between actors in a social debate on these risks, and the resulting political action. The methodological developments in this chapter make the case for the 'extended participation' model.

CONCLUDING REMARKS

Despite the evolution in the relationship between science and policy, this relationship is still a privileged one, since science is a primary source of legitimization for policy arguments. Hence, it is still commonly accepted that a good policy must have scientific underpinning.

This volume shows that science cannot be considered as a unique input, as other knowledges and its sources are often directly, even crucially relevant. If science is considered as an exclusive source of evidence for the policy discourse it can be vulnerable to defects in quality in a variety of ways. It then becomes a less robust basis for policy making. The context where policy-relevant science is deployed is often complex, subject to several types of uncertainty, and requires a plurality of perspectives to be taken into consideration. We can identify three types of vulnerability that can undermine the robustness of policy-relevant science: uncertainty, ambiguity, and quality.

Participatory activities endorsed by regulation and formal institutions are often used for political reasons, as rubber stamp and moral justification to legitimate a certain policy. There is, however, a great deal of literature that lists more genuine, as well as 'scholarly' motivations for participatory action. We would argue that, in relation to policy making, the vulnerabilities listed above can be addressed through extended peer review (Funtowicz and Ravetz 1990), which is the basis of the extended model of science and policy described earlier. Through participatory action, management of uncertainties may be shared; ambiguity can be tamed through the extension of the process of framing; and quality is enhanced through co-production of knowledge (Jasanoff 2006). Hence, policy making becomes a shared exercise legitimated by more broadly accepted narratives and justifications.

The contributions to this volume corroborate this perceived need for extended involvements of the concerned public in managing the above-mentioned vulnerabilities. They show how post-normal science and extended peer review are relevant frameworks in which current policy relevant science production should be looked at in order to assure the value of scientific knowledge in policy contexts.

REFERENCES

Funtowicz, S.O., (2006), 'Why Knowledge Assessment?' in A.S. Guimarães Pereira, S. Guedes Vaz and S. Tognetti (eds), *Interfaces between Science and Society*, Sheffield: Greenleaf Publishing, pp. 138–45.

Funtowicz, S.O. and J.R. Ravetz, (1990), *Uncertainty and Quality in Science for Policy*, Kluwer: Dordrecht.

Funtowicz, S.O., and Jerome R. Ravetz, (1992), 'Three Types of Risk Assessment and the Emergence of Post Normal Science', in Sheldon Krimsky and Dominic Golding (eds), *Social Theories of Risk*, London: Praeger, pp. 251–73.

Goldston, D. (2007), 'Technical Advice', *Nature*, Vol. 448, No. 2, p. 119.

Guimarães Pereira, A., S. Guedes Vaz and S. Tognetti (eds) (2006), *Interfaces between Science and Society*, Sheffield: Greenleaf Publishing.

Jasanoff, S., (1996), 'Beyond Epistemology: Relativism and Engagement in the Politics of Science', *Social Studies of Science*, Vol. 26, No. 2, pp. 393–418.

Latour, Bruno, (1993), *We Have Never Been Modern*, Cambridge: Harvard University Press.

Stern, N., (2006), *Stern Review on the Economics of Climate Change*, UK Government Economic Service, London, *http://www.sternreview.org.uk*.

PART 1

Methodological Perspectives in Policy-Relevant Science: Knowledge Assessment

2

Uncertainty Assessment in a Deliberative Perspective

JEAN-MARC DOUGUET, MARTIN O'CONNOR, ARTHUR PETERSEN, PETER H.M. JANSSEN, AND JEROEN VAN DER SLUIJS

This chapter provides an overview for uncertainty assessment relating to complex science-policy problems. It is proposed that tools to assess uncertainty must take into account three types of concerns. The first concern relates to the identification and analysis of the various forms of uncertainty that stakeholders and decision makers have to face. The second concern is linked to the quality of knowledge and its evaluation by the scientific community and/or an extended community of peers. The third concern relates to the pertinence and 'fitness for purpose' of our knowledge, including knowledge about uncertainties, in a given decision, policy, or governance context. The chapter, therefore, considers topics related to the characterization of uncertainty; to the complementarity of analytical and deliberative methods in the evaluation of the quality of knowledge; and to deliberation support tools intended to facilitate communication, structuring, and framing of knowledge in different socio-cultural and political contexts.

COMPLEXITY AND UNCERTAINTY IN THE 'POST-NORMAL' TRADITION

While science and technological advances bring benefits and attractive novelty to many sectors of our lives, the new knowledge will sometimes also lead to significant new sources of bother, inconvenience, and risks, such as negative health and environmental effects and societal tensions and stresses. In recognition of this, there has emerged, since at least the time of Frankenstein's Monster and the Luddites, a heterogeneous 'social demand' to reappraise, publicly and in a reflexive way, the place of science and technology as a vehicle for society's aspirations.

As science-related policy issues have come to be recognized as complex and difficult of solution, the conception of the role of science has itself evolved. Today, when science is deployed in the policy context, there is awareness of the possibility that facts are uncertain, values in dispute, stakes high, and decisions urgent.[1] Progress in science and technology is associated not just with greater productivity but with a 'deepening and widening' of our interventions in natural processes. Mankind has gone far beyond the mere macroscopic intervention in materials (such as building a dam) and is now capable of intervening simultaneously in organization at the scale of atoms (nuclear fission and fusion), of molecular and cellular structures (notably in genetic heritage, for example, gene splicing and cloning technologies), of ecosystems, and of planetary atmosphere and ocean current circulation systems. Because the forms of organization in question are dynamic (gene stocks, ecosystem change, hydrological cycles, atmospheric circulation), and the perturbing factors may have a long active life (radioactivity, other toxins) or are potentially self-renewing (modified life forms), our technological prowess constitutes a self-renewing source of problems that are intrinsically more complex than the productivity or performance efficiency calculations that may have guided the initial actions. More science and new technology applications can sometimes solve the emerging problems. But, as a 'general rule', the systems complexity is richer than our capacity to pilot the change!

Scientific assessments of complex risks such as climate change, biodiversity loss, bird flu, natural resource depletion, or particulate matter involve uncertainties of many sorts, not all of which can be effectively controlled in practice. Decisions need to be made before conclusive supporting evidence is available, while at the same time the potential impacts of wrong decisions can be huge. Governmental and intergovernmental agencies that inform the policy and the public about such risks increasingly recognize that uncertainty cannot convincingly be suppressed or denied, but needs to be dealt with in a transparent and effective manner.

But what is a transparent and effective treatment of uncertainty? It is useful here to evoke the emergent diversity of conceptual models

[1]This formulation is adapted directly from Silvio Funtowicz and Jerome Ravetz who have led the emergence of the perspective of a 'post-normal' practice of science (see Funtowicz and Ravetz 1990, 1994a, b). See also the overviews of science, complexity, and risk governance in Funtowicz et al. (1997) and Gallopin et al. (2001).

of the relation between science and decision making in policy processes. Silvio Funtowicz and Jerry Ravetz and others, in their ongoing articulation of a 'post-normal' science practice, have proposed a sequence of five models (Funtowicz 2006) whose emergence and criticism can be considered as a historical and cultural process of deepening—and progressively more reflexive—understanding of the 'emergent complexities' in the process of the use of science in policy. These are presented synthetically in Guimarães Pereira and Funtowicz (in this volume).

The proposal of 'post-normal science' (the fifth model in the Funtowicz and Ravetz typology) is to adopt a pluralistic, participatory, and democratic view of the knowledge and judgement base for policy actions. Dealing with contemporary knowledge problems requires opening the analytical and formal decision-making processes to broader categories of facts and actors than those traditionally legitimated.

The old distinction between hard facts and soft values is being replaced by a 'soft facts/hard values' framework—admitting the complexity of emergent system properties (and hence uncertainties, etc.) and admitting the plurality of quality and legitimating criteria (for example, there are different definitions of the problem, different ways of selecting and conceiving its relevant aspects, as well as different goal definitions, depending on cultural factors and not only on conflict of interests).

The highly asymmetrical distinction between experts and non-experts is losing its classical status. In a sense, when facing a 'post-normal' problem, all stakeholders are partially experts—in different ways, from different points of view, and with regard to different aspects of the problem. Hence, it is necessary to extend the number and type of actors, both individual and collective, legitimated to intervene in the definition of the problems as well as the selection and implementation of the connected policies (Faucheux, S. and M. O'Connor [2000]; O'Connor M. et al. [1996]). This extension does not just fulfil the requirements of democratic decision-making; it also improves the quality of decisions. The way of conducting a decision process can dramatically influence its results. The dialogue between different actors is essential for quality, credibility, legitimacy, and hence the prospects of success of policy implementation.[2]

---

[2]See also the discussions by van den Hove (2000, 2001) and O'Connor and van den Hove (2001) of the variety of participatory processes and their typology in terms of expected substantive, procedural, and contextual effects.

Alongside 'extended facts' and hand-in-hand with them, we are encouraged to recognize 'extended peer communities'. Implementing this deliberative model emerges, for those persuaded by the arguments, as one of the key science-governance challenges of our time.

In this view, uncertainty is understood as an intrinsic property of complex systems and it is affirmed that not all uncertainties can be quantified. The 'post-normal' perspective, therefore, proposes, as a way forward, to deal openly and publicly—deliberately and deliberatively—with the deep dimensions of uncertainty (in particular, uncertainty that results from problem framing, system boundaries, indeterminacy, ignorance, assumptions, value loadings, institutional dimensions, and of arbitrariness choices made in scientific analysis). The governance style with which the post normal perspective on science resonates is thus one of deliberative negotiated management of risk and argued choice. This chapter makes a succinct review of the state of the art of this reflective approach to Knowledge Quality Assessment (KQA).

The following section presents key features of an 'uncertainty diagnostic' or framework of enquiry into the quality and pertinence of scientific knowledge for complex problems. In particular, the approach is presented in terms of questionnaires developed by European researchers with the aim of characterizing the nature and extent of uncertainty in any specific scientific field. The question of relevant tools for knowledge quality assessment is considered; highlighting the complementarity between formal tools of mathematical (including statistical) analysis and the mobilization of qualitative insights through various forms of expert and wider stakeholder deliberation. The next section discusses the roles that can be played by interactive 'deliberation support tools' that highlight the ways in which fitness for purpose (or pertinence) cannot be dissociated from establishing appropriate procedures for sharing and communication of knowledge and of judgements about knowledge. We consider partIcularly some recent experiments with on-line tools (the KerBabel™ Indicator Kiosk and Deliberation Matrix) for integration of concerns related to uncertainty in dialogues about the selection of indicators in the context of comparisons of decision options or scenarios.

Uncertainty Diagnostic

Following the classic conception of scientific policy advice, certainty is the 'first best' knowledge situation for the management of complex problems. However, uncertainty is a fact of life. Scientific assessments today have to integrate information across a wide spectrum from well-established scientific knowledge to educated guesses, preliminary models, and tentative assumptions. In such contexts, uncertainty is endemic and, in general, can mostly not be remedied through additional research or comparative evaluations of evidence by expert panels searching for a consensus interpretation of the risks.

The challenge to scientific advisers in a deliberative governance or inclusive risk management perspective is to be as transparent and clear as possible in their treatment of uncertainties. Several institutions that interface science and policy have adopted knowledge quality assessment approaches in response to emerging needs. One example is the Netherlands Environmental Assessment Agency (Milieu en Natuur Planbureau, MNP), which recently commissioned Utrecht University to develop, together with MNP, a Guidance for Uncertainty Assessment and Communication,[3] a state-of-the-art reflective approach that is summarized below. This guidance has been developed in close consultation with international uncertainty experts. It aims to facilitate the process of dealing with uncertainties throughout the whole scientific assessment process and explicitly addresses institutional aspects of knowledge development, openly deals with indeterminacy, ignorance, assumptions, and value loadings. It thereby facilitates a profound societal debate and a negotiated management of risks. The Guidance is not set up as a rigid protocol. Instead, it provides a heuristic that encourages self-evaluative systematization and reflexivity on pitfalls in knowledge production and use. It also provides diagnostic help as to where uncertainty may occur and why. This can, its originators hope, contribute to more conscious, explicit, argued, and well-documented choices.

Following a diagnostic checklist approach, the Guidance consists of a layered set of instruments (Mini-Checklist, Quickscan, and Detailed Guidance) with increasing level of detail and sophistication (Janssen et al. 2005; van der Sluijs et al. 2008). It can be used by practitioners as a (self-) elicitation instrument or by project managers as a guiding instrument in problem framing and project design. Using the Mini-Checklist and Quickscan Questionnaire, the analyst can flag key issues that need further consideration. Depending on what is flagged as salient, the analyst is referred to specific sections in a separate Hints and Actions document and in the Detailed

[3] *http://www.nusap.net/guidance*

Guidance. Since the number of cross-references between the documents comprising the Guidance is quite large, a publicly available interactive web application has been implemented. This web application also offers a prioritized to-do list of uncertainty assessment actions, and generates reports of sessions (traceability and documentation), which enables internal and external review.

Six foci are distinguished where systematic critical reflection on uncertainty and quality can help to gain a better understanding of knowledge. These are: problem framing, stakeholder participation, indicator selection, appraisal of the knowledge base, mapping and assessment of relevant uncertainties, and reporting of the uncertainty information. Table 2.1 summarizes key issues that require systematic reflection for each of the six foci.

In order to facilitate communication about the different types of uncertainty that arise in scientific assessments, an uncertainty typology is part of the Guidance. The typology is based on a conceptual

Table 2.1:   Foci and Key Issues in Knowledge Quality Assessment

Foci	Key Issues
Problem Framing	Other problem views; interwovenness with other problems; system boundaries; role of results in policy process; relation to previous assessments; pertinence of framing
Involvement of Stakeholders	Identifying stakeholders; their views and roles; controversies; mode of involvement
Selection of Indicators	Pertinence of indicators in view of problem and context; adequate backing for selection; alternative indicators; support for selection in science, society, and politics
Appraisal of Knowledge Base	Pertinence of knowledge in view of problem and context; identify and acknowledge gaps in knowledge and understanding; quality required; bottlenecks in available knowledge and methods; impact of bottlenecks on quality of results
Mapping and Assessing Relevant Uncertainties	Identification, typification, and prioritization of key uncertainties; choice of methods to assess these; assessing robustness of conclusions
Reporting Uncertainty Information	Context of reporting; robustness and clarity of main messages; policy implications of uncertainty; balanced and consistent representation in progressive disclosure of uncertainty information; traceability and adequate backing

Source: (Van der Sluijs et al. 2003; Petersen et al. 2003; Janssen et al. 2003), available at *http://www.nusap.net/sections.php?op=viewarticle&artid=17*.

framework that resulted from a process involving an international group of uncertainty experts, most of whom participated in developing or reviewing the Guidance. Uncertainty can be classified along the following dimensions: its 'location' (where it occurs), its 'level' (whether it can best be characterized as statistical uncertainty, scenario uncertainty, or recognized ignorance), and its 'nature' (whether uncertainty primarily stems from knowledge imperfection or is a direct consequence of inherent variability). In addition, the typology distinguishes the dimensions 'qualification of knowledge base' (what are weak and strong parts in the assessment) and 'value-ladenness of choices' (what biases may shape the assessment). Below, we go further into the description of the typology.

The dimension 'location' indicates where uncertainty can manifest itself in the problem configuration at hand. Five categories are distinguished along this dimension:

- The 'context' concerns the framing of the problem, including the choices determining what is considered inside and outside the system boundaries ('delineation of the system and its environment'), as well as the completeness of this representation in view of the problem issues at hand. Part of these context-related choices is also reflected in the other location categories, such as 'data' that are considered to play a role, 'models' that are chosen to be used, and 'outcomes' that are taken to be of interest.
- 'Data' refers to measurements, monitoring data, survey data, etc. used in the study, that is, information that is directly based on empirical research and data collection. Also the data that are used for calibration of the models involved are included in this category.
- 'Model' concerns the 'model instruments' that are employed for the study. This category can encompass a broad spectrum of models, ranging from mental and conceptual models to more mathematical models (statistical models, causal process models, etc.) that are often implemented as computer models. Especially for the latter class of models, subcategories have been introduced, distinguishing between model structure (relations), model parameters (for example, process parameters, initial and boundary conditions), model inputs (input data, external driving forces), as well as the technical model, which refers to the implementation in hardware and software.
- 'Expert judgement' refers to those specific contributions to the assessment that is not fully covered by context, models, and data,

and that typically has a more qualitative, reflective, and interpretative character. As such, this input could also alternatively be viewed as part of the 'mental model'.
- The category of 'outputs' from a study refers to the outcomes, indicators, propositions, or statements that are of interest in the context of the problem at hand.

The various uncertainties on the location axis can be further characterized in terms of four other uncertainty features/dimensions, which are described below.

The dimension 'level of uncertainty' expresses how a specific uncertainty source can be classified using three distinct classes:
- 'Statistical uncertainty': this concerns the uncertainties that can adequately be expressed in statistical terms, for example, as a range with associated probability (examples are statistical expressions for measurement inaccuracies, uncertainties due to sampling effects, uncertainties in model-parameter estimates, etc.). In the natural sciences, scientists generally refer to this category when they speak of uncertainty, thereby often implicitly assuming that the involved model relations offer adequate descriptions of the real system under study, and that the (calibration)-data employed are representative of the situation under study. However, when this is not the case, 'deeper' forms of uncertainty are at play, which can surpass the statistical uncertainty in size and seriousness and which require adequate attention.
- 'Scenario uncertainty': this concerns uncertainties that cannot be adequately depicted in terms of chances or probabilities, but which can only be specified in terms of (a range of) possible outcomes. For these uncertainties it is impossible to specify a degree of probability or belief, since the mechanisms which lead to the outcomes are not sufficiently known. Scenario uncertainties are often construed in terms of 'what–if' statements.
- 'Recognized ignorance': this concerns those uncertainties of which we realize—some way or another—that they are present, but of which we cannot establish any useful estimate, for example, due to limits to predictability and knowability ('chaos') or due to unknown processes.

Note that these classes need not necessarily be on one scale; all three classes can be present at the same location in a model, but usually one of the three dominates. Continuing on the 'scale' beyond recognized ignorance, we arrive in the area of complete ignorance ('unknown unknowns'), of which we cannot yet speak and where we inevitably grope in the dark.

Notice that the uncertainties which manifest themselves at a specific location (for example, uncertainties on model relations) can appear in each of the above-mentioned guises: while some aspects can adequately be expressed in statistical terms, other aspects can often only be expressed in terms of 'what–if' statements; moreover, there are typically aspects judged relevant but about which we know that we are (still) largely 'ignorant'. Judging which aspects manifest themselves in what forms is to some degree subjective, and therefore practitioners that make these judgements should provide and document their argumentations, so that in the review peers can criticize these where they disagree.

The third dimension in the typology adds the distinction whether uncertainty is primarily a consequence of the incompleteness and fallibility of knowledge ('knowledge-related', or 'epistemic', uncertainty) or that it is primarily due to the intrinsic indeterminate and/or variable character of the system under study ('variability-related', or 'ontic', uncertainty).

- Knowledge-related uncertainty can possibly, though not necessarily, be reduced by means of more measurements, better models, and/ or more knowledge.
- Variability-related uncertainty is typically not reducible by means of more research (for example, inherent indeterminacy and/or unpredictability, randomness, chaotic behaviour).

The fourth dimension that is relevant for characterizing uncertainty concerns the 'qualification of the knowledge base'. This refers to the strength of underpinning of the established results and knowledge claims. The phrase 'established results and knowledge claims' can be interpreted in a broad sense here: it can refer to the policy-advice statement as such (for example, 'the norm will still be exceeded when the proposed policy measures have become effective', 'the total yearly emission of substance A is X kiloton') as well as to assertions about the uncertainty in this statement (for example, 'the uncertainty in the total yearly emission of substance A is...(95 per cent confidence interval)'). The degree of underpinning is divided into three classes: weak; fair; strong. If the underpinning is weak, this indicates that the statement of concern is surrounded by much (knowledge-related) uncertainty, and deserves further attention. This classification, moreover, offers suggestions about the extent to which uncertainty is reducible by providing a better underpinning.

Note that this dimension in fact characterizes the reliability of the information (data, knowledge, methods, argumentations, etc.) that is used in the assessment. Criteria such as empirical, theoretical, or methodological underpinning and acceptance/support within and outside the peer community can be used for assessing and expressing the level of reliability.

If required, a so-called 'pedigree analysis' can be done, which results in a semi-quantitative scoring of the underpinning on the basis of a number of qualitative criteria such as the aforementioned ones (see the Tool Catalogue for Uncertainty Assessment).

The final dimension for characterizing uncertainties denotes whether a substantial amount of 'value-ladenness' and subjectiveness or arbitrariness is involved in making the various—implicit and explicit—choices during the environmental assessment. This concerns, among other things, the way in which (i) the problem is framed vis-à-vis the various views and perspectives on the problem (ii) the knowledge and information (data, models) is selected and applied, and (iii) the explanations and conclusions are expressed and formulated. If the value-ladenness is high for relevant parts of the assessment, then it is imperative to analyse whether or not the results of the study are highly influenced by the choices involved, and whether this could lead to a certain arbitrariness, ambiguity, or uncertainty of the policy-relevant conclusions. This could then be a reason to explicitly deal with different views and perspectives in the assessment and to discuss the scope and robustness of the conclusions in an explicit manner.

This typology can be presented schematically as a matrix (Table 2.2). This 'uncertainty matrix' is an instrument for generating an overview of where one expects the most important (policy-relevant) uncertainties to be located (the first dimension), and how these can be further characterized (in terms of the other uncertainty dimensions mentioned). The matrix can be used as a scanning tool to identify areas where a more elaborate uncertainty assessment is required. The different cells in the matrix are linked to available uncertainty assessment tools suitable for tackling that particular uncertainty type. These tools are described in a Tool Catalogue that aims to assist the analyst in choosing appropriate methods (see the following section).

Deliberative KQA: Tools to Assess Uncertainty

Many methodologies and tools suitable for supporting uncertainty assessment have been developed and reported in the scientific literature. In line with recent reviews and discussions, 12 of the most commonly applied methods and tools can be identified as: Error Propagation Equations; Expert Elicitation; Extended Peer Review (review by stakeholders); Inverse Modelling (parameter estimation); Inverse Modelling (predictive uncertainty); Monte Carlo Analysis; Multiple Model Simulation; Numerical, Unit, Spread, Assessment, and Pedigree (NUSAP); Quality Assurance; Scenario Analysis; Sensitivity Analysis; and Stakeholder Involvement.[4]

Only a subset of this spectrum is reviewed below, namely those methods that specifically engage expertise and reflection in a dialogic or deliberative fashion. These are: Stakeholder Involvement; Extended Peer Review; Expert Elicitation; Quality Assurance; and Scenario Analysis (here considered as a terrain for collaborative learning). This selection is not to imply the irrelevance of the other, more analytical KQA techniques. Rather it is because the focus in this chapter is placed on the specific contributions of dialogue and deliberation processes as complementary to the analytical techniques.

Stakeholder Involvement

Stakeholder involvement—not only in the decision-making process, but also in modelling and scenario development processes—can help to assess and manage complex (environmental) problems in a better way. This potential can be tapped in various ways, notably: (i) by enabling stakeholders to articulate issues of concern and to improve the problem framing for research and policy; (ii) by utilizing their own (non-scientific) knowledge and observations and their capacity to invent new options; and (iii) by involving them actively in the quality control of the operational knowledge that is co-produced (extended peer review).[5]

---

[4]References to detailed descriptions and to supporting software tools for this spectrum of KQA methods and tools are provided in Refsgaard et al. (2005b, 2007). For several of the methodologies, more extensive descriptions are available in the RIVM/MNP Tool Catalogue that served as a starting point for the overviews presented by Refsgaard et al. (2005b, forthcoming) and Van der Sluijs et al. (2004).

[5]The RIVM/MNP Guidance for Uncertainty Assessment and Communication

Table 2.2: The Uncertainty Matrix of the Tools

Type → / Location ↓	Level of uncertainty (From determinism, through probability and possibility, to ignorance)			Nature of uncertainty			Value-ladenness of choices
	Statistical uncertainty (range+ probability)	Scenario-uncertainty ('what-if' option)	Recognized Ignorance	Knowledge related uncertainty	Variability related uncertainty	Qualification of knowledge base (backing)	
Context — Ecological, technological, economic, social, and political representation	SA, QA, EE	Sc, QA, SI, EE	Sc, MQC, QA, SI, NUSAP/EP, EE	NUSAP/EP, MQC, QA, EE	NUSAP/EP, MQC, QA, EE	NUSAP/EP, MQC, QA, PR, EPR, EE	CRA, PRIMA, Sc, AA, SI, EE, PR, EPR
Data (in general sense) — Measurements+ Monitoring data; Survey data			Sc, QA, NUSAP, MQC, DV, MV	NUSAP, MQC, DV, QA, EE	NUSAP, MQC, DV, QA, EE	NUSAP, MQC, QA, PR, EPR, EE	CRA, PRIMA
M o d e l — Model inputs — Measurements monitoring data; survey data	SA, Tier 1, MCA, EE	Sc, EE					Sc, PR, EPR, SI
Model structure — Parameters			EE	EE	EE	EE	SI

(contd...)

Table 2.2 (contd...)

Location ↓ / Type →	Level of uncertainty (From determinism, through probability and possibility, to ignorance)			Nature of uncertainty			
	Statistical uncertainty (range+ probability)	Scenario-uncertainty ('what-if' option)	Recognized Ignorance	Knowledge related uncertainty	Variability related uncertainty	Qualification of knowledge base (backing)	Value-ladenness of choices
Relations	SA, MMS, EE, MQC, MC	Sc, MMS	NUSAP, MQC, MC, MV	MQC, NUSAP, QA, EE	MQC, NUSAP, QA, EE	MQC, NUSAP, MC, MV, PR, EPR, EE	CRA, PRIMA, MMS, PR, EPR, SI
Technical Model — Software and hardware-implement	QA, SA	QA, SA	QA, SA	PR	PR	PR	SA, PR
Expert Judgement — Narratives; storylines; advice	SA, QA, EE	Sc, QA, SI, EE	Sc, MQC, QA, SI, NUSAP/EP, EE	NUSAP/EP, MQC, QA, EE	NUSAP/EP, MQC, QA, EE	NUSAP/EP, MQC, QA, PR, EPR, EE	CRA, PRIMA, Sc, AA, SI, PR, EPR, EE
Outputs — (indicators; statements)	Sc, SA, Tier1, MC, EE	Sc, SA, EE	NUSAP, EE	NUSAP, MQC, PR, EPR, EE	NUSAP, MQC, PR, EPR, EE	NUSAP, MQC, QA, PR, EPR, EE	CRA, PRIMA, PR, EPR

Note: Entries printed in italics are not described in this toolbox because there are no standard methods to perform these tasks; AA: Actor Analysis; CRA: Critical Review of Assumptions; DV: Data Validation; EE: Expert Elicitation; EP: Extended Pedigree scheme; EPR: Extended Peer Review (review by stakeholders); MC: Model Comparison; MCA: Tier 2 analysis/Monte Carlo Analysis; MMS: Multiple Model Simulation; MQC: Model Quality Checklist; MV: Model Validation; NUSAP: Numerical, Unit, Spread, Assessment, and Pedigree PR: Peer Review; PRIMA: Pluralistic Framework for Integrated Uncertainty Management and Risk Analysis; QA: Quality Assurance; SA: Sensitivity Analysis; Sc: Scenario Analysis; SI: Stakeholder Involvement; Tier 1: Tier 1 analysis (error propagation equation).

Among the strengths of stakeholder involvement are that it increases the level of public accountability and, through the common ground built up and collaborative learning between technical experts and others that it entails, it may increase public confidence in and support for implementation of subsequent management decisions.

Extended Peer Review (review by stakeholders)

Extended peer review is, in this case, the involvement of stakeholders in the quality assurance of the modelling process. Stakeholders' reasoning, observation, and imagination are not bounded by scientific rationality. This can be beneficial when tackling ill-structured, complex problems. Consequently, the knowledge and perspectives of the stakeholders can bring in valuable new views on the problem and relevant information on that problem. The latter is known as 'extended facts'. This is clearly related with Funtowicz extended model of science and policy (see Introduction in this volume). Stakeholders can contribute to the quality of knowledge in a number of ways. These include improvement of the quality of the problem formulation and the questions addressed by the scientists; the contribution of knowledge on local conditions, which may help determine which data are strong and relevant or which response options are feasible; providing personal observations, which may lead to new foci for empirical research addressing dimensions of the problem that were previously overlooked; criticism of assumptions made by the scientist, which may lead to changes towards assumptions that better match real life conditions; and creative thinking of mechanisms and scenarios through which projected environmental and hydrological changes may affect different sectors of society.

The main strength of extended peer review is that it allows the use of extra knowledge (or in the words of Collins and Evans (2002) 'uncertified expertise') from non-scientific sources. The key limitations lie in the difficulty for stakeholders to understand the sometimes complex and abstract concepts, to ensure representativeness of the selected stakeholders, and in the power asymmetries that may be reproduced.

(Van der Sluijs et al. 2004) has a section on stakeholder involvement, including an instrument for discourse analysis. The HarmoniCOP project has developed a typology to characterize tools to support the public participation process in relation to implementation of the Water Framework Directive (Maurel 2003).

Expert Elicitation

Expert elicitation is a structured process to elicit subjective judgements from experts. It is widely used in quantitative risk analysis to quantify uncertainties in cases where there are no or too few direct empirical data available to infer on uncertainty. Usually the subjective judgement is represented as a 'subjective' probability density function (PDF) reflecting the expert's degree of belief. Typically it is applied in situations where there is scarce or insufficient empirical material for a direct quantification of uncertainty, and where it is relevant to obtain defensible results (Hora 1992).

Several elicitation protocols have been developed, amongst which the much-used Stanford Research Institute Protocol is the first one (Spetzler and von Holstein 1975). Expert elicitation typically involves the following steps: (i) identify and select experts; (ii) explain to the expert the nature of the problem and the elicitation procedure; create awareness of biases in subjective judgements and explore these; (iii) clearly define the quantity to be assessed and chose a scale and unit familiar to the expert; (iv) discuss the state of knowledge on the quantity at hand (strengths and weaknesses in available data, knowledge gaps, qualitative uncertainties); (v) elicit extremes of the distribution; (vi) assess these extremes: could the range be broader than stated? (vii) further elicit and specify the distribution (shape and percentiles or characterizing parameters); (viii) verify with the expert that the distribution that you constructed from the expert's responses correctly represents the expert's beliefs; and (ix) decide whether or not to aggregate the distributions elicited from different experts (this only makes sense if the experts had the same mental models of the quantity for which a distribution was elicited).

Expert elicitation has the potential to make use of all available knowledge that cannot easily be formalized otherwise. The limitations are linked to the subjectivity of the results that are sensitive to the selection of experts. In case of differences among experts it may be difficult to reach consensus on the uncertainties.

Quality Assurance

Quality assurance (QA) for present purposes is defined as protocols and guidelines to support the proper application of models. Important aims of QA are to ensure the use of best practice, to build consensus among the various actors involved in the modelling process, and to ensure that the expected accuracy and model performance are in accordance with the project objectives.

Key elements of QA procedures include: (i) framing of problem and definition of the purpose of the modelling study; (ii) assessment of sources of uncertainties jointly with managers (public administration, company strategists, policy makers, etc.), modellers, and stakeholders and establishment of accuracy requirements by translation of the manager and stakeholder needs to preliminary performance criteria; (iii) performance of model validation tests, that is, testing of model performance against independent data that have not been used for calibration in order to assess the accuracy and credibility of the model simulations for situations comparable to those where it is intended to be used; and (iv) reviews carried out by independent auditors with subsequent consultation between the modeller, the managers, and possibly the stakeholders at different phases of the modelling project.[6]

QA improves the chances that best practice is used, it makes it possible to involve stakeholders in the modelling process in a formalized framework, and it improves the transparency and reproducibility. However, if not designed and performed thoroughly, QA may become a 'rubber stamp' and generate false credibility.

Scenario Analysis as a Terrain of Collaborative Learning

Scenario Analysis, in its formal usage, aims to describe credible and internally consistent sequences of events to explore how the future may, could, or should evolve from the past and present (van der Heijden 1996). A wide spectrum of alternative futures can be explored through scenario analysis and, as such, scenario analysis is also a tool or method that can deal explicitly with different assumptions about the future and about our knowledge of the future.

Explicit use of scenario methods can help to ensure that assumptions about future developments are made transparent and documented. For quantitative scenarios, the analysis is limited to those aspects of reality that can be quantified. However, through incorporation of

---

[6]Many QA guidelines exist such as Middlemis (2000) and Van Waveren et al. (1999). The HarmoniQuA project (Scholten et al. 2007; Refsgaard et al., 2005a) has developed a comprehensive set of QA guidelines for multiple modelling domains combined with a supporting software tool, MoST (downloadable via *www.harmoniqua.org*).

qualitative narrative with quantification, scenario development and comparison is, indeed, one of the few ways that it is possible to organize reflection about the unknown future, in a way that permits a diversity of points of view to be expressed in description (the possible futures) and in judgement—first, concerning the plausibility of assumptions leading to different futures; and second, in normative terms concerning the acceptability or not (and the reasons why or why not) of the various postulated futures.[7]

INTEGRATION OF UNCERTAINTY IN A DELIBERATIVE APPROACH

For a given social concern or policy problem there are always, both in theory and in practice, many feasible procedures for obtaining scientific and policy-relevant information. This implies the permanent possibility of considering the same object or method of enquiry from two or more quite distinct normative and epistemological positions. The approach of post-normal science advocates the enrichment of understanding of complex problems by interpersonal dialogue and debate. It thus poses the question of how the pursuit of knowledge quality can be framed in relation to the challenge of reconciling different points of view (O'Connor 1999).

Putting an emphasis on plurality does not mean to say that all methods and perspectives are assessed as 'equally good'. Rather, the question arises as to how to assess the merit of different insights, claimed insights, and knowledge claims? How might we decide what constitutes mere opinion, erroneous belief, ideological preconception, scientific observation, hypothesis, or inference? And how might we develop a useful knowledge base for policy action?

Deliberation Support Tools for KQA

The underlying KQA problem is reflexive (with a problem of infinite regress), because it leads to ask: how do we assess different perspectives on the assessment of KQA. As is already illustrated by the diversity of methods and protocols, etc. highlighted above for uncertainty characterization and appraisal, a great variety of justifications and 'tests' of adequacy can be invoked in relation to knowledge claims about any given situation. These include traditional scientific quality

---

[7]We return to some aspects of scenario analysis, as a support for extended peer review, later in the chapter.

criteria such as internal coherence, falsifiability, ability to account for observed phenomena, and fecundity for orienting research. They also include considerations that we might term religious, cultural, aesthetic, or social, and that answer in various ways to such considerations as perceived usefulness for the daily business of life, guidance as to right action, effectiveness for conflict resolution, and convenience in the exercise of power.

Hence, judgements about pertinence and adequacy of knowledge claims and about the significance of uncertainties do not relate just to the scientific quality (or defensibility) of the knowledge, information, or opinion as assessed by scientific criteria alone. They relate also and above all to the roles that can be played by (and claimed for) different sorts of knowledge in their diverse cultural, social, and policy contexts.

This raises the question as to what extent is it possible and appropriate to be attentive to different points of view on KQA? To what extent and in what sense might 'integration' of different opinions, understandings, and perspectives be desirable? In what terms might this integration be attempted?

In the dialogical perspective adopted here (see also O'Connor 1999), the emphasis is on exploring knowledge 'fitness for purpose' through reciprocal communication and the mutual learning capacity of persons-in-society. The starting point in a KQA enquiry would be to seek to understand the ways that the concerned individuals and populations (or, in a policy context, the stakeholders) themselves understand, account for, and judge events and possible futures (with their risks and uncertainties). In this way, we give weight to the reasoning and reasons underlying people's own actions, preoccupations, and opinions. In this approach, scientific enquiries and analyses are to be judged—validated or invalidated—only partly by reference to their affirmed 'internal' norms of coherence, fecundity, and rigour. What is just as fundamental is to situate scientific knowledge claims and processes by reference to the 'social', 'cultural', and 'stakeholder' considerations of quality relating to the particular situation and circumstances of the enquiry.

As has been suggested in the themes of post-normal science, where decision stakes are high and there are scientifically non-resolvable uncertainties, value-plurality and social controversies over decision criteria tend to emerge as glaring social facts. What this means is that many different points of view can be expressed about what matters and why, none of which is wholly convincing (to everybody, all of the time) and none of which deals entirely adequately with all aspects of the situation, but none of which can be wholly rejected (by everybody) as having nothing at all relevant to say about the situation and about what should be done and why. Claims of knowledge and opinion are thus bound together with sentiments about meaning and significance—the properly social dimensions—and science practice has to find its roles in this sea of meanings and passions and aspirations and convictions.

Knowledge in the sense of inter-subjective understanding is thus to be distinguished from the sort of knowledge obtainable through measurement of objects and physical processes and the scientific prolongations such as modelling based on logics of deductive explanation or geared to prediction. Two irreducible dimensions along the plane of social science knowledge—and, in particular, knowledge about uncertainty—are, first, the need to interpret social events and their significance, and, second, the need for this knowledge to be expressed socially, that is, shared and communicated. In other words, such dimensions of KQA are accessible through dialogue, and can be the object of structured elucidation and communication through tools and methods designed to facilitate such dialogues and to structure exchanges between concerned parties and the documentation of these exchanges and their results.

In line with this deliberative approach to knowledge quality assessment, a number of multimedia tools have recently been developed that permit a community of users to evaluate the pertinence of knowledge in environmental socio-economic and cultural contexts. The rest of this section discusses two such tools: the 'KerBabel™ Indicator Kiosk' (KIK) as a deliberation support tool designed to establish a dialogue around indicators; and the 'KerBabel™ Deliberation Matrix' (kerDST) designed to structure information, judgements, and communication in the assessment of options for action or prospects for the future.[8]

---

[8]The *Kerbabel©* tools are developed by IACA team (Incertitudes, Analyses, Concertation & Aménagements) at the C3ED (Research Centre on Economics and Ethics for Environment and Development) based at the University of Versailles Saint-Quentin-en-Yvelines, Guyancourt, France. These developments have been substantially funded through European projects (notably GOUVERNe, ViRTUALiS, SRDTOOLS, PASARELAS and ALARM).

Extended Peer Community and Judgements about Pertinence of Indicators

In a multi-stakeholder deliberation context, the role of scenario development is the construction of a set of exploratory views of the future that acts as a support allowing stakeholders to discuss and appraise the relevant action, policy, decision or uncertainty, and governance issues. Except in very extreme situations (dictatorship, etc.), the evaluation of scenarios—or of options for action—takes place from many different points of view. In participatory or deliberative assessment processes this is by design. As multiple perspectives are brought to bear on a common ground (the scenario set) then the tensions, conflicts of interests, uncertainties, and dissent (amongst scientists as well as decision makers, administrators, and stakeholders from different walks of commercial activity and civil society) can be expressed and explored in a structured way.

The evaluation process, therefore, is not purely analytical. Rather, it is a social process that may have strong interactive and inter-subjective dimensions, opening up the possibility of 'emergent' properties. In this context, a social process of comparative evaluation of scenarios or options for action can readily become a framework for *inter alia* appraisal of knowledge quality and uncertainties.

We take the example of kerDST (O'Connor 2006a,b; O'Connor et al. 2007) that provides a framework for carrying out an indicator-supported multi-stakeholder multi-criteria assessment. With this evaluation tool,[9] the basic idea is that Each Stakeholder type will make a judgement (good, fair, bad etc.) about each option with reference to each performance criterion or issue. These judgements produce a composite picture, visualized on-screen as a three dimensional array of 'cells' somewhat akin to the well-known Rubik's Cube. For example, from one angle of observation, one obtains rectangular arrays of cells, each being a layer of the Matrix, within which each row represents the evaluations (issue by issue) furnished by a given class of stakeholders for successive scenarios (see Figure 2.2). Or, looked at from another angle, one obtains the evaluations by each stakeholder, of a given scenario. And so on.

Several variations for the use of kerDST are available, with increasing structure. The first and simplest variation is simply to colour the

---

[9]Available on-line since 2006 at *http://kerdst.c3ed.uvsq.fr/*

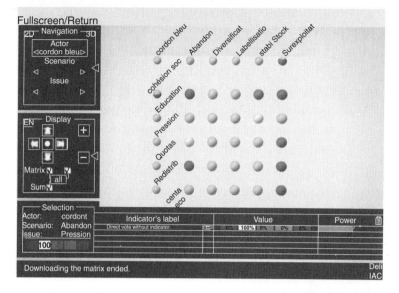

Figure 2.1   Screen image from the KerBabel™ Deliberation Matrix

Source: O'Connor (2006a, b. 2007).

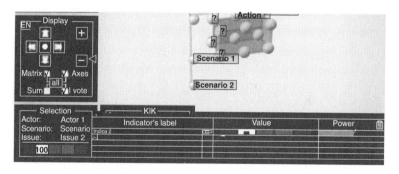

Figure 2.2:   Snapshot of the KerBabel™ Deliberation Matrix

Source: O'Connor (2006a, b, 2007).

cells (stakeholder x scenario x performance issue) using an intuitive code such as [red = bad], [yellow = not so bad], [green = good], [white = no idea], [blue = don't care]. A second, slightly more sophisticated variant is 'colouring the cells of the Deliberation Matrix' but with, at the same time, use of a text box for adding an explanation or commentary of the judgement (colour) made.

Moving beyond this impressionistic evaluation process, a more 'objective' basis or motivation for the judgement (colour) proposed in each cell can be constructed through the selection, for each cell of the Deliberation Matrix, of a 'basket' of indicators that are taken to characterize relevant attributes of the scenario or choice/action under scrutiny. With this procedure, the judgement at the cell level in the Matrix is obtained not by a simple choice of colour for the cell, but as a weighted 'amalgam' of the qualitative judgements assigned to each indicator in the 'basket'. (In the case shown below, only one indicator has so far been put in the 'basket', its colour code being Yellow). In general, the colour (or composite) of each matrix cell is a function of the relative weight and significance attributed to each indicator in the corresponding basket.

The kerDST evaluation process and outcome is thus built by several layers of judgements: the selection, from amongst the range of 'candidate indicators' available, of a set of (not more than five) indicators for each basket; the interpretation (significance) to be attributed to each indicator in a basket; the relative or absolute importance (weight) of each indicator in relation to the others in the basket, for arriving at a synthetic judgement for the cell as a whole; the overall comparison, via the Deliberation Matrix, between scenarios based on the multi-stakeholder multi-criteria profile of each one. The underlying vision of collaborative learning is based on the hypothesis that individual reflection and/or exchanges of views between protagonists in a deliberation/negotiation process may lead to modifications at any or all or the steps of the choices and judgements leading up to an entry in a cell of the Matrix table. Those 'representing' stakeholders of one type may try to persuade stakeholders of another type to modify their criteria or relative weighting; and so on.

The indicator mobilization process with kerDST has several successive cycles or components that can be pursued in a progressive way. This is the feature that allows, by design, a progressive initiation to KQA considerations:

- It may well be that, to start with, the indicators selected for each 'basket' are simply declared, without their exact values being yet known, specified, or estimated. In such a situation, the evaluation process is still qualitative and functions as an 'alignment exercise', where indicators, through being placed in 'baskets', are being linked (by or on behalf of different actors) to specified categories of performance or social values. In this sense, a judgement is being made about the pertinence of the indicator or 'fitness' for its evaluation function.[10]

- As indicators are identified in this way as pertinent, it becomes clear to those involved that it will be necessary to measure or estimate the values (qualitative or quantitative) for each site, strategy, policy option, or scenario etc., and also to specify Reference Values (RVs) against which an indicator will be scored as good (green) or bad (red), etc. The process of RV specification (or debate) reinforces the alignment exercise, through the focus being placed not on what indicators or what scores for the indicators, but rather on why (and by whom) this or that indicator is considered to signal something of societal importance.

- Thereafter, an iterative process can be developed, for as long as deemed interesting (within the available resources for the analysts and stakeholders concerned), of focusing analytical work (models, scenarios, maps, etc.) in order to improve estimates for high-pertinence indicators; of putting money values onto key indicators for that part of the appraisal that is deemed 'monetizable', of discussing RVs relative to community goals, and so on. In this context, there will in general be uncertainties and controversies; these fundamental issues of KQA are thus posed plainly within the context of the evaluation or governance problem being appraised.

[10]In fact, the on-line kerDST system generates statistics on the use of indicators within a given Deliberation Matrix and, in this way, provides data about a user's or user community's judgements about information pertinence. The sources of candidate indicators at this stage are complex. On the one hand, scenarios may be described and portrayed using a great variety of types of information, including qualitative descriptions (for example, the scenario 'storyline' and information on institutional changes) and also quantitative indicators (for example, numerical and visual information specifying land uses, fish species catches, demographic profiles, prices and costs, etc. through time and on a geographically distributed basis portrayed through analytical models, maps, and so on). A diversity of performance concepts are thus already incorporated as components of the scenario descriptions and, as such, are already presumed or immediately lend themselves to exploitation as indicators. On the other hand, there may be key performance concepts identified through interactions with stakeholders (formal research, public debate, etc.) that are not analytically incorporated into scenario descriptions but which are nonetheless considered as potentially interesting types of 'observations about' the situation. The kerDST system allows such concepts to be declared for their pertinence, thus opening up the question of their measurability, etc.

The Deliberation Matrix framework for indicator-based evaluation thus highlights the information requirements for, on the one hand, representing the situation and its possible evolution (via, we presume, a set of options or scenarios) and, on the other hand, making judgements about the present and eventual future situation (via a battery of indicators). More particularly, kerDST provides a framework for a structured discussion and evaluation of the significance, for the policy or governance issues being addressed, of the different forms of uncertainty that may be associated with the various classes of empirical information, modelling, and simulation results being introduced into the deliberation.

KQA through Dialogue on Indicators

The kerDST scenario evaluation framework, like many other systems and situations mobilizing models, data, and indicators, highlights the need for cataloguing systems that can organize and make accessible a great diversity of information with reference to, on the one hand, the various sources and, on the other hand, the envisaged contexts of use.

We present here, as exemplary of recognition of this double need, the on-line meta-information systems developed by the KerBabel™ team at the Research Centre on Economics and Ethics for Environment and Development (C3ED) in France, with the generic name KIK. The KIK is conceived, broadly, as a 'forum' permitting users to build up a catalogue of 'candidate indicators' for a decision or governance problem, and allowing an on-going dialogue between the producers and users of information (O'Connor 2004, 2007). As a function of need, there are more or less elaborate formats.

The on-line kerDST system, as described above, offers the facility for declaring indicators and building up an indicator catalogue (or KIK) adapted directly to the problem being addressed.

- In order to facilitate quick progress in mobilizing indicators in an assessment process, the kerDST system proposes a 'mini-KIK' catalogue, with a very restricted number of meta-information fields. At the moment of declaring an indicator within the mini-KIK, the user on line is invited to declare the name (or 'label') of the indicator, and there is also the opportunity to provide a short 'description', and to add 'comments'.
- In the process of selecting indicators for 'baskets', the person or group undertaking the assessment with kerDST can either choose indicators from amongst those already defined in the mini-KIK

catalogue, or contribute their own indicator suggestions into an evolving mini-KIK catalogue.

A full documentation of an indicator-based assessment requires not only that estimates be recorded for an indicator's value (or level, score, etc.) for each situation or scenario, but also that information be given about the basis for estimation, the sources, the uncertainties, and the controversies. Within the mini-KIK, the comments text-box may be used in a pragmatic way to signal RVs and other classes information (for example, controversies and uncertainties) that may bear on the judgement made. However, full treatment of the KQA issues requires a much more comprehensive meta-information framework, and this is the vocation of the full KIK described below.

The detailed KIK design considerations follow the principle of a 'progressive disclosure of information' (Guimarães Pereira et al. 1998; Guimarães Pereira and O'Connor 1999). For each indicator (and thus, for the KIK system as a whole) three levels of meta-information are established.

- At level 1, the user sees the overall structure and profile of meta-information offered for an indicator (see Figure 2.1 showing a screen-copy from a KIK implementation at the C3ED).

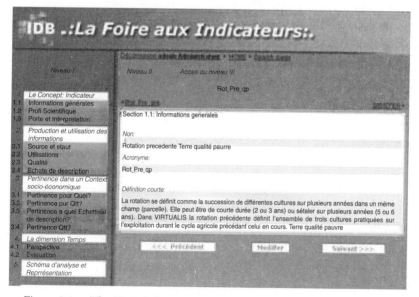

Figure 2.3:   The KerBabel™ Indicator Kiosk

Source: O'Connor (2004).

- At level 2, a standard format is offered for the characterization of individual indicators, covering both (i) the scientific and technical considerations of rigour, coherence, measurement, uncertainty, validation, and interpretation and (ii) the user-oriented considerations of pertinence for framing a decision problem and for supporting a multi-user learning activity. This framework includes provision for judgements and 'comments' to be offered by 'producers' and 'end-users' of the information (both of whom are considered to be among the stakeholders in the deliberation problem being addressed).

- Finally, at level 3, the user may be referred to elements of supplementary information (which may, depending on character and availability, include access to the 'data' itself). Notably, the user is offered, throughout level 2 of the main KIK, opportunities to consult (through hyperlinks) the components of complementary information.

The level 1 structure shows the KerBabel™ Indicator Kiosk as built up in five main sections. Section KIK.1 and Section KIK.2 characterize the information category 'in itself', that is, its 'content'. In these sections, some standard information and meta-information for KQA is provided (for example, measurement units, data sources, characterization of uncertainty, etc.).

Subsequent sections of the KIK then propose meta-information relating specifically to the envisaged contexts of 'use' of the information in multi-stakeholder multi-criteria deliberation processes. Section KIK.3 relates the information category to the 'issues' being addressed, including attention to the spectrum of stakeholders, the different scales of observation and action, and the range of sites under consideration. Postulates of an indicator's evolution through time, for example, in the case of a comparative scenario analysis, require distinct considerations as framed in Section KIK.4; this includes uncertainty in all its forms. Finally, the KIK has a reflexive component, containing in Section KIK.5 a documentation of the ways that the information is mobilized/exploited in the representation framework of the reference study or project.

Our focus here is on Sections KIK.3 and KIK.4, as an example of how a framework for science–policy/researcher–stakeholder dialogue can be built up, making a platform for accessing and judging the reliability and pertinence of information produced and used in widely disparate contexts. Looking at Sections KIK.3 and

KIK.4, it can be seen that, in effect, the definition of contexts of information production and use in the KIK privileges five axes:

- The scale(s) at which observation, analysis, and/or measurement takes place;
- The geographical places or site(s);
- The decision making, management, evaluation, or governance issues that are or might be in mind;
- The stakeholders that might have something to contribute;
- The scenarios within which the information may play a descriptive or evaluative role.

The role of the Section KIK.3 meta-information is to frame indicator pertinence as a function of physical and societal contexts of use or, in other words, a portrayal of the information's 'fitness for purpose'. The situation-specific facets include, notably, the set of 'performance issues' that are identified for the organization of the multi-criteria evaluation (KIK.3.1) and the set of stakeholder categories to be distinguished in the framing of deliberation perspectives (KIK.3.2). Beyond these aspects, depending on the overall framework of analysis and representation, there may (or may not) be a need to specify the organizational scale(s) at which the information is applicable (KIK.3.3) and/or the range of sites for which a characterization (description, evaluation and/or comparison, and/or aggregation) is envisaged (KIK.3.4).

The role of Section KIK.4 is to frame the time-development of indicators. Provision is made for characterizing whether and how each indicator is engaged for exploration of 'what if?' situations, for example, in the (comparative) characterization of scenarios. This constitutes Section KIK.4.1 of the KIK. Provision is also made for characterizing the uncertainties and inherent indeterminacies of any futures/scenario perspective. This constitutes Section KIK.4.2.

Overall, KIK is envisaged as an interactive knowledge management system that complements other tools of representation and evaluation. For example, it can be a framework for the documentation of information categories employed in integrated environmental assessment and modelling, map representations, transects, etc. used in scenario and policy evaluation work. This would allow scientists and other stakeholders ready access to the definitions of information concepts, the sources, their uses in models, and considerations of the pertinence of the information as a function of need and context. It can also, as highlighted above, be a framework for the management and accessing of 'candidate indicators' that are proposed for application in a multi-criteria multi-stakeholder deliberation framework.

In this context, it is useful to note that the considerations offered here about building dialogues between 'producers' and 'users' of information remain applicable even if there is not a fully integrated analysis going on. The KIK can be used to organize a documentation of views about the pertinence of information sets, as a function of need and context (that is, for one site or another, for one issue or another, for this or that stakeholder group, at different scales of observation and governance, and so on), even in the absence of any formal modelling, policy evaluation, or decision scenario framework.

The reason for this robustness is that clear communication of 'context' is more important than detailed 'content' for building meaningful dialogue. Neither 'knowledge' nor 'information' means anything without reference to a context that permits the data, measures, or ideas to be interpreted and to take on significance or meaning. A good indicator set, modelling exercise, map representation, etc. must not just carry cogent information, it must also clearly connote frameworks of purpose and collective action.

CONCLUSIONS

In this chapter, three features have been highlighted as complementary in the effort to integrate and to articulate uncertainty across its technical, methodological, epistemological, and societal dimensions. The first concerns diagnosis of uncertainty. The second is characterization and analysis, which is linked to the quality of knowledge and its evaluation by the scientific community and/or an enlarged community of peers. The third deals with the pertinence of knowledge, here illustrated by integrating uncertainty in a dialogue about mobilizing indicators for multi-criteria evaluation in a comparative scenario perspective.

The post-normal perspective on science and technology encourages us to adopt a dialogue model of knowledge (Funtowicz and Ravetz 1990; O'Connor 1999). But, an 'epistemology of dialogue' has many facets. Different components of social science evoke a spectrum of social and institutional dimensions, including the pertinence of multi-stakeholder dialogue and of 'concertative' governance. Common to all these is the notion of a 'dialogue' that can be proposed—and deliberatively constructed—between the disparate components of society, including dialogues between different perspectives on science and on the science-policy interface, between different social science models and perspectives of governance, and so on.

Two themes are fundamental for this dialogue model of knowledge. First, under prevailing conditions of 'imperfection of knowledge', it is not necessarily to be presumed that disciplinary sciences advance towards a full unity of knowledge. This 'full unity', even if in some metaphysics it exists, is infinitely removed from our sight. What we are left with is the perspective of mobilizing incomplete knowledge and exploring considerations of pertinence of knowledge as a function of context. Accepting this standpoint means reappraising the role and status of science as a help for navigating in complexity. Not only is knowledge always 'incomplete' in ways that can pose real practical dilemmas, but there can also, at any time, be an irreducible and legitimate plurality of theoretical perspectives and frameworks of analysis. This seems true for the natural science of complex systems and, even more so, for the conditions of social life and, *a fortiori*, for the social sciences. Hence, the theme of dialogue is particularly pertinent for the interdisciplinary domain of policy science at the crossroads of complex systems sciences and the social sciences.

Second, knowledge in the sense of inter-subjective understanding and meaningful relations is fundamentally to be distinguished from the sort of knowledge obtainable uniquely through measurement of objects and physical processes and the scientific prolongations such as modelling based on logics of deductive explanation or geared to prediction. Two irreducible dimensions along the plane of social science knowledge are (i) the need to interpret social events and their significance, and (ii) the prospect and desire for this knowledge to be expressed socially, that is, shared and communicated. Moreover, the structures of meaning, symbolic reference, and so on are 'cultural' forms that are largely pre-existent for each individual and that 'condition' and permanently socialize the individual just as much as the physical circumstances of life.

These points of epistemology help to illuminate the hopes placed in 'stakeholder dialogue' and deliberation. One of the central tenets of 'deliberative democracy' as a political model is that socially robust and legitimate decisions on complex subjects cannot rely on elites or on professional expertise alone; there also needs to be the expression of the wider 'social demand' through the integration of a broad spectrum of society's stakeholders. Many distinct principles, justifications, and ethics about what is fair and right can and will be put up for consideration. Evaluation of choices will be framed within a socio-political process where conflicts emerge and must be resolved between competing interests, between people holding different value systems and different principles of judgement, and also between different representations of future states and different visions of the world. The challenge then is to work with a permanent exchange, argumentation, and sometimes compromise between different principles of choice.

REFERENCES

Collins, H.M. and R. Evans, (2002), 'The Third Wave of Science Studies: Studies of Expertise and Experience', Working Paper Series Paper, Vol. 25, School of Social Sciences, Cardiff University.

Faucheux, S. and M. O'Connor, (2000), 'Technosphère versus ècosphère. Quel arbitrage? Choix technologiques et menaces environnementales: signaux faibles, controverses et décision', *Futuribles*, Vol. 251.

Funtowicz, S., (2006), 'Why Knowledge Assessment?' in A. Guimarães Pereira, S. Guedes Vaz, and S. Tognetti (eds), *Interfaces between Science and Society*, Sheffield: Greenleaf Publishing, pp. 138–45.

Funtowicz, S.O. and J.R. Ravetz, (1990), *Uncertainty and Quality in Science for Policy*, Dordrecht: Kluwer.

_____, (1994a), 'La science post-normale et les systémes complexes émergents', *Revue Internationale de SystÈmique*, Vol. 8, nos. 4–5, pp. 353–77.

_____, (1994b), 'The Worth of a Songbird: Ecological Economics as a Post-Normal Science', *Ecological Economics,* Vol. 10, pp. 197–207.

Faucheux, S. and M. O'Connor, (2000), Technosphère versus ècosphère. Quel arbitrage? Choix technologiques et menaces environnementales: signaux faibles, controverses et decision?, Futuribles, Vol. 251.

Funtowicz, S., M. O'Connor, and J. Ravetz, (1997), 'Emergent Complexity and Ecological Economics', in J. Van den Bergh and J. Van der Straaten (eds), *Economy and Ecosystems in Change: Analytical and Historical Approaches*, Cheltenham: Edward Elgar, pp. 75–95.

Gallopin, G.C., S.O. Funtowicz, M. O'Connor, and J.R. Ravetz, (2001), 'La science pour le XXIème siècle: du contrat social aux fondements scientifiques', *Revue internationale des Sciences Socials*, No. 168, June, pp. 239–50.

Guimarães Pereira, A. and M. O'Connor, (1999), 'Information and Communication Technology and the Popular Appropriation of Sustainability Problems', *International Journal of Sustainable Development,*Vol. 2, No. 3, pp. 411–24.

Guimarães Pereira, A., C. Gough, and B. De Marchi, (1998), 'Computers, Citizens and Climate Change: The Art of Communicating Technical Issues', *International Journal of Environment and Pollution*, Vol. 11, No. 3, pp. 266–89.

Hora, S.C., (1992), 'Acquisition of Expert Judgement: Examples from Risk Assessment', *Journal of Energy Engineering*, Vol. 118, pp. 136–48.

Janssen, P.H.M., A.C. Petersen, J.P. van der Sluijs, J.S. Risbey, and J.R. Ravetz, (2003), *RIVM/MNP Guidance for Uncertainty Assessment and Communication: Quickscan Hints and Actions List*, Bilthoven, The Netherlands: RIVM/MNP, ISBN 90-6960-105-2.

———, van der Sluijs, J. Risbey and J.R. Ravetz, (2005), 'A Guidance for Assessing and Communicating Uncertainties', *Water Science and Technology*, Vol. 52, No. 6, pp. 125–31.

Maurel, P. (ed.), (2003), 'Public Participation and the European Water Framework Directive: Role of Information and Communication Tools', Workpackage 3 Report of the HarmoniCOP Project, Cemagref, Montpellier, *www.harmonicop.info*.

Middlemis, H., (2000), 'Murray-Darling Basin Commission: Groundwater Flow Modelling Guideline', Project Report No. 125, South Perth, Western Australia: Aquaterra Consulting Pvt Ltd.

O'Connor, M., (1999), 'Dialogue and Debate in a Post-normal Practice of Science: A Reflexion', *Futures*, Vol. 31, pp. 671–87.

———, (2004), *The KerBabel Indicator Dialogue Box: Generic Design Specifications for the 'Indicator Dialogue Box'*—Version 3, Rapport de Recherche du C3ED, Guyancourt: UniversitÈ de Versailles St-Quentin-en-Yvelines.

———, (2006a), 'Building Knowledge Partnerships with ICT? Social and Technological Conditions of Conviviality', in A. Guimarães Pereira, S. Guedes Vaz, and S. Tognetti (eds), *Interfaces between Science and Society*, Sheffield: Greenleaf Publishing. pp. 298–325.

———, (2006b), *Deliberative Sustainability Assessment: Multiple Scales, Multiple Stakeholders, Multidisciplinarity and Multiple Bottom Lines*, Methodological study for Work Package WP6 of the SRDTOOLS Project (Methods and tools for evaluating the impact of cohesion policies on sustainable regional development, EC 6th Framework Programme, Contract No. 502485, 2005–2006), Rapport de Recherche du C3ED No. 2006–01, Guyancourt: Université de Versoilles St-quentin-en-Yvelines.

———, (2007), 'Multi-mediated Indicators and Deliberation: Knowledge Quality, Societal Choices and Environmental Learning through Multi-stakeholder Dialogues', *International Journal of Sustainable Development*, Vol. 10.

O'Connor, M. and S. van den Hove, (2001), 'Prospects for Concertation on Nuclear Risks and Technological Options: Innovations in Governance Practices for Sustainable Development in the European Union', *Journal of Hazardous Materials*, Vol. 86, pp. 77–99.

O'Connor, M., S. Faucheux, G. Froger, S. Funtowicz, and G. Munda, (1996), 'Emergent Complexity and Procedural Rationality: Post-Normal Science for Sustainability', in R. Costanza, O. Segura, and J. Martinez-Alier (eds), *Getting Down to Earth: Practical Applications of Ecological Economics*, Covelo, CA: Island Press, pp. 223–48.

O'Connor, M., P. Bureau, V. Reichel, and C. Sunde, (2007), 'Deliberative Sustainability Assessment with the on-line kerDST Deliberation Support Tool', *Cahiers du C3ED* No. 07–03, C3ED, Guyancourt: UVSQ.

Petersen, A.C., P.H.M. Janssen, J.P. van der Sluijs, J.S. Risbey, and J.R. Ravetz, (2003), *RIVM/MNP Guidance for Uncertainty Assessment and Communication: Mini-Checklist and Quickscan Questionnaire*, Bilthoven, The Netherlands: RIVM/MNP.

Refsgaard, J.C., H.J. Henriksen, W.G. Harrar, H. Scholten, and A. Kassahun, (2005a), 'Quality Assurance in Model based Water Management: Review of Existing Practice and Outline of New Approaches', *Environmental Modelling and Software*, Vol. 20, pp. 1201–15.

Refsgaard, J.C., J.P. van der Sluijs, A.L. Hojberg, and P.A. Vanrolleghem, (2005b), *HarmoniCa Guidance Uncertainty Analysis*, Report Commissioned by European Commission, Brussels, Belgium.

——, (2007), 'Uncertainly in the Environmental Modelling Process: A Framework and Guidance', *Environmental Modelling and Software*, Vol. 22, No. 11, pp. 1543–56.

Scholten, H., A. Kassahun, J.C. Refsgaard, T. Kargas, C. Gavardinas, and A.J.M. Beulens, (2007), 'A Methodology to Support Multidisciplinary Model-based Water Management', *Environmental Modelling and Software*, Vol. 22, pp. 743–59.

Spetzler, C.S. and S. von Holstein, (1975), 'Probability Encoding in Decision Analysis', *Management Science*, Vol. 22, No. 3.

van der Heijden, K., (1996), *Scenarios: The Art of Strategic Conversation*, John Wiley & Sons.

van den Hove, S., (2000), 'Participatory Approaches to Environmental Policy-making: The European Commission Climate Policy Process as a Case Study', *Ecological Economics*, Vol. 33, issue 3, June, pp. 457–72.

——, (2001), 'Approaches participatives la governance en matiere de development durable: une analyse en termes d'effects', in G. Froger (ed.), *Governance et Développement Durable Helbing & Lichtenhahn*, Bâle/Geneva/Munich.

Van der Sluijis, J.P., A.C. Petersen, P.H.M. Janssen, J.S. Risbey, and J.R. Ravetz, (2008), Exploring the quality of evidence for complex and contested policy decisions, Environmental Research Letters, 3, 024008 (9pp).

van der Sluijs J.P., P.H.M. Janssen, A.C. Petersen, P. Kloprogge, J.S. Risbey, W. Tuinstra, and J.R. Ravetz, (2004), *RIVM/MNP Guidance for Uncertainty Assessment and Communication: Tool Catalogue for Uncertainty Assessment (RIVM/MNP Guidance for Uncertainty Assessment and Communication Series, Volume 4)*, Report no.: NWS-E-2004–37, Utrecht/Bilthoven: Utrecht University and RIVM.

van der Sluijs, J.P., J. Risbey, P. Kloprogge, J. Ravetz, S. Funtowicz, S. Corral Quintana, A. Guimarães Pereira, B. de Marchi, A. Petersen, P. Janssen, R. Hoppe, and S. Huijs, (2003), *RIVM/MNP Guidance for Uncertainty Assessment and Communication: Detailed Guidance*, Copernicus Institute for Sustainable Development, Utrecht University, and RIVM–MNP, Utrecht, The Netherlands, Available at *www.nusap.net*.

van Waveren, R.H., S. Groot, H. Scholten, F. Van Geer, H.W^sten, R. Koeze and J. Noort, (1999), *Good Modelling Practice Handbook*, STOWA, Utrecht, The Netherlands (in Dutch). English version from *http:// www.landandwater.tudelft.nl/Downloads/GMP-uk.pdf*.

3

A Quality Assurance Framework for Policy Making
Proposing a Quality Assurance Assistant Tool (QAAT)

Serafin Corral Quintana

Public Policy Making: A Complex Process

Policy making cannot be looked at as a technocratic process. Governance issues imply, in many cases, interactions between Society and Nature. Such processes involve human beings' limited capacities for inquiry into issues characterized by different types of uncertainty (Simon 1957; Kahneman 2003), the frequent conflict between reasoned judgement and the exercise of political power (Lindblom 1959), as well as the central role of some stakeholders in policy making and social and political inequality (Crosby 1992; Dahl and Lindblom 1976).

One of the most prominent features of policy processes is their social nature. Policy issues cannot be analysed in isolation from the social context in which they occur. They are bound by different perceptions, perspectives, opinions, knowledges, and interests. As Lindblom (1993) argues, 'there is a deep and persistent unwillingness in Western culture to acknowledge the difficulties arising from the world's complexity and human's modest cognitive abilities...and unless political action is adjusted to take into account of the fact that complex problems cannot be understood fully, policy-making will fare much worse than it needs to'.

Different types of scientific uncertainties inherent to socio-environmental planning processes influence the planning processes. Uncertainty and ignorance are often evident when attempt is made to understand policy processes (Gibbons et al. 1994; Wynne 2005). Such ignorance requires new approaches for science and decision making. The assumption that more information means better decisions does not always hold. Techniques may now be more sophisticated, but they also unearth basic dilemmas at the heart of decision making. Can we attribute monetary values for the 'services' provided by the environment? Do we have to expand the scope of research to embrace ethical, social, and political issues?

Even though, traditionally the so-called problem-solving process—the framing process and the selection and implementation of the evaluation methodology in decision-making processes—has been considered to be the result of an objective scientific practice, this conception may be argued when decision making processes deal with socio-environmental matters. As suggested by the World Bank (1997), 'the application of evaluation methodologies requires a careful interpretation, and the limits of the analysis have to be understood completely from the base'.

Policy-making processes present an important degree of subjectivity due to social and scientific uncertainties. These processes cannot be seen as technocratic spaces where decisions are taken neutrally by a decision maker based on neutral scientific advice. The decision-making space is influenced by interests, value judgements, opinions, and perceptions; social actors will try, according to their possibilities, to manipulate that process to their own benefit, thus affecting the quality of the process and its outcome. This subjectivity is incorporated into the process from the earlier steps of the problem-solving process itself. During that process the context of analysis is framed and relevant subjects of analysis are chosen: impacts and relationships (including disregarded ones) taken into account; timing and spatial scale of the study decided; the decision-aid approaches applied, etc.

Schematically, the process of elaboration of public policies may be seen as the interaction of two dimensions (Figure 2.1):

 (i) the 'framework or decisional process', in which the process will be carried out. Actors interact among them, based on their perspectives and values, to reach their objectives and defend their positions, and

(ii) the 'analysis or problem-solving phase', which is related to the process of 'translating' the *problematique* into a decisional issue. The different problem-solving procedures, such as the information used, the choice of alternatives and criteria to be analysed, and the type of policy-aid model applied will determine the results obtained from this decisional procedure.

The recognition of such interaction modifies the commonly accepted role of neutrality played by the analysis within decision-

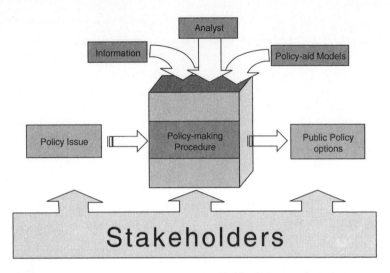

Figure 3.1:   Dimensions Interacting in a Public Policy-making Process

making process. Decision-aid procedures cannot be understood independently from the whole decision-making process (Becker 1978; Sen 1987; Coleman 1990; Dunleavy 1991). The analysis is not an alternative to policy[1] but it is a key component in the decision-making process, affecting and being affected by it. In some cases, these procedures may also be used to influence the results of a decision-making process. Following Lindblom (1993), 'more than facing directly the issue of public policies, the analysis frequently responds to certain agent's needs, especially public officers (with the aim of controlling other agents in interactive policy-making processes) or interest groups (to defend their interests or status)'.

Usually, the process of structuring public policy issues corresponds to the moment in which the ignorance and the uncertainty related to the subject of analysis disappear. The context framing, the selection of the variables to be analysed, the impacts to be measured, as well as the choice of the model imply the definition of a set of assumptions that move us from a 'world of uncertainty and ignorance' to which the socio-environmental questions beholds to a framework of constructed certainty in which the evaluation processes are carried out.

[1]The author refers to the divergent positions that schools of thought, such as the Incrementalism and the Policy Analysis, present while describing the characteristics and objectives of decision making processes and the role played by the decision-aid procedures. For a more detailed analysis, see Lindblom (1991) and Wildavsky (1984).

Thus, in the policy analysis only some types of uncertainty are stated and managed (generally those related to inexactness) while ignorance is driven out of the framework of analysis. Unknown impacts and its social effects, as well as some social and economical relations may rest outside the analysis. Together, the selection of approaches and evaluation techniques that only assess some aspects of the issue (usually the quantifiable ones) or look for an optimum solution will not allow a complete understanding of the *problematique*. The quality of a policy-making process will be strongly influenced by the choices taken during that framing process.

The methodology developed in the remaining sections of this chapter will explore a QA approach of the problem-solving phase of the elaboration of public policies. A QA Framework is proposed together with a set of quality assurance criteria as the basis for a quality assurance process. These criteria are tailored for a particular case study and address more specifically: the available information, the role of the analyst, and the decision model chosen during the problem-solving phase.

A QUALITY ASSURANCE FRAMEWORK FOR PUBLIC POLICY-MAKING PROCEDURES

In these terms, the full understanding of public policy-making processes requires a quality assurance process of the procedures used during the analysis phase (see Figure 3.1). Since the analysis phase may seriously influence the decision making process itself and its outcomes, it cannot remain as a 'black box' independent of some type of quality control.

When dealing with complex issues, a flexible methodology is necessary to allow the exploring of different aspects of the issue of concern. A term of reference is also necessary to facilitate the exploration and assessment of the characteristics of the planning processes. In this sense, the concept of quality, initially suggested by Funtowicz and Ravetz (1990, 1992, 1993) will be considered in the methodology proposed here.

Several definitions of quality have been proposed so far in the literature; the British Standard Institution (1979) and the ISO 8402 (ISO 1986) define quality as 'The totality of features and characteristics of a product or service that bear on its ability to satisfy stated or implied needs'. Crosby (1979) and Crosby (1996) define quality as 'adequacy to some requirements'. In these definitions, quality is considered as a pragmatic concept, or as Plato stated, 'the quality of something is measured by its ability of reaching its goal'. So, in all definitions the main idea is the necessity of satisfying the needs and expectations of the users, what could be defined as 'fitness for use'.

In the last few decades, the quality control process has been considered a fundamental practice for industrial activity, in this sense, the ISO 9000 in its section 0 considers that:

Most organizations—industrial, commercial or governmental—produce a product or service intending to satisfy a user's needs or requirements. Such requirements are often incorporated in 'specifications'. However, technical specifications may not in themselves guarantee that a customer's requirements will be consistently met. For example, there may be deficiencies in the specifications or in the organizational system to design and produce the product or service. Consequently, this has led to the development of quality system standards and guidelines that complement relevant product or service requirements given in the technical specification.

Public decisions are usually adopted in contexts of uncertainty, based on data and processes of moderate or unknown quality. Although there is a growing concern by experts, policy-makers, and the community at large on the uncertainties related to the available (and non-available) information about socio-environmental issues,[2] quality assurance procedures of decision-making activities have not been encouraged.

The QA Framework proposed here allows users (experts, decision makers, and stakeholders involved in decision-making processes) to explore the key aspects of such decision-making processes. According to that idea, the previous ISO 9000 statement could be rewritten as follows:

Most organizations (governments) produce a product or service (policies) intending to satisfy a user's needs or requirements (citizens). Such requirements are often incorporated in 'specifications'. However, technical specifications (decisions) may not in themselves guarantee that a customer's requirements (objectives) will be consistently met. For example, there may be deficiencies (uncertainties) in the specifications (information) or in the organizational system (decision-aid modelling) to design and produce the product or service. Consequently, this has led to the development of quality system standards and guidelines that complement relevant product or service requirements given in the technical specification.

[2]Examples of environmental issues are climate change and genetically modified organisms.

An Extended Quality Assurance Framework for Public Policy-making Processes

The QA Framework here proposed provides elements on quality, legitimacy, and reliability of the above-mentioned spheres of planning processes. It is based on the work done earlier by Funtowicz and Ravetz (1990) on the NUSAP system.[3] More concretely, this framework follows the idea behind the category Pedigree as presented in the NUSAP scheme and extends it to enable the assessment of the quality not only of quantitative information, but also of other types and sources of information and the uncertainty associated with other elements of the decision-making process.

Contrary to the production process of many products and services in which quality guidelines and standards can be designed by scientists and experts, the uncertainty inherent in socio-environmental decision matters and the difficulties of scientists not only in giving advice on them but also in characterizing them completely has suggested in recent years claims for extended processes. These extended processes require the inclusion of a plurality of perspectives into the process, the competence of experts being crucial; yet the inclusion of social actors[4] involved in the process is considered necessary. This implies a combination of knowledges that will facilitate a better comprehension of the *problematique*.

The need for new approaches openly challenges the dominance of technical expertise. The public has a wide range of views and understandings about the environment. People's knowledge is experience-led and is embedded in their social and political relationships. Relying solely on formal scientific knowledge to make decisions is short-sighted: public perspectives can also help frame the

[3]NUSAP is 'a notational system that enables different sorts of uncertainty in *quantitative* information to be displayed in a standardised and self-explanatory way. It enables providers and users of such information to be clear about its uncertainties. Since the management of uncertainty is at the core of the quality-control of *quantitative* information, the 'NUSAP' system also fosters an enhanced appreciation of the issue of quality in information'.

[4]Those are frequently called social actors, as well as stakeholders (North American school) and also in Dutch and German literature, the *bettrofenen* (those concerned). Although through this chapter, the word actors is used and while waiting for a better name, by 'actors' it is meant here, those that may affect or are affected by a '*problematique*', and this includes not only those that have a stake or interest, those that play a role but also those that are concerned or affected by a situation. (Corral Quintana et al. 2002).

issues. This is not to say that 'citizen' science or 'indigenous technical knowledge' is better than formal science; simply that engendering a wider range of perspectives can help cope with uncertainty.

Simultaneously, the involvement of actors is viewed as a step of quality assurance of the decision processes and corresponds to the principles of extended peer review (Funtowicz and Ravetz 1990), that is involving those that affect or are affected by a *problematique* to ensure higher quality of decision processes and identify different alternative courses of action (CEC 2001).

In this context, QA processes and their attributes should be a joint result of a scientific peer review together with an extended peer review. Hence, the determination of the QA attributes and criteria should be carried out through the society, bearing in mind the notion of quality previously defined, that is, 'fitness for use'.

Together with a better understanding, extended QA processes will allow addressing the dynamicity showed by decision-making processes. Environmental *problematiques* are framed in a social setting, affected by changing values, interest, and objectives. An extended framing as well as implementation of the QA process reflects that changing actors' perceptions provide the analysis with the capability of adaptation necessary to assess dynamic issues.

An everyday example could be the determination of the attributes used for the election of a new car—what criteria will allow characterizing a car as a 'quality' car? While in recent years, the importance of safety has grown, such attribute was less important 20 years ago. The changing framework (increased number of traffic accidents, faster vehicles, etc.) has generated the transformation of societal values and concerns. Those changes may be observed when the notion of quality is adopted and an extended peer community defines the assurance attributes.

The QA Framework is conceived as an exploring tool through which three main components of decision-making problem-solving phase could be understood: (i) the information used and its processing, (ii) the decision-aid tool applied, and (iii) the role played by the analyst.

The QA Framework is organized into two categories: attributes and criteria. Attributes are closely related to the 'virtues' of the components of the decision process, while characteristics and criteria extend them into more precise elements of analysis, being the criteria used to carry out the quality assurance process.

The QA criteria are implemented using matrices that embrace all the criteria related to each attribute. For each criterion, different definitions are suggested to facilitate the process of quality assurance. For instance, regarding a quality assurance process of the information used in a case of atmospheric pollution, the criterion 'Accessibility'[5] is presented as follows:

Accessibility of information categories:

Total Access	Without diffusion	Academic sphere	Not public: need for permits and credentials	Unknown

A QUALITY ASSURANCE FRAMEWORK FOR ATMOSPHERIC POLLUTION POLICY PROCESS

In the following section, the QA Framework is implemented in a case study consisting of the analysis of a set of policy options regarding the effects of atmospheric pollution in an urban area of Tenerife (The Canary Islands).[6] This case study assesses the effects of three sources of pollution: two stationary sources, that is, a refinery industry and a power generator station, and a mobile source, that is, the traffic in the urban area. Throughout the research process a set of feasible policy alternatives (in fact, these options were defined by local authorities and stakeholders) and their impacts on human health, agriculture production, and forest areas were assessed.

Besides, four different policy-aid methodologies were used to asses these alternatives and their impacts. A physical valuation, a monetary valuation, a multi-criteria evaluation, and a social multi-criteria evaluation were carried out.

The QA Framework discussed in the previous section was applied to explore the quality of the procedures and results obtained from the implementation of those evaluation processes. In this sense, both the framing process and the implementation procedures will be assessed through the development of a set of attributes, which will later on be specified in a set of quality assurance criteria implemented in the quality assessment process. More concretely,

[5]*Accessibility*. Shows the degree of accessibility to both the information used and the information needed in the planning process. It is an important aspect in the quality assurance of these types of studies where there is a high dependency on the availability of the information. Thus, if the information is not openly available (or available to a restricted audience), the entire process (for example, review) will be affected. This category is divided into five types ranging from the highest availability and accessibility to the lowest where the information is unavailable.

[6]For a detailed description of the case study and the assessment carried out, see Corral Quintana (2000).

the role played in the planning process by the information available, the analyst, and the decision-aid model chosen will be the aspects under analysis.

Following the claim for extended quality assurance processes the quality criteria were defined within a consultation process together with dialogue and debate among experts, decision makers, and other relevant sectors of the relevant social actors in the policy issues at hand. Hence, public authorities, experts, non-governmental organizations (NGOs), farmers, and people representing the local source of polluting industry and citizens were involved in the process of design and implementation of the QA criteria.

Attributes in the Quality Assurance of Information

The information required and usually used in decision-making processes of public policies—particularly those oriented to environmental issues—is frequently characterized as being:

- Information of diverse type. Quantitative information ('hard facts') (i.e., biological, meteorological, epidemiological or statistical data, etc.) and qualitative information (legislative and normative aspects, economic or monetary elements, opinions, perceptions, etc.) are usually implemented in conjunction in decision-making processes.
- Information coming from different sources. It does not always present the same level of adjustment to the *problematique* analysed; in many cases we are dealing with estimations, incomplete series, unclear legislation, contradictory information, etc.

This diversity of sources and types of knowledge influences the quality of planning processes, which entails the need of assessing the type of information used in such processes. Three complementary attributes have been defined to explore the quality of the Information used in the problem-solving process: Fitness for purpose, Applicability and Confidence (see Figure 3.2).

One of the requirements asked from any kind of software, instrument, or object is its 'Fitness for purpose' to reach the aims for which it was designed or applied. Similarly, the information or the knowledge used in planning processes must fulfil that requisite. In QAAT, this adjustment is analysed on the basis of three characteristics: Adequacy, Accuracy, and Completeness. Adequacy shall reflect the sensitivity of the information to reach the envisaged aims, that is to say, their adequacy to the problem. Completeness is intended to examine whether the available data are complete or, on the contrary,

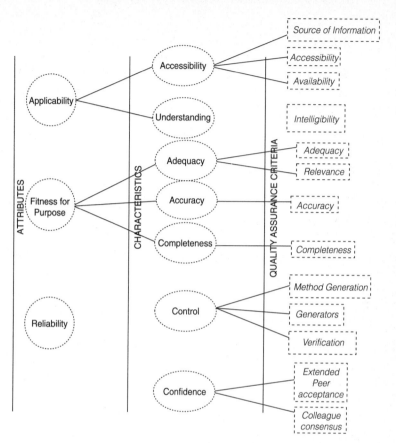

Figure 3.2:   Attributes, Characteristics, and QA Criteria of Information in Planning Processes

they show some 'lacks' (i.e. incomplete series, stakeholder opinions not available, etc.). Last, but not least, Accuracy states the uncertainties related to the information analysed.

As important as the fitness for purpose is 'Applicability'; when the information cannot be used during decision-making processes, its quality will certainly be affected (independently of the degree of adjustment of the information). Applicability is defined on the basis of 'Accessibility' and of 'Understanding'. Accessibility to the information and its sources plays an important role in the planning process—the information 'to be applicable has to be available'. Understanding reflects the intelligibility of the information by the various stakeholders as well as by the community at large. When data are not comprehensible, situations where some variables or effects are less valued (or on the contrary, valued in excess) may arise, affecting the quality of the decision process.

The information used in problem-solving processes should be 'Reliable', mainly when dealing with environmental planning, where the stakes are high, decisions are urgent (and in many cases, irreversible), and there is irreducible uncertainty and ignorance. The assessment of reliability will be implemented through the use of two complementary characteristics: Control and Confidence. The former relates to both the description of the sources and the process of verification of the information while the latter deals with the degree of legitimacy of the data.

These three attributes represent the quality characteristics the information used in planning processes should fulfil. To allow the quality assurance process, attributes are typified using different criteria, each of them reflecting a particular aspect of the attribute. So, for each attribute, usually several complementary criteria are defined.

In practice, the quality assurance process is the result of the assessment carried out through the implementation of specific criteria.

ATTRIBUTES IN THE QUALITY ASSURANCE OF THE ANALYST'S ROLE

Analysts play an important but frequently forgotten role in the problem-solving process that accompanies decision-making processes. They are in charge of transforming the socio-environmental issue at hand into a decisional problem, defining criteria and alternatives that reflect socio-political perceptions about the issue, and choosing the evaluation engine to be applied in the assessment process.

Usually the role played by experts in a process is considered neutral in that it is commonly assumed that they shall not influence this tailoring phase. This belief should be revisited when dealing with complex issues, where the degree of uncertainty and ignorance, as well as the need for urgent decisions in a context of high stakes and social, economical, environmental, and political interests and conflicts, are more than evident. Hence, the analysts' experience and their acceptance by social actors will play a crucial role in the process of framing the problem-solving process.

Experts are not intended to replace the decision maker in solving the problem, but to formulate the peculiarities of the problem in a clear, concise, and structured way. On the basis of the objectives expressed in relation to the recognized *problematique*, analysts will examine the existing data in order to develop the hypothesis and criteria to be used during the analytical phase of the decision-making process.[7]

Recognizing experts' capability of translating the decision issue into alternatives and criteria it must also be recognized that the planning process, and therefore its quality, may be influenced by that process of transformation. QAAT is used in this case to assess that process, paying special attention to (i) understanding the issue to be dealt with, and (ii) transforming information into alternatives, hypothesis, and criteria.

Experts also choose the decision-aid tool that will be used to assess the different policy alternatives. It is clear that the selection of one technique over another will influence the results of the analysis and hence the planning process itself.

Two attributes have been chosen to tackle the role of the analyst: Competence and Legitimacy (see Fig 3.3). Competence is intended to assess the experience of the analyst in addressing a particular policy issue, in terms of three characteristics: the Experience of the experts in processing these problems; their Adaptability to deal with new components or characteristics of the issue; and the way in which problems are Structured.

Legitimacy copes with the process of verification passed by the methodology—either developed or implemented—by the analyst. A process of verification where both the scientific community and the community at large—those relevant in planning issues; namely stakeholders and population—are involved. Legitimacy is assessed by means of two categories: Control and Acceptance.

ATTRIBUTES IN THE QUALITY ASSURANCE OF DECISION-AID TOOLS

Models used in environmental planning processes are not only evaluation tools, they should also be considered as instruments to structure significant issues as well as to facilitate and engage the relevant community in a dialogue leading to the resolution of conflicts arising in the decision-making processes.

Quality Assurance processes of models applied in problem-solving procedures should consider the following:

[7]It has to be noted that in relation to planning alternatives, frequently these can be either defined by the expert, or suggested by the political sphere.

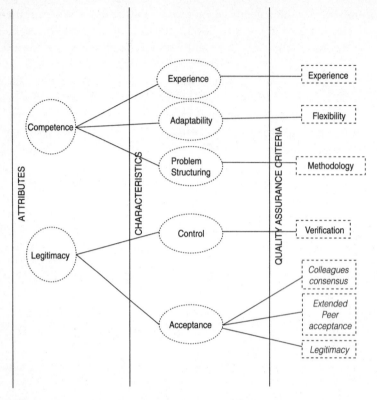

Figure 3.3: Attributes, Characteristics, and QA Criteria of the Role of Analysts in Planning Processes

(i) the ability of the model to internalize the information, alternatives, and criteria with minor loss of information;

(ii) the recognition of the model and its results by the scientific community as well as by the agents involved in the process; and

(iii) the transparency of the model, defined in terms of facility to handle and interpret results and the procedure's transparency itself.

With these concepts in mind the following attributes, Fitness for Purpose, Legitimacy, and Transparency will be set up to explore the quality of the decision-aid tools used in planning processes (see Figure 3.4).

The model's Fitness for Purpose will make explicit whether the methodology suits the issue under analysis. It tries to answer an important question (fundamental in the quality assessment of a tool or object): does the model fit the problem or is the problem being adapted to fit the model? Attempt is made to answer this

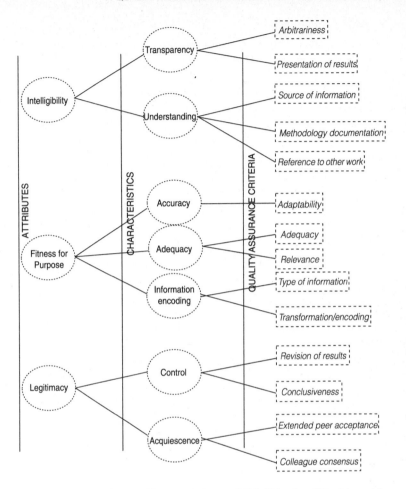

Figure 3.4:   Attributes, Characteristics, and QA Criteria of Decision-aid tools in Planning Processes

question by defining three categories: Adequacy, Accuracy, and Information Encoding. The model's specificity will be analysed in terms of whether it was developed to deal with the specific type of issues or whether it is a generic methodology used in several different spaces of decision-making processes. The adaptability of the methodology to the problem influences the way in which it can tackle non-envisaged aspects. Encoding Information refers to data processing issues, namely the necessity to transform, to codify, or to translate the information in order to be used during the model process.

Models not only have to be appropriate to the issue under analysis, but they should also be 'certified' by the experts and accepted by the actors involved in the process. This acceptance by social actors is crucial in the case of decision issues where there are conflicts of interests and compromise solutions perhaps might be needed. The Legitimacy attribute addresses this idea through two aspects: (i) the level of acquiescence of such methodology by the scientific community, the stakeholders and the extended community, and (ii) the kind of control procedure (if it does exist) applied to the obtained results.

The Transparency attribute is defined to assess the decision-aid model's ability to achieve this objective, exploring the understanding of the used methodology for both their internal mechanisms or procedures and the results generated through its application.

Operationalizing the Quality Assurance Framework: The Development of a Quality Assurance Assistant Tool

As discussed in the case study here, a QA process of the different dimensions involved in the elaboration of public policies implies the development and application of a large number of QA criteria. The importance of transparent procedures is due to the complexity inherent to most planning processes, where multiple dimensions and actors' perspectives should be taken into account to assure stable and legitimate decision processes. That multi-perspective implies not only comprehensible quality exploring criteria but also a comprehensible process of designing and implementing those criteria.

In this context, a computer application, namely the Quality Assurance Assistant Tool (QAAT), was developed to assist the exploration by the user of the previously discussed elements of the decision procedure through the application of the QA criteria. QAAT is intended to facilitate the definition of the different QA criteria for each attribute and their later implementation, as well as the posterior analysis of the results. The criteria are easily accessed from the main panel of the application, so the results of the analysis may be presented either individually for each of the three areas or globally through the radar.

With the purpose of visualizing in a clear and comprehensible way the results of the assurance process, a radar type plot is used (Figure 3.5). This choice is due to several reasons. A radar chart is a graphical representation that allows displaying in a clear way the criteria used to assist the quality assurance process. In addition, a representation

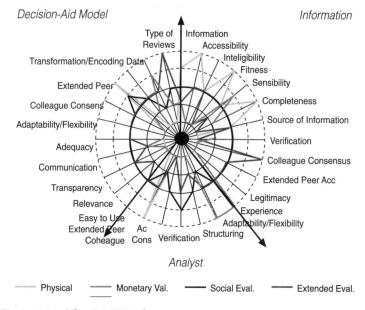

Figure 3.5:   The QAAT Radar

of radar type, unlike other types of chart representations—where results are displayed following a sequential structure (first the information, next the analyst, and finally the models)—due to its circular form, enables the analysis of different matrices in a contemporary way.

Indeed, in the QAAT Radar, the different categories do not need to be analysed following a pre-established order because of its circular form. It also gives the impression of the interconnectedness of criteria because of the circular adjacency: the dimension 'information' is adjacent to the 'role of the analyst' and also to the 'model', which is not possible in other types of charts.

The axes representing the QA criteria are grouped into three 'areas' that reflect the scopes of the present analysis: Information, Analyst, and Decision-aid Methods, facilitating the reading and understanding of this scheme.

For these areas each criterion is showed in individual axes. The surface of the radar chart is split into five concentric areas, each of them representing the assessment elements in which the criteria are divided. Graphically, the criteria scores placed closer to the centre of the diagram represent the categories located at the bottom of the criterion column, while those elements at the top of the criterion column are represented in the outer rings of the radar.

Box 3.1: Water Framework Directive

The Water Framework Directive (WFD) (CEC 2000) does not provide an implicit request for quality control of river basub management plans; yet, its Article 14 refers in point 1 that 'Member states shall encourage the active involvement of all interested parties in the implementation of this Directive, in particular in the production, review and updating of the river basin management plans.' The text of this Article does not explicitly recommend that consultation is made for quality assurance purposes: it only refers to '(a) a timetable and work programme for the production of the plan, including a statement of the consultation measures to be taken (...)' whereas in the subsequent points emphasis is clearly put in the review of the plan, i.e. ex-post knowledge reviews instead of ex-ante knowledge co-production. This could be interpreted as a way through to seek for 'external' (extended) legitimacy and accountability of public policies, for which QAAT and the QA Framework suggested here, may facilitate this process.

CONCLUDING REMARKS

In this chapter, a quality assurance framework for policy-making processes was discussed. The quality characteristics of three key components of the problem-solving phase of a planning process were discussed, that is, the type of information used and its processing, secondly the decision-aid tool applied, and finally, the role played by the analyst. A set of attributes was defined to typify their quality characteristics. These attributes were more deeply specified through a set of more specific QA criteria, in a case study dealing with some policy options of an atmospheric pollution policy making process, aimed at assisting the quality assurance process of those problem-solving components.

Finally, the QAAT was presented. This is conceived as a flexible and transparent tool to facilitate the quality assessment of the problem-solving framework implemented in planning processes.

Although QA procedures have not been implemented in decision making processes yet, they could play an important role in the policy-making process when dealing with complex *problematiques*, such as those related to sustainable development.

Socio-environmental policy issues are characterized by inherent scientific uncertainty and ignorance and frequently by social discrepancies. The development of quality assurance procedures for planning processes aims at recognizing the different types of uncertainty related to the issue and the limits of the problem-solving analysis. Additionally, quality assurance processes provide policy processes with a level of transparency considered essential when dealing with conflict policy issues where different opinions, perceptions, and interests are at stake.

The QA Framework here discussed constitutes a starting basis to assure the quality of policy making processes, also through the attributes and criteria suggested in this chapter. Framing the evaluation processes as a quality assurance process where at each level an extended community intervenes in order to ensure that the outcomes are fit for use does not seem an unviable proposal. The real issue is the articulation of quality checks with installed institutional practices.

REFERENCES

Becker, G.S., (1978), *The Economic Approach to Human Behavior*, University of Chicago: Chicago Press.

British Standard Institution, (1979), *The British Standard for Quality Assurance*, BS 4778. London: British Standard Institution.

Commission of the European Communities (CEC), (2001), European Governance: A White Paper, COM(2001) 428, Brussels, 25 July 2001. Available at *http://europa.eu.int/comm/governance/white_paper/index_en.htm*, Last accessed 15 July 2007.

Council of the European Communities (CEC), (2000), Directive 2000/60/EC of the European Parliament and of the Council establishing a framework for the Community action in the field of water policy. Published at *Official Journal (OJ L 327)* on 22 December.

Coleman, J.S., (1990), *Foundations of Social Theory*, Harvard University Press. Cambridge, Massachusetty.

Corral Quintana, S., (2000), *Una Metodología Integrada de Exploración de los Procesos de Elaboraciún de Políticas P´blicas*, Universidad de La Laguna, Tenerife, EC, Ispra: EUR 19724 ES.

Corral Quintana, S., S. Funtowicz and Â Guimarães Pereira, (2002), 'GOUVERNe: New Trends in Decision Support for Groundwater Governance Issues', in Guimarães Pereira, Â, S. Corral Quintana, S. Funtowicz, *Environmental Modelling and Software*, Vol. 20, No. 3, pp. 111–18. Venice.

Crosby, B., (1992), *Stakeholder Analysis: A Vital Tool for Strategic Managers*, Washington DC: USAID.

Crosby, P.B., (1979), *Quality is Free*, New York: McGraw-Hill.

_____, (1996), *Quality is Still Free: Making Quality Certain in Uncertain Times*, New York: McGraw-Hill.

Dahl, R. and C.E. Lindblom, (1976), *Politics, Economics and Welfare*, 2nd edn, New Cork, NY: Harpers.

Dunleavy, P., (1991), *Democracy, Bureaucracy and Public Choice: Economic Models in Political Science*, London: Pearson.

Funtowicz, S.O. and J.R. Ravetz, (1990), *Uncertainty and Quality in Science for Policy*, Dordrecht: Kluwer Academic Press.

_____, (1993), 'Science for the Post-Normal Age', *Futures*, Vol. 25, No. 7, pp. 739–55.

_____, (1992), 'The Role of Science in Risk Assessment', in S. Krimsky and D. Golding (eds), *Social Theories of Risk*, Westport: Praeger, pp. 59–88.

Gibbons, M., C. Limoges, H. Nowotny, S. Schwartzman, P. Scott and M. Trow, (1994), *The New Production of Knowledge: The Dynamics of Science and Research in Contemporary Societies*, London: Sage.

International Standard Organisation (ISO), (1987), ISO 8402, *Quality Management*, Geneva: ISO.

_____, (1986b), ISO 9000, *Quality Management*, Geneva: ISO.

Kahneman, D., (2003), 'Maps of Bounded Rationality: Psychology for Behavioral Economics', *The American Economic Review*, Vol. 93, No. 5, pp. 1449–75.

Lindblom, C.E., (1959), 'The Science of 'Muddling Through', *Public Administration*, Vol. 19, pp. 79–88.

_____, (1977), *Politics and Markets*, New York: Basic Books.

_____, (1993), *The Policy-Making Process, 3rd. ed.* with Edward J. Woodhouse, Englewood Cliffs, New Jersey: Prentice Hall.

_____, (1991), *El Proceso de Elaboracion de Politicas Publicas*, Madrid: Ministerio para las Administraciones Publicas.

Sen, A., (1987), 'Rational Behaviour', in J. Eatwell, M. Milgate, P. Newman (eds), *The New Palgrave: A Dictionary of Economics*, Vol. 3, pp. 68–76 Macmillan, London.

Simon, H., (1957), 'A Behavioral Model of Rational Choice', in *Models of Man, Social and Rational: Mathematical Essays on Rational Human Behavior in a Social Setting*, New York: Wiley.

Wildavsky, A., (1984), *The Politics of the Budgetary Process*, Boston: Little Brown.

World Bank, (1997), *Pollution Prevention and Abatement Handbook*, Part II, World Bank.

Wynne, B., (1992), 'Uncertainty and Environmental Learning', *Global Environmental Change*, Vol. 2, pp. 111–27.

_____, (2005), 'Reflexing Complexity: Post-genomic Knowledge and Reductionist Returns in Public Science Theory', *Culture & Society*, Vol. 22, No. 5, pp. 67–94.

4

Multi-causal Relationships in their Socio-political Context

LAURA MAXIM AND JEROEN P. VAN DER SLUIJS

FRAMING CAUSAL RELATIONSHIPS IN SCIENCE FOR POLICY

Identification of causal relationships has a lot to do with control. Understanding which phenomenon determines another increases the ability of human beings to cope with their environment.

At present, scientists and philosophers have difficulty in specifying when a relationship between two events is causal (Pearl 2000). In epidemiology, different models of causality exist, which Vineis and Kriebel (2006) divide into two classes. The first is characterized by a linear monocausal pattern of explanation, based on the concept of necessary cause (that is, the disease does not develop in the absence of exposure to the agent). The second is characterized by the concept of causal web (that is, a concurrence of different conditions is required to induce disease). A widely used multicausal model is Rothman's 'pie' model, in which a sufficient causal complex (a pie) is represented by a combination of several component causes (Rothman and Greenland 2005). The disease appears when the pie is completed. Such multi-causality provides the opportunity for removing only one or a small number of factors for preventing harm (Gee 2003). Other causality models have been developed in epidemiology but they have many limitations, mainly related to the low degree of accounting for interactions between causal factors, to their dynamic character over time, and to the differences between individual and population levels (Valleron 2000; Vineis and Kriebel 2006). The usual scientific approach to untangling such complex cause–effect relationships is to isolate one possible causal factor by statistically accounting for all others (EEA 2005).

For distinguishing between a chance association and a true cause and effect, Sir Austin Bradford Hill (1965) proposed nine criteria, widely used by epidemiologists and tested in environmental risk assessment (Collier 2003): strength of association, consistency, specificity, temporality, biological gradient, biological plausibility, biological coherence, experimental evidence, and analogy. Only one of these criteria indisputably revokes a cause-and-effect hypothesis (that is, temporality).

In environmental studies, research of causal relationships has the advantage of being able to test the experimental evidence in the laboratory, in controlled conditions. However, in natural systems, many factors may interfere with the researcher's ability to assess causality: the multitude of toxicants, their interactions with non-contaminant stressors, and the high biological variability. Furthermore, effects issued from different stressors might not be comparable and their synergic or antagonistic interactions make their combined effects to be greater or lesser than the sum of their individual effects. These gaps in knowledge add to those concerning compensatory processes that influence population dynamics, to the general lack of data, and to the difficulties associated with communication between several disciplines (Munns 2006). Moreover, assessment may concern several groups of organisms, at different levels of organization, and with different patterns of response to stressors. To date, there is no widely accepted and proven approach for establishing causality in natural systems (Collier 2003) or for dealing with multi-causality.

A simple conclusion that may be drawn from the above is that multi-causality is actually inseparable from uncertainty. Therefore, an aspect that has to be dealt with is the relevance of this uncertainty for action. How do people take decisions and what are the patterns of interaction between science and policy in conditions of uncertainty?

For dealing with the relatively new situations of hard political pressure, disputed values, high decision stakes, and major epistemological and ethical system uncertainties, science is called upon to answer with new practices. Funtowicz and Ravetz (1993) coined these emergent scientific patterns 'post-normal science', whose main features are the appropriate management of uncertainty, acknowledgment of the plurality of problem perspectives, and the extension of the peer community to include non-scientific actors.

The dominant belief in science for policy inquiries is that inappropriate control of environmental risks is due only to insufficient scientific knowledge. However, this ignores both the socio-economic influence on the construction of the scientific evidence and the influence of political contexts on the use of such evidence for communication and action. Stakeholders can strategically use science in public debates (Hellström 1996; van der Sluijs 2006). In some cases, the existence of contradictory expertise can be the result of a 'manufactured uncertainty', which is intended to favour the settling down and prolongation of the debate (Michaels 2005; Maxim and van der Sluijs 2007). The consequence is mistrust, conflict, and low chances for mutually respectful dialogue among interested parties.

The extended quality control through broad participation of the stakeholders involved is proposed by post-normal science as a method for increasing the quality and acceptability of the risk assessment process and of its outcomes, and is embedded in the 'extended participation' model (Funtowicz 2006) of science and policy (see Introduction by Guimarães Pereira and Funtowicz in this volume). Reducing the potential of conflict associated with mistrust is one of the results intended. Interested and/or affected parties may lack technical expertise but might have essential information and often hold strong views, which have to be considered in any democratic society (Kloprogge and Van der Sluijs 2005). However, the stakeholders' involvement process needs very careful architecture, as the quality of the process itself and the openness of participants to compromise are crucial for the outcome (Renn 1995).

The following case study is an exemplification of the need for post-normal science in case of contested (multi)causal explanations of environmental risks. First, we assert that the articulation of a particular causal link has, beyond its scientific basis, a social dimension that is strongly influenced by the actors' stakes. In the following, we compare two parallel processes of constructing knowledge for decision making with regard to the influence of socio-economic context on each and their respective consequences for policy. For this, we use the discourse analysis framework proposed by Hajer (1995). For him, the discourse coalitions that form around causal explanations ('story-lines') are meant to represent a particular definition of the environmental problem, on which the decision making critically depends. Second, the case presented below represents the first application of the precautionary principle in France for an environmental issue. The conditions and the consequences of applying the precautionary principle are analysed below. Third, we expand on what should not be done regarding stakeholders' involvement. The chapter concludes by examining how key elements of post-normal science have been reflected in the process(es) of knowledge construction.

SOCIAL INGREDIENTS OF CAUSAL RELATIONSHIPS: THE CASE OF HONEYBEE COLONIES DECLINE IN FRANCE

The Problem

In 1994–6, French beekeepers first noticed symptoms that they had never previously observed: in several days of sunflower foraging, honeybee populations were suddenly and massively falling. The foraging honeybees almost completely disappeared from the hives or, sometimes, were dying by the thousands in front of the hives. These mortalities were accompanied by behavioural symptoms (trembling honeybees and forming of moulds in front of the hives) and by a 30–70 per cent loss in sunflower honey yield (GVA 1998–2006). High honeybee losses were also seen during the winter or in early spring. Given the novelty of the symptoms with regard to their previous experience, beekeepers tried to find if a new element had appeared in the environment of the hives or if previously known factors had changed patterns. It was communicated to local farmers that a new insecticide, Gaucho®, was first used in sunflower seed-treatment also in 1994. This was the first of a new generation of insecticides, applied on the plant not by spraying, but in seed-dressing, which dispersed to all plant tissues during the plant growth. Since the symptoms were particularly recorded for bees foraging sunflower crops and beekeepers learned from farmers that many of these were treated with Gaucho®, the beekeepers suspected there to be a toxic effect of this insecticide on the honeybees. Consequently, they asked Bayer, the producer of the insecticide, to inform them about its potential toxicity for honeybees. This was the start of a long series of scientific studies involving experts from Bayer, the Ministry of Agriculture, beekeepers, and independent researchers. Many of the studies of independent researchers yielded arguments supporting the causal link with seed-dressing and Gaucho®, whereas all the studies undertaken by Bayer during this period reported that Gaucho® did not form a risk for honeybees. The symptoms continued to be observed year after year and the economic status of many beekeepers was severely affected. Despite the initial statement of Bayer that the active substance was not present in nectar and pollen at the flowering time, imidacloprid was found by researchers in both. The combination of findings obtained by independent research, social pressure, and media attention led to the first application of the precautionary principle for an environmental issue in France. In 1999, the Minister of Agriculture ordered a two-year ban on the use of Gaucho® in sunflower seed-dressing. This ban was renewed in 2001 for two years and again in 2004 for three years. Because the symptoms continued to be observed even after this year, two more hypotheses were raised: (i) honeybees were still being exposed to the pollen of maize treated with Gaucho®; and (ii) imidacloprid persisted in the soils, that is, the chemical was present in untreated crops growing in soil on which a seed-dressed crop had been grown one year earlier. Furthermore, another insecticide quickly replaced Gaucho® in sunflower seed-dressing. This new product, called RégentTS® (active substance: fipronil) was owned by BASF.

Discourse Coalitions

During the debate, all stakeholders acknowledged the influence on honeybees of several factors at the same time. However, the balance between the role of Gaucho® and the role of other causes has been framed differently according to the different stakeholders.

The debate on causal relationships can be structured around three story-lines. The first storyline is represented by beekeepers and independent researchers. Based on field observations and experimental evidence, they claim Gaucho® to be the main, if not sole, contributor to the damage caused to honeybee colonies observed after 1994 in sunflower/maize extensive crops areas (even if not the only contributor to all the honeybee problems in France). Their arguments built upon the results of numerous studies made in France after 1997 on the effects of imidacloprid on honeybees.

The second storyline argues for a non-causal relationship between Gaucho® and honeybees, articulating that other causes are to blame. This view was represented by Bayer and generally by the French Food Safety Agency (AFSSA). Their argument builds on the 'lack of evidence of harm' in their research carried out in controlled conditions of access of honeybees to food containing imidacloprid or in field conditions, whose results did not reproduce the symptoms observed by beekeepers. These two actors proposed several potential causal factors, including genetic origin of imported queens and low adaptation to local conditions, unfavourable climatic conditions, honeybee diseases and viruses, inadequate or illegal use of pesticides and mixes of pesticides by farmers, an insufficient quantity of pollen, and changes in sunflower strains.

Finally, the position of the Ministry of Agriculture was ambiguous, considering Gaucho® as one possible cause among others, with unclear contribution on the final effects.

The Socio-economic Stakes

For Bayer, the new generation of systemic insecticides used in seed-dressing represented an important opportunity for changing production patterns. Moreover, insecticides containing imidacloprid had a large international market.

Results for the honey yields published by the Coopérative France Miel for western France showed the year 1995 as the starting point for the abnormal losses. The sector passed through difficult times, as nearly 15,200 beekeepers left this occupation between 1994 and 2004 (most of them were small producers).

The Ministry of Agriculture, confronted with contradictory demands from the two sectors, had a hesitating attitude. The main stake was to defend its legitimacy, given that the debate on Gaucho® revealed important dysfunctions related to the process of authorization of pesticides. Thus, in a letter published in *Le Point* journal on 21 November 2003, the Head of the Bureau of Regulation of Anti-Pest Products, Direction Générale de l'Alimentation (DGAL) described its lack of capacity as follows: 'three public servants for dealing with 20,000 demands of authorisation per year, a joint management of the risk assessment with industrials, lack of transparency in the procedures...it is impossible for the bureau to comply with its missions'.

The Research

Starting with 1994, the symptoms described by beekeepers were confirmed by different local or regional state services, documents produced by beekeepers for communicating their problems (GVA 1998–2006), and several research reports. The use of Gaucho® in sunflower/maize seed-dressing was found to be a necessary cause (without which the symptoms do not appear) for the lethal and sublethal symptoms, because the symptoms were very characteristic (never seen before 1994) and no other cause among all those investigated could explain the specificity of these symptoms for sunflower flow or their novelty. A second reason for having considered Gaucho® as being a necessary cause is that in its absence, beekeepers found that the same symptoms were not appearing (for example, hives from the same apiaries placed in the forest during the same period of the season were behaving fine). The other factors potentially having an influence were found to be present all over the year and not only in areas of extensive cropping, without producing the set of symptoms observed. The use of RégentTS® brought an additional symptom, meaning intoxications during the spring sowing (the active substance was depositing with the dust spread during sowing on wild plants which were foraged by honeybees). Significant honeybee mortalities were signalled in 2003 in these conditions.

The first indications of reframing the issue of honeybee colonies decline as a multi-causal one can be traced to January 1999, when the Ministry of Agriculture announced an epidemiologic study intended to determine the other factors that could have contributed to the honeybees' problems, along with the ban on the use of Gaucho® in sunflower seed-dressing.

The first monitoring study based on an 'all symptoms and all factors at the time' ('multi-factor') approach was carried out by AFSSA in 1998–2001, producing only very vague results. In 1999, the results of another study of AFSSA were not considered relevant because of the lack of data representativeness (Faucon 1999).

In 2000, a booklet meant to argue for the multi-causal origin of honeybee colonies decline found in France was brought out by Bayer. Based on the statement that the 'mystery of the "disappearing disease" in France has not been solved', the main arguments of the booklet pointed towards 'the many diseases to which bees are prone' and more generally towards 'the various causes of the bee problem' (Jacobs et al. 2000, p. 8). Beekeepers replied under the title 'The art of seed-dressing and of making fools of us' by pointing out the disproval of the discursive practices employed in Bayer's booklet: selective use of information, tendentious interpretation, absence of critical approach regarding the knowledge available on the risks of Gaucho® for honeybees, and lack of rigour.

Some attempts to survey honeybees' intoxications were made in 2000 by the National Centre for Beekeeping Development (CNDA) within which the DGAL (General Directorate for Food, from the Ministry of Agriculture) engaged only formally (financing promised has not been accorded). A monitoring network in which the DGAL really participated was not started until August 2002 (eight years after the start of the debate and three years after the Minister's announcement regarding the creation of a monitoring network). In 2002–3, four monitoring networks superposed. For each of them, the definition of 'honeybees' problems' was different, referring to honeybees' diseases, to 'general' problems encountered by honeybees, respectively to intoxications. Their spatial coverage was also different. Most monitoring survey was based on calls from beekeepers (when problems arose) and on confirmation by sanitary agents (trained persons approved by the State). However, in many cases the sanitary agents arrived too late to confirm the symptoms. Moreover, in the cases of disappearance of honeybees from the hive, the symptom could not have been confirmed without trusting the beekeeper who had actually observed it.

From all the existing monitoring studies and networks, neither a clear description of field symptoms nor a coherent analysis has been produced. These exercises were neither peer-reviewed by researchers nor had relevance for decision making.

Being directly interested in monitoring the symptoms in order to see their problem acknowledged and solved, beekeepers had proposed in 1998 to use the Vendée department (one of the most affected) as an experimentation field resembling real-life conditions. Later, confronted with the ambiguity of successive surveys, they stepped back and felt the initiatives of field monitoring to be illegitimate and intended to bring confusion and prolong the debate. The passing of each year meant important losses for them, whereas the protocols of the multi-factor studies had low consideration for their description of symptoms. Beekeepers criticized the 'paralysis by analysis' and the diversion of the research towards too 'complex' subjects.

Seed-dressing insecticides have a high toxic activity at very low doses. Over several years, the precision of analytical methods for measuring low exposures was refined for reaching very low detection and quantification limits. This allowed precise measures of imidacloprid and fipronil in the nectar and pollen of sunflower and maize. Simultaneously, methods for assessing the sublethal and chronic effects of imidacloprid and fipronil on honeybees were developed in the laboratory. The values found for exposure in the field were comparable with the values found for negative effects in the laboratory. In 2003, field experimentations made an explicit link between fipronil used in seed-dressing and honeybee mortalities during spring sowing.

In 2001, an interdisciplinary expert group called the Scientific and Technical Committee for the Multifactor Study of the Honeybees Colonies Decline (CST), comprising 19 experts, was set up by the Ministry of Agriculture. The CST decided to start by carrying on the study of Gaucho®, because this was the most socially and politically sensitive factor among all those potentially involved. In the same time, the CST proceeded to the survey of honeybee problems in the field and envisaged effects of other factors (that is, other types of intoxications, honeybee diseases, etc.). In 2003, the CST published its final report on the risk of Gaucho® for honeybees (CST 2003), based on the detailed study of the 480 documents available. Temporal and spatial correlations between symptoms and sunflower/maize flowering led to focusing on these two crops, which were representing 'the problem' invoked by beekeepers. The CST agreed on criteria of quality for the studies and their results. These favoured transparency and allowed their comparative assessment. Their report published in 2003 was well organized and the methods and results were clear. It gave recommendations for continuing the study of the other factors involved and was approved by all the members of the CST. This report produced the first clear conclusion in the history of the debate, namely that the risk of Gaucho® for honeybees is worrisome, both in sunflower and in maize seed-dressing. A second assessment, which came one year later, confirmed the risk of RégentTS® on honeybees.

THE APPLICATION OF THE PRECAUTIONARY PRINCIPLE

The case of honeybee colonies decline was, at the beginning of the debate in 1994, a 'perfect case of post-normal science', in which uncertainty and stakes were high and in which values were in dispute. The interactions between stakeholders started under good signs, through several meetings bringing all of them 'around the table', in 1995–7. However, the situation degraded slowly, along with the progressively disappearing mutual trust. This can be attributed to several factors. First, several times the scientific evidence provided by the two companies was found to lack scientific quality and was contradicted by findings of independent researchers. Despite this, regulatory decision-making (that is, authorization for marketing) relied exclusively on evidence coming from the industry. This led to doubts both on the reliability of the information on risks produced by the company and on the role of the State. A second reason was the absence of an 'arbiter' able to mediate the relationships between actors. The legitimacy of the Ministry of Agriculture was contested both by beekeepers and by chemical companies, the former suspecting a policy of partisanship in favour of the industry, while the latter was suspecting decision-makers of weakness. The position of the Ministry in the debate was systematically confused, contradictory, and opaque. This changed the perception of the State from being the traditional provident 'social peace-maker' to being an actor as any other, with its own interests. Consequently, stakeholders felt abandoned to their own ability of defending their interests.

The debate embodied not only high political stakes, but also ethical values, related to the definition of democracy, the power of the State to control economic interests for protecting its citizens, and to the moral responsibility for the protection of the environment. The beekeepers received support from the civil society also because their case was relevant for larger preoccupations in the French society, such as the right to contest priority to be given in decision making to the criterion 'economic weight' to the disadvantage of 'equity'. Furthermore, the cultural and symbolic connotations of the honeybee contributed much to the public sympathy regarding the decline of apiaries.

By applying the precautionary principle and banning Gaucho® for sunflower seed-dressing, the Minister of Agriculture tried to strike a compromise between the economic stakes for Bayer (only 10 per cent of the benefits issued from selling Gaucho® were obtained from use on sunflower), the economic stakes for beekeepers, and the socio-political context reflected by the media. This decision calmed down the conflict for the moment and boosted investigations on the effects on honeybees of RégentTS® and of Gaucho® used in maize seed-dressing. However, further political action proved to be much more difficult. The surface cultivated with sunflower in France comprised only about 40 per cent of the surface cultivated with maize, which represented, therefore, a much more important market opportunity for Bayer. The decision to ban Gaucho® in maize seed-dressing did not come until very late, in 2004.

After the ban of the two products, the social tension diminished and beekeepers recorded positive effects on their honeybees. In 2005, the honey yield, despite the negative influence of the hot summer, started to improve progressively. Sudden depopulation during sunflower and maize flowerings has not been observed any more

(Clément 2005). Recent reports indicate that the situation of apiaries was good in the early spring of 2007 (Clément 2007).

Given the inadequacy of the available testing procedures for assessing the risks of new generations of insecticides on honeybees, acknowledged during the debate, a group of honeybee experts was appointed by the French Ministry of Agriculture, with the mission to develop new tests for honeybees. In 2006, a new unit was created at the AFSSA, responsible for risk assessment, while risk management continues to be the responsibility of the Ministry of Agriculture. The questions raised today relate to whether enough independence and resources are allocated to this unit for assuring its good functioning, and whether the choice of experts will allow a non-biased appreciation of the potential risks for honeybees.

Following the public acknowledgement of the role of the honeybee as pollinator and bioindicator for the environment, a 'Honeybee, sentinel of the environment' programme was initiated by the National Union of French Beekeepers (UNAF), a syndicate representing about 22,000 beekeepers. The coverage of the case in the media also demonstrated the importance of a partnership between beekeepers and farmers and raised consciousness among them.

CONCLUDING REMARKS

The analysis of the two processes of building knowledge on honeybees' problems shows the relevance of post-normal concepts of knowledge quality assessment and of involving the interested parties for contributing to informed policy decisions and for dealing with conflicting situations.

The multifactor approach had not provided answers to scientific or social purposes. The knowledge production was dealt with as being a general process of understanding the situation of honeybees in France, because it considered all the potential symptoms and all the potential factors indistinctively, instead of addressing the very particular problem of societal concern (honeybees' symptoms related to sunflower and maize crops). This 'general' approach could have been appropriate for an investigation in 'normal' conditions, but it proved to be inadequate for such a conflicting case in which research and decision needed to be quick and targeted towards limiting a specific harm. The monitoring schemes were implemented too late, when the relationships between beekeepers and the DGAL were already marked by profound mistrust. This led to low interest of beekeepers in monitoring, which they suspected of being only a tool for the DGAL for seizing the subject and legitimizing decisions already taken.

Beekeepers' involvement had an instrumental view, in which they would have automatically provided the knowledge that experts (DGAL, AFSSA) wanted for telling the beekeepers back as to 'what is wrong'. But beekeepers had their own capacity of expertise, which was not technical but which arose from their everyday experience with honeybees, and thus already had views on 'what is wrong'.

Independent researchers focused on assessing the exposure of honeybees for the two crops that constituted 'the problem', that is, sunflower and maize, and on understanding the symptoms described by beekeepers. For the researchers involved in the CST, the main resources for dealing with the social conflict were their competence and their commitment to transparency. During its work, the CST invited interested parties to communicate on their experience. Thus, it assured the scientific quality of the knowledge produced (through reviewing and validation of available studies) and its social relevance.

The most sensitive point in dealing with complex issues is not how to describe complexity as such, but how to choose the right manner to simplify it for decision making. As Hewitt et al. (2003) suggested, for some situations it may not be necessary, nor affordable, to attempt to determine precise causality. The level of investigation needs to be established with inputs from stakeholders (EEA 2001) from the very beginning of the research. This process of building the knowledge as a 'hybrid' presumes negotiations of each one's responsibility in the problem (Wynne 1996), enriches the assessment with information that can positively contribute to the results, and represents a democratic exercise of arrangement of (possibly) unbalanced power relationships through argumentation and expression of value diversity rather than through addled conflict.

REFERENCES

Clément, H., (2005), 'Premier bilan', Abeilles et fleurs, Editorial n 664, available at *http://www.unaf-apiculture.info/*, accessed on June 2007.

——, (2007), 'La situation n'est pas irréversible!', Abeilles et fleurs, Editorial n°684, available at: *http://www.unaf-apiculture.info/*, accessed on June 2007.

MULTI-CAUSAL RELATIONSHIPS IN THEIR SOCIO-POLITICAL CONTEXT 79

Collier, T.K., (2003), 'Forensic Ecotoxicology: Establishing Causality between Contaminants and Biological Effects in Field Studies', *Human and Ecological Risk Assessment*, Vol. 9, No. 1, pp. 259–66.

CST, (2003), 'Imidaclopride utilisé en enrobage de semences (Gaucho®) et troubles des abeilles, rapport final', Paris: Ministère de l'Agriculture.

European Environmental Agency (EEA), (2001), *Late Lessons from Early Warnings*, Copenhagen: EEA.

———, (2005), 'An Approach to Multi-causality and Health: BH Background Paper No. 2, Part A and B', London: Bradford Hill Workshop, Imperial College, 12–14 December.

Faucon, J.P., (1999), 'Etude des comptes rendus des visites : dépopulations des colonies d'abeilles', Sophia Antipolis : Frech Food Safety Agency (AFSSA).

Funtowicz, S.O. and J.R. Ravetz, (1993), 'Science for the Post-Normal Age', *Futures*, Vol. 25, No. 7, pp. 735–55.

Gee, D., (2003), 'Presentation at the Stakeholder Forum on Environment and Health Strategy', 11 July 2003, Brussels, Belgium.

GVA (Galerie Virtuelle Apicole), (1988–2006), 'Apiservices—Le Portail Apiculture. Dossier Intoxications', available at *www.beekeeping.com.*, 1998–2006, accessed on June 2007.

Goodman, K.J. and C.V. Phillips, (2005), 'Hill's Criteria of Causation', in B.S. Everitt and D.C. Howell (eds), *Encyclopedia of Statistics in Behavioural Science*, Volume 2, Chichester: John Wiley & Sons Ltd.

Hajer, Maarten, (1995), *The Politics of Environmental Discourse*, New York: Clarendon Press, Oxford University Press.

Hellström, T., (1996), 'The Science-Policy Dialogue in Transformation: Model-Uncertainty and Environmental Policy', *Science and Public Policy*, Vol. 23, No. 2, pp. 91–7.

Hewitt, L.M., M.G. Dub, J.M. Culp, D.L. MacLatchy, and K.R. Munkittrick, (2003), 'A Proposed Framework for Investigation of Cause for Environmental Effects Monitoring', *Human Ecological Risk Assessment*, Vol. 9, No. 1, pp. 195–211.

Hill, A.B., (1965), 'The Environment and Disease: Association or Causation?', *Proceedings of the Royal Society of Medicine*, Vol. 58, pp. 295–300, available at *http://www.edwardtufte.com/tufte/hill.*

Jacobs, Frans, Wolfgang Pflüger, Hans-Werner Schmidt, Richard Schmuck, and Octaaf Van Laere, (2000), *A propos de la santé des abeilles*, Paris: P.R. Editions, Bayer CropScience.

Kloprogge, P. and J.P. van der Sluijs, (2006), 'The Inclusion of Stakeholder Knowledge and Perspectives in Integrated Assessment of Climate Change', *Climatic Change*, Vol. 75, No. 3, pp. 359–89.

Maxim, L. and J.P. van der Sluijs, (2007), 'Uncertainty: Cause or Effect of Stakeholders' Debates? Analysis of a Case Study: The Risk for Honeybees of the Insecticide Gaucho®', *Science of the Total Environment*, Vol. 376, pp. 1–17.

Michael, D., (2005), 'Industry Groups are Fighting Government Regulation by Fomenting Scientific Uncertainty: Doubts is their Product', *Scientific American*, pp. 96–101.

Munns, W.R. Jr., (2006), 'Assessing Risks to Wildlife Populations from Multiple Stressors: Overview of the Problem and Research Needs', *Ecology and Society*, Vol. 11, No. 1, available at *http://www.ecologyandsociety.org/vol11/iss1/art23/*

Pearl, Judea, (2000), *Causality: Models, Reasoning, and Inference*, Cambridge: Cambridge University Press.

Renn, O., T. Webler, and P. Wiedemann (eds), (1995), *Fairness and Competence in Citizen Participation: Technology, Risk and Society*, Dordrecht, Boston, London: Kluwer Academic Publishers.

Rothman, K.J. and S. Greenland, (2005), 'Causation and Causal Inference in Epidemiology', *American Journal of Public Health*, Vol. 95, No. S1, pp. 144–50.

Valleron, A.J., (2000), 'Mise en évidence des faits et recherche des causes en épidémiologie environnementale: enjeux méthodologiques', C.R. Academy of Science, Paris, *Sciences de la vie/Life Sciences*, Vol. 323, pp. 617–28.

van der Sluijs, J., (2006), Uncertainty, Assumptions, and Value Commitments in the Knowledge Base of Complex Environmental Problems', in Â Guimarães Pereira, S. Guedes Vaz, and S. Tognetti (eds), *Interfaces between Science and Society*, London: Greenleaf.

Vineis, P. and D. Kriebel, (2006), 'Causal Models in Epidemiology: Past Inheritance and Genetic Future', *Environmental Health: A Global Access Science Source*, Vol. 5, No. 21, available at *http://www.ehjournal.net/content/5/1/21*.

Wynne, B., (1996), 'May the Sheep Safely Graze? A Reflexive View of the Expert–Lay Divide', in S. Lash, B. Szerszynski, and B. Wynne (eds), *Risk Environment and Modernity: Towards a New Ecology*, London: Sage.

PART 2

Science in the GMOs Policy

5

The Future of Agriculture
GMOs and the Agonizing Paradigm of Industrial Agriculture

Mario Giampietro

The Present: the Crisis of the Paradigm of Industrial Agriculture

The Paradigm of Industrial Agriculture

The paradigm of industrial agriculture can be defined as the existence of an uncontested consensus over the idea that a massive use of technology (capital) and fossil energy in agriculture is justified in order to achieve two key objectives: (i) boosting the productivity of labour in the agricultural sector; and (ii) boosting the productivity of land in production. The priority given to these two objectives, in the definition of technological progress in agriculture, has been generated, in the last century, by two crucial transformations typical of modern societies: (i) a dramatic socio-economic re-adjustment of the profile of investment of human time, labour, and capital over the different economic sectors in industrial and post-industrial societies, with such transformation requiring the progressive elimination of farmers from the workforce; and (ii) the worldwide demographic explosion that has taken place—first in the developed world and then in the rest of the world—linked to the phenomenon characterized as 'globalization of the economy'. This explosion has led to a requirement for boosting the yields on the land in production, due to the progressive reduction of available arable land per capita.

In technical/scientific terms the paradigm of industrial agriculture entails a major simplification of the functional and structural organization of traditional agro-ecosystems. That is, it entails the abandonment of traditional, integrated systems of agricultural production based on cycles of nutrients. These cycles of nutrients were guaranteed by the interaction of different species present in pre-industrial agricultural systems, which, for this reason, can be characterized as Low External Input Agriculture (LEIA). The industrial paradigm requires a linearization of flows of nutrients obtained with the massive use of commercial fertilizers and irrigation. Such a linearization is possible only because of a large use of technical inputs (for example, machinery, pesticides, commercial seeds), which are heavily dependent on fossil energy. For this reason, an agriculture based on the industrial paradigm can be characterized as High External Input Agriculture (HEIA). However, this massive use of input is based on a progressive depletion of stocks (for example, fossil energy, soil erosion, loss of biodiversity) and the progressive filling of sinks (for example, pollution of the environment, greenhouse gases). The elimination of the biophysical constraints associated with natural patterns of cycling of nutrients in terrestrial ecosystems represents a major plus provided by the paradigm of industrial agriculture in relation to the socio-economic dimension. In this way, HEIA can boost the yield per hectare and the productivity of labour at the same time. However, HEIA has serious negative effects on the environment. These negative effects include loss of biodiversity generated by the destruction of natural habitats, and a continuous erosion of the genetic variety of cultivated crop species. Within the paradigm of industrial agriculture, traditional varieties are increasingly replaced by hybrid seeds produced by a few big commercial corporations. Additional negative side effects include: soil erosion; high consumption of freshwater; accumulation of residues of pesticides in the environment; and leakage of large quantities of phosphorus and nitrogen both in the water table and rivers, which leads to eutrophication of water bodies. Biophysical constraints on the indefinite expansion of humans on this planet do exist (Pimentel and Giampietro 1994).

It should be noted, however, that in spite of the seriousness of its environmental impact, the crisis of the paradigm of industrial agriculture is nowadays perceived by the general public mainly because of its bad performance on the socio-economic side.

THE GROWING AWARENESS OF THE CRISIS OF THE PARADIGM OF INDUSTRIAL AGRICULTURE

A clear example of the current crisis of the paradigm of industrial agriculture, within developed countries, is given by the predicament faced by the Dutch government in relation to the development of Flevoland. Flevoland is the last piece of land that has been claimed in the legendary fight of the Dutch people against the sea. For centuries, this fight required the continuous construction and operation of dykes, dams, channels, and pumping stations (the Dutch windmills). Thanks to new technology and much more power available, by taking advantage of the opportunity provided by the gigantic Zuiderzee project, the Dutch people would now have the possibility of winning their war for good. But, unexpectedly, in spite of the strong cultural tradition, the traditional narrative that technical progress means 'the ability of claiming as much agricultural land as possible from the sea' was abandoned.

In the last decades in the Netherlands, it has become evident that nobody wants to become a farmer in Flevoland as farming is no longer perceived, at the level of individual households, as an attractive economic activity. It is also evident that the Dutch society is happy that nobody wants to become a farmer in Flevoland. The agricultural sector is no longer perceived as an economic sector driving the growth of the economy. That is, increasing the amount of agricultural land in production would represent, first, a drain on the Dutch economy because of the subsidies needed for new farmers starting on marginal land, and second, an additional load for the environment, because of an additional boost in the pace of pollution of the water table.

This predicament applies to the rest of Europe too, where agriculture is the economic sector with the highest demand of capital investment per job, lowest economic returns on the economic investment, and the largest environmental impact per unit of added value generated. Furthermore, in Europe, guaranteeing a high quality of social services to the rural population is more expensive than to the urban population.

Thus, in spite of their strong sense of cultural identity, formed through the centuries by the continuous fight to claim land from the sea, the Dutch had to recognize that today, in post-industrial Europe, increasing the land under agricultural production (under the industrial paradigm) is not a step in the right direction, neither for the farmer nor for the society, let alone the environment.

The metaphor of Flevoland describes well the crisis experienced by the agricultural sector in Europe that has led to a public acknowledgment of the need for a total rethink of the CAP (Common Agricultural Policy). There are at least three clear reasons for moving away from the old system of incentives:

(i) from an economic point of view, it does not make sense to subsidize the farmers to produce a surplus of commodities, which do not have a demand in developed countries and are too expensive for the poor in developing countries;

(ii) from a food security point of view, it does not make sense to subsidize the farmers to adopt expensive farming techniques that have a negative impact on the environment and deplete more and more natural resources, since there is no longer a food shortage in Europe; and

(iii) from a social point of view, it does not make sense to operate a system of subsidies supposed to protect farmers and rural communities, in which the money allocated to the agricultural sector ends up in other economic sectors (those producing technical inputs and services) and not in the pockets of the farmers and those living in the countryside.

This latter point indicates the second critical aspect of the paradigm of industrial agriculture, which is more related to the social dimension. This is a critical aspect which is becoming more and more evident both in developed and in developing countries. Technological progress of agriculture, under the industrial paradigm, translates into an increased stress on farmers and more in general on rural communities. In Australia, the farmers are so dispersed in the countryside that special TV programmes—for example, 'desperately seeking Sheila', are available to help them look for a wife (*http://www.sbs.com.au/sheila/*). Similarly, in some rural areas Canadian children have to use the internet to reach a critical mass of interaction (for example, Canada's School Net). The situation in Europe is slightly different, because of a higher demographic density. Yet, in marginal rural areas, especially in the mountains, the steady trend in emigration of young people, which translates into an increase in the average age of farmers, is alarming. Whole villages have to be closed during winter for lack of a critical mass of people living in them.

In the rural areas of developing countries, if possible, things are even worse. In India, the phenomenon of suicides of farmers unable to pay their debts is massive. Estimates of the number of suicides in the decade going from 1996–2006 are between 15,000 and 50,000 (for more, see *http://en.wikipedia.org/wiki/Farmer_Suicides_in_India*). Rural areas all over the developing world share a similar situation— of the social fabric disintegrating and disappearing everywhere because of crumbling rural communities. New generations are abandoning the traditional way of farming, since the industrial paradigm is providing neither a viable nor a desirable alternative. As soon as agricultural production is regulated by the market, farmers learn quickly that the cost of the inputs grows faster than the price at which they can sell their output. The resulting lack of rural development entails a massive abandonment of traditional farming systems, made no longer viable due to the increase in demographic pressure, and a migration to the cities or to other countries.

Before closing this section, the following additional points should be noted:

(i) the current clash against ecological constraints at the global level has been recently described and documented by a large-scale project, Millennium Ecosystem Assessment, *http://www.millenniumassessment.org/en/index.aspx*—which provides an integrated assessment of the negative impact on the health of ecosystems all over the world; and

(ii) in relation to the heavy dependency of agricultural production on fossil energy (entailed by the paradigm of industrial agriculture), without getting into the debate on the exact date of the Peak Oil, we can assume as valid three predictions about which there is total agreement among energy analysts (for example, *http://www.chim.unisi.it/portovenere/*): (a) the era of cheap oil is over; (b) for the moment (in the short/medium term) humans do not have large-scale alternatives to oil; (c) fossil energy will remain crucial to sustain the existing economic development for the next 25 years. This means that the problems of increasing price for energy and climatic change are here to stay.

THE PAST: THE SUCCESS OF THE PARADIGM OF INDUSTRIAL AGRICULTURE

Achievements in Terms of Food Production

The industrial paradigm of agriculture is the legacy of one of the most extraordinary successes of technological progress for the whole humankind. This explains the ideological intoxication and the lock-in about the uncontested acceptance of the underlying narrative. In the last century, world population increased three-fold, rising from two billion at the beginning of 1900 to more than six billion at the beginning of the year 2000. Even more impressive has been the increase in the pace of population growth. World population increased from 3.5 billion at the beginning of the 1970s to 6.5 billion in 2005. That is, in 35 years the population increased more— by three billion people—than in the previous 35,000 years! In spite of the accompanying skyrocketing increase in the amount of required food, humans were able to increase their ability to produce it. According to the Millennium Ecosystem Assessment, 'since 1960, population doubled while the economic activity is increased of 6 times, food production is increased 21/2 times'.

The stunning performance of the industrial paradigm is, however, not only related to its ability to produce much more food on less land per capita, but also to its ability to produce much more food using much less human labour. In the industrial era there is no country with a gross domestic product (GDP) higher than US$10,000 per capita with more than 5 per cent of the workforce allocated in agriculture. The richest countries have a fraction of farmers—lower than 2 per cent—in the workforce.

Therefore, technical progress in agriculture managed to achieve two main objectives:

(i) the increasing use of technical inputs (based on fossil energy) made it possible to use less agricultural land per capita, and produce more food per capita. In developed countries, the consumption of grain per capita is around 1,000 kg per year (direct consumption plus the indirect consumption in the food system for animal production, the making of beer, and other industrial products). This value is almost four times the consumption of 250 kg of grain per capita per year typical of pre-industrial societies.

(ii) the increasing use of technical inputs (based on fossil energy) made it possible to use less hours of agricultural labour while producing more food per capita. For example, the entire amount of food consumed per capita in the year 2002 by a US citizen (the US is among the countries with the highest consumption of food items per capita) was produced using only 17 hours of work in the agricultural sector (Giampietro 2003).

The Economic Mechanism to Sideline Farmers: 'Agricultural Technology Treadmill'

The process of dramatic reduction in the number of farmers, necessary for the socio-economic transformations leading to modern societies, can be analysed in economic terms. Such an analysis has been proposed by Willard Cochrane (1958), who identified the mechanism through which the market can be used, in the agricultural sector, to get rid of the farmers. Cochrane called this mechanism the 'agricultural technology treadmill'. This mechanism works in five steps, iterated in time, which are summarized in Box 5.1.

Box 5.1: The Five Steps of the 'Agricultural Technology Treadmill'

Step 1: Many small farms all produce the same product. Because not one of them can affect the price, all will produce as much as possible against the going price;

Step 2: A new technology enables innovators to capture a windfall profit—'innovation';

Step 3: After some time, others follow—'diffusion of innovations';

Step 4: Increasing production and/or efficiency drives down prices. Those who have not yet adopted the new technology must now do so lest they lose income—'price squeeze';

Step 5: Those who are too old, sick, poor, or indebted to innovate have to eventually leave the scene. Their resources are absorbed by those who make the windfall profits. This is called 'scale enlargement', but it should be called 'farmers elimination'.

Technical Solutions Behind Success in Agriculture

The data and the statements presented in this section are elaborated in several studies analysing and comparing the use of technical inputs in world agriculture [Giampietro 1997, 2002b, 2003; Giampietro et al. 1999]:

Two different types of pressure, namely demographic and socio-economic pressure, can be seen as drivers of technical progress in agriculture. First, the higher is the demographic pressure (proxy: population divided colonized land) the higher is the productivity of land (proxy: yields of cultivated crops). Second, the higher is the socio-economic pressure (proxy: the fraction of the workforce allocated in the industrial, services, and government sectors) the higher is the productivity of labour (proxy: the amount of food produced per hour of work in agriculture).

The combination of these two different types of pressure entails a different combination of use of technical inputs: (i) irrigation and fertilizers are required to deal with the demographic pressure; whereas (ii) machinery is required to deal with the socio-economic pressure. Looking at the use of irrigation and fertilizer over different countries of the world, these inputs are used more in crowded countries, independently of the level of economic growth. Looking at the use of machinery over different countries of the world, these inputs are found to be used basically only in developed countries.

These points will be used later in the chapter when discussing the possibility of continuing in the future within the same trajectory of technical progress entailed by the paradigm of industrial agriculture.

Side Effects of the Success Obtained in the Past

Economic Development and Increase in Food Consumption Per Capita

Looking at the direct consumption of food energy in the diet can be misleading when assessing the total requirement of agricultural production per capita. For example, in 1997 the energy consumed in the diet per capita in developed countries was 13.6 MJ per day as compared to a slightly lower value for developing countries at 11.1 MJ per day. However, when considering the differences in 'quality' of the diet we get a completely different picture. For example, the presence of animal products requires the production of plant calories, which have to be fed to the animals. When considering the energy intake from animal products the difference between developed and developing countries becomes much wider (3.6 MJ per day of animal products in developed countries as compared to 1.3 MJ per day in developing countries). This entails that the diet typical of developed countries requires 28 MJ per day of plant calories versus the 13 MJ per day consumed right now in developing countries, that is, more than double the primary agricultural production per capita. It should be noted that as soon as the income of consumers in developing countries grows, richer consumers tend to follow the pattern of consumption adopted in developed countries.

Differences in the Pattern of Use of Technical Inputs between Developed and Developing Countries

By assessing the amount of fossil energy backing up an hour of work in agriculture, a proxy of the level of capitalization of the agricultural sector can be obtained. The rationale of this analysis is that the ability to harness a larger quantity of fossil energy per hour of labour indicates the availability of more technology and capital per worker. In this way, it is possible to notice that between developed and developing countries the difference in this value is huge. In 1997, in developed countries this value was 152 MJ per hour, versus 4 MJ per hour in developing countries, a difference of 38 times! This huge difference is due to: (i) the almost total absence of machinery in developing countries (low socio-economic pressure); and (ii) the limited availability of land per agricultural worker, which reduces the consumption associated with irrigation and fertilizers (much higher demographic pressure). As a matter of fact, the difference in hectares of cultivated land per worker was of 12 times—12 ha per worker in developed countries and only 1 ha per worker in developing countries. It is remarkable that in spite of the large difference in the level of energy and capital per agricultural worker, the production of food per hectare in developing countries, at 24.2 GJ per ha, is more than double the production achieved in developed countries, 10.1 GJ per ha. This difference can be explained by various factors: the mix of produced crops (mainly cereals in developing countries); multicropping patterns (especially relevant for rice production); and the different yields of the individual crops.

Differences in Density of Flows of Added Value Generated in Different Typologies of Farming Systems

When performing a comparison of the density of flows of added value over different typologies of farming systems of the world, the differences are found to be so big that one has to use a logarithmic scale! Figure 4.1 shows that the three main typologies of agricultural production— (i) production systems operating in developed countries within the industrial paradigm; (ii) mixed systems of production operating partially in the market; and (iii) subsistence farming systems;—are characterized by numerical values separated by orders of magnitude.

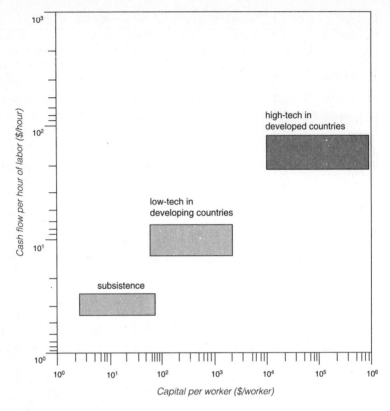

Figure 5.1:   Difference in Density of Flow of Added Value and Level of Capitalization in Various Typologies of Farming Systems

THE FUTURE: IS IT POSSIBLE TO GO ON WITH THE INDUSTRIAL AGRICULTURE PARADIGM?

Future of Technical Progress in Agriculture in Developing Countries

Looking at existing benchmarks and trends, it seems that it will be very unlikely that the technical development of agriculture in developing countries will follow the same pattern (going through the industrial paradigm) experienced by developed countries. In fact, because of the very high demographic pressure, developing countries are already using, per hectare, more fossil energy per capita (only for fertilizer and irrigation) than developed countries. When considering only the fossil energy relative to these two types of input, in 1997 developing countries used (Giampietro 2006) more fossil energy per hectare (4.9 GJ per ha) than developed countries (7.4 GJ per ha). This entails that in relation to the use of technical inputs, developing countries are already in the part of the curve with decreasing marginal returns. An additional intensification in the use of technical inputs will not pay.

Furthermore, in relation to the very low level of socio-economic pressure, to follow the same pattern of development adopted by developed countries, developing countries would have to replace farmers with capital and fossil energy. This would require a dramatic increase in the current economic investment in agriculture per worker. The investment would have to be accompanied by a massive restructuring of rural infrastructures since traditional agriculture is organized at the moment in very small units of production. In turn, these investments would provide an additional boost to the process of urbanization, which is already excessive and out of control. But even more perplexing is the idea that it would be convenient to opt for such a massive flow of economic investments. As a matter of fact, if one had US$100,000 to invest in a rural area in China, looking at the availability of land and the existing infrastructures, it would be unwise to invest it in a big tractor!

In relation to the biophysical constraints limiting the possibility of expanding economic activity, it is easy to predict that, if possible, things can only get worse. The vast majority of the 2 billion people, the expected increase in world population by the year 2050, will arrive in those areas of the planet in which the problems generated by demographic pressure are already serious. Writing down a relation linking the various factors determining the income of farmers:

$$\text{Added Value/worker} = \text{profit/kg} \times \text{kg/ha} \times \text{ha/hours of workload} \times \text{hours of workload/worker,}$$

it can be seen that: (i) the profit per kg tends to go down in agriculture; (ii) the value 'kg/ha' is already higher in developing countries—when considering the aggregate values of yields of China, India, and other South-East Asian countries; (iii) the number of ha per worker is much lower in developing countries and will remain so, because of demographic pressure. This means that the workload per worker cannot be increased, since the existing combination of factors generates a systemic surplus of labour in rural areas.

An additional problem is generated by the quick demographic changes taking place in developing countries. Changes in the profile of the population over different age classes translate into a change in the supply of hours of work per year in the society (see Figure 5.2). The consequences in time of these changes are not easy to control. For example, in China the 'one child only' policy implemented for demographic control has induced a population structure of a peculiar shape: 60 per cent of the population is economically active at present. The economic effect of this structure can be appreciated against the age structure determining a 50 per cent of economically active population in OECD countries, or that of Italy, where, due to the progressive ageing of the population, the economically active population is just 40 per cent. This explains how it is possible for the Chinese economy to deal with a huge demographic pressure in agriculture (using massive quantity of fertilizers and irrigation wherever possible) without using large amounts of machinery. That is, right now in China, this large supply of labour makes it possible to produce both food in the agricultural sector, without the use of machinery and at the same time, 'labour intensive' industrial products in other economic sectors (Ramos et al. 2007). But what will happen when this wave of adults will become a wave of elderly?

Even more complicated is the situation of those countries that experienced in the preceding decade a demographic boom—(lower graph on the right in Figure 5.2). They have a distribution of

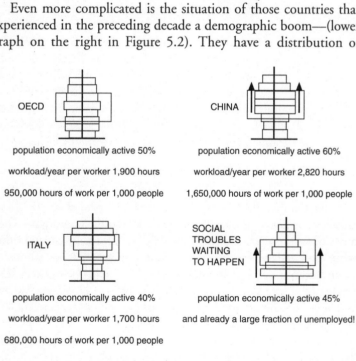

OECD

population economically active 50%

workload/year per worker 1,900 hours

950,000 hours of work per 1,000 people

CHINA

population economically active 60%

workload/year per worker 2,820 hours

1,650,000 hours of work per 1,000 people

ITALY

population economically active 40%

workload/year per worker 1,700 hours

680,000 hours of work per 1,000 people

SOCIAL TROUBLES WAITING TO HAPPEN

population economically active 45%

and already a large fraction of unemployed!

Figure 5.2: The Effect of Changes in Demographic Structure on Work Supply

population over age classes with large waves (or rather 'tsunamis') of youngsters that will enter the workforce looking for a job. For these countries it will be impossible to generate jobs at a pace that will be able to provide a level of employment capable of avoiding social tensions and conflicts. The majority of Islamic countries provide a clear example of this typology of problem. A rural development based on systems of production adopting the industrial paradigm will represent the worst-case scenario (the highest requirement of capital invested per job generated) for these countries.

To sum up, the future of agriculture in developing countries can be looked at from the following perspectives: It is very unlikely that the industrial paradigm of agriculture will be useful to solve the problems of rural development in developing countries, except in special niches. Even increasing the actual productivity of labour in agriculture by 100 per cent will not provide a viable and acceptable alternative for rural development in many areas of the world. In a globalized world, rural development has to be based on something completely different (multifunctional use of the landscape) based on a progressive integration of agricultural activities with non-agricultural activities. Further, it is not clear as to why developing countries should invest an important fraction of their limited endowment of financial resources in the type of technical capital required by the paradigm of industrial agriculture. In fact, in developing countries, capital investment would provide the lowest economic return, the highest requirement of capital per job created, and significant environmental impact.

Future of Technical Progress in Agriculture in Developed Countries?

The socio-economic transformations typical of modern societies entail a dramatic change in the 'costs'—either defined in terms of energy (Joules) and/or in terms of money ($)—of food security within the food system. For example, in a developed society, what is paid for in a food product is related to its convenience (that is, reduced time and easy preparation), rather than to its content in nutrients. Therefore, the food system of a modern society no longer supplies raw materials for the cook, but rather pre-prepared components of meals or even ready-to-eat meals to be processed in a microwave or eaten outside (Figure 5.3). Because of this change in the meaning of a 'food product', the food system is now performing

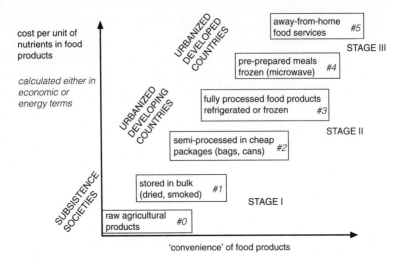

Figure 5.3:   Changing Meaning of 'Food Products' in Post-industrial Society

several functions that were performed by the households (in particular, by housewives and children) in pre-industrial societies.

In spite of the high cost—either in terms of energy or money—of the step of agricultural production, the 'cost' of agricultural products is only 20 per cent of the overall cost of the production and consumption of food in a food system. For example, in the USA (data from Heller and Keoleian 2000)—left graph of Figure 4.4—the amount of money spent on food and going to the farmers is US$680 per capita per year. This amount of money is several times higher than the overall amount of money spent per capita for food in developing countries. However, this amount is only 20 per cent of the total of the money spent on food per person per year in the USA, that is, US$3,400. The rest of the money goes to economic activities performed in the post-harvest sector. The same breakdown of relative costs is found when considering energy expenditures. The amount of energy spent per person per year to produce food in the agricultural sector is 9.2 GJ (Heller and Keoleian 2000). However, when considering the energy expenditures of the rest of the food system—post-harvest handling, processing, packaging, transportation, and home preparation—the overall energy expenditures reach the value of 42.4 GJ per person per year, that is, almost five times more!

In spite of the large energy costs (Joules) and economic costs ($) per person for food security at the level of the whole food system, in developed countries these costs are less than 12 per cent of the total. For example, in the USA (data from Heller and Keoleian 2000)—right graph of Figure 5.4—the amount of US$3400 spent per person per year on food represents only 11 per cent of the total amount of money spent per year per person, that is US$31,400. In the same way, the 42.4 GJ per person per year spent in the food system is only 12 per cent of the total amount of energy expenditure per person and per year in the USA at 355 GJ.

To sum up, the future of agriculture in developing countries can be looked at from the following perspectives:

(i) Looking at the data presented in the previous section, we can say that either in energy or economic terms the phase of agricultural production is quite irrelevant for the costs of a modern society—it represents around 2 per cent (11 per cent × 20 per cent) of the overall expenditures of a society. This is to say, that working on technical innovations, within the industrial paradigm, to reduce the costs of agricultural production of 20 per cent or 30 per cent (of 2 per cent!) should not be given a high priority by society. This is especially true when other factors such as the integrity of the social fabric and ecosystems are in great danger.

(ii) Put in another way, in developed societies the agricultural sector is clearly a victim of its own success. At present, 'producing more food' is no longer a priority for society. The availability of food is considered as given, and other criteria of performance are being given importance. This change in the perception of the role of the food system in a society should be reflected in a change in the priorities to be given to the technological development of agriculture. However, this change has not been perceived yet by those working on technological innovation. This is at the basis of the development of the Concorde Syndrome.

WHAT WENT WRONG?: THE 'CONCORDE SYNDROME' AND GENETICALLY MODIFIED ORGANISMS IN AGRICULTURE

The 'Concorde Syndrome'

The expression 'Concorde syndrome' refers to a form of lock-in that often takes place in the field of technical innovations. This syndrome occurs when the narrative used to provide the terms of reference of the problem to be solved is obsolete and no longer reflects the social perception of what the problems to be solved are. In the case of the

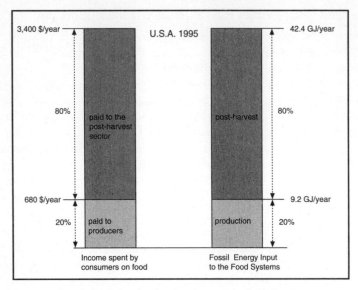

'Costs' of agriculture against the other costs in the food system

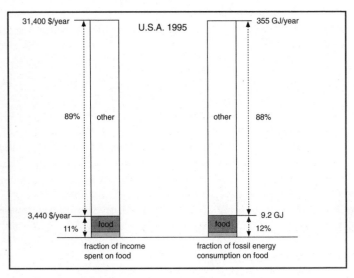

'Costs' of food system against the other costs in the economy

Figure 5.4:   Contextualizing the 'Costs' of Food Production within Society

Concorde, the problem to be solved was to build an airliner capable of cruising above the speed of sound, much faster than its competitors. However, besides the actual flying time, other criteria of performance—the cost of the ticket and the variety in the options of time schedule—turned out to be relevant for the customers. These neglected criteria provided a clear edge to the competition which went for a strategy based on large airliners flying below sound speed. Therefore, the fundamental mistake of those running the Concorde project was that of ignoring a set of key criteria relevant for the customers. Similarly, the fundamental mistake of those still looking at technical innovations within the paradigm of industrial agriculture is to ignore a set of key costs of the food systems, which are rapidly gaining relevance for society. These are:

- costs on the public health: obesity, diabetes, cardiovascular diseases, and negative effects of the heavy use of hormones and pesticides in the food system;
- environmental costs: soil erosion, loss of biodiversity, pollution of the water table, excessive withdrawal from the water table and rivers, and interference—at the level of the landscape—with bio-geochemical cycles of matter and nutrients;
- social costs: loss of social fabric in rural areas, loss of cultural traditions and the symbolic/cultural dimension of food, and negative impact on rural landscapes;
- economic costs: increasing requirement of economic resources for subsidies, which keep increasing in the face of an increasing cost of energy. Possible indirect costs may include the loss of image of traditional food products, the loss of traditional rural landscapes—for example, in relation to alternative uses of the land for residential, recreational, or touristic purposes.

Put in another way, the Concorde syndrome of the paradigm of industrial agriculture has been transferred into the strategy of development of genetically modified organisms (GMOs) by the endorsement of a series of assumptions/simplifications about the future role of agriculture in society which are not longer shared by the rest of society. In particular, the most contested simplifications are:

(i) agriculture is just another economic activity having the goal of producing commodities and profit;

(ii) the various food products can be effectively considered in generic terms as commodities. In technical jargon, this assumption is carried out under the claim of 'substantive equivalence'. This means assuming that independently from their taste, texture, smell, cultural traditions, and—above all—independently from the way they are produced, food products assigned to the same category have all the same quality: for example, any kg of corn, apples, potatoes, or beef is the same (for more, see Giampietro 1994). Obviously, this assumption must be based on an uncontested agreement on the definition of quality for the chosen categories of food products. The question then is: how many categories are needed to describe our food and who decides about the definitions to be adopted for the various categories?;

(iii) the existing environmental, social, and economic costs associated with technical progress of agriculture within the industrial paradigm are negligible or can be handled by using reliable regulations. This assumption entails the idea that it is possible to deal with the assessment of negative consequences of technological innovation in terms of risk analysis, that is, that large-scale development of technical innovations does not entail large doses of uncertainty and genuine ignorance (Giampietro 2002a).

Sunk Cost and Technical Innovation within the Paradigm of Industrial Agriculture

It should be noted that the vast majority of technical innovations in agriculture in the last decades can be easily characterized as belonging to the Concorde Syndrome. A very good example is represented by the introduction of the Bovine Growth Hormone (BGH, also called Bovine Somatropin or BST), to boost the production of milk in cows, which was introduced in the 1990s in the USA. The similarity between the Concorde and the BGH projects is striking:

A. The steps that took place in the Concorde Project were as follows:

(i) the goal given to the scientists was to 'produce an airliner flying faster';

(ii) the scientists worked successfully on a HOW defining what should be considered as a more efficient system, but in relation to a WHY which was not shared by society;

(iii) the reality check was negative—it looked like a good idea, but it resulted in a flop. Too much speed! It translated into small and expensive airliners, with no adequate demand;

B. The steps that took place in the BGH/BST project were as follows:

(i) the goal given to the scientists was to produce a hormone capable of boosting the production of milk in cows;

(ii) the scientists worked successfully on a HOW defining what should be considered as a more efficient system, but in relation to a WHY which was not shared by society;

(iii) the reality check was negative—it looked like a good idea, but it resulted in a flop. Too much milk! The resulting production of milk was too much both for the physiology of the cows and for the functioning of the market. In this particular case, in the state of New York, the introduction of BGH/BST represented a classic example of 'agricultural technology treadmill', Basically, it drove a large part of the small dairy farms in that state out of business.

The Curse of 'Sunk Cost'

When working on technological innovations, the worst case scenario is to discover that the original choice of a narrative about the problem to be solved with the innovation was wrong. This acknowledgment that the initial choice of a narrative was bad entails the need for dealing with a 'sunk cost', which can be pretty high at times. The standard reaction to the existence of large sunk costs is 'we cannot stop now, otherwise what we invested so far will be lost...'. This seems to be the situation of those that have been developing GMOs in order to make profit within the field of technological innovations in agriculture, in the last decades. While the reaction stated above is certainly true, this is irrelevant in relation to the fact that it does not make any sense to keep investing in a bad idea. Moreover, when trying to avoid the 'sunk cost' in the short term, one may adopt a strategy based on convincing the rest of the society that the bad idea is good and that, therefore, it should be implemented, even if this will result, in the long run, in even larger social, economic, and ecological costs.

CONCLUDING REMARKS

Alternatives to irrational investments based on bad ideas about technical innovations determined by the Concorde syndrome do exist. Finding these alternatives, however, would require that before jumping into a frantic search for magic technological solutions— the mythical 'silver bullets'—one should reflect using common sense.

First of all, it is important to understand better the nature of the problems that we want to solve.

For example, nobody would like to go to a dentist who is paid in terms of a given amount of dollars per kg of teeth extracted from the mouth of the patient. As a matter of fact, dentists have to take care of the health of the mouth of their patients and not just extract kilos of teeth. It is not clear, therefore, why we accept a mechanism of characterization and regulation of the agricultural sector which describes farmers as economic agents paid to extract biomass from terrestrial ecosystems at a given ratio of dollars per kg.

On the contrary, common sense says that agriculture should play an essential role for society, which cannot be fully captured when adopting an economic perspective: (i) it produces food which is needed for life: it guarantees the health of individual human beings; (ii) it preserves existing landscapes: it guarantees the health of ecosystems; (iii) it preserves important aspects of existing culture: it contributes to the health of society.

Thus, agriculture should be assessed, regulated, and remunerated in relation to these services, many of which are very difficult to quantify in monetary terms. Acknowledging the crucial importance of these services entails acknowledging that agriculture is not about producing economic commodities, which can be successfully assessed in terms of dollars per kg.

What are the implications of this fact on the activity and investments for technical innovations in agriculture?

- In developed countries, the priority of 'producing more', is no longer there; on the contrary there is a clear alternative priority to be given to 'producing better'. In terms of technical progress, this means that the two historic objectives of: (i) eliminating farmers; and (ii) eliminating the cycles of nutrients by simplifying the agro-ecosystems are no longer valid.—Rather, new priorities should be: (i) re-connecting the cities and urban dwellers with their rural roots; and (ii) reinforcing the ability of agro-ecosystems, plus the natural ecosystems embedding them, to provide ecological services.

  For these reasons, a change in the narrative about the role of agriculture in society would require a fresh societal debate about how to negotiate a new 'social contract' for agriculture. It is important that the society (and not transnational corporations having as their main goal the maximization of profit) starts a deliberation and a negotiation about what meaning should be assigned to the expression 'producing better' within the agricultural sector.

- In developing countries, it is extremely clear that the last thing that is needed is a strategy aimed at eliminating farmers as quickly as possible by boosting their already high stress, putting them on the 'agricultural innovation treadmill'. As a matter of fact, the level of stress and the pace of elimination of farmers is already too high! In order to slow down the uncontrolled and desperate migration toward urban areas and toward developed countries, what is needed is a pattern of rural development that is effective in reducing the stress of farmers and in keeping them in rural areas.

- There is a wild card that can have important implications on this discussion. In the last World Trade Organization (WTO) trade talks, the Doha Round, an agreement (at least in principle) was reached about commodity support programmes. Crop insurance, export subsidies, loan deficiency payments, and countercyclical payments have been considered to distort production and trade and, therefore, were listed in the Amber Box, including those subsidies to be restricted by WTO Trade Agreements. This would translate to an amount of subsidies to be cut in the order of US$19 billion for the USA and of US$80 billion for the European Union (EU). If ever implemented, this agreement could make available money that could and should be spent in getting a better agriculture. This money could and should be used to help a change in the existing paradigm about how to produce and consume food, rather than in keeping alive the agonizing industrial paradigm. In the same way, a more effective integration of the agriculture of developing countries within that of developed countries could provide new opportunities for a re-discussion of the direction of technical progress in agriculture within developing countries.

- It is possible to get out of the 'Concorde syndrome' associated with the paradigm of industrial agriculture. This would require looking for new trajectories of rural development based on different narratives about technical progress in agriculture. These alternative trajectories cannot be found or implemented by scientists working on 'silver bullets' following an agenda set by transnational corporations. A viable and desirable solution cannot be found on the basis of models that optimize technical coefficients and generation of profit. Yet, science and technology are crucial in the task of finding desirable solutions to existing problems. However, technical solutions will have to be found within new problem structuring provided by fresh narratives about development based on wisdom, vision of the future, shared values, ability to consider different points of views, and the will to negotiate in good faith. This has nothing to do with looking for maximization of productivity or a higher return on the investment.

REFERENCES

Cochrane, W., (1958), *Farm Prices: Myth and Reality*, Minneapolis, MN: University of Minnesota Press.

Conforti, P. and M. Giampietro, (1997), Fossil Energy Use in Agriculture: an International Comparison', *Agriculture, Ecosystems and Environment*, Vol. 65, No. 3, pp. 231–43.

Giampietro, M., (1994), 'Sustainability and Technological Development in Agriculture: A Critical Appraisal of Genetic Engineering', *BioScience*, Vol. 44, No. 10, pp. 677–89.

_____, (1997), 'Socioeconomic Pressure, Demographic Pressure, Environmental Loading and Technological Changes in Agriculture', *Agriculture, Ecosystems and Environment*, Vol. 65, pp. 201–29.

_____, (2002a), 'The Precautionary Principle and Ecological Hazards of Genetically Modified Organisms', *AMBIO*, Vol. 31, No. 6, pp. 466–70.

_____, (2002b), 'Energy Use in Agriculture', in *Encyclopedia of Life Sciences*, Nature Publishing Group, accessible at *http://www.els.net/* (accessed on 15 July 2007).

_____, (2003), *Multi-Scale Integrated Analysis of Agro-ecosystems*, Boca Raton: CRC Press, pp. 472.

Giampietro, M., S.G.F. Bukkens, and D. Pimentel, (1999), 'General Trends of Technological Changes in Agriculture', *Critical Reviews in Plant Sciences*, Vol. 18, No. 3, pp. 261–82.

Heller, M. and G. Keoleian, (2000), 'Life-Cycle Based Sustainability Indicators for Assessment of the U.S. Food System', Report 2000–4, Center for Sustainable Systems, University of Michigan, Ann Arbor, MI, December, accessible at *http://www.public.iastate.edu/~brummer/papers/FoodSystemSustainability.pdf* (accessed on 15 July 2007).

Pimentel, D. and M. Giampietro, (1994), 'Implications of the Limited Potential of Technology to Increase the Carrying Capacity of our Planet', *Human Ecology Review*, Vol. 1, No. 2, pp. 249–52.

Ramos-Martin J., M. Giampietron, and K. Mayumi, (2007), 'On China's Exosomatic Energy Metabolism: An Application of Multi-scale Integrated Analysis of Societal Metabolism (MSIASM)', *Ecological Economics*, Vol. 63, No. 1, pp. 174–91.

6

Mexico' s Biosafety Policy Regime
A Critical Analysis

ALEJANDRO NADAL

In March 2005, Mexico's Congress enacted a new Biosafety Law for Geneticaly Modified Organisms (BLGMO),[1] a public interest law that explicitly states its objective as providing adequate protection for human health and the environment from possible risks related to activities involving genetically modified organisms (GMOs). However, the analysis of the main components of this law show that the basic premise of the new legislation is that GMOs do not pose a serious risk to the environment or to human health. In fact, the new legislation contains a special chapter on the promotion of the development of biotechnology in Mexico. From this perspective, Mexico's biosafety regime is marked by a peculiar stance concerning risk management, liability and redress mechanisms, and the role of GMOs in the agricultural system of a megadiverse country.

The Biosafety Law devotes most of its initial contents to the procedures surrounding permits for experimental and commercial planting of GMOs. There are three types of permits involved in the new legislation: experimental, pilot scale, and commercial release of GMOs. Although this part of the law appears to be rather lenient with companies and laboratories interested in the release of GMOs, there are important barriers that emerge due to other sections of the law. Recent events in Mexico concerning the request of permits for experimental planting of Bt corn by three multinational companies (Monsanto, Pioneer, and Dow) help understand the mechanics and risks of the new legislation.[2] In what follows, we

---

[1]*Diario Oficial*, 18 March 2005.

[2]Bt corn is a genetically modified variety of corn in which a gene of the common *Bacillus thuringiensis* that synthesizes an insect repellent is inserted through various methods into the genome of the host plant.

106 SCIENCE FOR POLICY

will consider these elements in order to provide a systemic analysis to the law.

In the second section of this chapter we focus on the relation between GMOs and Mexico's ecosystems, covering the law's references to centres of origin, natural protected areas, and GMO-restricted areas. The third and fourth sections examine the labelling and liability and redress systems, respectively. The fifth section analyses the institutional framework and the relationship between this law and the Cartagena Protocol. The final section presents the main conclusions.

BIOSAFETY AND MEXICO'S ECOSYSTEMS

Mexico is located at the crossroads of the Nearctic and Neotropical biogeographic regions. It possesses approximately 1.4 per cent of the world's surface (two million square kilometers) but ranks third in biological diversity (Mittermeier 1988). It is host to almost 12 per cent of the total number of known species (Toledo and Ordoñez 1993). With a coastline of nearly 12,000 kilometres, rugged topography, and a rich combination of ecosystems, Mexico is a megadiverse country with a very high level of endemism: the percentage of endemic species is in the range of 40–63 per cent for plants and 30 per cent for vertebrate animals (INE 2000). It ranks second in total number of reptiles and first in number of endemic reptile species. It holds fifth place in total species of mammals. Harbouring 30,000 species of plants, of which 21,600 are flowering plants (Rzedowski 1993), Mexico occupies fifth place in the world with respect to the total number of vascular plant species. It also ranks fourth in total number of amphibians. Together with China and India, Mexico is a country where megadiversity coexists with a centre of agricultural origin of several critical crops, including corn, *Zea mays*.

The new Biosafety Law, that is, BLGMO, recognizes the importance of Mexico's biodiversity in its preamble and many of its articles. Article 2 states that the objective of the BLGMO is to guarantee an adequate level of protection for human health, the environment, and biodiversity with respect to the risks that activities with GMOs may pose. In order to unravel how effective the new law is in providing this 'adequate level of protection' we need to examine the policy regime for centres of origin, natural protected areas, and GMO-free areas.

Centres of Origin

The Biosafety Law states (Article 88) that in centres of origin and of genetic variability of animal and plant species, liberation of GMOs will only be authorized when these GMOs are different from native species, and only in those cases in which there will be no negative effects on human health and/or biological diversity.

This article involves several important qualifications. In order to be eligible for a full-fledged commercial permit, GMOs must differ from native species. This may appear as an important safeguard, but it excludes the more comprehensive environmental effects of GMOs. Although potential negative effects may be significantly reduced by the safeguard clause, effects on other non-target species (for example, in the case of Bt GMOs) are ignored.

The definition of 'centres of origin' in this article does not help to clarify the scope of the protection given to these regions. Article 87 asserts that centres of origin and of genetic diversity are defined as 'regions that are hosts to populations of wild relatives of a GMO, including different races or varieties, which constitute a genetic reservoir'. It adds that in the case of crops, centres of origin are geographical regions in which an organism was domesticated if those regions are also centres of genetic diversity.

The scientific merits of this legal definition are rather questionable. Today there is a genuine controversy within the scientific community regarding the concept of centre of origin. Typically the concept of centre of origin pertains to a geographical region where domestication of a crop took place, and/or where there is greater genetic variability of a crop. Although these two criteria may appear rather straightforward, there are serious obstacles in the determination of a precise area as a centre of origin.

Another debate concerns the methodology to determine the scope of a given centre of origin. A good example is the case of corn in Mexico. There appears to be a rather robust consensus in the scientific community that *Zea mays* finds its centre of origin in Mexico in the two senses defined in Article 87. Corn was domesticated in Mexico approximately 6,000 years ago and today there are more than 59 races of that crop, each with a large number of varieties. However, it is difficult to pinpoint the precise areas in which corn was domesticated. According to some researchers, the cradle of corn domestication lies in the Balsas river basin, in the states of Guerrero and Michoacán (Serratos and Turrent 2004).

Other researchers propose a multiple origin theory, ranging from central Mexico to the highlands in Guatemala (Serratos and Turrent 2004). This uncertainty has serious legal implications.

In addition, genetic diversity is a trait that exists in many regions of Mexico. In the process of domestication, corn travelled on a northward path, leading to to further diversification. This process may have been the result of conscious decision-making to influence probabilities of different outcomes in plant, ear, and kernel morphologies. Also, because of the strong interaction between genetic traits and ecosystem characteristics, genetic variability is a distinct feature in many corn producing regions in Mexico. From this perspective, it is a rather difficult task to identify and isolate a region that hosts a 'centre of origin'. A great number of Mexico's agroecosystems would qualify as a 'centre of origin'. In addition, the BLGMO ignores the fact that *in situ* conservation is an ongoing process closely associated with the deepening of genetic diversity and leaves out of the definition of centres the role of the communities and individual producers that are the curators of genetic diversity and the development of genetic resources.

Establishing the precise boundaries of a 'centre of origin' as prescribed by the BLGMO is a delicate task. Article 86 announces that these boundaries will be determined jointly by the Ministry of Agriculture and the Ministry of the Environment with information from their data banks and information provided by several specialized official agencies (notably, by the National Commission for Biodiversity, CONABIO). However, these descriptive references do not help much in solving the basic problem of drawing limits and boundaries.

Perhaps the most important objection to the law in this context is that protecting centres of origin becomes a policy regime based on an exception, instead of relying on a general rule. Instead of defining exceptional areas where liberation of GMOs to the environment is to be permitted, the law works the other way around: it sets a procedure to identify the exceptional areas that are to be protected (through restrictions on GMOs). The corollary of this is that the rest of Mexico's rural landscape will be available for the release of GMOs. This is in accordance with the basic premises of the BLGMO and the untenable position that GMOs pose no risks to the environment. We return to this point below.

Article 2 states that one of the objectives of the law is to determine the basis for the establishment of GMO-free zones and zones in which GMO activities are to be restricted, 'as well as of crops which find their center of origin in Mexico, especially maize, for which there will be a special protection regime'. This special protective regime does not exist as yet and is a powerful barrier to current efforts to deregulate GMO commercial planting.

Natural Protected Areas

The surface of natural protected areas (NPAs) has experienced significant growth in the past decade. This may explain why the Biosafety Law gives special attention to the relation between GMOs and NPAs. Unfortunately, the end result is rather disappointing.

Article 89 of the BLGMO prohibits the introduction and release of GMOs in the core zones of NPAs. This is a good start, given the uncertainties surrounding the effects of GMOs in ecosystem dynamics. However, the law allows the use of GMOs as bio-remedial agents in NPAs when specific GMOs have been engineered to prevent or counter pests or contaminants that may endanger the lives of animal or plant species. Article 89 also tries to discipline this by stating that in all cases there must be scientific evidence 'supporting the environmental benefits that are being sought'.

Unfortunately, this discipline is insufficient. The ecosystems of NPAs are endowed with a very dense network of interdependencies between the living species they harbour. Introducing GMOs in a buffer zone of a biosphere reserve, for example, poses a serious risk for the entire protected area. Prohibiting the release of GMOs in core zones of NPAs only to allow their use in the buffer zones is a contradictory approach to GMOs in NPAs. Once introduced in a buffer zone, there may be nothing to prevent the spillover of these GMOs into the core zone.

Because the introduction of alien invasive species is the second most important cause for extinctions, it would have been better to prohibit the release of GMOs in all NPAs, without distinguishing between buffer and core zones. Because of the strong natural presence of comensalism and parasitism in NPAs, it would have been better to look at GMOs as invasive alien species which may pose a serious risk. In fact, on this point the new Biosafety Law contradicts Mexico's Federal Law on Ecological Equilibrium and Environmental Protection (LGEEPA, for the acronym in Spanish), which defines GMOs as contaminants.

GMO-free Areas

In one of its most important articles, the law defines the possibility of establishing GMO-free areas in Mexico in order to protect organic producers. Article 90 states that these zones will be established when GMOs are of the same species as the crops of organic producers and it is 'scientifically and technically' demonstrated that the coexistence of these two products is not viable or that the requirements for certification will not be met.

There are several problems with this article. First, conventional producers who do not use GMOs are ignored. It is not inconceivable that groups of these producers would want to preserve their crops free of genetically modified constructs. The law does not provide them with the necessary protection to safeguard their crops.

In addition, it is difficult to think of a case in which GMOs cannot coexist with crops of the same species. Coexistence does not necessarily imply innocuousness; if there is introgression between these plants, genetically modified constructs will find their way into the non-GMO plants. Non-coexistence is going to be very difficult to prove, but the article states that if loss of certification is involved, that is sufficient to provide the foundation for a GMO-free zone.

In order to determine a GMO-free zone the interested communities must make an explicit request to the Ministry of Agriculture. This request must be accompanied by 'the favourable opinion' of state-level and municipal authorities. Questions remain on the truly representative nature of state-level governments in Mexico, and recent experience shows that the power of lobby interest groups is significant. Thus, this provision is a formidable barrier to the emergence of GMO-free zones anywhere in Mexico.

The BLGMO is also deficient because it ignores the importance of organic and sustainable agricultural practices. Instead of promoting and fostering this set of agricultural practices, the Biosafety Law places organic producers in a defensive position without adequate legal instruments. This law contains a long chapter on the promotion of molecular biotechnology in Mexico, but has nothing to offer for sustainable agriculture and organic producers.

Finally, the notion of a GMO-free zone is treated as an exception instead of the other way around. It would make more sense to deal with GMOs on an exceptional basis, instead of opening the entire territory to their release and putting the burden of proof on producers and communities that want to refrain from using this technology. This is especially important in a country that is the centre of origin of commercial crops.

LABELLING

The labelling of GMO products is closely related to the rights of consumers and producers to be informed about the contents of the products or inputs used by them. The crucial principle of consumer sovereignty is at stake here. The Biosafety Law contains provisions concerning the labelling of GMOs for direct human consumption and for planting and uses as inputs in production processes. In the case of GMO products destined for direct human consumption which receive an authorization from the Ministry of Health, labels explicitly mentioning that the product contains GMOs are mandatory. These labels must contain information regarding their food composition and nutritional properties. However, Article 101 states that compulsory labelling is only required when 'these characteristics are significantly different from those of conventional products'. Thus, the principle of essential equivalence predominates and consumers are deprived of their right to know if they are consuming GMO or non-GMO products.

As regards GMO products destined for planting, mandatory labelling is established. These labels must make explicit references to the fact that these products contain GMOs. Although this is a step in the right direction, one problem is that in rural Mexico illiteracy rates are still important. This is why overdoses of pesticides and fertilizers are frequent in spite of the fact that labels must indicate correct dosages. The most important problem here in this context is that poor and marginalized producers who are under severe economic pressure may pay little attention to labels.

Mandatory labelling for GMO seeds cannot be considered as the solution to the problem of inadvertent release of these products. Releasing GMO seeds in Mexico's rural landscapes will continue to pose risks for agro-biodiversity. The traditional multi-cropping systems used by many subsistence and commercial producers will be subject to new sources of stress if a generalized process of liberation of GMOs takes place (Ortega Paczka 2003).

A final remark on labelling is that the discrimination between consumers of final products and agricultural producers is not justified. The right to know and discern between GMO and non-GMO products is inherent to every consumer, whether he/she is buying an input for agricultural production or for final consumption. This part of the Mexican biosafety regime is in stark contrast to the experience of other countries, and in particular with the federal Swiss Gene Technology Law which explicitly states (Article 17) that 'any person marketing genetically modified organisms must label them as such for the benefit of the recipient, in order to ensure freedom of choice for the consumer and to prevent product fraud'.

LIABILITY AND DAMAGE REDRESS SYSTEM

The liability and redress system in biosafety is a critical component of the policy regime. An effective liability regime allows for successful use of the polluter-pays principle and sets incentives for agents to introduce precautionary measures in their activities. Finally, it helps balance technical innovation with the need to protect human health and the environment.[3]

The liability regime of Mexico's biosafety law is determined in Section XI on violations to the law and sanctions. In this section, Article 119 contains a list of possible violations to the law. This inventory of possible infringements must not be considered an exhaustive catalogue of all possible violations to the law, but rather a simple record of examples of cases that breach the law.

Article 120 then proceeds to set forth a series of penalties for infringers. These sanctions range from fines to administrative detention, passing through the temporary or definitive closing of businesses that are implicated in illegal actions involving GMOs. However, Article 121 states that resort to these administrative sanctions does not preclude applying other sanctions when the acts or omissions related to GMOs entail other penalties, and most notably those related to the relevant articles of Mexico's Federal Criminal Code. This is an important point because the Criminal Code contains a chapter on biosafety with a strongly worded article that involves a harsh penalty of up to nine years in prison. The wording of the article deserves to be quoted *in extenso*:

Article 420 ter: A penalty of one to nine years of prison and a fine of three hundred to three thousand days [of minimum wage] will be imposed on whoever, in violation of applicable norms, introduces, extracts, trades, transports, stocks or liberates into the environment a genetically modified

---

[3]It is important to note that the liability and redress mentioned in this article are not related to responsibilities due to breach of contract.

organism that negatively alters or may alter the components, structure or functioning of natural ecosystems.

This is indeed a very strong precept because the article contains the clause 'may alter'. The wording of this article clearly assumes that strong protection is required against the illegal introduction or release of GMOs, in stark contrast with the basic premise of the BLGMO.

This contrast is nowhere clearer than in the chapter on liability and redress of damages. Article 121 states that any person who, in full knowledge of the fact that he/she is using GMOs, causes damages to third parties in their property or health 'through wrongful use or manipulation of said organisms will be liable and required to redress those damages in accordance with Federal civil law'. The article also specifies that the same obligation will be acquired by any person who damages the environment or biological diversity through the wrongful use or handling of GMOs in accordance with the LGEEPA. As we shall see, Article 203 of the LGEEPA adds nothing new to civil liability, except that it establishes a distinct statute of limitations with a period of five years, instead of two years as specified by civil law, for legal action to claim damages.

Through Article 121 the BLGMO establishes a system of wrongful liability, something similar to what is known in tort law as subjective liability. This means that for a party to be held responsible for damages, he/she must engage in some wrongful behaviour. This may be an act of negligence or omission, or an imprudent or reckless conduct, whereby the physical integrity or health of another person is affected or put at risk. A typical example of this fault-related responsibility is when somebody drives a car without the proper precautions, or without obeying traffic rules. Damages must be redressed by the agent engaged in faulty behaviour. Wrongful conduct ranges from negligence to imprudence.

How can this be translated to the case of GMOs? It may not be difficult to think of examples of wrongdoing. Any of the violations mentioned in Article 119 which caused damages to third parties would fall in this category. However, in cases where GMOs have received a go-ahead from authorities for commercial release, the liability practically disappears. Consider the following example. Once approval for commercial release has been given, a producer buys and plants GMO seeds. Suppose organic producers have fields nearby and their crops are contaminated with these GMOs. Any complaints against this producer will have to prove that he/she did not follow the instructions of the manufacturer. However, this will be meaningless because the permit for commercial release entails that there are virtually no restrictions for planting. There will be exceptions, such as centres of origin, NPAs, or GMO-free areas. But in the general case, any organic producer who finds genetic constructs in his/her plants and that as a result loses his/her certification, will not be able to obtain compensation because planters of GMOs will not have engaged in any wrongful behaviour.

There are several important drawbacks with wrongful-dependent liability. One of them is that for redress to be effectively implemented it is necessary to prove the direct link between the wrongful conduct and the damages. This is not always an easy task. In many instances of non-point pollution, it has been known to be almost impossible to prove the existence of direct linkages between sources of contamination and negative effects on human health. In the case of GMOs, the existence of a linkage of causality between the wrongful action and damages will not be easy to prove. This allocation of the burden of proof is unfair and will open many avenues for defence attorneys; it is a powerful deterrent against potential plaintiffs.

This system of wrongful liability emanates from tort legislation. There are other liability systems. For example, strict liability affects a person who is in possession of objects that bear nuisances or engage in production processes that are risky. By simply fulfilling these conditions, a person is directly liable, aside from the fact that he/she may or may not have engaged in any wrongful behaviour. This is a stronger regime and is reserved for cases where it is an imperative to put the full weight of precautionary measures on agents who engage in these activities.

It is important to note that strict liability is present in several important cases in Mexico's legislation, including civil law. Article 1913 of Mexico's Civil Code states that when a person manipulates substances, or uses mechanisms, instruments, or devices that pose a danger due to the speeds that they reach, or due to their explosive or flammable nature, that person will be liable and must engage in reparation and damage redress, even if he/she does not act wrongfully.

In Mexican environmental law, those that cause damages to soils and ecosystems are also subject to strict liability and must redress damages and restore the environment to its original status.[4] Also,

---

[4]Law on Ecological Equilibrium and Environmental Protection (LGEEPA), Article 152 *bis*.

operators of nuclear plants (reserved for public sector firms) are subject to a regime of strict liability.[5] Finally, strict liability exists in the realm of labour relations and industrial accidents, as well as in consumer protection law. In spite of this, the BLGMO rejected the principles of strict liability for GMOs.

Strict liability is an important component of legislation in other countries. One important example is the Swiss Gene Technology Law,[6] which is based on the early application of the precautionary principle and on strict attachment to the polluter-pays principle (Article 2). According to the Swiss Law, 'any person subject to the notification or authorization requirement, who handles genetically modified organisms in contained systems, releases such organisms for experimental purposes or markets them without permission is liable for damage that occurs during this handling that is a result of the genetic modification'. The only limitation to this application of strict liability comes from the doctrine of so-called 'Acts of God' and through gross misconduct of the injured party.

The statute of limitations states that the right to claim damages expires after three years from the time the injured party becomes aware of the damage and the liable agent, but at the latest 30 years from the time on which the GMOs were marketed. Also, the person claiming damages bears the responsibility to prove cause, but if this proof cannot be provided with certainty the court may be satisfied with 'overwhelming probability'.

Another example can be found in the amendment to the German Genetic Modification Act approved by the Bundestag in 2004.[7] This amendment aims to protect GMO-free farming through its 'coexistence provisions' designed to prevent material negative effects of GMOs. These material negative effects arise when products cannot be placed in the market due to cross-contamination with GMOs or must be labelled as GMO products, and when producers cannot label their products as 'organic'. Strict liability and no recourse to wrongful acts is required to file claims.

To summarize, by adopting the wrongful liability regime, the Mexican Biosafety Law adopts a very soft approach to GMOs and

[5]Law on Civil Liability from Nuclear Damages, Article 23.

[6]Swiss Federal Law Relating to Non-Human Gene Technology (21 March 2003).

[7]Amendment to the Genetic Modification Act (implementing Article 26A of Directive 2001/18/EC). The Genetic Modification Act is also known as the Gene Technology Act.

their risks and fails to provide adequate incentives for the adoption of precautionary measures. These incentives work through the direct mechanism of possible payment to redress damages, and indirectly through the cost of insurance (when risks are perceived through strict liability, insurance premiums increase). Thus, Mexico's Biosafety Law fails to provide the correct market incentives for risk management and prevention of damages. Strict liability, on the other hand, represents an adequate balance between risk and technological innovation.

INSTITUTIONAL FRAMEWORK AND RELATIONS WITH OTHER LEGAL INSTRUMENTS

Article 1 of the new Biosafety Law explicitly recognizes that the BLGMO is a 'public interest' law. This has important implications in Mexico's legal system. In the realm of public interest law, the interpretation of a legal instrument must be more generous and comprehensive whenever protection of the public sphere is concerned. Thus, the reference to public interest implies greater, not less, protection against potential damages. It is critical to recognize in good faith that there is currently a genuine scientific controversy surrounding these risks and this is why, if the biosafety regime is based on public interest legislation, the conclusion is straightforward: when dealing with the environment and human health, the strictest possible interpretation of the law is required. This line of reasoning leads to the issue of the precautionary principle.

The Cartagena Protocol is a legal instrument under the Convention on Biological Diversity (CBD) dealing with the transfer, handling, and use of GMOs which may have an adverse effect on biodiversity. Several key aspects of the Cartagena Protocol are relevant to our discussion on Mexico's biosafety regime. The main component of the Cartagena Protocol is a procedure of advanced informed agreement allowing importing parties to evaluate and authorize or reject the movement of GMOs.

GMOs intended for direct use as food or feed, or for processing, are not subjected to this requirement. This is an important lacuna considering the fact that the presence of transgenic constructs in Mexico's traditional corn varieties belongs to a family of cases that is not covered by the Cartagena Protocol. In addition, the question of liability and damage redress mechanisms is still the object of complex negotiations. The existing framework is too general and does not provide the basis for a reasonable balance between risks and potential benefits from innovation.

Another critical issue pertains to the relations between the Cartagena Protocol and the rules defined by the WTO. The important question here is whether rules emanating from multilateral environmental agreements (MEAs) are trumped by WTO rules. The most important testing ground for this question was the case presented in 2003 by the United States, Argentina, and Canada against the EU's rules for approving and marketing biotech products. A WTO ruling in September 2006 faulted the EU for undue delay in approving GMO products and of establishing in this manner a *de facto* moratorium. It also ruled that national bans in six EU member states were in violation of WTO rules because they had already been found safe at the EU level.

There is a very important lesson here that is quite relevant for the debate on the relations between environmental and trade rules. The WTO ruling focused on a technicality (undue delay) and thus avoided to settle the substantive differences between GMO regulatory regimes.[8] More important, the ruling refused to recognize the right of the EU to apply the precautionary principle in regulating GMO imports consecrated in the Cartagena Protocol. This is a dangerous precedent for future disputes involving environmental and trade rules.

To conclude this section, it is important to note that Mexico is a party to the Cartagena Protocol on transboundary movements of GMOs and Article 14 of this instrument states that parties to the Cartagena Protocol cannot have a level of protection that is inferior to the level set forth in this legal instrument. Also, the basic premise of the Cartagena Protocol is that GMOs entail risks and this is why they must be regulated. However, the starting point of Mexico's BLGMO is exactly the opposite: GMOs do not involve objective risks. This is why the BLGMO does not make any significant reference to the Cartagena Protocol. This, of course, leaves the application of the precautionary principle hanging on a very weak

---

[8]The ruling rejected the claim that the EU regulations were illegal, but it also refused to rule on the issue of whether biotech foods are safe or not. To a large extent, the ruling remains an interesting theoretical case because the EU had already lifted the *de facto* moratorium in 2005. The EU Commission is trying to reach an agreement with its national member states which still have bans incompatible with WTO rules.

limb. Therefore, from the perspective of Constitutional Law, it can be argued that the Biosafety Law is unconstitutional.

CONCLUDING REMARKS

The Biosafety Law is, in effect, a law designed to open the door for full commercial release of GMOs into the environment. The Biosafety Law itself provides a very strong contradiction because, on the one hand, public interest is explicitly upheld, while, on the other, this legislation is too lax and establishes a permissive regime for GMOs.

In addition, Chapter VI of the new law is devoted to the promotion and fostering of molecular biotechnology in Mexico. This represents a serious problem because the main objective of a biosafety law is to protect human health and environmental integrity from risks emanating from the release of GMOs. The regulatory components of the law may enter into severe contradictions with the promotional contents of the law. The parallelisms with the revolving-door approach taken in the nuclear industry should be taken into account.

In spite of this permissive approach to GMOs, the law does contain a formidable obstacle to the full commercial release of certain GMOs in the environment. This is the special protection regime for corn and other crops which find their centre of origin in Mexico. Without this regime, GMOs which have been constructed on crops that fall into this category cannot be released into the environment. Just precisely how this regime is going to be established is still an open question.

The Biosafety Law was enacted more than three years back, and it still does not have a set of by-laws and regulations that allow for its full implementation. Several serious lacunae still persist. One of them is the void related to the special protection. Another pertains to the precise identification of the centres of origin. Our hypothesis is that these two aspects of the law pose almost insurmountable obstacles to implementation.

REFERENCES

Diario Oficial, April 2005.

Instituto Nacional de Ecologia (INE), (2000), *Estrategia nacional sobre biodiversidad de México*, México: INE.

Mittermeier, R.A., (1988), 'Primate Diversity and the Tropical Forest: Case Studies from Brazil and Madagascar and the Importance of Megadiversity

Countries', in E. Wilson (ed.), *Biodiversity*, Washington, D.C.: National Academy Press.

Ortega Paczka, Rafael, (2003), 'La erosion genética del maíz en México y sus causas', paper presented at the conference on *Gene Flow: What Does it Mean for Biodiversity and Centres of Origin*, The Pew Initiative on Food and Biotechnology, 29–30 September, available at *http://pewagbiotech.org/events/0929/presentations/ortega.pdf.*

Toledo, V.M. and M.J. Ordoñez, (1993), 'The Biodiversity Scenario of Mexico: A Review of Terrestrial Habitats', in T.R. Ramamoorthy, R. Bye, and A. Lot y J. Fa (eds), *Diversidad biológica de México: Orígenes y distribución*, Mexico: Instituto de Biología, Universidad Nacional Autónoma de México, pp. 757–77.

Ramamoorthy, T.R., R. Bye, and A. Lot y J. Fa (eds), (1993), *Diversidad biológica de México: Orígenes y distribución*, Mexico: Instituto de Biología, Universidad Nacional Autónoma de México.

Rzedowski, Jerzy, (1993), 'Diversity and Origins of the Phanerogamic Flora of Mexico', in T.R. Ramamoorthy, R. Bye, and A. Lot y J. Fa (eds), *Diversidad biológica de México: Orígenes y distribución*, Mexico: Instituto de Biología, Universidad Nacional Autónoma de México, pp. 129–44.

7

Spain and the European Debate on GM Moratoria vs Coexistence

ROSA BINIMELIS AND ROGER STRAND[1]

Agricultural GMOs have generated substantial controversy in Europe since their introduction and commercialization in 1998. On the one hand, GMOs were promoted as 'high-yield sustainable agriculture' (Serageldin 1999), playing a central role for supporting economic growth and increasing competitiveness of European agriculture (European Commission 2002). On the other hand, opponents challenge the potential benefits and raise questions on the purposes and uncertainties related to this technology (Altieri 2005; Carr and Levidow 2000; Schubert 2002). As is well known, the resistance towards GMOs resulted in a 'de facto moratorium' on new GMO approvals in the EU during 1999–2003.[2]

In recent years, the European GMO controversy has crystallized, both in political and technical terms, into the debate on the principle of coexistence. The concept was first introduced by the European Commission in 2002 to face the emerging concerns about admixture between GM, conventional, and organic crops. This is especially relevant for organic crops, as there is a worldwide consensus among organic farmers not to use GMOs (IFOAM 1998; Barth et al. 2002). This consensus was incorporated into the EU norm concerning organic food and feed production (Council Regulation (EEC) No. 1092/91). Despite this agreement, the Council of Agriculture Ministers—in apparent disagreement with the European Parliament—voted for allowing products containing up to 0.9 per

[1]The authors express their sincere gratitude to Kamilla Kjølberg for her help in the revision of this chapter.

[2]For a complete list of deliberate releases and placing on the EU market of GMOs, see *http:www.gmoinfo.jrc.it* or *http://www.gmo-compass.org/eng/gmo/db/*.

cent of 'adventitious or technically unavoidable' GMO content to be labelled and sold as organic (European Commission 2007).

One perspective upon the coexistence policy framework is that it provided an opening for the definitive end of the European *de facto* moratorium, by supporting 'the ability of farmers to make a practical choice between the conventional, organic and GM-crop production' (European Commission 2003a). In order to implement coexistence measures, the European Commission issued non-binding recommendations to be developed and put into practice by the member states. However, the issue is still unsettled and controversial, as both the foundations of the concept of coexistence and the specific measures to be applied have been contested. Indeed, coexistence itself has become a contentious notion, and various authors challenge the compatibility between organic and conventional agriculture and transgenic crops. Marvier and van Acker (2005) discuss the feasibility of GM crop containment. Haygood et al. (2004) model hybridization and conclude that even small leakages can have a significant effect over time, confirming the conclusion of Snow (2002). Coexistence with organic agriculture has also been discussed in terms of a clash of rationales or conflicting paradigms (Altieri 2005; Ponti 2005; Lyson 2002; Levidow and Boschert 2007).

In spite of the EU *de facto* moratorium commercial cultivation of GM maize started in Spain in 1998. This chapter provides a first *ex-post* analysis of aspects of the legal, economic, and social processes emerging during the introduction of GM crops. In this respect, the chapter aims at contributing to the on-going debate on the implications and feasibilities of developing the coexistence policy framework. Particular emphasis is laid on the organic farmers' situation.

The chapter is structured as follows. First, we review the emergence and development of the concept of coexistence, with particular emphasis on the implications that coexistence has had for the *de facto* moratorium in EU. Next, the case study is introduced, characterising the situation regarding maize production and management in Lleida, Catalonia. After a brief description of methodology, results pointing out a number of challenges related to coexistence not accounted for in the official EU discourse are presented.

COEXISTENCE VS *DE FACTO* MORATORIUM

The insect resistant maize Bt-176 was approved for all uses, including commercial cultivation in EU in 1997. Since this first approval, two other products have been authorized for their cultivation in 1998. Maize with the modifications Bt-176 and Mon-810 has been farmed since then in Spain at a commercial scale, although not in other EU countries.

As a response to the public disquiet, however, Denmark, France, Greece, Italy, and Luxembourg declared in the Environmental Council in June 1999, that they would 'take steps to have any new authorisation for growing and placing on the market suspended', until a more stringent legal framework was established (Cantley 2004). This initiated the so-called '*de facto* moratorium', which provoked a complaint by Argentina, Canada, and the United States, asking for a WTO dispute settlement panel in 2003, arguing that the *de facto* moratorium was restricting imports (de Chazournes and Mbengue 2004).[3] By April 2004, the EU-required full normative 'package', with a more transparent risk-assessment procedure and full traceability and labelling across the agro-food chain, had been approved. However, the *de facto* moratorium was only lifted—with the approval of Bt11 maize in May 2004—for imports. New GM varieties for cultivation still require authorization.

By that time, a third concept, the coexistence of GM crops with conventional and organic agriculture, emerged. For some, it was a matter of concern due to the repercussions of the so-called 'transgenic contamination' into natural or agricultural ecosystems (Barth et al. 2000; Bock et al. 2002). For others, through the establishment of some technical measures, it was a way to lift the moratorium because, as the European Agricultural Commissioner Franz Fischler stated: 'no form of agriculture should be excluded in the EU' (European Commission 2003b). Finally, in July 2003, the European Commission issued the 'Guidelines for the Development of National Strategies and Best Practices to Ensure the Co-existence of Genetically Modified Crops with Conventional and Organic Farming' (European Commission 2003a). These were non-binding recommendations to be developed and implemented by the Member States. Implementation of measures at the national level varies. By the end of 2005, specific coexistence legislation had been adopted in Denmark, Germany, Portugal, and six of the Austrian Länder, while in the majority of other states only draft measures have been issued (European Commission 2006).

---

[3]Dispute Settlement: European Communities—Measures Affecting the Approval and Marketing of Biotech Products. Dispute DS293, 17 June 2007. See *http://www.wto.org/english/tratop_e/dispu_e/cases_e/ds293_e.htm*

A corpus of literature attending the design of coexistence measures has emerged. In 2002, the European Environment Agency (EEA) published a first report considering the significance of pollen-mediated gene flow from six major crops. Conclusions showed difficulties in isolating maize, oilseed rape, and sugar beet, advising the implementation of barrier crops and information systems, as well as increasing the current isolation distances (Eastham and Sweet 2002). At the national level, Denmark was the first European country to publish a major study on the technical measures for ensuring coexistence, including protocols for segregation along the production chain (Tolstrup et al. 2003). Austria has warned about the limitations of this approach, highlighting uncertainties and irreversibilities (Müller 2003). Other technical perspectives have comprised legal aspects, including liability schemes (Barth et al. 2002), agronomic (Ma et al. 2004; Messeguer et al. 2006), and economic analysis (Smyth et al. 2002). Most of these studies have been done *ex-ante*, based on modelling or experimental case studies, due to the lack of commercial fields in most European countries. In the United States, Byrne and Fromherz (2003) describe a real public process to design protocols to encourage coexistence. We now proceed to our *ex-post* analysis of the introduction of GM agriculture in Lleida (Catalonia, Spain).

THE CASE STUDY: LLEIDA (CATALONIA)

Introduction of GM maize in Spain started in 1998, when 16 insect-resistant maize varieties (five with the modification Bt-176 and 11 of maize Mon810) were included in the Register for Commercial Varieties. Since then, the number of commercial GM varieties has increased to 42 in 2006. All of them contain the modification Mon810, as the Bt-176 varieties were withdrawn due to the EFSA recommendations (EFSA 2004).

Only preliminary documents on the implementation of coexistence have been released by the Spanish administration. No agreement has been reached so far. Instead, some guidelines on good practices for cultivating GM maize have been promoted by the seed producers association (APROSE 2006). There are, furthermore, no official data on the surface planted with GMOs in Spain, but data from the Ministry of Agriculture indicate 56,000 ha were sown with GM maize in 2006 (Ortega 2006), representing an overall 14.5 per cent of the total area with grain maize. The highest concentration of use is in Catalonia and Aragon (North-East Spain).

Production of maize in Spain amounted to 3.7 million tonnes in 2003. In addition, Spain imports around 2 million tonnes of Brazilian, American, and Argentinean maize, presumed to be largely GM maize (European Commission 2005). Another 2 million tonnes of maize are imported from France (Ministry of Agriculture 2004a). Moreover, standard feed contains around 20 per cent of soy. Estimations from the Ministry of Agriculture calculate that 98.7 per cent of this soy is GM. As a consequence, almost all feed manufactured in Spain is labelled as GM (Ortega 2006). Although Spain produces maize seeds, it also imports a substantial quantity (Ministry of Agriculture 2004b).

This study was undertaken in the Catalan province of Lleida. Catalonia is one of the Spanish regions with a high degree of autonomy, in particular with regard to areas such as agriculture. In 2007, Catalonia had started developing its own coexistence legislation.

Maize production is a key agricultural activity in Catalonia, mainly related to the meat industry. The province of Lleida alone accounts for 7 per cent of the Spanish production of maize. Among the Spanish provinces Lleida is also the province with the highest percentage of GM maize relative to conventional and organic maize. In 2005, 27,000 ha were cultivated with maize in Lleida—of which around 15,000 were GM maize.

With more than 3 million pigs, 600,000 cows, over 350,000 sheep, and a production of avian meat of 356,000 tonnes, Lleida has become a leading region for meat processing in Europe. It is also in the lead of Spanish production on feed and fodder (DARP 2003, 2005, 2006). Although the surface allocated to crops remains stable, the number of agrarian exploitations is decreasing because of land concentration. Still, however, the average size of exploitations is small (5.45 ha) (IDESCAT 2003). Prices received by maize farmers have been constant or slightly decreasing during the last decade or so. GM and conventional maize have the same price, as it is mainly for feed production, which is generally labelled as GM anyway.

In Lleida, there are around 40 cereal cooperatives, which integrate the production process from the seed to the grain commercialization. Cooperatives sell the inputs (seeds, fertilizers, herbicides) to the farmers, rent machinery, give technical assessment, and buy and process—for instance, drying—the final product. Moreover, the cooperative will often grant the farmers credit during the season: the value of the products and services is subtracted from the money that the farmer will receive after the grain is dried in the cooperative (personal interviews with cooperative managers). Through this process, the cooperative's manager or technician turns into a fundamental actor in the introduction of new technologies at the local level.

Simultaneously, organic agriculture is in expansion, with a rapid increase both in the number of producers, manufacturers, and hectares. It is estimated that about 80 per cent of the organic food produced in Spain is exported to other European countries, mainly Germany and the United Kingdom (Junta de Andalucía 2004). Regarding the area planted with organic maize in Spain, there is limited data available. The Spanish Ministry of Agriculture has published only the figure for the total amount of cereals and legumes: 100.860 ha in 2003 (Ministry of Agriculture 2004b). However, a frequently used approximation was made by Brookes and Barfoot (2002), who estimated the area of organic maize in Spain to be 1000 ha. It would represent less than 2 per cent of the total surface sown with maize. In Catalonia, the area sown with organic maize was 97.6 ha in 2003, which serves as a baseline.

There have been emergent social reactions with the parallel increase of land cultivated both with GMOs and organic agriculture. The controversy has grown in intensity. Although public participation during the introduction of GM crops in Spain was almost non-existent, more recently, and especially within the framework of negotiations on the coexistence legislations, the discussion has been opened by relevant stakeholders, such as environmentalist or farmer associations. It seems fair to say that it has been difficult to establish a real, transparent dialogue between the stakeholders.

METHODOLOGY

The study was performed in two parts. First, information available on this issue was compiled. This included the European Commission's official press releases and communications, legislative documents, and technical reports as well as other type of documents (press releases, statements, pamphlets, web pages) produced by other stakeholders. Other secondary sources include results of different research projects, scientific meetings, and round tables conducted at the European, Spanish, and Catalan levels. This part also comprises an extensive literature review on key issues such as coexistence, technical measures, and liability.

The second part of the study is an on-going field research, initiated in 2002 (Binimelis 2008). It aims to incorporate stakeholders' viewpoints and experiences at the local level. It targets two groups of stakeholders, namely Catalan farmers and actors at the Catalan policy level. Initially, 25 farmers (8 organic farmers, 9 farmers cultivating conventional maize, and 8 farmers using both conventional and GM maize), 8 technicians or managers of agricultural cooperatives related to the maize sector, and 2 purchasing managers of starch and glucose companies were interviewed. Qualitative techniques including workshops, group, and individual in-depth interviews were used, as well as participant observation. Most of the participants were located in Lleida, although four of the informants were inhabitants or worked in the neighbouring province in Aragon. Second, in parallel, relevant stakeholders at the policy level related to the coexistence debate in Catalonia were interviewed. Nineteen semi-structured interviews, which included the completion of a quantitative questionnaire, were conducted. Stakeholder informants were selected among politicians and public administrators, representatives from agricultural unions, experts in the genetic engineering and organic agriculture areas, consumers' organizations, and environmental and development NGOs, also at the advice of other informants. In total, 51 persons were interviewed. Most interviews (31) were recorded, transcribed, and sent back to participants for posterior review. Twenty interviews were recorded with field notes as the informants did not wish audio recordings to be performed.

RESULTS AND DISCUSSION

This section is divided into three parts. The first part briefly analyses the framing of the notion of coexistence. The second part identifies some assumptions behind the principles framing the proposed coexistence measures. Finally, these assumptions are contrasted with examples of problems and dilemmas experienced by farmer informants.

Different Approaches to Coexistence

Two different approaches to the principle of coexistence can be found in the policy discourse. The first approach, developed by the European Commission, defines coexistence as the farmers' right to choose the type of crop production (European Commission 2003). Therefore, the focus is put on the farm level. A clear distinction is made between the economic aspects of coexistence and the environmental and health aspects, assuming that the latter two aspects are covered by the risk assessment enforced by Directive 2001/18/EC. Accordingly, unless the risk assessment process concludes otherwise, there is no need to regard GM and non-GM organisms as inherently different. Thus, the concept of contamination is rejected, as it assumes an unfavourable value judgement on GMOs.

This division is based in the separation between the aspects that can be evaluated through expert advice (mainly environmental, human, and animal health) and those that relate to policy (social or ethical concerns), drawing a strict demarcation between risk assessment and risk management (van den Belt and Gremmelt 2002), or, if one so wishes, between 'facts' and 'values'. Within this scheme, Directive 2001/18/EC defines regulation of GMOs as an expert scientific issue, to be kept apart from social and ethical issues (Levidow et al. 2005). When concerns about admixture between GM, conventional, and organic crops emerged, the debate was again 'technified' and the coexistence issue reduced to the quantification of 'the potential economic loss and impact of the admixture' (European Commission 2003). In other words, the coexistence issue is a compensatory mechanism of the costs derived from the market-driven differentiation between GM and non-GM products; and the efforts are devoted to designing the technical measures to minimize the costs caused by the implementation of the labelling normative 'in a proportionate manner'.

The second approach shifts the focus from the farmer to consumer or societal rights (for example, European Parliament 2003) and includes the possibility of fundamental differences between GM and conventional/organic agriculture, in particular with respect to the quality aspect. An example is the characterization of admixture as 'contamination'. This perspective suggests the incompatibility of these practices and promotes for instance the creation of European GMO-free zones. The scope of this second definition is wider, both for the impacts taken into account (for instance, regional and local land use and economic development, consumer and environmental protection, cultural aspects, and those related to local identities and to the integrity of organic agriculture) (European Economic and Social Committee 2004) and for the shift from a supply-driven food chain to a demand-driven one (Wolf and Nilsagård 2002).

A fundamental point of the argument is the discussion on the admixture thresholds to be tolerated. The first approach defines coexistence on the basis of 'practical thresholds' for the presence of GMOs in non-GMOs. There is an obligation to label a product if the GM content exceeds 0.9 per cent (following Regulation (EC) No 1830/2003). This practical threshold is established so that no economic loss should be suffered by the organic or conventional farmer if the GM content exceeds 0.9 per cent. Thus, the conflict is removed in theory: '[on the one hand] the organic farming regulation establishes that no GMOs shall be used in production. Thus, materials, including seeds, which are labelled as containing GMOs, cannot be used. However, [on the other hand] seed lots containing GM seeds below the seed thresholds (which would not need to be labelled for this GMO presence) could be used' (European Commission 2003). The second approach establishes that consumers' right to choose non-GM products should prevail and, therefore, coexistence measures should be able to pursue a 100 per cent GMO-free product for the final consumer. The reasoning behind is that there is a difference between containing GMOs and being labelled as a GM product. This threshold is implemented in organic agriculture certification so far.

These different approaches would drive divergent policy actions. The first approach defines coexistence as desirable, and technically feasible. Therefore, the issue under analysis is the design of the technical solutions to achieve it. The second approach challenges the idea of a desirable coexistence, placing the focus on the societal choices about the agricultural system. Conflicts in discussing the underlying practical problem(s)—the ultimate purpose—could result, as it will be seen later, in difficulties to concur on the technical measures to be applied (Ravetz 1971; Strand 2002).

Assumptions Underlying the First Approach

The definition of coexistence used by the European Commission has been the definition adopted in the development of normative measures. Three general assumptions that appear to underlie the European Commission's approach to coexistence can be identified. The first assumption follows directly from the above description:

- Assumption 1: Coexistence is possible and desirable, and an opportunity for maximizing income of all agricultural practices simultaneously.

  Next, the principles of transparency and stakeholder involvement for cooperation, as well as the idea of coexistence measures through voluntary agreements, logically presuppose as conditions for their successful implementation that:

- Assumption 2: There is a sufficiently equal distribution of power among different stakeholders.

Another additional assumption of this approach may be distilled from the official documents:

- Assumption 3: A civil regulatory framework supporting liability schemes will compensate losses produced if admixture takes place.

Lleida Farmer Experiences Casting Light upon the Assumptions

- Assumption 1: Coexistence is possible and desirable, and an opportunity for maximizing income of all agricultural practices simultaneously.

Some trade-offs are found to be associated in practice with the implementation of different agricultural models. The existence of one type of agriculture could imply the impossibility of practising another type in the vicinity. The first draft of the Catalan decree on coexistence proposed an isolation distance between GM and non-GM maize fields of 25 metres, which was criticized as unsafe and increased up to 200 metres in the last proposal. In fact, prescribed isolation distances in literature vary from 25 metres to 10 kilometres, depending on the study and the chosen level of acceptance of impurity (Binimelis 2004). However, 200 metres isolation distances would result in the impossibility of growing GM maize in vast areas of cultivation due to the limited size of plots. The solution would be the creation of either GM or conventional and organic homogeneous regions. In Lleida, coexistence is thus sometimes not practically possible.

- Assumption 2: There is a sufficiently equal distribution of power among different stakeholders.

In Lleida, organic farmers are a minority and environmentalist groups are on the defensive. In the words of one informant farmer, who explains that he fears the ridicule of the local community if his neighbours learn that he is into organic farming: 'I am going to do organic [agriculture] next year but in an area where nobody sees it, so they won't laugh at me' (interview, conventional farmer, August 2005). This view is rooted in the intense farming modernization in Spain, which started in the mid 1960s, reorienting agrarian land to produce feed and fodder crops, as maize (Domínguez-Marín 2001), including the introduction of hybrid maize. In that sense, the agrarian cooperatives have played a key role in the introduction and diffusion of new technologies. This preference for mechanized and technified agriculture is exemplified by a cooperative technician when asked about their sales: 'Pioneer is now selling the most because the

Syngenta gene is old, and people always want the latest [technology]' (interview, September 2005).

As stated by most of the informants, cooperatives are the objective of the agribusiness companies' sales strategies. The cooperative structure also implies that infrastructures are concentrated, it being technically difficult and expensive to isolate the GM production chain from the conventional and organic one. As the price for GM and conventional maize is the same, the final product for feed production is labelled as GM. The relatively fewer and socially inferior organic farmers are the ones forced to implement their own independent production system and usually they are the ones who implement the measures to prevent gene flow. As explained by an organic farmer when interviewed on his reasons for postponing sowing with a consequent loss of income: 'my neighbour plants GMOs.... What can I say? My neighbour is not my enemy. He is my colleague, from the school...We are a small community and we have a community life. He is my friend. I cannot say anything. He is trying to survive and he does what he can. I prefer quitting agriculture to having bad relations' (organic farmer, April 2005). Under these circumstances a decline in organic maize surface has been reported by the organic certification bodies in Catalonia and Aragon (from 97.6 ha in 2001 to 345 ha in 2007 in the case of Catalonia; from 120 ha in 2002 to 30 ha in 2007 in Aragon). To sum up, the inferior social, cultural, and economic position of organic farmers affects the possibility of cooperation and stakeholder involvement on equal terms.

• Assumption 3: A civil regulatory framework supporting liability schemes will compensate losses produced if admixture takes place. Apart from the problems associated with economic quantification of non-marketable goods (for example, admixture of GM maize with traditional non-hybrid varieties; threats to local cultures or identities), fieldwork also highlights the social aspects of liability frameworks. This point is exemplified by the following assertion an organic farmer: 'they want to make farmers responsible, they want that we face each other. The future normative is saying that who sows GMOs must say so and has to be responsible in case of contamination, for example to an organic farmer. Then, this organic farmer can take reprisals through legal means.... Let's see: where are we? In what country are we? What do they want? That we open war in the villages, in the fields?' (Interview of organic farmer, November 2005). In other words, the liability schemes foreseen in the Commission recommendations disregard the social and cultural implications of raising liability claims in a community.

CONCLUDING REMARKS

There is a clear evidence of a lack of common purpose (for example, the definition of what agricultural models are being targeted) linked to the different approaches for coexistence. In spite of this conflict, unwanted admixture between GM crops and conventional and organic crops is handled by the implementation of technical measures and reduced to the economic aspects, as an example of the so-called 'science-based regulation'. This presumes that such measures are independent of socio-cultural, political, and economic conditions, assuming this independence as a source for legitimation. However, on the one hand, the question of unwanted admixture—or contamination—has conflicting framings. Any formulation of rules to ensure coexistence depends on the options taken at the policy level. On the other hand, the analysis of the implementation of the GMOs in Lleida has shown that even when coexistence would be possible, its desirability needs to be discussed with attention to the social and cultural aspects of the regulation of coexistence.

REFERENCES

Altieri, M., (2005), 'The Myth of Coexistence: Why Transgenic Crops Are Not Compatible with Agroecologically based Systems of Production?', *Bulletin of Science, Technology and Society*, Vol. 25, No. 4, pp. 361–71.

APROSE, (2006), Guía 2006 de buenas pr·cticas para el cultivo del maíz Bt, available at '*www.monsanto.es/Novedad/Folleto per cent20aprose per cent202006.pdf*, accessed on 15 July 2007.

Barth, R.R. Brauner, A. Hermann, R. Hermanowski, K. Nowack, H. Schmidt and B. Tappeser, (2002), 'Genetic Engineering and Organic Farming', Freiburg, Darmstadt, Berlin, FIBL-Öko-Institut e.V.

Binimelis, R., (2004), 'Co-existence of Organic and GM Agriculture in Catalonia', Master Thesis, Universitat Autònoma de Barcelona, Bellaterra.

———, (2008), 'Coexistence of Plants and Coexistence of Farmers: Is an Individual Choice Possible?', *Journal of Agricultural and Environmental Ethics*, Vol. 21, No. 5, pp. 437–57.

Bock, A.K., K. Lheureux, M. Libeau-Dulos, H. Nilsagård, and E. Rodrãguez-Cerezo, (2002), Scenarios for Co-existence of Genetically Modified, Conventional and Organic crops in European Agriculture', Seville: Joint Research Centre, Institute for Prospective Technological Studies.

Brookes, G. and P. Barfoot, (2003), 'Co-existence of GM and Non GM

132 SCIENCE FOR POLICY

Crops: Case Study of Maize Grown in Spain', in B. Boelt (ed.), *Proceedings of the First European Conference on the Co-existence of Genetically Modified Crops with Conventional and Organic Crops*, Slagelse: Danish Institute of Agricultural Science, Research Centre Flakkebjerg, Available at *http://www.agrsci.dk/gmcc-03/gmcc_proceedings.pdf.*

Byrne, P.F. and S. Fromherz, (2003), 'Can GM and Non-GM Crops Coexist? Setting a Precedent in Boulder County, Colorado, USA', *Food, Agriculture and Environment*, Vol. 1, No. 2, pp. 258–61.

Cantley, M., (2004), 'How Should Public Policy Respond to the Challenges of Modern Biotechnolology?' *Current Opinion in Biotechnology*, Vol. 15, pp. 258–63.

Carr, S. and L. Levidow, (2000), 'Exploring the Links between Science, Risk, Uncertainty, and Ethics in Regulatory Controversies about Genetically Modified Crops', *Journal of Agricultural and Environmental Ethics*, Vol. 12, pp. 29–39.

DARP, (2003), Estadístiques del sector avícola a Catalunya, 2003', available at *http://www.gencat.net/darp/dades.htm.*

———, (2005), 'Estadísitiques ramaderes: Censos de bestiar porcí: Enquestes 2005, Available at *http://www.gencat.net/darp/dades.htm.*

———, (2006), 'Estadístiques ramaderes: Censos de bestiar boví: Enquestes 2006', Available at *http://www.gencat.net/darp/dades.htm.*

De Chazournes, L.B. and M.M. Mbengue, (2004), 'GMOs and Trade: Issues at Stake in the EC Biotech Dispute', *Review of the European Community and International Environmental Law*, Vol. 13, No. 3, pp. 289–305.

Domínguez-Martín, R., (2001), 'Las transformaciones del sector ganadero en España (1940–1985)', *Ager, Revista de Estudios sobre Despoblación y Desarrollo Rural*, Vol. 1, pp. 47–83.

Eastham, K. and J. Sweet, (2002), *Genetically Modified Organisms (GMOs: The Significance of Gene Flow through Pollen Transfer*, Luxembourg: European Environment Agency, Environmental issue report No. 28, Office for Official Publications of the European Communities.

European Commission, (2002), 'Life Sciences and Biotechnology: A Strategy for Europe', Luxembourg: Communication from the Commission to the European Parliament, the Council, the Economic and Social Committee, and the Committee of the Regions, COM(2002)27 final, 23 January; Available at *http://europa.eu.int/comm/biotechnology/pdf/com2002-27_en.pdf.*

———, (2003a), 'GMOs: Commission Addresses GM Crop Co-existence', Brussels: Press Release, IP/03/324, 5 May.

———, (2003b), 'Commission Recommendation of 23 July 2003 on Guidelines for the Development of National Strategies and Best Practices to Ensure the Coexistence of Genetically Modified Crops with Conventional and Organic Farming', Notified under document number C(2003) 2624, (2003/556/EC).

European Commission, (2005) Final Report of a Mission Carried Out in Spain 07/03/2005 to 11/03/2005 Concerning Controls on Food and Feed Containing, Consisting or Produced from GMO', DG(SANCO)/ 7632/2005-MRFinal Directorate F—Food and Veterinary Office, Health and Consumer Protection Directorate General.

_____, (2006), 'Report on the Implementation of National Measures on the Coexistence of Genetically Modified Crops with Conventional and Organic Farming {SEC(2006) 313}', Brussels: Communication from the Commission to the Council and the European Parliament, COM(2006) 104 final, 9 March, available at *http://ec.europa.eu/ agriculture/coexistence/com104_en.pdf.*

_____, (2007), 'Organic Food: New Regulation to Foster the Further Development of Europe's Organic Food Sector', Brussels: Press Release, IP/07/807, 12 June.

European Economic and Social Committee, (2005), 'Opinion on the Co- existence Between Genetically Modified Crops, and Conventional and Organic Crops', (2005/C 157/29), 28 June.

European Food Safety Authority, (2004), 'EFSA Provides Scientific Advice on the Use of Antibiotic Resistance Marker Genes in Genetically Modified Plants', Press Release, 19 April.

European Parliament, (2003), 'Report on Coexistence between Genetically Modified Crops and Conventional and Organic Crops', Committee on Agriculture and Rural Development, 2003/2098(INI).

Haygood, R., A.R. Ives, and D.A. Andow, (2004), 'Population Genetics of Transgene Containment', *Ecology Letters*, Vol. 7, pp. 213–20.

IFOAM, (1998), 'The Mar del Plata Declaration: Not to Genetic Engineering', September, available at *http://www.ifoam.org/press/ 1998marp.html.*

Junta de Andalucía, (2002), *Plan Andaluz de la Agricultura Ecológica*, Seville: Consejería de Agricultura y Pesca.

Levidow, L. and K. Boschert, (2008), 'Coexistence or Contradiction? GM Crops versus Alternative Agricultures in Europe', *Geoforum*, Vol. 39, No. 1, pp. 174–90.

Levidow, L., S. Carr, and D. Wield, (2005), 'European Union Regulation of Agri-biotechnology: Precautionary Links between Science, Expertise and Policy', *Science and Public Policy*, Vol. 32, No. 4, pp. 261–76.

Lyson, T.A., (2002), 'Advanced Agricultural Biotechnologies and Sustainable Agriculture', *Trends in Biotechnology*, Vol. 20, No. 5, pp. 193–6.

Ma, B.L., K.D. Subedi, and L.M. Reid (2004), 'Extent of Cross-Fertilization in Maize by Pollen from Neighboring Transgenic Hybrids', *Crop Science*, Vol. 44, pp. 1273–82.

Marvier, M. and R.C. van Acker, (2005), 'Can Crop Transgenes be kept on a Leash?', *Frontiers in the Ecology and the Environment*, Vol. 3, No. 2, pp. 99–106.

Messeguer, J., G. Peñas, J. Ballester, M. Bas, J. Serra, J. Salvia, M. Palaudelmàs, and E. Melé, (2006), 'Pollen-mediated gene flow in maize in real situations of coexistence', *Plant Biotechnology Journal*, Vol. 4, pp. 633–45.

Ministry of Agriculture, (2004a), 'Anuario de estadística agroalimentaria, 2004', available at *http://www.mapa.es/es/estadistica/pags/anuario/Anu_04/indice.asp?parte=2&capitulo=6.*

_____, (2004b), 'Producción nacional de semillas (histórico 2003)', available at, *http://www.mapa.esbvi.*

Müller, W., (2003), *Concepts for Coexistence*, Vienna: Office of Ecological Risk Research, Commissioned by the Austrian Federal Ministry of Health and Women.

Ortega Molina, J.I., (2006), 'La coexistencia de los cultivos modificados genéticamente con los ecológicos', VII Congreso de la Sociedad Española de Agricultura Ecológica/III Congreso Iberoamericano de Agroecología, Zaragoza, 2 September.

Ponti, L., (2005), 'Transgenic Crops and Sustainable Agriculture in the European Context', *Bulletin of Science, Technology and Society*, Vol. 25, No. 4, pp. 289–305.

Ravetz, Jerome R., (1971), *Scientific Knowledge and its Social Problems*, Oxford: Clarendon Press.

Schubert, D., (2002), 'A Different Perspective on GM Food', *Nature Biotechnology*, Vol. 20, No. 10, p. 969.

Serageldin, I., (1999), 'Biotechnology and Food Security in the 21st Century', *Science*, Vol. 285, pp. 387–89.

Smyth, S., G.G. Khachatourians, and W.B. Phillips, (2002), 'Liabilities and Economic of Transgenic Crops', *Nature Biotechnology*, Vol. 20, pp. 537–41.

Snow, A.A., (2000), 'Transgenic Crops: Why Gene Flow Matters', *Nature Biotechnology*, Vol. 20, p. 542.

Strand, R., (2002), 'Complexity, Ideology and Governance', *Emergence*, Vol. 4, Nos. 1–2, pp. 164–83.

Tolstrup, K., S.B. Andersen, B. Boelt, M. Buus, M. Gylling, P.B. Holm, G. Kjellsson, S. Pedersen, H. Østergård, and S.A. Mikkelsen, (2003), 'Report from the Danish Working Group on the Co-existence of Genetically Modified Crops with Conventional and Organic crops', Danish Institute of Agricultural Sciences (DIAS), Tjele DIAS report Plant Production No. 94.

Van den Belt, H. and B. Gremmen, (2002), 'Between Precautionary Principle and "Sound Science": Distributing the Burdens of Proof', *Journal of Agricultural and Environmental Ethics*, Vol. 15, pp. 103–22.

Wolf, O. and H. Nilsagård, (2002), 'Reversed Food Chain—From the Plate to the Farm: Priorities in Food Safety and Food Technology for European Research', Seville: Joint Research Centre, EUR 20416EN.

8

Critical Issues in the Regulation of Genetically Modified Organisms

Lim Li Lin and Lim Li Ching

Genetic engineering, also called modern biotechnology or genetic modification, involves the transfer of genetic material from one organism to another, often unrelated, species. This results in a transgenic or genetically modified organism (GMO) containing new genes or novel combinations of genes. The potential applications are wide ranging, including GM crops, GM animals and fish, GM trees, GM virus vector vaccines, GM micro-organisms, and GM insects. GMOs and their products are used in food and animal feed, in industrial processing and applications, and to produce pharmaceuticals and chemicals.

However, the introduction of the technology has been accompanied by controversy, particularly over the role of genetic engineering in addressing agricultural problems in both developing and developed countries. Advocates cite potential yield increases and reductions in pesticide applications for GM crops, among other factors. Critics point to environmental and health risks as well as to socio-economic impacts as significant drawbacks.

Scientific Uncertainties Pose Regulatory Challenges

One of the most characteristic components of the debate relates to the scientific uncertainties surrounding the technology. This is exacerbated by the fact that while there has been a large research focus on GM technology advances, there has been rather less focus on biosafety research, that is, looking at the health, environmental, and socio-economic risks (Myhr and Traavik 2002).

In spite of the obvious need, few studies investigating the effects of GM food/feed on animals or humans have been published in peer-reviewed journals (Domingo 2000). While many opinions and comments have been offered, these are not based on experimental data. In 2003, a review of *in vivo* studies on possible health consequences of GM food and feed found that a total of only ten studies had been published on this issue (Pryme and Lembcke 2003). Furthermore, the few studies that have been designed to reveal physiological or pathological differences demonstrate a worrying trend: studies conducted by the industry find no differences, while studies by independent researchers show differences that merit immediate follow-up. This lack of published scientific papers, particularly by independent researchers, means that a reliable database of safety cannot yet be established for GM food and feed (Pusztai et al. 2003; Pusztai and Bardocz 2005), still leaving many unanswered questions and uncertainties (Traavik and Heinemann 2007; Wilson et al. 2006).

More recently, concerted effort has been made to look at the potential environmental effects of GM crops (for example, Squire et al. 2003), particularly with the discovery of introgression of transgenes in Mexican maize landraces (Quist and Chapela 2001). The gaps in scientific knowledge with regard to environmental impacts are also increasingly being acknowledged (for example, Snow et al. 2003; Wolfenbarger and Phifer 2000). The scientific uncertainties pose challenges for the regulation of GMOs. Moreover, it is clear that any introduction of GMOs must assess not just potential health, environmental, and socio-economic impacts, but must also take into account the economic, political, social, and scientific contexts (Myhr and Traavik 2002).

One response to the scientific uncertainties has been the use of the precautionary principle in regulation (Myhr and Traavik 2002, 2003). Essentially, the lack of sufficient scientific evidence does not prevent one from taking action to prevent or mitigate the potential adverse impacts of GMOs. In the international regulatory framework governing GMOs, the Cartagena Protocol on Biosafety (2000) has established precaution as the basis for decision-making and risk assessment in the face of scientific uncertainty due to insufficient relevant scientific information and knowledge regarding the extent of the potential adverse effects (see also Chapter 6 in this volume).

THE CARTAGENA PROTOCOL ON BIOSAFETY

Efforts to establish legally-binding rules on GMOs were first introduced onto the international agenda during the discussions leading to the Rio Earth Summit, particularly under the negotiations of the CBD. Finalized in 1992, the CBD, in its Article 19(3), provided governments the mandate to consider the need for a protocol on biosafety to address the risks of genetic engineering (CBD 1992).

After long and at times acrimonious negotiations, the Cartagena Protocol on Biosafety was finally concluded in 2000. It entered into force on 11 September 2003 after obtaining the requisite number of ratifications, acceptances, approvals, or accessions. It is the first and only international law to specifically regulate genetic engineering and GMOs. (In the Protocol, GMOs are known as living modified organisms or LMOs.)

The Cartagena Protocol is legally binding in the international legal system and in the legal systems of countries that have ratified, approved, accepted, or acceded to it. As of 4 March 2009, there were 155 Parties to the Protocol. Four meetings of the Conference of the Parties serving as the meeting of the Parties to the Cartagena Protocol on Biosafety were held in February 2004, May/June 2005, March 2006, and May 2008.

SIGNIFICANCE OF THE PROTOCOL

For the first time in international law, there is recognition that GMOs are inherently different from other naturally occurring organisms and may carry special risks and hazards and, therefore, need to be regulated internationally. The Protocol addresses the fact that GMOs may have biodiversity and human health impacts, and that these impacts need to be risk assessed. The Protocol also recognizes that socio-economic considerations can be taken into account when making decisions on GMOs, an issue that is particularly significant for developing countries. The crucial importance of centres of origin and genetic diversity of plant and animal genetic resources is acknowledged, and due regard for the risks posed by GMOs in these centres is one of the underlying concerns of the Protocol.

Importantly, the Cartagena Protocol puts the precautionary principle into operation in decision making (that is, in the absence of scientific certainty, a Party should err on the side of caution and could restrict or ban the import of GMOs on account of their potential adverse effects) and this further establishes the precautionary principle in international law.

The Protocol deals mainly with the transboundary movement (import and export) of GMOs. Its 'advance informed agreement' (AIA) procedure governs the first international transboundary movement between Parties, of GMOs for intentional introduction into the environment. This procedure essentially establishes the principle that there should be no export of GMOs unless the importing country approves its transboundary movement.

The AIA procedure involves three key steps. First, the Party of import must be notified by the Party of export/exporter that it intends to send GMOs. Thus, countries now have an international right to be notified that a GMO is going to be shipped to them. The Party of import then evaluates the risk assessment that has been submitted by the Party of export/exporter and can conduct its own risk assessment if it is not satisfied with the risk assessment submitted, which is usually conducted by the developer of the GMO. Risk assessment can take into account the expert advice of, and guidelines developed by, relevant international organizations. Precaution is also one of the general principles of risk assessment. Finally, the Party of import makes its decision based on precaution. The decision could be for unconditional approval, approval with conditions, prohibition, a request for additional relevant information, or extension of the time period for further consideration of the application.

The AIA procedure thus places obligations on exporting Parties, to first seek the informed approval of importing Parties before any transboundary movement can occur. It reverses the burden for importing countries that have little capacity and information to know what is entering into their territories, and to regulate them accordingly. It also affords corresponding rights and places obligations on the importer countries.

However, the Protocol excludes some GMOs—GMOs in transit, GMOs in contained use, GMOs that are intended for food, animal feed, or for processing—from the AIA procedure. Nonetheless, they are still covered by the Protocol and all other provisions apply to these categories of GMOs. For GMOs that are intended for food, animal feed, or for processing a separate procedure applies.

Parties to the Protocol can, moreover, choose to implement the AIA procedure at the national level in relation to all GMOs. Within the domestic regulatory system, this principle can also apply to nationally developed GMOs that undergo an approvals process.

SOME KEY REGULATORY ISSUES TO BE CONSIDERED IN BIOSAFETY REGULATION

Scope of Regulation

The scope of any regulation is very important as it sets out the extent to which the regulation is applicable. For example, the Cartagena Protocol's scope extends to all activities and all GMOs, whether or not classified as GMOs for deliberate release into the environment, or for food, animal feed, or for processing, GMOs in agriculture, GMOs in industrial use, GM trees, GM animals, GM pharmaceuticals, etc. This is a reflection of the concern about the possible impacts of any application of genetic engineering. It is also significant because the methods and techniques for genetic engineering are the same, regardless of the application, and carry the same inherent risks and hazards.

Thus, in principle, the same fundamental safety issues apply to all GMOs. If we are concerned about biosafety, then it is an issue of 'technology' regulation, not merely of regulating some of the different applications. Nonetheless, the different applications and specific GMOs may also have distinctive biosafety concerns, which should be assessed and regulated separately.

Furthermore, while the Cartagena Protocol only covers 'living modified organisms' (LMOs), products derived from GMOs could also be included in the scope of national regulation because the transgenic DNA may not be degraded, and hence may still cause potential adverse effects. Notably, GM pharmaceuticals for humans are excluded from the scope of the Protocol, but only if they are addressed by other international agreements or organizations. No further development of this has taken place at the Meetings of the Parties (the decision making body of the Protocol), and as such this provision is open to interpretation. Arguably, no other international agreements or organizations to date regulate GM pharmaceuticals for humans in the same way that the Protocol regulates other GMOs, and as such they are still covered under the scope of the Protocol. GM pharmaceuticals for animals, however, are clearly within the scope of the Protocol.

The Cartagena Protocol explicitly recognizes the right of Parties to regulate all these GMOs at the national level. Further, there can and should be differential regulation on the different GMO applications and products. This in itself is a challenge, to not generalize the regulations and assessments, but to be specific to the intricacies and demands of the different GM applications in question.

'Contained Use' vs 'Release'

The intended use of a particular GMO should not be the basis of any critical distinctions in regulation. A GMO may only be intended for animal feed (that is, not for planting), for example, but when it is present in a developing country in particular, there is a high chance that it will not remain confined to its intended use, and will be planted. The Starlink scandal where a variety of GM maize that was only approved for animal feed was found in food across the US and in a number of other countries, and the contamination of native varieties of maize in Mexico, demonstrate that contamination will happen. In Mexico, the GM maize imports from the US were intended for 'food or feed, or for processing', but nonetheless probably ended up in the fields.

What is, therefore, important in regulation is the distinction between what is 'contained use' and what is 'released'. Regulation and risk assessment should then be conducted on this basis. GMOs are self-replicating organisms that cannot be recalled once they are released into the environment. Any regulation must, therefore, be careful to define 'contained use' very strictly, that is containment that is truly contained, for example in laboratory conditions where there is no possibility of contact with the external environment. Whatever is not 'contained' is thus a 'release' and should be regulated accordingly. 'Contained use' occurs inside a physical facility that is designed to prevent escape into the open environment. It can be controlled in principle, and made as safe as possible, though the current laws on contained use are far from adequate, and in most developing countries there are no laws at all.

Nevertheless, the possibility of an accident or accidental release from containment cannot be ruled out. There is thus good reason to regulate 'contained use' as strictly as 'release'. In addition, policy supervision over research that usually begins in 'contained use' is critical, as by the time considerable resources have been spent developing a GMO, the push for eventual commercialization is very great, sometimes even at the expense of biosafety.

Releases of GMOs into the environment consist of all uses that occur outside a physical facility. All of these are capable of spreading transgenic DNA by (trans)gene flow. Released GMOs and transgenic

DNA cannot be controlled nor recalled, and hence great care must be taken in advance of the release. This is particularly important in centres of origin and diversity of genetic resources.

Field trials must also be risk assessed as releases. Certain requirements to limit contact with the external environment can and must be put in place if the decision is taken to release a GMO in a field trial. A key question for consideration would be: 'Should the decision about conducting field trials be made according to the same requirements as commercial releases?' There have already been cases where GMOs in field trials have ended up planted commercially and sold in the market.

Liability and Redress

The issue of liability and redress for damage arising from GMOs is critical, and international rules to deal with this are currently being negotiated under the Cartagena Protocol. It is very important to have an international liability and redress regime in place in the event that there are negative health, environmental, or socio-economic impacts, given the difficulties of assessing liability caused by GMOs, in the context of international trade and transboundary movements. Such a regime should also ensure a remedy for any damage.

Many countries support an international legally-binding liability and redress regime in relation to GMOs. Developing countries, in particular, are concerned about the potential for damage to the environment and health from GMOs, which are largely developed and produced outside their countries, and which have not been tested in their specific environments. Countries are also concerned about economic damage to their export markets from contamination by GMOs. Such damage also includes the remediation costs needed to clean up contamination or to recall contaminated products.

The issue is so important that national level regimes for liability and redress relating to GMOs should also be put in place as soon as possible. This will also assist the development of the international liability regime. Several countries have already adopted national liability regimes, including Austria, Germany, New Zealand, Norway, and Switzerland.

Identification Requirements

The bulk of traded GMOs is comprised of GMOs intended for direct use as food or feed, or for processing. These GMOs include, for example, GM foods, GM animal feed, and GM microbes used in industrial production. The issue of their identification has been very contentious. The main disagreement was because the majority of countries wanted such shipments to be clearly identified as containing GMOs that are not intended for intentional introduction into the environment, while the GMO exporting countries would only agree to identify such shipments as those that 'may contain' GMOs not intended for intentional introduction into the environment.

At stake was whether the world community would continue to allow contamination of bulk commodity shipments of GMOs, or whether a system would be put in place that would remove ambiguity, allowing Parties of import to know exactly what GMOs there are in a shipment, and which would protect Parties without the laws or regulations (most developing countries) that many exporting countries themselves have to protect against this contamination. At stake was also the ability to track and trace particular GMOs, allowing correlation with risk assessments for that particular GMO and which is necessary for important biosafety functions such as monitoring, emergency measures, liability and redress, and meaningful labelling.

After years of discussions under the Cartagena Protocol, consensus was finally reached in 2006 at the Third Meeting of the Parties. In situations where the identity of the GMO is known through 'means such as identity preservation systems', the shipment must be identified as one that 'contains' GMOs that are for direct use as food or feed, or for processing. A two-stage approach is set out for cases where the identity of the GMO shipment is not known; the shipment can be identified as one that 'may contain' one or more GMOs that are intended for direct use as food or feed, or for processing, but there is an in-built review and assessment process to eventually ensure that the shipment is identified as one that 'contains' GMOs.

Details in the documentation accompanying both categories of shipments must include, among other things, the common, scientific, and, where available, commercial names of the GMOs and transformation event code of the GMOs or, where available, as a key to accessing information in the Biosafety Clearing House, its unique identifier code. Such clear identification of GM commodities indicate that a system of testing, segregation, and identity preservation would need to be set up in the exporting countries. Exporting countries should rightfuly bear the burden of ensuring that contaminated shipments do not leave their country and of ensuring that the exact GM components and all necessary information linked to those events are communicated to the country of import.

It would also help to ensure that the burden of making sure that contaminated shipments are not entering the country does not rest on the importing countries. Most developing countries are importing countries, and lack the capacity and resources to test shipments at the port. There are also many difficulties with sampling and detection, and trying to always ensure that all contaminated shipments are accurately detected is difficult.

Even if the main exporting countries are not Parties to the Cartagena Protocol, the decision reached by the Parties in 2006 means that Parties will have to implement it at the national level as a minimum standard. Exporting countries, whether or not they are Parties, will have to comply with the laws of the importing countries.

Other Key Issues

Other important provisions in the Cartagena Protocol, which are also considerations for national biosafety regulations, include socio-economic considerations, public awareness, and participation, risk assessment and risk management, review of decisions in the light of new scientific information, unintentional transboundary movements and emergency measures, and illegal transboundary movement of GMOs.

Parties to the Cartagena Protocol may take socio-economic considerations into account when making decisions on GMOs. This issue is particularly important for developing countries, where small farmers, who could be adversely affected by GMOs, may make up the majority of the population.

The Protocol also places a clear obligation on Parties to promote and facilitate public awareness, education, and participation, including access to information. It also requires mandatory public consultation and disclosure of results of decisions to the public in the decision-making process. Parties will have to implement these provisions nationally.

Risk management measures, unintentional transboundary movements and emergency measures, and measures to deal with illegal transboundary movement of GMOs are all important elements in the Protocol, which must be implemented nationally and which are important in any national regulatory regime in order to deal with post-release monitoring and regulation.

Monitoring for environmental/ecological effects and effects on human and animal health is critical if releases are approved and GMOs are planted and eaten in the country, for example. It is important that this is worked in as part and parcel of the information provided and considered when making decisions, as this is the true cost and responsibility of releasing a GMO. It should not just be considered as something to put in place once a release has taken place.

It is important to monitor unintentional and illegal releases of GMOs. The capacity of any country to detect such releases is critical for compliance with national legislation and for safety. If this capacity does not exist, countries must proceed with caution in allowing the domestic development of GMOs, and must be vigilant if GMO imports are allowed into the country. This may happen accidentally or illegally, even if a country does not allow GMOs to enter its territory, and the capacity to detect and enforce needs to be built urgently.

In such situations, emergency measures need to be taken. It is critical for countries to evaluate whether or not they know what to do, and whether the damage is repairable. All these are also important factors to consider before any releases are authorized.

National Implementation of the Cartagena Protocol

At the national level, the implementation of the Cartagena Protocol is only one part of the national biosafety law and regulation that countries should put in place for biosafety. National implementation is an obligation on countries that are Parties to the Protocol. It is important to recall that the Protocol is a negotiated international law framework that sets minimum standards for national biosafety implementation. This is clearly established in Article 2(4) (Cartagena Protocol on Biosafety 2000):

Nothing in this Protocol shall be interpreted as restricting the right of a Party to take action that is more protective of the conservation and sustainable use of biological diversity than called for in this Protocol, provided that such action is consistent with the objective and the provisions of this Protocol and is in accordance with that Party's other obligations under international law.

Sovereign countries interpret and implement the Cartagena Protocol, and can do so in a comprehensive manner, and with higher standards for biosafety. The Protocol primarily deals with the transboundary movement of GMOs. In national legislation on biosafety, countries also need to regulate research, field trials, placing on the market, etc. Any international law that is negotiated is the lowest common denominator that is able to reflect agreement by all Parties. It is in national implementation that countries are able to reflect their concerns, and put in place strong and robust legislation.

What is the ideal domestic policy and law on biosafety? This should be the starting point for any discussions on the appropriate national policy and legal response. Then consideration should be given to the rights and obligations of Parties under the Cartagena Protocol on Biosafety, and then to other international obligations and agreements that affect national legal and policy options. For countries which are members of the WTO, the rights and obligations under the WTO Agreements should also be considered.

The implementation of biosafety at the national level involves a complex piecing together of the national policy on biosafety, together with the rights and obligations that a country is committed to at the international level. At the national level, the chosen policy direction can also be a complicated process, sometimes involving the weighing up and balancing of competing interests (such as genetic engineering research and development priorities, biosafety research and considerations, sustainable agriculture policy and direction, technology assessment, socio-economic considerations, etc.). The challenge for any country is to ensure a coherent policy that takes into account possibly differing interests, but which moves the country down the path of sustainable development.

It is also important to begin by identifying national priorities and needs for biosafety, and then integrating a country's commitments under the Cartagena Protocol, as the primary international legal instrument on biosafety that many countries are now Party to. This involves interpreting and implementing the binding international rights and obligations according to the policy space and flexibilities accorded to a Party under the legal instrument and in the light of national needs and priorities on biosafety policy, law, and regulation.

The next step is then to integrate into national biosafety implementation other biosafety-relevant legally binding rights and obligations such as those under the WTO Agreements, and the biosafety-relevant standards set by international bodies such as the Codex Alimentarius Commission (for food safety), the International Plant Protection Convention (for plant health), and the World Organisation for Animal Health (OIE) (for animal health).

Some Options for Biosafety Regulatory Systems

There are options a country has when putting in place its biosafety regulatory system. These are policy decisions that should be taken early on, and real public participation in this decision is critical. The options include a 'GM-free' decision, a moratorium, or a case-by-case assessment system. All of these should require a legal instrument, regulation, and administration. WTO members would need to assess the compatibility of any restrictions or moratoria with the relevant WTO agreements. A 'GM-free' decision may be made at the national, county/region/province, or local level. Many local authorities at the town, municipal, regional, or state level have already chosen to declare themselves 'GM-free', and have put in place policies, and sometimes laws, to support this.

Other countries have opted to put in place a moratorium, some for a specific period of time, others until certain criteria are met. A moratorium may be established until omitted research on biosafety risks are conducted, until a law is implemented, until there is capacity to implement biosafety regulation, until concerns around genetic engineering and GMOs are resolved, until a country is able to assess its needs and priorities and take an informed decision, etc.

Many countries have adopted a case-by-case risk assessment system—for example, the EU biosafety laws put such a system in place. A case-by-case assessment system would involve setting up a system for receiving and processing individual applications, risk assessment (for example, ecological, health, social, economic), and decision making. This means that each GMO event is risk assessed, followed by the rejection or approval of an application.

Restrictions may also be included, for example, bans or restrictions on the hostile use of genetic engineering, on the use of antibiotic resistance marker genes, on releases in centres of origin and diversity, on releases in organic/ecological farming areas, on releases where there are wild relatives, on releases in protected areas or in areas which are socially and culturally important to indigenous peoples, and a ban on genetic use restriction technologies, also known as 'Terminator Technology'.

Any restrictions require an enforcement mechanism for discovery of any violations and legal sanctions when these restrictions are violated. This also applies in cases where the region or country is GM-free or if there is a moratorium in place. There need to be provisions for monitoring and detection, unintentional/illegal releases, and emergency measures because there is the risk of contamination, and illegal entry and spread of GMOs. In addition, when there are violations, there should be some means of dealing with the problem of accidental or illegal release, and some measures that should be activated immediately to mitigate the problem, and if possible, reinstate the original situation as far as possible. Liability and redress provisions that take into account the special case of GMOs are needed.

Biosafety laws are thus important whatever be the option that is chosen. If there is no biosafety law, there are no legal requirements that require biosafety risk assessment before any GMO activity takes place, and no recourse to any biosafety specific action when legal requirements are violated. One has to be mindful of the danger of a weak biosafety law, in that it could facilitate 'rubber stamping' of GMOs, and may pave the way for the introduction of GMOs without proper assessment.

In any case, the worst-case scenarios, and the 'what-if' questions, must be asked when designing any regulation. If these problems cannot be prevented or dealt with satisfactorily by national legislation, then there should be no approvals or releases. This is because the damage could be irreversible if the GMO concerned is problematic.

It is very important to understand that we do not fully know the risks of GMOs. Risks are defined as the consequence of a negative impact, multiplied by the likelihood of it happening. A risk can be very great if the consequence is catastrophic, even though the likelihood of it happening is small—it needs to happen only once. At this point in time, not enough research has been done to know what the negative impacts may be or even the likelihood of its happening. Early warnings are, however, starting to emerge, with new scientific evidence, from biosafety research and field monitoring of environmental and health hazards.

In addition, before approving or releasing GMOs, it is critically important to consider whether or not we know what to do if something goes wrong. Can the negative impacts be reversed? Is remediation possible? Is coexistence possible? Is contamination inevitable? If these are questions that cannot be answered, then the precautionary principle dictates that there should be no releases or approvals until independent biosafety research has shown that these GMOs are safe beyond reasonable doubt.

References

Cartagena Protocol on Biosafety, (2000), Montreal: CBD Secretariat.
Convention on Biological Diversity (CBD), (1992), Montreal: CBD Secretariat.

Domingo, J.L., (2000), 'Health Risks of Genetically Modified Foods: Many Opinions but Few Data', *Science*, Vol. 288, pp. 1748–49.

Myhr, A.I. and T. Traavik, (2002), 'The Precautionary Principle: Scientific Uncertainty and Omitted Research in the Context of GMO Use and Release', *Journal of Agricultural and Environmental Ethics*, Vol. 15, pp. 73–86.

——, (2003), 'Genetically Modified (GM) Crops: Precautionary Science and Conflicts of Interests', *Journal of Agricultural and Environmental Ethics*, Vol. 16, pp. 227–47.

Pryme, I.F. and R. Lembcke, (2003), '*In vivo* Studies on Possible Health Consequences of Genetically Modified Food and Feed—with Particular Regard to Ingredients Consisting of Genetically Modified Plant Materials', *Nutrition and Health,* Vol. 17, pp. 1–8.

Pusztai, A. and S. Bardocz, (2005), 'GMO in Animal Nutrition: Potential Benefits and Risks', in R. Mosenthin, J. Zentek and T. Zebrowska (eds), *Biology of Nutrition in Growing Animals*, London: Elsevier Limited, pp. 513–40.

Pusztai, A., S. Bardocz, and S.W.B. Ewen, (2003), 'Genetically Modified Foods: Potential Human Health Effects', in J.P.F. D'Mello (ed.), *Food Safety: Contaminants and Toxins*, London: CABI, pp. 347–72.

Quist, D. and I.H. Chapela, (2001), 'Transgenic DNA Introgressed into Traditional Maize Landraces in Oaxaca, Mexico', *Nature,* Vol. 414, pp. 541–43.

Snow, A.A., D.A. Andow, P. Gepts, E.M. Hallerman, A. Power, J.N. Tiedje, and L.L. Wolfenbarger, (2003), 'Genetically Engineered Organisms and the Environment: Current Status and Recommendations', Ecological Society of America position paper, available at *http://www.esa.org/pao/ esaPositions/Papers/geo_position.htm#top*, accessed on 24 August 2006.

Squire, G.R., D.R. Brooks, D.A. Bohan, G.T. Champion, R.E. Daniels, A.J. Haughton, C. Hawes, M.S. Heard, M.O. Hill, M.J. May, J.L. Osborne, J.N. Perry, D.B. Roy, I.P. Woiwod, and L.G. Firbank, (2003), 'On the Rationale and Interpretation of the Farm Scale Evaluations of Genetically Modified Herbicide-tolerant Crops', *Philosophical Transactions: Biological Sciences*, Series B, Vol. 358, pp. 1779–80.

Traavik, T. and J. Heinemann, (2007), *Genetic Engineering and Omitted Health Research: Still No Answers to Ageing Questions*, TWN Biotechnology and Biosafety Series 7, Penang: Third World Network.

Wilson, A.K., J.R. Latham, and R.A. Steinbrecher, (2006), 'Transformation-induced Mutations in Transgenic Plants: Analysis and Biosafety Implications', *Biotechnology and Genetic Engineering Reviews*, Vol. 23, pp. 209–34.

Wolfenbarger, L.L. and P.R. Phifer, (2000), 'The Ecological Risks and Benefits of Genetically Engineered Plants', *Science,* Vol. 290, pp. 2088–93.

9

Role of Scientific Information in Food Policy Making
The Case of GMOs

SAMARTHIA THANKAPPAN

One of the principal characteristics during the end of the twentieth century was the mounting public concern in Europe about new (and often unsuspected) food-related threats to human health. In the 1990s, there was particular focus on unsafe food and threats to the human food chain. Fears and uncertainties about the Bovine Spongiform Encephalopathy (BSE) agent, GMOs, and dioxins in food attracted a vast amount of media coverage. The modern industrial civilization was witnessing the advent of 'Risk Society' as foretold by Beck (1992) a few years earlier. In this framework, risk begins to structure and condition social institutional relations with risk allocations, replacing the distribution of monetary wealth and cultural privilege that marked industrial society, giving rise to distributional tensions and political conflict.

Food scares continue and indeed these are said to be inevitable unless the way we produce food is changed (Lawrence 2001). The application of science in modern agriculture and the use of large-scale production methods have made it possible to produce food that is plentiful and cheap. Yet such methods have done little, in the wake of an unrelenting diet of food scares, to promote public confidence in food production. New concerns have prompted reappraisals of food regulation and the ever more elaborate strategies and methods adopted have dramatically increased the cost of supporting and managing agriculture. The attention given to regulatory reform has itself generated media attention to matters of food safety while complicating and problematizing the regulatory role of government in this area.

An editorial in the Irish Times[1] reviewed a decade of alarms about the safety of European agriculture and food production:

The emergence of mad cow disease (BSE) in Britain gave way to dioxin-infected food in Belgium and sewage-contaminated meat in France before Britain again hit the headlines by originating a foot-and-mouth epidemic in cattle and sheep.

Though it has been more than a decade since GM crops were first cultivated commercially, the debate over whether they should be grown at all continues. Today, around 8.5 million farmers in 21 countries grow GM crops, according to Brookes and Barfoot (2006). In recent years, debates over GM food and agricultural biotechnology have substantially increased all over the globe. Agricultural biotechnology has both been appreciated by its promoters as a solution to world hunger and depreciated by critics as a means to environmental destruction. We have also witnessed of late the rejection of GM food aid by Zambia; a WTO dispute over Europe's refusal to accept GM food; and fiascos related to Bt cotton crops in India. On the other hand, however, consumers in the United States continue to accept GM foods and agricultural biotechnology continues to expand its global reach.

The GM controversy is fundamentally about the future of food and farming and what it implies for development. For some, the debate is about politics (Torgerson 1986), control, and access in agri-food systems, with issues of corporate dominance, patenting, and the changing nature of public sector research and development at the forefront (Schenkelaars 1996). For others, it is about ethics, morals, and rights (Arvanitoyannis and Krystallis 2005), centred on the value of nature, the role of science, and the opinions of farmers, consumers, and future generations (Tokar 2001; Gaskell 2004). Still others focus on the potential risks and uncertainties for biodiversity, for agro-ecosystem stability, for human health, etc. The issue, therefore, is how to develop an effective regulatory system in the face of scientific uncertainty, public disquiet, and mistrust in formal risk management institutions.

However, there are a few issues upon which science and politics disagree, for example: the assessment of risk; the management of risk; and the interconnectedness of risk assessment, risk communication, and risk management. A significant driver towards greater consumer

[1] *Irish Times*, 21 June 2001.

involvement in food is a new approach to risk governance, a process by which risks are assessed, managed, and communicated (Rothstein 2006). Risk assessment is based on differential notions of psychological assumptions, and this in turn is connected to the level of public involvement in risk assessment (Hood and Rothstein 2001; Hood et al. 2001). Consumers say they care how natural or healthy food is or how and where it was produced. Some consumers want to see their views represented in decisions about food and agriculture. Consequently, there is unease when decisions or actions are taken that appear to ignore the needs or values of ordinary consumers.

In many respects, the GM crop issue provides a window through which to examine a range of current development policy issues. What role should the private sector play? What complementary roles are there for public sector research and development? What form should state-led regulation take? How safe is 'safe'? How can public trust in regulatory institutions be improved? What role can a more democratized science and technology effort play in addressing the diverse development challenges of developing countries?

By exemplifying the case of GM, this chapter explores the public debates and concerns over GM products that afflict food science. The chapter looks at the analytical perspectives on regulatory science and the question of what role scientific information and advice has played and can and should play in food policy making.

TECHNICAL ASPECTS OF CURRENT AND FUTURE RISKS: THE CASE OF GMOS

The introduction of GM foods into the EU has been extremely controversial, and there are numerous dimensions to that controversy. One of the most vigorous controversies focuses on the issue of whether or not, and to what extent, it is possible to reliably assess the risks that may arise from the consumption of GM foods. Several official expert advisory committees, such as the UK government's Advisory Committee on Novel Foods and Processes, have indicated themselves to be satisfied that sufficient theoretical knowledge and empirical evidence are available to enable them to reliably judge whether or not GM foods can safely be consumed. They contend that the risks from GM foods can be and are being reliably assessed and that their findings provide a robust basis for policy decisions.

Whenever official approval for the introduction of GM foods has been given in Europe (or in the US), regulatory committees have invoked the concept of 'substantial equivalence', which means that if an expert advisory committee deems a GM to be 'substantially equivalent' to its natural antecedents, it can be presumed to pose no new health risks and hence to be acceptable for human consumption (OECD 1993). The concept of substantial equivalence in itself is, however, the focus of a vigorous controversy (Millstone et al. 1999).

It has been argued that the concept of 'substantial equivalence' does not provide an adequate basis for reliable assessments of risks of consuming GM foods. Millstone et al. (1999) have argued that judgements of substantial equivalence are based upon the chemical analyses of the food products, and that knowledge of chemical analyses does not provide an adequate basis for predicting their biochemical, immunological, and toxicological action. Therefore, they contend that until some other more comprehensive and sophisticated approach involving biochemical, immunological, and toxicological tests is developed and adopted, it will not be possible to say how reliably those risks are being assessed.

There is no evidence that any of the relatively small number of GM foods that have been permitted is toxic. It is possible now to know the precision and lack of precision with which risks to public health from consuming GM foods may currently be estimated. Scientists cannot, however, estimate the magnitude of the uncertainties with which consumers are confronted.

At the European Commission Conference on Risk Perception,[2] there was a unanimous acceptance that the public/consumers look at risk very differently from risk assessors. However, public perceptions can also be fragmented and this seems to be due to the complex interplay of implicit or inherent cultural models that human beings use to interpret their environment and the world around them. Thus, the public seems to perceive risk in their own cultural models. Risk perception influences all steps of the risk analysis process and this may explain such intriguing situations as to why scientists from different parts of Europe come up with different conclusions, despite following similar risk assessment approaches. Risk perception plays a much larger role than perhaps previously considered in the risk assessment procedure and indeed may explain such divergence in views.

[2]'Risk Perception: Science, Public Debate and Policy Making', Conference held on 4–5 December 2003, Brussels.

It is possible, however, to bring this apparently unbalanced perception of risk into a clear political focus. A study of the contemporary politics of risk does offer some insights into the seeming absence of balance in the perception and reaction to new and unlikely risks. It also suggests a general explanation for the high levels of public anxiety and intense press interest in novel and unanticipated threats to human well-being. The public now appears to be much more reactive to a mixture that brings together the novel and bewildering with an ill-defined potential for great harm and combines fear of the unknown with distrust of commerce, government, and science.

The catalyst for a good deal of the loss of confidence in the integrity of both British and European governments was undoubtedly the BSE saga; it has been the most important, though not the only, 'food scare' to fashion contemporary attitudes to the reliability of public policy makers and those who advise them about threats to food safety and human health. The European Commission accepted as much when it presented its detailed legislative proposal for an EFSA in June 2001, stating that:

.... there has been a reduction in the confidence of consumers and trading partners in the public authorities' ability to regulate and control the safety of food supply, in the systems under which European food law is made, and in the European institutions themselves.

While there may have been a general decline in public respect for public bodies and scientific expertise, the growing distrust of the public authorities and of scientific experts in relation to food safety has closely paralleled a series of food scandals and crises that have been the subject of extensive, and often unflattering, media coverage.

It is evident from the above discussion how uneven, policy related to food science can be. The uncertainties that afflict some of food science highlight the question of what role scientific information and advice has played and can and should play in food policy making. This is especially so in the light of the UK government's initiative in creating the Food Standards Agency (FSA) with a mandate to provide objective and reliable scientific advice to policy makers.

THE RELATIONSHIP BETWEEN SCIENCE AND PRECAUTION

The nature of science has for many years been a relatively familiar and well-explored subject. Science is conventionally held to imply a series of key properties, including a systematic methodology, scepticism, transparency, quality control by peer-review, professional independence, accountability, and an emphasis on learning.

The formal regulatory concept of precaution, on the other hand, is more specific, less familiar, and a much more recent innovation. General notions of precaution have arisen repeatedly in different guises in national and international legislation since the 1972 Stockholm Environment Conference. The concept of 'precautionary principle' has been widely adopted in the regulation of marine pollution, climate change, biodiversity loss, dangerous chemicals, and most recently in the release of GMOs. One classic and globally influential formulation is Principle 15 in the 1992 Rio Declaration on Environment and Development, which holds that:

Where there are threats of serious irreversible damage, lack of full scientific certainty shall not be used as a reason for postponing cost-effective measures to prevent environmental degradation.

One of the most prominent axes for the emerging debate over the precautionary principle concerns a contrast that is often drawn between precautions on the one hand and science-based regulation on the other. The implication of this distinction is that the adoption of a precautionary approach might somehow be seen *a priori* as being opposing or at least in tension with the principles of scientific rigour in the regulation of risk (Legge and Durant 2003). Under such a view, the implementation of the precautionary principle becomes essentially a politically-determined compromise on what are held to be the otherwise clear dictates of the sound science of risk assessment.

Whether viewed from the point of view of policy analysis, science and technology studies, decision analysis, or risk assessment, notions of a unitary definitive concept of sound science are highly problematic (Goklany 2001; Raffensperger and Tickner 1999). In situations where different bodies of scientific evidence, alternative theoretical paradigms, or different disciplinary perspectives appear to be in tension, it is often far from clear what criteria are to be employed in determining the practical substance of sound science.

Given the polarization and strength of feeling so often encountered in discussions over the role of science in the regulation of risk, the implication is that a number of things may be equally true in the appraisal of risk (Fraiberg and Trebilcock 1998; Bohanes 2002). It is of course uncontentious that policy making regulation and the day-to-day management of risk must be informed by all the available empirical evidence and should be consistent with prevailing scientific understandings. However, this does not mean that science on its own should be assumed to determine particular regulatory or policy responses.

It would be more apt to say that when ignorance and disproportionality are acknowledged to be firmly grounded in the science of risk assessment, then it follows that a more broadly-based, pluralistic precautionary approach is more scientific than traditional risk assessment. Either way, it remains an indispensable element in the effective management of risk (Diahanna 2006).

Given an acknowledgement of the scientific uncertainties, discussions concerning the role of science in policy making are typically embedded in terms of when, and how, to adopt and apply a precautionary approach. From Article 7 of the EU General Food Law,[3] it is clear that the precautionary principle can only be considered when the following prerequisite conditions are satisfied:

 (i) There are potentially harmful effects deriving from a phenomenon, product, or process that have been identified;

 (ii) That scientific evaluation does not allow the risk to be determined with sufficient certainty; and

 (iii) There has to be an objective evaluation of available scientific data and other information before any decision is made to invoke the precautionary principle.

Precautionary measures are by nature provisional. The European Court[4] has endorsed the philosophy behind the principle and its application and has clarified the steps that need to be followed. A public authority cannot take a purely hypothetical approach to risk and may not simply base decisions of 'zero risk'. Existing relevant scientific data should always be evaluated before the precautionary principle is invoked.

The Sanitary and Phytosanitary Agreement (SPS), which forms part of the rules of the WTO, stipulates that in the face of scientific uncertainty, precaution is appropriate and legitimate, but that whenever precaution is deemed appropriate, steps should also be taken to diminish the scientific uncertainties.[5] The scientific uncertainties can be diminished only by research. The issue of how most effectively to diminish the key scientific uncertainties is a challenge to all EU member states. One question with which we all struggle is: to what

[3]Regulation (EC) No. 178. 2002, Article 7.

[4]Case T-13/99, judgement of 11 September 2002 of the court of First Instance (Pfizer Animal Health SA against Council of the European Union).

[5]Sanitary and Phytosanitary Agreement, Article 5(7).

extent should public policy makers be obliging the corporate sector to invest in research which would serve to reduce many of the key uncertainties and to what extent should public resources be invested in research which could help to diminish the scientific uncertainties with which public policy makers are currently struggling.

THE SOCIAL SCIENCE BEHIND POLICY MAKING

A new food policy is emerging. The character of the food system and the nature of food policy are both changing as change in technology and industrialization of the food system has transformed the way food is produced, marketed, and consumed.

Policy makers in both the public and private sectors have struggled to cope with technical and political challenges on food safety issues, especially the implications for trade policy. More generally, there is a widespread perception that we face a crisis in science and governance. For example, the UK government has created the FSA, which, as a science-based organization, encourages research in assessing risks across the food chain with the aim of ensuring that risks are minimized. Science is the key factor for the FSA to help meet its strategic targets. This view is also highlighted in the following excerpt from an interview with the FSA by the author.

We're not basing purely on science, we're dealing, obviously public health; food safety is our primary concern. But we're also concerned with consumer choice for instance. We're involved in labelling and other areas of consumer choice. We have to think about things like, when we're doing risk management, is it appropriate to ban something, or is it more important to focus on the risk communication and say 'this is the situation' and we're giving you the choice, we've given you the information and you decide whether to eat this or not. I think we're doing this more than we used to.

The EC's justification on the science-based approach to risk management followed a similar line, as is evident from the following excerpt:

They [industries] like the science-based approach because they think it protects them against political indiscretion, so they, on the whole, are very much in favour of science-based approaches and somewhat suspicious of the supplementary necessity, which is the need, on some occasions to take precautionary measures. But we have managed to diffuse this over the last two years, by structuring the so-called precautionary principle in a way, which they can't really object as a kind of provisional system that you use when scientific information is at hand for a decision.

Governments have routinely referred to 'scientific findings' in their communications to the public on food safety, explicitly encouraging the public to rely upon this standard when forming their own judgements about the safety of food supply. However, experience has shown that consumers do not necessarily find these communications to be wholly persuasive. This is emphasized in a recent survey conducted by the UK FSA on public perceptions in Britain, which pointed to widespread unease among the public about food safety in general, and in particular, a huge increase in public concern about GM ingredients in foods. All major food retailing chains in the UK removed foods with GM ingredients from their shelves, and have been assiduously tracking back product lines in their supply chains to ensure that they can advertise their wares as 'GM free'. This, despite over a decade of consistent messages from industry and governments to the public, to the effect that GM crops for food products have been carefully assessed as to safety, using science-based approaches, and have passed all of the relevant tests. These experiences clearly show that factors other than science are important to consumers (Assael 2004; Becker et al. 1998; Imram 1999). Survey data, for example, show that people's concerns are related more to a desire for transparency in decision making about GM foods, a suspicion about the economic motives of multinational companies which sell such foods, a concern about the implications of GM products for the European agricultural system (which in turn connects to concerns about landscape and culture), and worries about the implications of globalization for quality of life (Marris et al. 2001; Gaskell et al. 2003; Rayner 2003). In the scientific controversy over GM foods, these diverse values have no legitimate part in the debate over levels of risk. Thus, not only are expressions of these values suppressed, but they are suppressed in favour of an alternative value, that is, economic openness, which remains camouflaged behind the commitment to carrying out the debate in scientific terms alone (Sarewitz 2000).

Given that science is so frequently contested, it cannot determine policy outcomes. Even when science is straightforward, decisions about which risks are acceptable, in exchange for particular anticipated benefits, may involve non-scientific considerations.

Science-based evidence does not seem to resonate well with many consumers (Leiserowitz 2004), at least so far, because it does not seem to necessarily respond well to diffuse consumer fears, especially when there are significant uncertainties in the scientific assessment. Considerable efforts have been made by scholars in the fields of science policy and political analysis to foster greater understanding of the ways in which science-based risk management policies are made. For the purposes of discussion, the key issue is the role that scientific information and advice can and should play in the policy making process.

CHANGING REGULATORY POLICY MAKING

Traditionally, regulatory policy making for the protection of consumers and public health has been officially represented as based upon sound science, where it is assumed that science operates in a sphere where social, political, cultural, and economic vacuity exists. Further, scientists are presumed to be in possession of the truth or a repository of reliable knowledge, whereas the general public is considered to be at best ignorant. Risk communication is then seen as the challenge of providing science-based representations of risk that are sufficiently simplified so as to be readily understood by the general public. A classic example worth presenting is that of the history of BSE policy making in the UK (at least up to March 1996).[6] In this case, assessment and representations of risk were not based on independent scientific advice, but on prior decisions concerning non-scientific judgements about the direction and parameters of policy. It is because of that case that the argument for separating risk assessment from risk management is so widely acknowledged.

Weinberg (1972) articulated the concept of 'trans-science' to refer to the intersection between policy making and scientific deliberation during the early 1970s. Since then, a growing proportion of academic policy analysts have acknowledged that because of uncertainties in the underlying science and for other reasons as well, scientific considerations can never by themselves determine policy decisions. The Commission's White Paper on Food Safety is a very good example of the Commission's move from a traditional policy making mould to one where there is a distinction between 'risk assessment' (purely scientific enterprise) and 'risk management' (involving non-scientific considerations) such as economic, social, cultural, and evaluative considerations.

[6]P. van Zwanenberg, E. Millstone, (1999), 'BSE and the UK National Action System', Report to the European Commission, SPRU University, Sussex.

The assumptions and empirical adequacy of the modern model have been repeatedly and effectively disproved by critics, who emphasize that risk assessments are framed by a range of non-scientific considerations—for example, which risks qualify to be significant; which evidences qualify as significant evidence; and the level of tolerance (Jasanoff 1990).

Policy making now assumes that science always operates within a specific social, political, cultural, and economic context, and that risk assessments involve the analysis of selected scientific information within a prior set of non-scientific considerations. Furthermore, it is assumed that once expert scientific risk assessors have reached conclusions about the existence of a risk, its probability and severity, and acknowledged the scientific uncertainties which they have had to tackle, policy makers need to make a further set of specific downstream evaluative judgements to decide how the conclusions of risk assessment will influence policy decisions.

CONCLUDING REMARKS

Some of the most important food safety issues of the day cannot be resolved by relying on scientific data and traditional risk assessment methods. As our understanding of risk has advanced, we have learnt that many questions about food-related risks cannot be answered with current knowledge. Precaution, sensibly applied, is one useful tool for making decisions of this nature (Giandomenico 2002).

A precautionary approach does not reject science and risk assessment (Wiedemann and Schütz 2005). More accurately, it requires an even more rigorous use of science. It pays greater attention to what science does not know, and to the possible consequences of knowledge gaps, when assessing risks (Cairns 2003).

The growing emphasis on precaution also implies a shift in philosophy on some long-standing conflicts in societal values. One involves the concept of 'burden of proof'. For decades, new technologies have been presumed safe until proven harmful. Today, there is a growing tendency to place a greater burden on proponents of a new technology, to demand that risk questions be better identified and addressed before innovations are widely adopted. This reflects social learning from past mistakes, and a greater sense of equity, an assertion that consumers and future generations have the right not to have risks imposed upon them without more discussion of who is benefiting, and of how much risk is acceptable.

The precautionary approach also implies a greater role for government, and less reliance on unrestrained market forces, to chart the course of technology. It requires a conscious effort to look for alternative solutions to food-related technical problems, and to choose options with the best risk/benefit ratios. Attempts to 'control' technology risk stifling innovation, and governments will proceed cautiously, seeking the right balance. But a better balance must be found.

The international health community is now becoming more precautionary, and this trend will continue. Adopting a more precautionary approach to risk assessment will not be easy. Dealing with science and value trade-offs is complicated enough, and in the international arena, national interests in promoting trade, private sector resistance to restrictions on markets, and other political factors have all confounded efforts to improve food safety risk analysis.

It must be recognized that the 'right' balance point will differ for different societies, and that a developing country may choose to pursue the benefits of rapid economic growth, and be less precautionary about risks than a wealthy nation with mature technologies might prefer. An international consensus on the 'right' amount of precaution may be nearly impossible to find.

There is a growing recognition that the scientific and technological aspects of food policy must be understood in terms of their implications for public health and public interest, rather than just in terms of their economic or industrial implications. Rather than merely ask 'will this work?', the question now asked is 'what impact will this have on public health and confidence?'

Debates over the relative merits of scientific and precautionary approaches to the management of risks falls easily into a dichotomy trap, in which productive and creative solution-oriented thinking is hampered by rigid contrasts and associated conflicts. It is true that neither a totally permissive approach nor a totally restrictive approach to regulation offers a valid, feasible, or a desirable way forward. Both precautionary and scientific approaches can be caricatured by stigmatizing them in a polarized way; further, both forms of rhetoric are equally vulnerable to manipulation by different parties in order to achieve political or commercial objectives.

Wynne (2004) shows how the public understanding of science questions raises issues of the epistemic commitments and institutional structures that constitute modern science. Wynne suggests that many of the inadequacies in the social integration and uptake of science might be overcome if modern scientific institutions were more reflexive and open about the implicit normative commitments embedded in scientific cultures.

Some of the key elements of a precautionary approach may be entirely consistent with sound scientific practice in responding to intractable problems in risk assessment, as for example, lack of knowledge and disproportionality. These problems are well-founded in the fundamental theoretical framework of the sciences underlying risk assessment. With different assumptions adopted in different risk assessment exercises often yielding results that vary by several orders of magnitude, the practical policy implications are equally profound. The acknowledgement of such difficulties under a precautionary approach may thus be seen as a more scientifically rigorous way of carrying forward the regulation of risks than would be their denial under a purely risk-based approach. Recognizing the unproductive nature of the science/precaution dichotomy, attention can then turn to the details of the measured and incremental application of an approach that is both scientific and precautionary in nature.

Firstly, there can be no simple analytical, instrumental, or institutional fixes for the complexities encountered in the management of risks. Policy making must be based, therefore, on the available scientific information, but science on its own is not enough. Scientific analysis of risk is inextricably intertwined with subjective framing assumptions, values, and trade-offs. The appraisal of risks should, therefore, be conducted in an open and pluralistic manner allowing for critical discourse as an essential part of the regulatory process.

Secondly, there is a need for flexibility and learning in regulation itself. The management of risks is necessarily an incremental and context-specific undertaking. Different risks will warrant greater or lesser degrees of precaution at different times, and different regulatory instruments would be appropriate in different contexts. Attention, therefore, should be given to focus on the different crucial characteristics of the different types of risks.

Recognising the unproductive nature of science/precaution dichotomy, focus should be on developing an approach that is both scientific and precautionary in nature. An essential complement to the science lies in the development of institutions and procedures for the fostering of social learning in different forms of discourse over risk and, in particular, for the provision of vital contextual information on values and priorities to inform the framing of science itself.

The issues surrounding GM food contain both scientific uncertainty and societal values. Within such a context, the process ultimately becomes political. Sarewitz (2004), for example, states that 'scientific inquiry is inherently unsuitable for helping to resolve political disputes. Even when a disagreement seems to be amenable to technical analysis, the nature of science itself usually acts to inflame rather than quench debate'. The reason Sarewitz gives for this outcome, which, according to his terminology, is an 'excess of objectivity', is that science seeks to come to grips with the richness and complexity of nature through numerous disciplinary approaches, each of which gives factual, yet always incomplete, views of reality.

When decision making processes become politicized as in the case of GM, it leaves the door open for the process where the intent is to protect and defend strongly held values, but the arguments are cast in the guise of scientific debate. So, the inherent uncertainty, however small, is exploited and can significantly influence decision making within the political process.

REFERENCES

Arvanitoyannis, I.S. and A. Krystallis, (2005), 'Consumers' Beliefs, Attitudes and Intentions towards Genetically Modified Foods, Based on the "Perceived Safety vs. Benefits" Perspective', *International Journal of Food Science and Technology*, Vol. 40, pp. 343–60.

Assael, Henry, (2004), *Consumer Behaviour: A Strategic Approach*, Boston: Houghton Mifflin.

Beck, Ulrich, (1992), *Risk Society: Towards a New Modernity*, London: Sage.

Becker, T., E. Benner and K. Glitsch, (1998), 'Summary Report on Consumer Behaviour toward Meat in Germany, Ireland, Italy, Spain, Sweden and the United Kingdom', Results from a consumer survey, Department of Agricultural Economics, University of Göttingen, Göttingen.

Bohanes, J., (2002), 'Risk Regulation in WTO Law: A Procedure-Based Approach to the Precautionary Principle', *Columbia Journal of Transatlantic Law*, Vol. 40, pp. 323–58.

Brookes, G. and P. Barfoot, (2006), 'GM Crops: The First Ten Years—Global Socio-Economic and Environmental Impacts', International Service for the Acquisition of Agri-Biotech Applications (ISAAA) Brief No. 36, Ithaca, New York: ISAAA.

Cairns, J., Jr., (2003), 'Interrelationships between the Precautionary Principle, Prediction Strategies, and Sustainable Use of the Planet', *Environmental Health Perspective*, Vol. 111, pp. 877–80.

Diahanna, L.P., (2006), 'The Precautionary Principle and Risk Assessment in International Food Safety: How the World Trade Organization Influences Standards', *Risk Analysis*, Vol. 26, No. 5, pp.1259–73.

Fraiberg, J. and M.J. Trebilcock, (1998), 'Risk Regulation: Technocratic and Democratic Tools for Regulatory Reform', *McGill Law Journal*, Vol. 43, pp. 835–63.

Gaskell, G., (2004), 'Science Policy and Society: The British Debate over GM Agriculture', *Current Opinion in Biotechnology*, Vol. 15, pp. 241–5.

Gaskell, G., N. Allum, M. Bauer, J. Jackson, S. Howard and N. Lindsey, (2003), 'Ambivalent GM Nation? Public Attitudes to Biotechnology in the UK, 1991–2002', London, UK: Methodology Institute, London School of Economics.

Giandomenico, M., (2002), 'The Precautionary Principle and its Policy Implications', *Journal of Common Market Studies*, Vol. 40, No. 1, pp. 89–109.

Goklany, I.M., (2001), 'The Precautionary Principle: A Critical Appraisal of Environmental Risk Assessment', Washington DC: Cato Institute.

Hood, C. and H. Rothstein, (2001), 'Risk Regulation Under Pressure: Problem Solving or Blame Shifting?', *Administration and Society*, Vol. 33, No. 1, pp. 21–53.

Hood, Christopher, Henry Rothstein and Robert Baldwin, (2001), 'The Government of Risk: Understanding Risk Regulation Regimes', Oxford: Oxford University Press.

Imram, N., (1999), 'The Role of Visual Cues in Consumer Perception and Acceptance of a Food Product', *Nutrition and Food Science*, Vol. 99, No. 5, pp. 22–3.

Jasanoff, Sheila, (1990), The Fifth Branch: Science Advisers as Policymakers, Massachusetts: Harvard University Press.

Lawrence, F., (2001), 'This is a Chance for Safer Food', *Guardian*, London, UK, 27 June.

Legge, J.S. and R. Durant, (2003) 'Public Opinion, the Precautionary Principle and GM Food Regulation: Assessing the Calculus of Dissent in the European Union' available at *http://www.allacademic.com/meta/ p62543_index.html*, accessed on 20 May 2007.

Leiserowitz, A., (2004), 'Before and After the Day After Tomorrow: A National Study of Climate Change Risk Perception and Behaviour', *Environment*, Vol. 46, No. 9, pp. 22–37.

Marris, C., B. Wynne, P. Simmons and S. Weldon, (2001), 'Final Report of the Public Attitudes to Biotechnology in Europe Research Project', FAIR CT98–3844 (DG12–SSMI), Lancaster, UK: Centre for the Study of Environmental Change, Lancaster University.

Millstone, E., E. Brunner, and S.Mayer, (1999), 'Beyond Substantial Equivalence', 7 October available at *http://www.biotech-info.net/ substantial_equivalence.html*, accessed on 7 April 2007.

Organization for Economic Cooperation and Development (OECD), (1993), *Safety Evaluation of Foods Produced by Modern Biotechnology: Concepts and Principles*, Paris: OECD.

Raffensperger, Carolyn and Joel Tickner, (1999), *Protecting Public Health and the Environment: Implementing the Precautionary Principle*, Washington D.C.: Island Press.

Rayner, S., (2003) 'Democracy in the Age of Assessment: Reflections on the Roles of Expertise and Democracy in Public-sector Decision Making', *Science Public Policy*, Vol. 30, No. 3, pp. 163–70.

Rothstein, H., (2006), 'The Institutional Origins of Risk: A New Agenda for Risk Research, *Health, Risk and Society*, Vol. 8, No. 3, pp. 215–221.

Sarewitz, D., (2000), 'Science and Environmental Policy: An Excess of Objectivity', in Robert Frodeman (ed.), *Earth Matters: The Earth Sciences, Philosophy, and the Claims of Community*, Upper Saddle River: Prentice Hall.

———, (2004) 'How Science Makes Environmental Controversies Worse', *Environmental Science Policy*, Vol. 7, pp. 385–403.

Schenkelaars, P., (1996), 'Outlooks on Public Information and Participation in the Context of the European Biotechnology Directives 90/219/EEC and 90/220/EEC', in Van Dommelen (ed.) *Coping with Deliberate Release: The Limits of Risk Assessment*, Tilburg, The Netherlands: International Centre for Human and Public Affairs,.

Torgerson, D., (1986), 'Between Knowledge and Politics: Three Faces of Policy Analysis', *Policy Sciences*, Vol. 19, pp. 33–59.

Tokar, Brian, (2001), *Redesigning Life: The Worldwide Challenge to Genetic Engineering*, London: Zed Books.

Weinberg, A., (1972), 'Science and Trans-science', *Minerva*, Vol. 10, No. 2.

Wiedemann, P.M., and H. Schütz, (2005), 'The Precautionary Principle and Risk Perception: Experimental Studies in the EMF Area', *Environmental Health Perspective*, Vol. 113, pp. 402–5.

Wiener, J.B. and M.D. Rogers, (2002), 'Comparing Precautions in the US and Europe', *Journal of Risk Research*, Vol. 5, No. 4, pp. 317–20.

Wynne, B., (2004), 'Misunderstood Misunderstandings: Social Identities and Public Uptake of Science', in Irwin Alan and Brian Wynne (eds), *Misunderstanding Science? The Public Reconstruction of Science and Technology*, London: Cambridge University Press, pp. 19–46.

PART 3

Science in Climate Change Policy

10

Is Climate Change Cost–Benefit Analysis Defensible?
A Critique of the Stern Review

PAUL BAER AND CLIVE L. SPASH

The threat of anthropogenic climate change raises numerous complex problems, but the issue is mainly framed as the need to cut global greenhouse gas (GHG) emissions, with often exclusive emphasis on carbon dioxide (CO_2). Environmental economists reduce the decision further to a monetary cost–benefit analysis (CBA), in which the costs of controlling GHG emissions are balanced against the benefits of avoiding induced climatic-related damages to human welfare. CBA climate professionals then claim an ability to calculate 'optimal' long-term policy choices. Such use of CBA, especially for global-scale problems, has been called into question on a variety of grounds by people inside (Vatn and Bromley 1994; Vatn 2000; Spash 2002b) and outside (Sagoff 1988; O'Neill 1993; O'Neill 1997) the economics profession.

Historically, CBA was developed to evaluate well-defined small-scale projects. Even at such a project level there is often scepticism relating to the necessary simplifications and assumptions. In particular, a host of controversial ethical choices are required because of the incommensurability of costs and benefits, the possibility of appropriate compensation, accounting for future generations and non-human species, income inequality, and the distribution of rights. The enormous uncertainties surrounding the relationship between causes of climate change, their potential impact, and valuation raise additional challenges. At the global and multi-century scale, the mismatch between the claims of robust and objective measurement and the realities of subjective and uncertain projection become profound. Yet, despite the considerable range and number of serious critiques, the CBA approach remains influential and continues to be applied to the debate over preventing human-induced climate change.

A recent example is the so-called Stern Review (SR) (Stern 2006a), an economic analysis commissioned by the United Kingdom's (UK's) ruling Labour Party and chaired by Sir Nicholas Stern, a former chief economist at the World Bank. This report, released in October 2006 with a good deal of fanfare, is known primarily for its headline message that straightforward economic (cost–benefit) analysis justifies 'prompt and strong action' to reduce GHG emissions. The SR favours stabilization of GHG concentrations at 450–550 parts per million (ppm) CO_2 equivalent with a target of 500–550 ppm CO_2 equivalent, said to be achievable at a cost of about 1 per cent of gross world product (GWP); business as usual is estimated to cause losses of 5–20 per cent of GWP.[1] Prior to the SR, most climate CBA professionals produced numbers supporting little or no mitigation,[2] while non-economists and critics of CBA called for stringent mitigation. The significance of the SR is that mainstream economists are found claiming that CBA 'done properly' shows that rapid and significant emissions reductions are economically warranted.[3] Professional climate economists have then felt the need to defend their own CBAs, and in particular their discounting of future harm (Mendelsohn 2006; Nordhaus 2006; Tol 2006; Yohe 2006). The main claim is that wrong conclusions are drawn due to the making of non-standard assumptions about discounting and so valuing future impacts more highly than those in conventional mainstream economics, that is, in the critics' own models.

The resulting debate has focused upon whether CBA does warrant a limit of 550 ppm CO_2 equivalent. As a result, the case for a limit at 450 ppm CO_2 equivalent has been neglected. This means effectively accepting global average temperature increases above 2°C, despite this being the limit previously endorsed by both the UK government and the European Commission.[4] The SR and

[1] The scenario was one selected from amongst those of the IPCC (SRES A2).
[2] Cline (1992) is the most prominent exception.
[3] A mainstream economic argument for strong mitigation suits a neo-liberal leaning UK Labour government seeking to placate the business class. We return to the political context later.
[4] The SR acknowledges that stabilization at 450 ppm CO_2 equivalent offers at best a roughly even chance of keeping global mean temperature increase below 2°C, with a significant (order of 20 per cent) likelihood of an increase over 3°C. The SR

others then seem happy to use CBA to debate upper but not lower emissions limits. This raises concerns both about the role of CBA in general and the quality of the SR's analysis in particular, for deciding upon GHG control measures.

The SR does express some humility and even scepticism concerning the ability of Integrated Assessment Models (IAMs) (linking emissions to economic losses) to produce precise quantified projections, saying at times that such calculations should be considered only as 'indicative'. Indeed, the fact that damages are attributed such a large range (5–20 per cent) makes uncertainty about the impacts of climate change—both their likelihood and their valuation—a central concern. Thus, a logical presumption would be that the choice of limits on emissions and climate was centrally determined by such uncertainties. However, it is shown here that the SR's own standards for addressing uncertainty and value controversy support neither the upper nor the lower bound with justifiable quantitative arguments.

In the remainder of this chapter, we consider how the SR conducts its quantitative analyses. Four subjects will be addressed in turn, namely the treatment of: future generations, risk and uncertainty, extreme and catastrophic impacts, and intra-generational ethics. These areas reflect the ways in which the SR claims to be innovative. We then discuss the issues raised by the reduction of all future climate damages to a single indicator of expected utility. We conclude with an assessment of whether the quantitative results are sufficiently robust to justify the policy conclusions and some interpretation of the role of the SR in the current climate policy context.

One background for our analysis is the framework of 'post-normal science'. Funtowicz and Ravetz (1994) used this approach to critique global CBA estimates of climate change control by Nordhaus (1991a; b). They showed that, in spite of appeals to various tenets of theory and economic estimates to several decimal places of accuracy, Nordhaus produced results on the basis of ad hoc assumptions, educated guesses, and controversial value judgements. Funtowicz and Ravetz (1994) focused on many of the same issues—scientific uncertainty, discounting of future generations, the valuation of impacts—that the SR highlights to differentiate itself from Nordhaus and others. However, the PAGE2002 model used by the SR is directly related

---

suggests fairly strongly that achieving 450 ppm CO_2 equivalent is already too expensive to be 'worth' the extra risk reduction it accomplishes, but does not rule it out.

to the model developed by Nordhaus and, in addition, the similar basic methodology means identical problems despite the attempted differentiation.

A key aspect of what follows is to show that the SR's argument for stabilization at 550 ppm lacks quantitative economic justification. Subtly different modelling choices allow a case for more stringent mitigation of 450 ppm or even lower. Precisely because the numbers are so pliable, they fail to show that lower targets are economically unwarranted. In addition, non-economic arguments are centrally important and the expression of plural incommensurable values essential in the policy debate. Thus, for many, a highly persuasive argument exists due to the expected physical impacts under 'business as usual' and the resulting inequitable distribution and imposition of harm on the innocent.

THE SR'S CBA ARGUMENT

Two main arguments are made in support of the SR's policy recommendations. First is a justification of targets using a comparison of the marginal costs and benefits of a single ton of CO_2 equivalent emissions. Second is the assertion that the likely damages from business as usual can be equated to a GDP loss of 5–20 per cent, while control costs equate to 1 per cent of GDP to stabilize atmospheric GHGs at 500–550 ppm CO_2 equivalent, which is claimed to avoid 'most of the worst impacts'.

The first argument relates to the theoretical holy grail of CBA. If an analyst could define and equalize the costs with the benefits of reducing a ton of carbon, they would be able to meet the conditions for defining the 'optimal' point for efficient pollution emissions reduction. In the SR, the comparisons are actually never made explicitly. However, in chapter 10 (with estimates based on Grubb et al. 2006), the SR reports that the marginal costs of emissions reductions for a 450 ppm CO_2 stabilization pathway (equivalent to around 500–550 ppm CO_2 equivalent) are around \$27 per ton CO_2 (±50 per cent) in 2030 and around \$15–\$70 per ton CO_2 in 2050.[5] The benefits of control are reported as being in the order of \$85 per ton of CO_2 equivalent for business as usual, versus about \$30 per

[5]Note that the actual figures reported in the SR (Stern 2006a: 248) are incorrectly converted from tons C to tons CO_2, resulting in numbers that are too high by a factor of 13!

ton if concentrations are stabilized at 550 ppm CO_2 equivalent, and \$25 per ton if concentrations are stabilized at 450 ppm CO_2 equivalent.[6] Taking these numbers at face value shows ambiguous support for even the 550 ppm upper limit.

The second argument is supposed to provide a relatively self-evident choice in favour of the 550 ppm target. However, as Mendelsohn (2006) has pointed out, this ignores the possibility that stabilization at, say, 650 ppm might also avoid 'most of the worst impacts' and have much lower mitigation costs. By the SR's own admission, picking a stabilization target that is to be defended on grounds of welfare economics still requires a comparison of marginal costs and benefits. Thus, the SR states:

Our work with the PAGE model suggests that, allowing for uncertainty, if the world stabilises at 550ppm CO2e, climate change impacts could have an effect equivalent to reducing consumption today and forever by about 1.1 per cent. As Chapter 6 showed, this compares with around 11 per cent in the corresponding 'business as usual' case—ten times as high. With stabilization at 450ppm CO2e, the percentage loss would be reduced to 0.6 per cent, so choosing the tougher goal 'buys' about 0.5 per cent of consumption now and forever. Choosing 550ppm instead of 650ppm CO2e 'buys' about 0.6 per cent.'(Stern 2006a: 295).

Note here that the authors claim that the 'marginal benefits' of moving from 650 ppm to 550 ppm and 550 ppm to 450 ppm are roughly the same—in both cases, about half a per cent of GDP 'now and forever'. This implies that the mitigation cost of moving from 650 ppm to 550 ppm would have to be less than half a per cent of GDP for 550 ppm to be clearly warranted on economic efficiency grounds. Yet in one table, the SR shows reductions of approximately this scale (some mismatch occurs because of the conversion of CO_2 to CO_2 equivalent levels), leading to costs at mid-century on the order of 1–4 per cent of GDP (Stern 2006a: 297, Table 13.4), and (in another table based on another meta-analysis), leading to discounted equivalent costs on the order of 0.3–0.8 per cent–(Stern 2006a: 296, Table 13.3). Thus, the marginal benefit of reducing CO_2 equivalent from 650 ppm to 550 ppm is not demonstrably larger than the cost.

[6]The SR reports on the 'Social Cost of Carbon', which is highly misleading terminology (on manipulation of cost terminology, see Spash 2002b: 172–77); this is actually referring to the marginal benefits of greenhouse gas reduction, and should not be confused with emissions control costs.

This shows that the quantitative analyses behind the policy recommendations are of questionable robustness, even at the level of the use of the numbers calculated. There is then good reason to be sceptical that monetary conversion and aggregation of impacts, and the appeal to 'state of the art' economic methods, actually can provide justification for policy recommendations. In addition, the case for setting a lower threshold of 450 ppm CO_2 equivalent remains open and may be as, or more, desirable on several grounds.

FUTURE GENERATIONS

The long time scale of human-induced climate change makes the question of our ethical responsibilities to future generations central to the framing of the problem. In economic analysis, this debate is centred on the concept of discounting. This is the practice of reducing the value of future costs and benefits in proportion to their distance in the future, typically through the use of an exponential discount rate (for more detailed discussion in the context of climate change, see Spash 1993, 2002a).

There is a consensus among philosophers—and some economists—that the economic practice of discounting can lead to a dangerous disregard for the well-being of future generations. There is an extensive literature on ethical issues relating to future generations that raises concerns over inter-generational justice, the role of rights and responsibilities, and the standing of future as opposed to present individuals.[7] No such literature is cited in the SR, making its claim to be a 'review' rather implausible. This merely perpetuates the failure of public discourse to address the ethical implications of multi-generational environmental problems. The fundamental reason for concern is straightforward: for any positive discount rate, a time in the future can be specified at which the effective destruction of civilization would be literally 'not worth preventing'. The high discount rates typically used in climate CBAs mean that the importance of global catastrophe just a few decades in the future is vastly reduced in present decisions, and those in a century or more are effectively written off completely.

The SR recognizes that the choice of a discount rate (or perhaps, more appropriately, a discounting model) is inescapably normative.

[7]See for example, Callahan (1981); d'Arge et al. (1982); Norton (1982); Barry (1983); Page (1983, 1988); Parfit (1983, 1984); Howarth (1997); O'Neill (1999); and Gardiner (2006).

In the mainstream debate within economics, the key question is whether the economic analyst should include a 'pure rate of time preference' as a component in the discount rate. In general, mainstream economists accept the validity of a pure time preference and then debate the size of the rate. Despite numerous qualifications, and claims which seem to undermine the practice, the SR does exactly the same. Conventional welfare economics takes for granted that commodity discounting—reducing the importance of future costs or benefits in proportion to the (assumed) increased consumption of future generations—is well justified. Indeed, commodity discounting is based on the assumption of declining marginal utility from consumption, which is itself treated as a self-evident fact requiring no proof.

The SR uses a standard formula for combining the pure rate of time preference and the declining marginal utility of income to define the discount rate r:

$$r = \delta + \eta g \qquad\qquad (10.1)$$

where δ (delta) is the rate of pure time preference, g is the growth rate of per capita consumption, and η (eta) determines the effect of economic (consumption) growth on the discount rate. The parameter η is also characterized as an 'inequality aversion' parameter in the SR, because of the way it is derived from the elasticity of the marginal utility of consumption. The higher the value of η, the greater the weight given to impacts on persons with lower consumption or income levels. Importantly, as we discuss below, η is also characterized as a 'risk aversion' parameter.

The dominant convention in CBA has been to use a relatively high discount rate (for example, 5–10 per cent). This includes, explicitly or implicitly, a significant positive pure rate of time preference (for example, 2–3 per cent). The term η is typically set to 1. The SR rejects such a high pure rate of time preference on ethical grounds, but then rather strangely reasserts a very small positive pure rate of time preference (0.1 per cent), based on the probability that human civilization may cease to exist in a century.[8] The SR uses $\eta=1$, although sensitivity analyses using higher values of η have been added post publication of the main report in an 'appendix to the postscript', as a response to critics. Under $\eta=1$, the

---

[8]In fact, the SR appears to pick the 0.1 per cent number and then use it to estimate what the likelihood of extinction must be! See Stern (2006a: 46–7).

discount rate is equal to 0.1 per cent plus the economic growth rate, which averages 1.3 per cent annually between 2000 and 2200 in the SR's baseline world without climate change (Stern 2006a: 161). Even using this relatively low rate, impacts which occur 200 years in the future have just 6 per cent of their value compared to their occurring today.

Discounting has some appeal as a way of representing certain types of properties in a quantitative way for lay and expert groups. At an intuitive level for lay persons, the more you have the less it is valued (that is, marginal utility of income declines), and people in industrialized economies have been lead to expect increases in real income over time. At a more theoretical level for experts, it fits into a family of models within which an ethical judgement (the relative value of consumption to different persons) can be reflected in a single parameter, and then (with a few additional assumptions) 'calibrated' on the basis of 'empirical data'. This ability to extract a rate from observations gives a supposed scientific objectivity that is employed to justify the policy consequences of using the selected parameter. For the analyst, then, all normative aspects are dispelled by a claim that discounting is an empirical fact which can be observed by an objective scientist regardless of any moral implications.

The formula in the SR is standard in welfare economics, and it is a classic example of the way in which economics mixes ethical and empirical claims in the justification of particular calculations. There are a range of problems with this whole approach. First, economists ignore empirical reality which shows individuals can and do hold negative discount rates for some impacts and positive ones for others, for example, bringing forward harms and delaying pleasures (Lowenstein and Prelec 1991). Second, there is no one discount rate in society and there are different rates for different groups, capitals, contexts, and so on. Third, different scenarios imply different rates, even in theory, which makes the rate endogenous to the climate change problem and its policy 'solution'. Fourth, merely observing that something occurs as an empirical fact says nothing of its moral acceptability or repugnance, for example, people murder, rape, torture, and commit genocide. Fifth, adding in risk to discounting conflates separate issues and makes untenable assumptions as to the nature of uncertainty. In brief, the SR fails to seriously address the arguments against discounting and lacks any reasoning as to why, even if one accepts discounting, zero or negative rates are inappropriate.

RISK AND UNCERTAINTY

Uncertainty over future human-induced climate change and impacts is a widely recognized major consideration affecting policy responses. The SR acknowledges this in a variety of places and claims that their approach to the incorporation of risk and uncertainty gives an improved estimate of the overall damages compared to previous climate CBAs. The authors discuss the relationship between risk and uncertainty referring to a variety of debates. However, the fundamental methodology employed reduces strong uncertainty (for example, partial ignorance, social indeterminacy) to known probabilistic events. There are also questionable assumptions about the characteristics of the resulting risk calculations in terms of risk aversion and the treatment of utility.

Economics and the related field of decision theory utilize an idealization of the problem of decision making under uncertainty in which actors—persons, firms, countries—are assumed to behave in such a way as to maximize 'expected utility'. The approach integrates the probability that specific future states of the world will occur with the 'utility' or welfare from the realization of those states. Underlying this is a set of conditions or axioms of assumed 'rationality' that impose a very specific model of human behaviour. There has actually been an extensive debate regarding whether persons do, in fact, act 'rationally' in this sense, whether the model is fundamentally normative rather than descriptive, and if it is normative whether it is well justified.[9] As a practical matter, there are clearly many cases where people fail to meet such expectations (for example, Gintis 2000). This brings into question the case for arguing that behaviour can generally be described by simple notions that abstract from the complexity of individual behaviour and empirical reality.

The approach also rapidly becomes messy because of the involvement of an increasing number of countries. Potential futures differ across multiple dimensions and different actors vary in their valuation of alternative states. Even if we assumed a finite number of possible outcomes, there is little reason to assume that there will be well-defined probabilities for those outcomes. Human-induced climate change holds the prospect of large-scale unique changes

[9]For a survey, see Smithson (1989); for a collection of articles, see Gärdenfors and Sahlin (1988).

outside human historical experience. The standard scientific approach of repeated experiments to produce an 'objective' probability distribution is then of no practicable use. Rather, the likelihood of some future state coming to pass is necessarily an opinion, perhaps a well justified opinion, perhaps a consensus opinion among a group, but an opinion nonetheless.

The problem confronting natural and social scientists in their role as policy advisers is how best to address this type of uncertainty. One approach is to take 'opinions' and create probabilities of future events and essentially treat these as if they were derived from empirically observed experiments. These subjective probabilities suffer from numerous problems, not least of which is who has the right to have their opinion determine the weight given to possible future events?

In terms of expected utility analysis, a method is required to incorporate 'loss aversion', that is, the recognized human preference to treat equivalent losses and gains asymmetrically. The SR addresses these concerns about uncertainty and risk aversion using two primary methods. First, a Monte Carlo model is used to create a probability density function (PDF) of climate outcomes and associated economic damages for a specified emissions pathway, based on 1,000 'runs' of the model (on the model, see Hope 2006). Second, a discount rate is employed in each run that varies with the 'realized' rate of economic growth, after climate damages have been subtracted. Since (as discussed above) the effective discount rate increases with economic growth, model runs with higher damages have lower discount rates. As a consequence, those runs with higher damages are weighted more heavily in the aggregation of the multiple Monte Carlo runs, creating loss aversion in a stylized fashion.

There are problems relating to both of these aspects. The model (PAGE2002) requires subjective PDFs for over 30 crucial inputs, everything from the climate sensitivity to the ratio of climate damages in different regions in response to temperature increase. In practice, for only climate sensitivity is there any significant literature on an appropriate PDF; for the remainder, the authors simply use their judgement based on any available evidence, however scanty.[10] Furthermore, the PDFs used are triangular, which means there is zero probability of a value above or below some arbitrarily specified point.

[10]Hope (2006: 21) states that 'Most parameter values are taken from the IPCC Third Assessment Report', but it is evident that a great deal of subjective judgement went into converting the numbers into PDFs.

The SR acknowledges that the input PDFs are not well constrained, and indeed they address one aspect of this strong uncertainty by running their baseline climate scenario (the SRES A2 scenario) with alternative formulations of the carbon cycle feedback and possible methane releases. This so-called 'high climate' scenario leads to an increase in expected damages of about 35 per cent (Stern 2006a: 154–5), and is an important contributor to the 5–20 per cent range of reported damages. They also run the model with a higher climate sensitivity PDF (the baseline PDF has a modal value of 2.5°C and under no possibility can it be higher than 5.0°C), although these results are reported only in a single place (Stern, 2006a: 156), are referred to as 'particularly speculative', and play no role in the decision analysis. In their sensitivity analyses, they use alternative PDFs for the primary damage function (Stern, 2006b: 7–10), although later essentially ignore the results.

In a further gesture at the significance of strong uncertainty, the SR discusses, in chapter 2, a specific methodology for dealing with unknown probabilities leading to alternative calculations of expected utility. Citing an unpublished paper by Henry (2006), the authors recommend taking a weighted average of the highest and lowest expected utilities, where the weights 'would be influenced by concern of the individual about the magnitude of associated threats, or pessimism, and possibly any hunch about which probability might be more or less plausible'. They conclude the discussion: 'We now have a theory that can describe how to act' (Stern 2006a: 34). Yet at the heart of the theory are concerns, pessimism, and hunches.

There are also good reasons to doubt the SR's claim that the differential weighting of damages in an expected utility calculation, based ultimately on a parameter used to describe the declining marginal utility of consumption, is an adequate reflection of loss aversion. This requires the assumption that the monetized valuation of all possible impacts captures everything we care about—impacts must be translated into equivalent monetized losses to count. For example, risks of catastrophic species losses of 25 per cent or even 50 per cent or more would only enter the decision calculus inasmuch as one could put a monetary value on them.

Finally, there is a very powerful normative assumption in the claim that policy should aim to maximize the expected value of a scenario—even if possible losses are weighted higher than possible gains—rather than, say, reducing the risk of crossing some threshold to an acceptably low level. In theory, almost any level of loss aversion could be 'programmed' into a model like PAGE2002. However, justifying the use of any particular function or parameter requires deciding in advance what risk of catastrophic outcomes should be accepted.

EXTREME AND CATASTROPHIC IMPACTS

The possibility of catastrophic impacts has been discussed in the context of possible states of the world or state changes called irreversible, non-linear, or discontinuous. In most climate CBA models, there is at best a highly stylized inclusion of catastrophic events. For example, Cline (1992) produced a central estimate of damages reaching 6 per cent of GDP with a 10°C warming, and 20 per cent of GDP lost under a pessimistic scenario. He showed that, even with a 5 per cent discount rate, incorporating only a small probability of catastrophe within such economic models is all that is required to justify 'aggressive' action (Cline, 1992: 6). In contrast, Nordhaus and Boyer (2000) estimated the 'willingness to pay' to avoid the risk of catastrophe by using a variety of ad hoc adjustments to an expert survey carried out much earlier (Nordhaus 1994). They used this to justify equating a 2.5°C warming to a 1 per cent loss of GDP and a 6°C warming to a 7 per cent loss of GDP. Even with the ad hoc adjustment (a large component of their estimated damages), 'optimal' global temperature increase is calculated to be 2.44°C above the 1900 level in 2105 (the end of the modelling horizon), just 0.09°C below the business as usual base case, and still rising at 0.20°C per decade.

The SR explicitly lists and represents graphically several of the risks associated with catastrophic impacts—most notably, the melting of ice sheets. However, this is then ignored. Instead, the PAGE2002 model used in the SR broadly follows Nordhaus and Boyer (2000) by including an aggregated probabilistic formulation in which, in every year of each model run, there is some probability (proportional to temperature) of extra GDP losses attributed to unspecified catastrophic impacts. The incorporation of this calculation in the end has the simple effect of raising the expected damages at any particular temperature, and thus at any specified level of emissions. The particular way in which the catastrophic damage function is calculated is necessarily quite arbitrary, as there is no well established basis for any such function or associated PDF.

All the impacts are monetized, and are by assumption presumed to be impossible below a 2°C increase, and never to exceed 20 per cent of GDP lost in the 'focal region'. A scatter plot of model results reproduced in Warren et al. (2006) suggests that there is essentially a zero possibility of any catastrophic impacts until temperature exceeds 3°C. This is at best inconsistent with the scientific literature. In the SR itself, a finite probability is attributed to the melting of the Greenland ice sheet even below 2°C, with a resulting rise in sea level by several metres. However, an effectively zero probability is then used in the model. This choice, whether conscious or not, shows that contentious scientific and value judgements are embedded within the mathematical analysis of catastrophic impacts. This is a crucial example of how strong uncertainty is converted into weak uncertainty and impacts treated as some quasi-monetized risk.

EQUITY AND DISTRIBUTION

This section considers the distribution of costs and benefits within a generation (although the inter-generational issues are inextricably linked). The premise of welfare economics is that the utility of different individuals can and must be aggregated to calculate the overall ranking of a possible state of the world or outcome. This assumes that in comparing two specific outcomes, the gains to some persons can be directly added to the loss for others. In the ideal world of economic theory, a social welfare function transforms specific gains or losses in utility to particular individuals into cardinal numbers.

In models, such as PAGE2002, one or more 'representative individuals' are used in the calculation. Common formulae assume a declining marginal utility of consumption, which means that the marginal gain or loss from a unit consumed (measured in money) is 'more valuable' to a poor person than to a rich person. Noting this and adjusting calculations to take it into account is known as equity weighting. Depending upon the function and parameters used to model the declining marginal utility of consumption, the relative impact on the poor and the rich of an equal amount of lost consumption can be larger or smaller.

EQUITY WEIGHTING OF THE BENEFITS OF MITIGATION

Most climate CBAs ignore equity weighting and, therefore, implicitly take the distribution of income in society as it stands as being justified. This means that if a person who lives on $2 a day or less loses $1 and a millionaire gains $2, the world is a better place. The few studies that have included equity weighting have typically shown greater reductions to be warranted since standard damage assessments assert that poor regions will suffer greater proportional harm from anthropogenic climate change. Two such studies that do include equity weighting are cited by the SR (Stern 2006a: 156): Nordhaus and Boyer (2000) claim damages at 5°C warming increase from about 6 per cent to 8 per cent of GDP, while Tol (2002) states damages at 5°C double.[11]

The SR asserts that equity weighting is appropriate. In fact, the model used is capable of providing regionally disaggregated damage estimates that could straightforwardly be used to calculate equity-weighted aggregate damages. The authors assert that a reasonable estimate of the impact of equity weighting would raise the maximum expected damage estimate associated with business as usual from 14.4 per cent to 20.0 per cent of GDP. This shows that the results of the model are quite sensitive to the use of a stylized incorporation of equity. Obviously, the move to 20.0 per cent of GDP has more to do with picking a nice round number rather than any specific and justifiable parameterization. The SR's authors could just as easily have picked any number—as long as the recommended mitigation remained acceptable to their political sponsors.

If the SR had actually calculated equity weights, this might have stimulated a debate over the numbers employed. The SR might have shown, for example, that equity weighting increased business as usual damages from 14.4 per cent to 19.7 per cent. Or perhaps, using different estimates for the relevant parameters, to anywhere from 17.3 per cent to 26.2 per cent. Or the equity weight could have followed Tol's analysis, which would have meant doubling the SR's damage factors. Such a debate would seem likely to have revealed the excessive precision being claimed on the basis of ad hoc assumptions—wrongly precise, and precisely wrong.

There is then a direct parallel with the estimate of GHG control benefits presented by Nordhaus (1991a; b) and criticized by Funtowicz and Ravetz (1994). After presenting a table of numbers with as many as three significant digits on some figures and not

[11]In fact, these numbers appear to be taken from a graph in the IPCC's Third Assessment Report (Smith et al. 2001: Table 19.4) which is reproduced in the SR (Stern 2006a: 147). The numbers on the equivalent graph in Nordhaus and Boyer (2000: 95, Figure 4.3) appear to be closer to 7 per cent and 8 per cent, while the numbers from Tol's study do not appear in the cited 2002 paper, but appear to be from a working-paper version of the same study used in the TAR.

even a clear sign on others, Nordhaus simply increased the total to 2 per cent GDP loss (for a doubling of CO_2) to account for his intuitions. The SR follows Nordhaus in producing a figure with a calculated deceptive precision, which is simply arbitrarily rounded off to another number.

The idea of inequality aversion, described by a function or parameter, suggests that a collective social attitude towards inequality can be modelled, and appropriate functional forms and parameter values inferred from observable data. Hidden in this debate is a question about exactly what this weighting is supposed to mean, and how it is supposed to justify policy choices. The methodology of welfare economics is prone to a relatively frequent slipping back and forth between ostensibly normative and empirical concepts. The fact that an 'equity' parameter can be set by the preferences of the modeller seems to imply that the aggregate value of the outcome is simply an expression of the CBA climate experts' concern, or lack of concern, over poverty.

EQUITY WEIGHING OF THE COSTS OF MITIGATION

In economic analysis of pollution control, income inequality is generally taken as given, as if a natural consequence of life, while the distribution of mitigation costs is presumed to be a consequence of policy. This would seem to make its analysis a self-evident requirement of policy design. Strangely then, the distributional impacts of mitigation costs are rarely modelled or even discussed.

In any model assuming a declining marginal utility of consumption, the aggregate pollution control cost will be affected as much by distributional considerations as will the aggregate benefits from pollution control (for example, climate change avoidance). Mitigation costs can be made to appear arbitrarily small by distributing them to ever smaller and wealthier fractions of the population. The welfare impacts of a policy that can be modelled as a tax (as climate mitigation can) tend toward zero as the tax is shifted towards the wealthiest fraction of the population.

Countries like USA and Australia, which have opposed GHG emission control, tend to reflect a view that the wealthy should refuse a distribution of mitigation costs that burdens them disproportionately, even if it demonstrably minimizes global welfare losses. Climate change economists are generally inconsistent in their analysis of this position. They, as in the SR, assume that global welfare maximization can be an effective justification for the choice of a stabilization target, but not for the distribution of mitigation costs. Yet, compared to control benefits, equity weighting might have a similar (or even greater) impact on the estimation of control costs to that for the estimation of control benefits. As a result, the actual emissions target being recommended would necessarily be different based upon the specific assumptions about the distribution of mitigation costs.

CBA Legitimacy and Equivalent Consumption Losses

Key to understanding the SR's argument for policy targets is to be aware of what the quantities measured as projected costs and benefits are intended to describe. The central figures fail to represent a range of possible impacts, but rather give a range of 'expected values' where a possible future in quasi-monetary terms is weighted according to its estimated likelihood.[12] We refer to quasi-monetary terms because both consumption (proportional to future GDP) and welfare losses (from climate harm) are transformed by a mathematical operation into utility. This move, which, as the SR authors note, is standard practice in applied economics, plays a variety of important roles in their analysis. Utility is then further aggregated, discounted, and compared at the margin, in order to allow comparison of control benefits (avoided damages) with the costs of reducing emissions.

There are several points that need to be made about this idea of expected utility. Crucially, there is no straightforward link to anything real in the world. Rather, it represents a hypothetical valuation of possible future worlds associated with some policy scenario, integrating the perceived likelihood of different possibilities with the presumed desirability of those possibilities. As such, it is a kind of judgement that can reasonably be expected to differ among different persons, and indeed the SR discusses the kinds of disagreements that might be expected to lead to different estimations of the value (expected utility) of a particular scenario. The idea that even a single individual could have a well-defined view of the expected utility of an uncertain future is open to serious question. As discussed, such projections involve addressing not merely processes that are well understood

---

[12]Indeed, if non-market impacts, catastrophic risks, and high feedbacks are taken into account, the SR's model calculates at least a 5 per cent likelihood of impacts exceeding 32.5 per cent of GDP (Stern 2006a:158).

but uncertain (in a probabilistic sense), but processes about which we are at least partially ignorant, or which are indeterminate due to human choice. The expected utility approach requires a world of 'weak uncertainty' in which the range of possible outcomes and their respective probabilities are well bounded (Spash 2002d), as opposed to one of 'strong uncertainty' (Spash 2002c). Thus, strong uncertainty must be reduced to weak uncertainty but such a move simultaneously undercuts the robustness of the resulting calculations.

A fundamental justification for such reductionism is the claim that choice amongst alternatives requires a single scalar index of 'value' to achieve a ranking. This conversion of all aspects of a scenario (from loss of life to the melting of the Greenland and West Antarctic ice sheets) into quantitatively commensurable objects is extremely controversial. Even supporters of such global CBA, like the SR authors, note that this is 'problematic' (Stern, 2006a: 145–146). There is no account of the involuntary imposition of physical harm and threat of harm to people spread across countries and generations. Framing the policy question as a trade-off between fewer commodities and greater risk of harm to the innocent is an ethical decision.

While plainly recognizing some of the issues, the SR is inconsistent in its treatment of the critical question about the ethical legitimacy of the conclusions reached by CBA. There are a variety of gestures towards questions about the priority of rights, the idea of stewardship, and other non-utilitarian approaches to justifying climate policy, and in these sections the SR appears humble about the role of economic considerations in such decisions. Yet the policy conclusions of the report fail to evidence this humility; rather they assert that economic analysis has set the upper and lower bound on reasonable policy objectives, and that ethical disputes about uncertainty, distribution, and fairness can only make adjustments within this range. As the SR states:

There will always be disagreements about the size of the risks being run, the appropriate policy stance towards risk, and the valuation of social, economic and ecological impacts into the far future. But the range suggested here provides room for negotiation and debate about these. And we would argue that agreement on the range stated does not require signing up to all of the judgements specified above. In presenting the arguments, for example, we have omitted a number of important factors that are likely to point to still higher costs of climate change and thus still higher benefits of lower emissions and a lower stabilisation goal. (Stern 2006a: 299–300).

In the section of the SR from which this is taken, the authors demonstrate the relationship between their argument, the ethical considerations that policy must address, and the many relevant kinds of uncertainty. This brings into question the ignoring of the case for a 2°C limit on allowable warming. The SR authors are asserting that people with differing values may differ on a stabilization target, but can only do so within the 450–550 ppm CO_2 equivalent range. They nonetheless admit to biasing their argument by omitting 'a number of important factors' that would have supported lower targets.

There is no specific reason given why people who reject the role of CBA in determining policy should accept the upper and lower ranges. On the contrary, people who support the 2°C target are simply classified as holding that the target should be met 'whatever the cost' and, hence, economically irrational. We suggest that the structure of the policy problem at hand includes an obvious asymmetry that has specific implications. Where, as a consequence of self-interested action, costs are imposed on others—a negative externality, in mainstream economic terms—we suggest that the burden of proof should be greater for arguing that a limit on pollution is too strict. If our emissions limits are too lax, more people will die from climate harm; if they are too strict, our economies will grow more slowly and some will have to consume a bit less than otherwise.[13]

Climate sceptics argue that the risks are in fact symmetrical. They argue that given the levels of global poverty—its relationship to preventable death, health risks, and indeed even vulnerability to climate extremes—reducing economic growth today will cause harm of the same moral consequence as humans-induced climate change. That is to say, millions of people may die as a consequence of climate change mitigation, due to slower economic growth in poor countries. This is an argument that must be taken seriously; clearly there are tens of millions of preventable deaths annually from causes related fundamentally to poverty, a number that greatly exceeds estimates of likely deaths from human-induced climate change in the near future. Put simply, in a world in which premature death is ubiquitous, there are opportunity costs to investing resources in any one approach to reducing it. This is the heart of the argument made by economists such as Schelling (1997) and Tol (2006) as well as by political lobbyists such as Lomborg (2006) and other professional environmental sceptics:

[13]This asymmetry could be a primary justification for the precautionary principle, though it is rarely articulated this way.

many more lives in poor countries could be saved by other ways of investing the same money than will be saved by emissions mitigation.

This is a relevant argument with regard to setting an emissions objective. However, turning the argument around slightly shows it is not decisive in favour of the sceptics. The structure of the case can be explained as follows: Group A is carrying out an activity (call it polluting) that causes X deaths to group B, and it would cost Group A $Y to eliminate those X deaths; but if Group A can reduce X deaths in Group B for $Z, which is less than $Y but does not address the pollution problem, that would be morally preferable and the two groups can negotiate how to divide the surplus; this potentially allows more lives to be saved than by eliminating the pollution. The point to this example is not that one solution is *a priori* right or wrong, but rather that neither solution is free of moral judgement or dilemma. On the one hand, we can save more lives and on the other, we choose that some people will die due to preventable pollution so that others might live. We have simply rediscovered the basic conflict between the utilitarian intuition, that the sum of all harm matters, and the deontological intuition, that some categories of harm should just be avoided. We might go further and raise some assessment of the democratic legitimacy of the process of making such a decision and the problems of who specifically dies being different and so on.

This gets to the heart of the debate over the applicability of CBA to climate change and other risk assessment problems. One obvious issue is that the policy choice at hand—how much to reduce greenhouse pollution—is not in fact being debated in the context of the question 'what would be the best way to save lives in developing countries?' No one is saying 'Instead of reducing emissions by such-and-such per cent, we will invest in sanitation, or malaria reduction, or whatever'. Furthermore, since those who are most at risk are the poorest people—who are not participating in policy debate—and also poor (as well as wealthy) people in the future, the procedural legitimacy of any decision to sacrifice the specific interests of those at risk from human-induced climate change faces a substantial challenge. This is magnified by the fact that those who benefit most from GHG emissions are today's wealthy.

The controversy over using CBA in this context is precisely about such issues as assuming we can legitimately trade lost lives for consumer goods—a dilemma which symbolizes debates about commensurability. The structure imposed by standard economic analysis makes inevitable the reduction of lost lives to their equivalent in lost consumption, a move that is in many contexts and to many people morally indefensible, and that is indeterminate even if it is accepted as necessary. In the end, the numbers produced by the SR are only meaningful if one accepts that the prospective human deaths (plus extinction of species and other losses) due to human-induced climate change can be defensibly converted into equivalent amounts of consumption today.

CONCLUDING REMARKS

Mainstream economics addresses all of the major areas of impact under the enhanced greenhouse effect (GHE)—future generations, risk and uncertainty, extreme and catastrophic impacts, distributional equity—through the unjustifiable reduction of complexity and ethical controversy into a single scalar value. Reasonable differences about choices in each of these areas lead to very wide variance in the possible valuation of alternative policy scenarios. There cannot be a 'correct' value associated with any specific scenario nor 'correct' selection of a limited set of future scenarios. Moreover, the claim of such reductionism to any authority at all depends upon the assertion that, in fact, the core problems of CBA—commensurability, compensation, and the distribution of impacts—can all be adequately incorporated in a scientifically objective framing by an elite group of professional climate CBA experts. Such authority is clearly unwarranted.

The SR's authors have plainly expressed their desire to be persuasive in the policy debate as they perceive it. To achieve this they have used a variety of methods of rhetorical and quantitative argument, but the SR's persuasiveness also depends upon the social and political context and the broader credibility of its authors. The credibility of mainstream economic analysis in general rests in part on three crucial factors: the disciplinary authority of mainstream economics in the elite academic world, the apparently robust quantitative measures it produces, and its flexibility in supporting policies desired by economic elites. We suggest that the apparent insensitivity, or lip service, of standard economic analyses to relevant alternative considerations (for example, justice) is not simply a regrettable flaw, but rather a critical failure undermining the justification for giving economic analyses such a great weight in policy making.

The SR makes some effort to point out that action is supported even without relying upon the aggregation of all mitigation costs and benefits into a single comparable figure. Nonetheless, at the heart of the analysis is a model which reduces uncertainty to risk and all climate impacts to a single quasi-monetary value, to be compared with an equivalent quasi-monetized pollution control cost. The SR recognizes the fallacy of a single number approach but proceeds regardless. Some carefully crafted arguments regarding the uncertainty of the results are then meant to justify the numbers calculated as upper and lower bounds on 'reasonable' stabilization targets.

Three points then need to be raised in drawing conclusions about the SR. First, addressing human-induced climate change has created a complex political debate, in which there is a vast distance between parties who see effectively no mitigation to be warranted, and those who see extremely stringent mitigation as warranted. The extreme positions can be caricatured as those who see a global average temperature increase of 4°C or more as no problem or even beneficial, and those who see a temperature increase of only 2°C as an unmitigated human disaster. Evidence supporting a middle path then has an air of respectability and political rationality, whether produced and paid for by an economic and political elite with vested interests of its own, whether right or wrong.

Second, in this debate, those who oppose stringent mitigation typically speak in the language of economics, and oppose mitigation on the basis of projected financial costs. Typically, the costs highlighted are aggregated at the national level, especially in the USA, although some reference may be made to the global economy and/or particular economic sectors. The fundamental method of reducing GHG emissions is perceived to be via the reduced usage of fossil fuel energy. Modern economies are heavily dependent on fossil fuels and stored energy in general. The idea of controlling consumption via demand management is outside the political frame. Short-term costs are then intuitively accepted to be high for any stringent mitigation effort.

This political economic battleground was staked out by the energy industry and the trenches dug some time ago. In this respect, perhaps there should be no surprise that the SR's major 'innovations' are not particularly innovative, and reflect work by other modellers. Similar problems to these are also evident in the treatment of catastrophes and the distribution of impacts. Rather than innovation, the SR delivers only highly subjective and scientifically questionable PDFs (in the case of catastrophic impacts), and an arbitrary multiplication factor and a gesture at 'further research' (in the case of distributional equity). A more thorough approach would have made the analysis appear less rather than more robust. In addition, the whole economic framing of the problem would have been brought into question.

Third, these debates take place across communities within a political economy. There is a more-or-less academic community, in which there is a presumption of commitment to reasoned and disinterested argument. Then there is a political community in which parties use arguments strategically, attempting to win support for the policies they prefer by selecting favourable evidence and attempting to discredit evidence which opposes their vested interests. The scientific foundations of human-induced climate change mean that political actors legitimize their policy arguments on the *prima facie* credibility of the academic community, and deploy a wide range of 'scientific evidence'. This is plainly not the conduct of a disinterested truth-seeking exercise. The approach assumes that the best process for seeking truth is to have zealous advocates make their case and weaken those of their opponents in the 'if you are not with us then you are against us' school of thought. In this regard, the primary focus on justifying the higher 550 ppm CO_2 equivalent upper limit is clearly a political statement.

The discounting in the SR is still substantial, and the justification is open to question on a variety of grounds. The reduction of strong uncertainty to expected utility with a particular function is methodologically flawed, and even putting this to one side, the treatment of weak uncertainty could easily justify more serious risk aversion. The treatment of catastrophic risk has implausibly low damages as temperature increases between 2°–3°C. The sources cited by the SR for calibrating equity weighting justify higher possible damage adjustments. All of these would argue for greater mitigation. Yet in the end, the SR chose to place a minimum stabilization level at a threshold which the authors themselves claim has at least even odds of exceeding a 2°C warming.

A close look shows many reasons why the critical issues concerning the enhanced GHE cannot be decisively resolved in any quantitative exercise. Each area of the modelling process requires subjective judgements about likelihood and valuation, which lead to large changes in the results. Metaphorically, the model has a bunch of control knobs that can be turned to different settings to represent different views of particular concepts, mixing (for example) views about ethical responsibilities to future generations with views about the risk of exceeding some climatic threshold. Despite the mathematical formalism and air of objectivity (employed by all global CBAs), no purely scientific determination is possible for the settings of these knobs, and there are plausible settings of the control knobs which would warrant even more stringent mitigation.

Among those most opposed to GHG regulation are the industries (notably oil, coal, electricity, and transportation) which suspect that the greatest impact will be on their power and profits. These industries include many of the world's largest multinational corporations and also corporations with enormous influence in particular countries and over ruling governments. Greenhouse gas regulation must literally be imposed against the will of many of these corporations, which can in turn count on popular support from politicians, consumers, and workers who expect to see prices increase and jobs lost. For those who most vehemently oppose mitigation on 'economic' grounds, the fact that 550 ppm has been shown to be economically warranted will not be convincing—since they are not interested in being convinced—and they will continue to use the opinions of Mendelsohn, Nordhaus, Tol, and their like to defend themselves. The point of the SR is to enlist the prestige of economics to persuade the uncommitted rather than to persuade the committed opponents of mitigation. In this regard, the fact that the analysis is not robust is of minor importance. No one whom it intends to persuade is expected to read or understand it any more than those appealing to the ad hoc numbers produced by Nordhaus for 20 years have ever paid any attention to their fallibility.

References

Barry, B., (1983), 'Intergenerational Justice in Energy Policy', in D. MacLean and P.G. Brown. (eds), *Energy and the Future*, Totowa, New Jersey: Rowman and Littlefield, pp. 15–30.

Callahan, D., (1981), 'What Obligations do We have to Future Generations?', in E. Partridge (ed.), *Responsibilities to Future Generations: Environmental Ethics*, Buffalo, New York: Prometheus Books, pp. 73–85.

Cline, W.R., (1992), *The Economics of Global Warming*. Harlow, Essex: Longman.

d'Arge, R.C., W.D. Schulze and D.S. Brookshire, (1982), 'Carbon Dioxide and Intergenerational Choice', *American Economic Association Papers and Proceedings*, Vol. 72, No. 2, pp. 251–56.

Funtowicz, S.O. and J.R. Ravetz, (1994), 'The Worth of a Songbird: Ecological Economics as a Post-normal Science', *Ecological Economics*, Vol. 10, No. 3, pp. 197–207.

Gärdenfors, P. and N.E. Sahlin, (1998), *Decision, Probability, and Utility: Selected Readings*, Cambridge: Cambridge University Press.

Gardiner, S.M., (2006), 'A Perfect Moral Storm: Climate Change, Intergenerational Ethics and the Problem of Moral Corruption', *Environmental Values*, Vol. 15, No. 3, pp. 397–414.

Gintis, H., (2000), 'Beyond Homo Economicus: Evidence from Experimental Economics', *Ecological Economics*, Vol. 35, No. 3, pp. 311–22.

Grubb, M., C. Carraro and J. Schellnhuber, (2006), 'Technological Change for Atmospheric Stabilization: Introductory Overview to the Innovation Modelling Comparison Project', *Energy Journal*, Vol. 27, Special Issue 1, pp. 1–16.

Henry, C., (2006), 'Decision-making under Scientific, Political and Economics Uncertainty', *Chaire Developpement Durable*, DDX-06-12 Paris: Laboratoire d'Econometrie de l'Ecole Polytechnique.

Hope, C., (2006), 'The Marginal Impact of CO_2 from PAGE2002: An Integrated Assessment Model Incorporating the IPCC's Five Reasons for Concern', *The Integrated Assessment Journal*, Vol. 6, No. 1, pp. 19–56.

Howarth, R.B., (1997), 'Sustainability as Opportunity', *Land Economics*, Vol. 73, No. 4, pp. 569–79.

Lomborg, B., (2006), (ed.), *How to Spend $50 Billion to Make the World a Better Place*, Cambridge: Cambridge University Press.

Lowenstein, G. and D. Prelec, (1991), 'Negative Time Preference', *American Economic Review*, Vol. 81, pp. 347–52.

Mendelsohn, R., (2006), 'A Critique of the Stern Review', *Regulation*, Winter, pp. 42–6.

Nordhaus, W.D., (1991a), 'A Sketch of the Economics of the Greenhouse Effect', *American Economic Review*, Vol. 81, No. 2, pp. 146–50.

———, (1991b), 'To Slow or Not to Slow: The Economics of the Greenhouse Effect', *Economic Journal*, Vol. 101, pp. 920–38.

———, (1994), 'Expert Opinion on Climate Change', *American Scientist*, Vol. 82, No. 1, pp. 45–51.

———, (2006), 'The Stern Review on the Economics of Climate Change', 16 November, *http://nordhaus.econ.yale.edu/SternReviewD2.pdf*.

Nordhaus, W.D. and J. Boyer, (2000), *Warming the World: Economic Models of Global Warming*, Cambrdige, MA: The MIT Press.

Norton, B.G., (1982), 'Environmental Ethics and the Rights of Future Generations', *Environmental Ethics*, Vol. 4, No. 4, pp. 319–37.

O'Neill, J., (1993), *Ecology, Policy and Politics: Human Well-being and the Natural World*, London: Routledge.

———, (1997), 'Managing without Prices: On the Monetary Valuation of Biodiversity', *Ambio*, Vol. 26, pp. 546–50.

O'Neill, J., (1999), 'Self, Time and Separability', in T.-C. Kim and R. Harrison (eds), *Self and Future Generations: An Intercultural Conversation*, Cambridge: White Horse Press, pp. 91–106.

Page, T., (1983), 'Intergenerational Justice as Opportunity', in D. Maclean and P.G. Brown (eds), *Energy and the Future*, Totowa, New Jersey: Rowman and Allanheld, pp. 33–58.

——, (1988), 'Intergenerational Equity and the Social Rate of Discount', in V.K. Smith (ed.), *Environmental Resources and Applied Welfare Economics*, Washington, DC: Resources for the Future, pp. 71–89.

Parfit, D., (1983) 'Energy Policy and the Further Future: The Social Discount Rate', in D. Maclean and P.G. Brown (eds), *Energy and the Future*, Totowa, New Jersey: Rowman and Allanheld, pp. 31–37.

Parfit, D., (1984), *Reasons and Persons*, Oxford, England: Clarendon Press.

Sagoff, M., (1988), *The Economy of the Earth: Philosophy, Law, and the Environment*, Cambridge: Cambridge University Press.

Schelling, T.C., (1997), 'The Costs of Combating Global Warming: Facing the Trade-offs', *Foreign Affairs*, Vol. 76, No. 6, pp. 8–14.

Smith, J.B., H.J. Schellnhuber, M.Q. Mirza, S. Fankhauser, R. Leemans, L. Erda, L. Ogallo, B. Pittock, R. Richels, C. Rosenzweig, U. Safriel, R.S.J. Tol, J. Weyant, and G. Yohe, (2001), 'Vulnerability to Climate Change and Reasons for Concern: A Synthesis', in J.J. McCarthy, O.F. Canziani, N.A. Leary, D.J. Dokken, and K.S. White (eds), *Climate Change 2001: Impacts, Adaptation, and Vulnerability*, Cambridge: Cambridge University Press, pp. 913–67.

Smithson, M., (1989), *Ignorance and Uncertainty: Emerging Paradigms*, New York: Springer-Verlag.

Spash, C.L., (1993), 'Economics, Ethics, and Long-term Environmental Damages', *Environmental Ethics*, Vol. 15, No. 2, pp. 117–32.

——, (2002a), 'Dividing Time and Discounting the Future', in C.L. Spash, *Greenhouse Economics: Value and Ethics*, London: Routledge, pp. 201–20.

——, (2002b) (ed.), *Greenhouse Economics: Value and Ethics*, London: Routledge.

——, (2002c), 'Strong Uncertainty: Ignorance and Indeterminacy', in C.L. Spash (ed.), *Greenhouse Economics: Value and Ethics*, London: Routledge, pp. 120–52.

——, (2002d), 'Weak Uncertainty: Risk and Imperfect Information', in C.L. Spash (ed.), *Greenhouse Economics: Value and Ethics*, London: Routledge, pp. 97–119.

Stern, N., (2006a), *Stern Review on the Economics of Climate Change*, UK Government Economic Service, London, available at *www.sternreview.org.uk*.

——, (2006b), 'Technical Annex to Postscript', *The Stern Review on the Economics of Climate Change*, London, available at *http://www.hm-treasury.gov.uk/media/1/8/Technical_annex_to_the_postscript_P1-6.pdf.*

Tol, R.S.J., (2002), 'Estimates of the Damage Costs of Climate Change: Part II Dynamic Estimates', *Environmental and Resource Economics*, Vol. 21, pp. 135–60.

———, (2006), 'The Stern Review on the Economics of Climate Change: A Comment', 2 November, available at *www.fnu.zmaw.de/fileadmin/ fnu-files/reporst/sternreview.pdf.*

Vatn, A., (2000), 'The Environment as Commodity', *Environmental Values*, Vol. 9, No. 4, pp.493–509.

Vatn, A. and D.W. Bromley, (1994), 'Choices without Prices without Apologies', *Journal of Environmental Economics and Management*, Vol. 26, No. 2, pp. 129–48.

Warren, R., C. Hope, M. Mastrandrea, R.S.J. Tol, N. Adger, and I. Lorenzoni, (2006), 'Spotlighting Impacts Functions in Integrated Assessment', *Tyndall Centre on Climate Change*, Working Paper No. 91, Norwich.

Yohe, G., (2006), 'Some Thoughts on the Damage Estimates Presented in the Stern Review: An Editorial', *The Integrated Assessment Journal*, Vol. 6, No. 3, pp. 65–72.

11

Uncertainty Communication
The IPCC Reports

TIAGO DE SOUSA PEDROSA[1]

Climate change is now an issue widely discussed by society at various levels. Almost every day we read or hear news about climate change (CC) and global warming. This is in part due to the raised public and media interest in the possible effects of CC on weather events patterns—not only tropical cyclone activity (Hegerl et al. 2007), but also heat waves, exceptionally dry summers, or floods. The association of weather events to GHE and anthropogenic GHG emissions (correctly or not) is not recent. While news about CC in the popular press may be traced since the 1950s (Henson 2006), it is only now that society has had a massive awareness of the importance of anthropogenic GHG emissions. At the present moment, any change in weather is easily associated with GHE and anthropogenic GHG emissions, but even with this popularization no one can deny that CC is now being taken much more seriously than in the recent past.

We may consider at least four main events in the last few years that have, directly or indirectly, triggered this wide discussion: (i) the increase in the intensity of extreme weather events such as Hurricane Katrina, with severe social and economic damages; even though 'determining whether a specific, single extreme event is due to a specific cause, such as increasing greenhouse gases, is difficult, if not impossible' (Hegerl et al. 2007, pp. 696), this event raised the discussion in the media and public; (ii) the mobilization by Al Gore to fight global warming with his book and later Academy Award®-winning (popularly known as the Oscar® award) documentary *An Inconvenient Truth* (which explained the complexity of CC in a few words and many figures); (iii) the recent planetarium event Live

[1]The opinions expressed here are those of the author and cannot be attributed to the European Commission.

Earth (similar to Live Aids and Live 8 events), with the objective of raising public as well as political awareness and also to pressurize decision makers to act; (iv) and finally, the release of the Intergovernmental Panel for Climate Change (IPCC) Fourth Assessment Report (AR4) gathering more than five years of research on CC, which had a noteworthy media coverage—even though not being prominent on the overall news agenda (PEJ 2007), which some argue to be a 'massive communication failure' (Nisbet 2007). This chapter will focus precisely on the latter, more specifically, about the role of IPCC in the communication of CC science to policy, media, and society at large.

The AR4 was mainly awaited by the scientific and policy community, and also by the media, non-governmental organizations (NGOs), as well as other stakeholders. In early March of 2007 there was a discussion meeting on the 'Science of Climate Change: A Royal Society showcase of the IPCC 4th Assessment Working Group I Report' at the Royal Society, London. The meeting was attended by some of the most renowned scientists in the field and lead authors of the IPCC report, providing an opportunity to discuss the main findings of the report.

A key aspect that one might value in the IPCC is the effort made over time to improve the assessment and communication of uncertainties (as discussed later). The meeting provided the opportunity to discuss with the scientists involved in the production of the report, how the IPCC Assessment Reports are carried out, with special focus on the science production process, how the main findings and uncertainties are communicated and expert judgements used.

From the several discussions among the participants and speakers of the meeting, it emerged that the statements included in the AR4 used two different language scales: one referring to levels of confidence and the other referring to likelihood of events—a system originally introduced in the Third Assessment Report (TAR) (Moss and Schneider 2000) and later improved (IPCC 2005). While the first one is based on expert judgements, the second is based on probabilities and statistical analysis. This appears to be a simple method to recognize and communicate uncertainties, ignorance, and even value-ladenness associated with several statements in the report. But when one tries to understand how the statements were produced, it is difficult to follow a traceable account of the scientific production method deployed. The attributions of levels of confidence were based on expert judgement agreed between the authors involved in the chapter drafting, but the distinction between likelihood and confidence is not straightforward. Also, the techniques applied to attribute the level of confidence are not stated. The statements need to be agreed on by representatives of governments. Levels of confidence have a value-laden component, and are based on expert judgement, not just on mathematical methods.

Given the need to better communicate CC science to policy makers and society, now that policy is starting to deal with adaptation issues, requiring the input of science to make decisions at the regional/local scale, the development of guidelines to deal with expert judgement, communicate uncertainties, and assess the knowledge pedigree, for example, of models or statements, is very important for an effective communication.

This chapter analyses the several assessment reports and how uncertainty was dealt with. It then provides a discussion about the importance of the pedigree of information. Finally, it analyses the communication process of IPCC and provides suggestions to improve its focus on the target audience, objectives, and format.

The IPCC Role

IPCC works under the auspices of the United Nations Environmental Programme (UNEP) Governing Council and World Meteorological Organization (WMO) Executive Council, as well as in support of the United Nations Framework Convention on Climate Change (UNFCCC) since 1988.

According to the Principles governing IPCC work [last amended at the 25th session (Mauritius, 26–28 April 2006) (IPCC 2006)]:

The role of the IPCC is to assess on a comprehensive, objective, open and transparent basis the scientific, technical and socio-economic information relevant to understanding the scientific basis of risk of human-induced climate change, its potential impacts and options for adaptation and mitigation. IPCC reports should be neutral with respect to policy, although they may need to deal objectively with scientific, technical and socio-economic factors relevant to the application of particular policies.

In other words, the IPCC should assess the scientific, technical, and socio-economic information relevant for understanding the risk of human-induced CC and communicate this information to governments and intergovernmental organizations to support their policies (Somerville et al. 2007).

Even if assessments do not mean carrying out new research [and are more about assembling, summarizing, organizing, interpreting, and communicating results to make them relevant and helpful for the policy-maker's deliberations (Sluijs 1997)], the IPCC process of synthesis and assessment has often inspired scientific research leading to new findings (Somerville et al. 2007).

The IPCC has three Working Groups (WGs)—WGI, WGII, and WGIII—and a Task Force. The three working groups deal with scientific aspects, vulnerability and adaptation, and mitigation options, respectively. The Task Force is responsible for the IPCC National Greenhouse Gas Inventories Programme.

UNCERTAINTY AT THE IPCC

IPCC classifies uncertainties into two primary types: 'value' or 'statistical uncertainties' and 'structural uncertainties' (Manning et al. 2004; Somerville et al. 2007). Value uncertainties arise when variables and functional relationships are known but there is an incomplete determination of particular values or results. Structural uncertainties arise from processes and conceptual frameworks or models that may be incomplete or incorrect, that is, it is not clear that all relevant variables and functional relationships are known.

While value uncertainties are generally estimated using statistical techniques and expressed probabilistically, structural uncertainties are more complex to assess and are usually described on the basis of expert judgement of their confidence in the correctness of a result. In the field of Integrated Assessment Models (IAM), uncertainty studies have mainly involved methods for quantitative uncertainty analysis, such as the Monte Carlo technique, but these quantitative mathematical techniques provide only partial insight.

The use of qualitative assessment technique in addition to these quantitative techniques can help to partly overcome problems of structural uncertainty (Kloprogge et al. 2005). In the chain of calculations that lead to end results, many assumptions need to be made that involve subjective judgements to some degree by the analysts (Kloprogge et al. 2005).

The question is to know the influence of such subjective component in the results of the scientific studies and the value-ladenness of such assumptions. Expert judgement is subject to cognitive processes and group dynamics, which tend to introduce imprecision, bias, and overconfidence (Morgan and Henrion 1990).

The decisions tend to be value-laden (see for example, Kloprogge et al. 2005). Different assumptions may lead to different outcomes and, consequently, to different interpretations of the problem, resulting in different political recommendations and measures, and hence they should be subject to a critical review.

It is in this field of structural qualitative uncertainties that much of the work on communication still needs to be done. Policy-making not only needs to be informed about science; it also needs to be informed about the values (Goldston 2007).

ASSESSMENT AND COMMUNICATION OF UNCERTAINTY

There are several methods for dealing with uncertainty (see Kloprogge et al. 2005 for an overview; see also Chapter 2 in this volume). The NUSAP method (Funtowicz and Ravetz 1990), already successfully applied to the IMAGE/TIMER model, and the Guidance for Uncertainty Assessment and Communication (Sluijs et al. 2003) are examples of such methods.

NUSAP has extended the statistical approach to uncertainty with the methodological and epistemological dimensions by adding expert judgements of reliability (assessment) and systematic multi-criteria evaluation of the underpinning of numbers (pedigree).

The guidance for uncertainty assessment and communication was developed by the Netherlands Environmental Assessment Agency (Sluijs et al. 2003). This guidance was complemented with methods and checklists (Petersen et al. 2003; Janssen et al. 2003; Sluijs et al. 2004) to support researchers, analysts, and policy makers, not only to communicate uncertainty but also to frame the way uncertainty is dealt with in the assessment.

TRACEABILITY

The importance of a traceable account on how science is produced is already recognized by IPCC in their guidelines to deal with uncertainty (Moss and Schneider 2000; Manning et al. 2004; IPCC 2005). However, this information is not easily found when exploring the background of IPCC statements (see Box 11.1 for some examples) and is expressed in languages and formats depending on the chapter or even statement.

Many times the problem of traceability is related with the recognition of the several options available before making a decision (for example, about an assumption, values, etc.; see Box 11.1) not only in the assessment but also in the supporting studies. A framework is created based on several assumptions but there is no record of the other alternatives, variables, or constraints available *a priori* and why these were discarded. This is a problem because many of the criteria evaluated are hard to measure in an objective way, and hence the assessment involves qualitative expert judgement.

When looking at the several assessments included in the Summary for policymakers of WGI, we see that the traceability varies significantly. While this may be due to the complexity of the issues covered, different authors for each chapter, or even to the use of different 'languages' and information representation to communicate, questions are also raised regarding the choosen alternatives, and the legitimacy of the studies.

Pedigree of information has a relevant role in quality and communication of uncertainty. If quality is crucial, pedigree is also essential. As described by the NUSAP method, pedigree is about an evaluative description of information (Funtowicz and Ravetz 1990). This adds transparency to the science used and eventually helps with the communication of uncertainty. Another advantage of constructing the pedigree of information is the clarity gained by the researchers about the characteristic uncertainties of their own field. It helps to identify the main processes and to establish key assumptions for each process.

Assessing the pedigree of knowledge generates insight into the many assumptions and choices that inevitably have to be made during the production process of science-for-policy. All values and assumptions should be explicit but attention should be paid to not producing a false sense of simplicity and clarity.

The importance of being explicit about potential value-ladenness of the assumptions made and about the potential outcomes and impacts of such assumptions in the assessments is also argued by Kloprogge et al. (2005) and Schneider (1997). The latter suggests that incorporating decision makers and other citizens into the early stages of assessments can help with increasing the transparency of such assumptions and suggests a partial checklist of issues or practices to have in mind to increase the transparency in IAMs. To fail to be transparent 'is to make IAMs irrelevant to policy-makers and at worst misleading' (Schneider 1997: 246).

Pedigree is not only about assessing the knowledge produced, it is also about communication. There are several methods to structure and communicate the pedigree of information. One of these methods

Box 11.1: IPCC Statement Examples

• *Positive examples—extended description*:
'The equilibrium climate sensitivity (…) is likely to be in the range
2°C to 4.5°C with a best estimate of about 3°C, and is very unlikely
to be less than 1.5°C. Values substantially higher than 4.5°C cannot
be excluded but agreement of models with observations is not as
good for those values. (…) {8.6, 9.6, Box 10.2}' (IPCC 2007a: 12).
    The reference chapters mentioned in this statement include an
extended description of the sensitivity analysis made and support
their findings with presentation of the frequency distributions.

• *Positive examples—expert judgement description:*
The IPCC report provides an extended description of how the level
of scientific understanding (LOSU) for the radiative forcing (RF)
values was established in terms of evidence and consensus. Evidence
is related to the observation of RF mechanisms and to the capability
of physical models to explain the RF while consensus is assessed by
ranking the number of studies, how well studies agree on quantifying
the RF, and especially how well observation-based studies agree with
models (Forster et al. 2007).

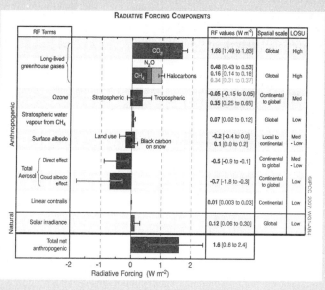

Figure 11.1: Global Average Radiative Forcing Estimates and Ranges in
2005 for GHG and Assessed Level of Scientific Understanding (IPCC
2007a).

Source: IPCC 2007: WG1-AR4 (IPCC 2007a)

An extended description on the existing research on the RF agents and mechanisms is made throughout chapter 2 of the IPCC report (IPCC 2007). However, it is not clear how the evidence and consensus' levels (both used to calculate LOSU) were reconciled, that is, what was the applied methodology. It is important to understand the dynamics through which the levels were agreed (for example, how much agreement or dissent between studies do you need to attribute a certain level of consensus). Different procedures may lead to different outcomes.

- *Missing links—Value-ladenness:*
'Carbon dioxide emissions associated with land-use change are estimated to be 1.6 [0.5 to 2.7] GtC (5.9 [1.8 to 9.9] GtCO2) per year over the 1990s, although these estimates have a large uncertainty. {7.3}' (IPCC 2007a: p. 2)

Analysing chapter 7.3 of the IPCC report (Denman et al. 2007), it is possible to find information regarding the several estimates made to the land use carbon source. This information is limited and does not provide information about the base estimates uncertainties, but more information can be read in the references provided. Nevertheless, there is an important aspect that was apparently superficially considered. To produce the official AR4 estimate, only two authors of a total of five reported were used. The argumentation was: 'For evaluating the global carbon budget, the mean of DeFries et al. (2002) and Houghton (2003a), which both cover the 1980s and the 1990s (Table 7.2), was chosen and the full range of uncertainty is reported' (Denman et al. 2007: p. 518). However, this is a very limited discussion, which may lead to the conclusion that the choice was based on the period range covered, and not on the quality of the estimates. Probably more criteria were taken into consideration but no references were made. This gives space to interpretation of the results and consequent controversy in their analysis.

is the Pedigree Exploring Tool (PET) scheme (Corral Quintana 2000; see also Chapter 3 in this volume).

The PET scheme allows the assessment of the quality of environmental decision-making processes, by the inclusion of an extended peer community in the quality assurance process. It has been conceived as an exploratory tool by which three main elements of policy-making processes—information used within the process, the influence of the decision tool, and the role of the analyst—can be assessed (Corral Quintana 2000).

Monbiot (2006) stressed the difficulties he had in writing about CC, namely deciding whom to trust, and that somehow he developed a sort of hierarchy of credibility. His major concern was related to the hidden interests and unsupported claims by several stakeholders (that is, industry, environmental NGOs, or others).

Increasing the level of the quality standards of IPCC studies and communications (namely in terms of transparency and traceability) can only improve their reliability and eventually reduce the controversy around the scientific facts, which become easier to review by the peers. This is not to be confused with dissent. Scientific facts may be accepted, but there may be dissent about their interpretation. However, an increase in such quality standards would contribute to a more informed discussion. Indirectly, others who challenge IPCC findings have at least the moral obligation of providing the same type of quality assessment and communicating it properly. This would also place and concentrate the debate in the political vs scientific arena.

While the IPCC internal guidelines only mention the inclusion of 'traceable account' (Moss and Schneider 2000), the inclusion of pedigree of information and use of NUSAP methodology to more easily evaluate the quality of the information assessed and used in the report would be of help.

COMMUNICATION OF UNCERTAINTY AT IPCC

Each IPCC Assessment Report is prepared at approximately five- to six-year intervals. The First Assessment Report (FAR), published in 1990 (IPCC 1990), provided the overall policy framework and legal basis for addressing CC issues, highlighting the possible link between man-made GHGs and potential global CC. The FAR supported the negotiations for the UNFCCC. Most conclusions from the FAR were non-quantitative and remain valid today.

While this first report hardly mentioned scientific uncertainty, it recognized the importance of identifying those areas where scientists had high confidence (Somerville et al. 2007). Shortly after the FAR a supplementary report (IPCC 1992) was issued but the treatment of scientific uncertainty remained as in the FAR.

The IPCC completed its Second Assessment Report (SAR) in 1995 (IPCC 1996), which supported the 1997 Kyoto Protocol negotiations. In this second assessment, uncertainty was defined in a number of ways (see Moss and Schneider 2000), but no reference was made to the expected likelihood or confidence levels. However, it was recognized that there was the need to draw formal methods for assessing more consistently the uncertainties (McBean et al. 1995). This second assessment provoked the reaction of some sceptics (mainly Global Climate Coalition), who criticized the process by which the wording used in some of the statements included in the summary for policy-makers was prepared (Henson 2006; Edwards and Schneider 1997). This lead to a review and improvement of the process for the next assessment.

With the IPCC special report on Aviation and Global Atmosphere (Penner et al. 1999) a consistent approach to assigning uncertainty to Radiative Forcing, based on mixed objective and subjective criteria, was introduced.

With the purpose of recommending a common approach for assessing, characterising, and reporting uncertainties in a more consistent—and to the extent possible, quantitative—fashion, a guidance paper (Moss and Schneider 2000) was developed. This was distributed to all WG authors for the drafting of the Third Assessment Report (TAR) released in 2001 (IPCC 2001). The main purpose of the recommendations were 'to enable authors to be more systematic in characterizing the types and sources of uncertainty' and, in turn, help to 'improve communication between the research community, decision-makers, and interested publics regarding what is known and unknown' (Moss and Schneider 2000: 35). A series of recommendations was made regarding sources of uncertainty, coverage of ranges, and distributions given in literature, nature of uncertainties and state of science, qualitative and quantitative description of values, and consistent use of confidence descriptors. This guidance paper focused on a 7-steps approach with the inclusion of two important aspects: one refers to the traceable account of how the estimates were constructed (maybe a first approach to the concept of Pedigree of information that we already discussed); the second, to the inclusion of formal methods for assessing expert judgement (considered optional).

One of the most visible outcomes of these recommendations is the use of the Bayesian paradigm, that is, the use of a formal and rigorous language to communicate uncertainty (Moss and Schneider 2000) translated into a five-level scale of confidence for assessing state of knowledge.

In the same year, another report was release by IPCC on *Good Practice and Uncertainty Management in National Greenhouse Gas*

Inventories (IPCC 2000), establishing a protocol for expert elicitation and methods for encoding expert judgements.

In 2001, IPCC released its TAR. The different approaches taken by WGs I and II highlighted the difficulties in the choice of the language. The WGI used the 'likelihood' wording to approach uncertainty, while the WGII used a level of confidence. Also when analysing the TAR, it is not easy to find a traceable account on how the estimates were constructed (as recommended by the guidance document of Moss and Schneider 2000). One of the most criticized aspects of this assessment by the CC sceptics was the 'hockey stick' graphic produced by Mann et al. (1999) for the IPCC (Henson 2006), even though these critiques were published mainly in non-peer-review literature (Daly 2000) and had little support in peer-reviewed papers (Soon and Baliunas 2003) and many other peer-reviewed literature have been published rebutting their claims (for example, Mann et al. 2003).

In May 2004, the IPCC organized a workshop on 'Describing Scientific Uncertainties in Climate Change to Support Analysis of Risk and of Options'. The workshop was held to consider past experiences and the latest developments in the determination and communication of uncertainties in order to improve the guidelines that would be made available to the lead authors of the AR4 (Manning et al. 2004). From the analysis of past experiences it emerged that the choice of language represents a critical aspect in the way uncertainties are understood (Manning et al. 2004). This resulted in several recommendations, which were presented as a result of this workshop.

Finally, in 2005, the IPCC released the 'Guidance Notes for Lead Authors of the IPCC Fourth Assessment Report on Addressing Uncertainties' (IPCC 2005). This document is supported by the previous documents released by IPCC, namely TAR Guidance Paper (Moss and Schneider 2000) and workshop report and background papers (Manning et al. 2004). The Guidance is structured in 15 points covering:

- Planning the treatment of uncertainty and confidence;
- Reviewing the information available;
- Making expert judgements;
- Using the appropriate level of precision to describe findings; and
- communicating using calibrated language (focusing mainly on the presentation of the uncertainty and language to be used).

Even though some progress has been made in the way IPCC

deals with uncertainty, this has been a long and slow process if one compares both the guidelines for TAR and for AR4, and their application by the WGs.

SCIENTIFIC CONTROVERSY

When attempting to learn about CC, the choice seems easy: the most credible source of information is peer-reviewed papers. But these may be confusing and contradictory. In order to provide an overview and reach a consensus over certain issues, scientific committees may be created (as is the case for IPCC). However, this may not be sufficient. As mentioned by Sarewitz (2004: 385), 'scientific uncertainty, which so often occupies a central place in environmental controversies, can be understood not as a lack of scientific understanding but as the lack of coherence among competing scientific understandings, amplified by the various political, cultural, and institutional contexts within which science is carried out'. The scientific debate conceals people's value preferences behind technical arguments. That is to say that an instrumentalization of science may take place. Scientists and scientific committees should be more explicit about their goals, rather than act as if they were only providing 'neutral' scientific information to support and inform policy processes.

An appropriate communication process, together with a pedigree of the information provided, would not only increase the robustness of the assessment, but would also raise the transparency and quality of the science provided and would eventually induce the counterparts, that is, scientists with different or even antagonist information and opinions, to do the same, adding some clarity in scientific disputes and related values, thus contributing to a more informed discussion.

Two examples of how scientific findings may create controversy and eventually be manipulated are the 'hockey-stick' graphic and the temperature ranges proposed by the IPCC. The first example was highly criticized as misleading by several sceptics. The graphic makes a reconstruction of the temperatures for the last millennium, with the claim that the 1990s had likely been the warmest decade of the last 1,000 years. Published in 1999 (Mann et al. 1999), the validity of the temperature reconstruction was questioned by several scientists. And even if none was able to back up their own claims in scientific peer-reviewed literature, there was the need to produce more studies to confirm its validity (Henson 2006) and support the policy purposes.

The second example relates to the range of temperatures that was used depending on groups' interests. The most widely accepted estimate for the rise in global temperature from a doubling of atmospheric CO_2 concentration in the atmosphere is 3°C, with a range of 2–4.5°C deemed likely by the IPCC (2007a). Some sceptics believe that the lower end of the range is the most likely outcome, while environmentalists argue that temperature has already increased by about 0.8°C with only up to 35 per cent of CO_2 since pre-industrial times (Henson 2006), and hence it is much more likely that the other end will be approached.

These ranges are not a probability distribution and the most likely value may not be the same as the temperature range mid-point. Considerable work has been done since the TAR to estimate climate sensitivity and to provide a better quantification of relative probabilities (Meehl et al. 2007). However, it should be made clear how the most likely value is achieved to reduce these controversies.

HUMBLE SUGGESTIONS FOR UNCERTAINTY COMMUNICATION AT IPCC

When communicating uncertainties and policy-relevant science in general, at least three issues ought to be considered: target audience; objectives (closely related with the content provided); and format (medium through which the *story* is conveyed).

Target Audience

At a first glance, the target audience of IPCC seems straightforward: policy-makers and scientists [as referred in the comments of the First Scoping Meeting of the IPCC's Fourth Assessment Report (IPCC 2003)]. But is this really the case?

The IPCC is the authorative voice in terms of CC, and its reports go much further than simply feeding directly the policy-making process. They provide the source of information (or disinformation) for media, NGOs, lobby groups, and even concerned citizens. Thus, it is not enough to be concerned about a specific target audience. The task is much more complex and should address several kinds of audience, with different technical capabilities. A broader communication, identifying and preparing communications for specific target audiences, not only media, NGOs, citizens, etc., but also looking at their own specificities and taking into consideration their needs and interests (e.g. radio, press, environmental or social NGOs, etc.), can bring at least two benefits: at first it may reduce the misuse of scientific information by media and citizens, and secondly it will assure that decision-makers are positively influenced by other sources of information (or at least they are not confused by them). Decision-makers receive information not only from scientific sources; several times their decisions are influenced by audience polls, newspapers, television, and pubic opinion. Ignoring the impact that the information provided can have in the spheres outside policy-making is jeopardizing the effectiveness of the communication to the policy-maker itself.

Taking this into consideration, three aspects are important: (i) socially robust knowledge (Gibbons 1999), that is, the information present should be relevant for the specific audience it is intended for; (ii) application of the principle of progressive disclosure of information (Guimarães Pereira et al. 1998), that is, the information is provided in a multi-layered fashion from simple to more detailed, disclosed upon users' demands, and the user has access to more specialized information navigating from upper layers to deeper layers; and (iii) presenting the pedigree of the information (Funtowicz and Ravetz 1990) provided (as mentioned earlier, this is necessary to raise the quality and transparency of the assessments and at the same time reduce the controversy).

Objective

It is important to consider what the main objective of the communication's message is. Each target audience has different needs and languages that should be reflected in the communication.

Though the primary objective of the IPCC is not to communicate CC science to all society (Browning 2005; IPCC 2006), indirectly this already happens, and in order to avoid misunderstanding and manipulation of the information, it is preferable to consider an extended communication prepared by IPCC [for different target audiences reflecting on their needs, interests, and relevance of the information provided. The structure and communication of IPCC reports, to some extent, already reflect these concerns, for example, the Summary for Policy Makers; the Technical Summary; 'figures and presentations'; and 'press releases and speeches' available at the IPCC webpage (IPCC 2007b)], but this could be further extended with the inclusion of new formats and contents for specific target audiences.

Format

At present, the main communications of IPCC are done through their printed reports and website. The printed version of the AR4 is organized by the WGs. Each WG provided a Summary for Policy Makers, Technical Summary, and WG contribution (the report itself). WGI also included an innovation regarding the TAR report: a chapter entitled Frequently Asked Questions.

At the time of writing this chapter, the on-line version of the AR4 was still not available. Taking into consideration the work developed for the TAR, the internet functionalities are limited to providing the information available in the reports in a similar structure as the one available in the printed version. Each topic of the chapter can be accessed individually but no other features that could eventually enhance the visualization of the information, make it easier to navigate between different contents, or increase the traceability of the information were implemented. It is also available as a list, with the most significant figures of the report and a set of power-point presentations for direct download.

The IPCC already deals with the most important mediums to convey their message, but nevertheless the communication could be further improved. For instance, the recent inclusion of a chapter about Frequently Asked Questions is already an improvement in the way information is presented and communicated to different audiences. The inclusion of chapters focused mainly towards citizens and the media could also be of added value.

However, the largest improvements could be made in the technological platform: the internet. This platform provides a medium of excellence to communicate the information in an effective way. Because we are considering communicating to different audiences, it is necessary to take into consideration the design of the principle of progressive disclosure of information. This would allow different audiences (stakeholders) to access the same information, depending on their interests.

The introduction of blog structures inside the IPCC framework of communication and dialogue could also be considered. These types of structured discussions have been receiving increasing interest, providing an accessible and open scientific discussion. A blog is a website where comments are written in chronological order. It may combine text, images, movies, and links to other sources of (scientific) information. There are already several blogs dealing with CC discussion (for example, *www.realclimate.org; www.climatesciencewatch.org; www.worldclimatereport.com*). The inclusion of blogs in the communication process could lead to a more informed discussion. Blogs tend to be hybrid forms of scientific communication, where different types and formats of knowledge are accessed.

However, the internet also poses the problem of information divide, given that not every one can have access to or is skilled to access information in such format. Thus, this format has a specific audience, and other formats (printed documents, videos, articles, etc.) should be considered to cover such audiences.

Concluding Remarks

As referred earlier, many of the controversies over the CC *problematique* are raised by an incomplete or at least insufficient communication of the uncertainties and assumptions. This leads to an increase in controversy about the CC science. The main purpose of the IPCC is to provide scientific input to policy-making, which should follow the principles of openness, participation, accountability, effectiveness, and coherence (EC 2001).

It is important to distinguish between value uncertainties and structural uncertainties, and ignorance. Often the word uncertainty is used to define the low level of knowledge about some system or process; this creates the sense that we are dealing with the same type of uncertainty as in models or statements about, for example, the rise in temperature. In several paragraphs of the AR4, uncertainty is used to define lack of knowledge about an issue and there is no associated assessment.

At least two types of improvements should be taken into consideration in future communications. The first is assessment of structural uncertainties through more transparent methods and techniques (this could be done through information pedigree). The second is improving the communication of the CC issues to a wider audience, taking advantage of new technologies such as the internet (this could reduce the noise created around the main findings and contribute to a sound discussion about CC).

The IPCC assessments gather and organize scientific information produced and published in international peer-review journals and selected non-scientific peer-reviewed literature but from widely recognized sources (such as industry or research institutes' reports or studies). In this process, where different sources of information are used at different levels of the assessment, it is difficult to present structured information about the quality of the science produced (for example, assumptions, sensitivity, value-ladenness, etc.). This information is lost in the several steps of the assessment procedure. The existence of information pedigree, not only for qualitative information but also for the numbers used, would simplify the task of presenting the information in a uniform format (see Chapter 3 and Chapter 15 in this volume). At each step the pedigree could be updated and information would not be lost, adding robustness to the assessments.

The IPCC has to innovate, extending the established methods of science communication (as it has been doing) and find new paths in the way scientific uncertainty is dealt with and communicated to inform the policy process.

REFERENCES

Browning, P., (2005), 'Framework Communications Strategy for Release and Dissemination of IPCC 4th Assessment Report, Communications & Network Consulting', Twenty-fourth Session of IPCC, IPCC-XXIV/INF. Vol. 3.

Bindoff, N.L., J. Willebrand, V. Artale, A. Cazenave, J. Gregory, S. Gulev, K. Hanawa, C. Le. Quéré, S. Levitus, Y. Nojiro, C.K. Shum, L.D. Talley, and A. Unnikrishnan, (2007), 'Observations: Oceanic Climate Change and Sea Level', in S. Solomon, D. Qin, M. Manning, Z. Chen, M. Marquis, K.B. Avert, M. Tignor, and H.L. Miller (eds), *Climate Change 2007: The Physical Science Basis. Contribution of Working Group 1 to the Fourth Assessment Report of the Intergovernmental Panel on Climate Change*, Cambridge and New York: Cambridge University Press.

Corral Quintana, Serafín, (2000), *Una Metodología Integrada de Exploración de los Procesos de Elaboración de Politicas Públicas*, Tenerife. España: Universidade de La Laguna.

Daly, J., (2000), 'Still Waiting for Greenhouse: A Lukewarm View of Global Warming', available at *http://www.john-daly.com/hockey/hockey.htm* accessed on 26 October 2007.

DeFries, R.S. et al., (2002), 'Carbon Emissions from Tropical Deforestation and Regrowth Based on Satellite Observations for the 1980s and 1990s', Proc. Natl. Acad. Sir., U.S.A., 99 (22), 14256–61.

Denman, K.L., G. Brasseus, A. Chidthaisong, P. Ciais, P.M. Cox, R.E. Dickinson, D. Hauglustaine, C. Heinze, E. Holland, D. Jacob, U. Lohmann, S. Ramachandran, P.L. da Silva Dias, S.C. Wofsy, and X. Zhang, (2007), 'Couplings between Changes in the Climate System and Biochemistry', in S. Soloman, D. Qin, M. Manning, Z. Chen, M. Marquis, K.B. Averyt, M. Tignor, and H.L. Miller (eds), *Climate*

Change 2007: The Physical Science Basis, Contribution of Working Group 1 to the Fourth Assessment Report of the Intergovernmental Panel on Climate Change, Cambridge and New York: Cambridge University Press.

Edwards, P. and S. Schneider, (1997), 'Climate Change: Broad Consensus or "Scientific Cleansing"?', *Ecofables/Ecoscience*, Vol. 1, No 1, pp. 3–9.

EC, (2001), *European Governance: A White Paper*, COM(2001) 428, Brussels: European Commission, pp. 1–29.

Forster, P., V. Ramaswamy, P. Artaxo, T. Berntsen, R. Betts, D.W. Fahey, J. Haywood, J. Lean, D.C. Lowe, G. Myhre, J. Nganga, R. Prinn, G. Raga, M. Schulz, and R. Van Dorland, (2007), 'Changes in Atmospheric Constituents and in Radiative Forcing', in S. Solomon, D. Qin, M. Manning, Z. Chen, M. Marquis, K.B. Averyt, M. Tignor, and H.L. Miller (eds), *Climate Change 2007: The Physical Science Basis. Contribution of Working Group I to the Fourth Assessment Report of the Intergovernmental Panel on Climate Change*, Cambridge and New York: Cambridge University Press.

Funtowicz, S.O. and J.R. Ravetz, (1990), *Uncertainty and Quality in Science for Policy*, The Netherlands: Kluwer Academic Publishers.

Gibbons, M., (1999), 'Science's New Social Contract with Society', *Nature*, Vol. 402, Supplement 1, pp. C81–C84.

Goldston, D., (2007), 'Technical Advice', *Nature*, Vol. 448, No. 2, p. 119.

Guimarães Pereira, A.C. Gough, and B. De Marchi, (1998), 'Computers, Citizens and Climate Change: The Art of Communicating Technical Issues', *International Journal of Environment and Pollution*, Vol. 11, No. 3, pp. 266–89.

Hegerl, G.C., F.W. Zwiers, P. Braconnot, N.P. Gillett, Y. Luo, J.A. Marengo Orsini, N. Nicholls, J.E. Penner and P.A. Stott, (2007), 'Understanding and Attributing Climate Change', in *Climate Change 2007: The Physical Science Basis. Contribution of Working Group I to the Fourth Assessment Report of the Intergovernmental Panel on Climate Change*, S. Solomon, D. Qin, M. Manning, Z. Chen, M. Marquis, K.B. Averyt, M. Tignor, and H.L. Miller (eds), Cambridge and New York: Cambridge University Press.

Henson, R., (2006), *The Rough Guide to Climate Change*, London: Rough Guide.

Houghton, R.A., (2003a), 'Revised Estimates of the Annual Net Flux of Carbon to the Atmosphere from Changes in Land Use and Land Management', 1850–2000. *Tellus*, 55B(2), pp. 378–90.

IPCC, (1990), *Climate Change: The IPCC Scientific Assessment*, J.T. Houghton, G.J. Jenkins, and J.J. Ephraums (eds), Cambridge and New York: Cambridge University Press.

―――, (1992), *Climate Change 1992: The Supplementary Report to the IPCC Scientific Assessment*, J.T. Houghton, B.A. Callander, and S.K. Varney (eds), Cambridge and New York: Cambridge University Press.

_____, (1996), *Climate Change 1995: The Science of Climate Change. Contribution of Working Group 1 to the Second Assessment Report of the Intergovernmental Panel on Climate Change*, J.T. Houghton, L.G.M. Filho, B.A. Callandar, N. Harris, A. Kattenberg and K. Maskell (eds), Cambridge and New York: Cambridge University Press.

_____, (2000), *Good Practice Guidance and Uncertainty Management in National Greenhouse Gas Inventories*, Hayama: Institute for Global Environmental Strategies.

_____, (2001), *Climate Change 2001: The Scientific Basis. Contribution of Working Group I to the Third Assessment Report of the Intergovernmental Panel on Climate Change*, J.T. Houghton, Y. Ding, D.J. Griggs, M. Noguer, P.J. van der Linden, X. Dai, K. Maskell and C.A. Johnson (eds), Cambridge and New York: Cambridge University Press.

_____, (2003), 'Summary of Comments relating to Scoping of the IPCC's Fourth Assessment Report (AR4)', available at *http://www.ipcc.ch/activity/ar4docs/synthesis.pdf*, accessed on 17 July 2007.

_____, (2004), 'Procedures: The Preparation of IPCC Reports', available at *http://www.ipcc.ch/about/faq/IPCC%20Procedures.pdf*, accessed on 17 July 2007.

_____, (2005), 'Guidance Notes for Lead Authors of the IPCC Fourth Assessment Report on Addressing Uncertainties', available at *http://www.ipcc.ch/activity/uncertaintyguidancenote.pdf*, accessed on 17 July 2007.

_____, (2006), 'Principles Governing IPCC Work', available at *http://www.ipcc.ch/about/princ.pdf*, accessed on 17 July 2007.

_____, (2007a), *Climate Change 2007: The Physical Science Basis. Contribution of Working Group I to the Fourth Assessment Report of the Intergovernmental Panel on Climate Change*, S. Solomon, D. Qin, M. Manning, Z. Chen, M. Marquis, K.B. Averyt, M. Tignor, and H.L. Miller (eds), Cambridge and New York: Cambridge University Press.

_____, (2007b), Intergovernmental Panel on Climate Change webpage, available at *http://www.ipcc.ch*, accessed on 28 September 2007.

Janssen, P.H.M., A.C. Petersen, J.P.v.d. Sluijs, J.S. Risbey and J.R. Ravetz, (2003), *RIVM/MNP Guidance for Uncertainty Assessment and Communication: Quickscan Hints & Action List*, Bilthoven: RIVM/MNP.

Kloprogee, P., J.P. van der Sluijs, and A.C. Petersen, (2005), 'A Method for the Analysis of Assumptions in Assessments' Exploring the Value-ladenness of Two Indicators in the Fifth Dutch Environmental Outlook', Report 550002010/2005, The Netherlands: Netherlands Environmental Assessment Agency.

Mann, M.E., R.S. Bradley, and M.K. Hughes, (1999), 'Northern Hemisphere Temperatures During the Past Millennium: Inferences, Uncertainties, and Limitations', *Geophysical Research Letters*, Vol. 26, pp. 759–62.

Mann, M.E., C.M. Ammann, R.S. Bradley, K.R. Briffa, T.J. Crowley, M.K. Hughes, P.D. Jones, M. Oppenheimer, T.J. Osborn, J.T. Overpeck, S. Rutherford, K.E. Trenberth, and T.M.L. Wigley, (2003), 'On Past Temperatures and Anomalous Late 20th Century Warmth', *Eos*, Vol. 84, pp. 256–58

Manning, Martin, Michel Petit, David Easterling, James Murphy, Anand Patwardhan, Hans-Holger Rogner, Rob Swart, and Gary Yohe (eds), (2004), *Workshop Report: IPCC Workshop on Describing Scientific Uncertainties in Climate Change to Support Analysis of Risk of Options*, Boulder: IPCC Working Group I Technical Support Unit.

McBean, G.A., P.S. Liss, and S.H. Schneider, (1996), 'Advancing Our Understanding', in *Climate Change 1995. The Science of Climate Change: Contribution of Working Group I to the Second Assessment Report of the Intergovernmental Panel on Climate Change*, J.T. Houghton, L.G. Meira Filho, B.A. Callander, N. Harris, A. Kattenberg, and K. Maskell (eds), Cambridge and New York: Cambridge University Press.

Meehl, G.A., T.F. Stocker, W.D. Collins, P. Friedlingstein, A.T. Gaye, J.M. Gregory, A. Kitoh, R. Knutti, J.M. Murphy, A. Noda, S.C.B. Raper, I.G. Watterson, A.J. Weaver, and Z.C. Zhao, (2007), 'Global Climate Projections', in *Climate Change 2007: The Physical Science Basis. Contribution of Working Group I to the Fourth Assessment Report of the Intergovernmental Panel on Climate Change*, S. Solomon, D. Qin, M. Manning, Z. Chen, M. Marquis, K.B. Averyt, M. Tignor, and H.L. Miller (eds), Cambridge and New York: Cambridge University Press.

Monbiot, G., (2006), *Heat: How We Can Stop the Planet Burning*, England: Penguin Books.

Morgan, M.G. and H. Dowlatabadi, (1996), 'Learning from Integrated Assessment of Climate Change', *Climatic Change*, Vol. 34, No. 3/4, pp. 337–68.

Morgan, M.G. and M. Henrion, (1990), *Uncertainty: A Guide to Dealing with Uncertainty in Quantitative Risk and Policy Analysis,* Cambridge: Cambridge University Press.

Moss, R. and S. Schneider, (2000), 'Uncertainties in the IPCC TAR: Recommendations to Lead Authors for More Consistent Assessment and Reporting', in *IPCC Supporting Material: Guidance Papers on Cross Cutting Issues in the Third Assessment Report of the IPCC,* R. Pachauri, T. Taniguchi, and K. Tanaka (eds), Geneva: Intergovernmental Panel on Climate Change.

Nisbet, M., (2007), 'Framing Science: Reticence? The IPCC's Communication Problem', available at *http://scienceblogs.com/framing-science/2007/06/reticence_the_ipccs_communicat.php*, accessed on 26 October.

PEJ, (2007), 'Project for Excellence in Journalism News Coverage Index: April 1–6, 2007', available at *http://www.journalism.org/node/4969*, accessed on 26 October.

Penner, J.E., D.H. Lister, D.J. Griggs, D.J. Dokken, and M. McFarland (eds), (1999), *Intergovernmental Panel on Climate Change Special Report on Aviation and the Global Atmosphere,* Cambridge and New York: Cambridge University Press.

Petersen, A.C., P.H.M. Janssen, J.P.v.d. Sluijs, J.S. Risbey, and J.R. Ravetz, (2003), *RIVM/MNP Guidance for Uncertainty Assessment and Communication: Mini-Checklist and Quickscan Questionnaire,* Bilthoven: RIVM/MNP.

Sarewitz, D., (2004), 'How Science makes Environmental Controversies Worse', *Environmental Science and Policy,* Vol. 7, pp. 385–403.

Schneider, S.H., (1997), 'Integrated Assessment Modelling of Global Climate Change: Transparent Rational Tool for Policy Making or Opaque Screen Hiding Value-Laden Assumptions', *Environmental Modelling and Assessment,* Vol. 2, pp. 229–49.

Sluijs, J.P. van der, (1997), *Anchoring amid Uncertainty: On the Management of Uncertainties in Risk Assessment of Anthropogenic Climate Change,* Ultrecht: Utrecht University.

Sluijs, J.P.v.d., J. Potting, J. Risbey, D. van Vuuren, B. de Vries, A. Beusen, P. Heuberger, S. Corral Quintana, S. Funtowicz, P. Kloprogge, D. Nuijten, A. Petersen, and R. Ravetz, (2002), 'Uncertainty Assessment of the IMAGE/TIMER B1 CO2 Emissions Scenario, Using the NUSAP Method'. Report No. 410200104. The Netherlands: Dutch National Research Program on Climate Change.

Sluijs, J.P.v.d., J.S. Risbey, P. Kloprogge, J.R. Ravetz, S.O. Funtowicz, S.C. Quintana, A.G. Pereira, B.D. Marchi, A.C. Petersen, P.H.M. Janssen, R. Hoppe, and S.W.F. Huijs, (2003), *RIVM/MNP Guidance for Uncertainty Assessment and Communication: Detailed Guidance,* Utrecht: Utrecht University.

Sluijs, J.P.v.d., P.H.M. Janssen, A.C. Petersen, P. Kloprogge, J.S. Risbey, W. Tuinstra, M.B., A.V. Asselt, and J.R. Ravetz, (2004), *RIVM/MNP Guidance for Uncertainty Assessment and Communication: Tool Catalogue for Uncertainty Assessment,* Utrecht: Utrecht University.

Somerville, R., H. Le Treut, U. Cubasch, Y. Ding, C. Mauritzen, A. Mokssit, T. Peterson, and M. Prather, (2007), 'Historical Overview of Climate Change', in *Climate Change 2007: The Physical Science Basis. Contribution of Working Group I to the Fourth Assessment Report of the Intergovernmental Panel on Climate Change,* S. Solomon, D. Qin, M. Manning, Z. Chen, M. Marquis, K.B. Averyt, M. Tignor, and H.L. Miller (eds), Cambridge and New York: Cambridge University Press.

Soon, W. and S. Baliunas, (2003), 'Proxy Climatic and Environmental Changes of the Past 1000 years', *Climate Research,* Vol. 23, No. 2, pp. 89–110.

12

Ecology and Economy in the Arctic
Uncertainty, Knowledge, and Precaution

IULIE ASLAKSEN, SOLVEIG GLOMSRØD, AND
ANNE INGEBORG MYHR[1]

The Arctic is in the centre of rapid and unpredictable change, with
respect to climate, economy, and social organization. Climate change
impacts manifest themselves more rapidly there than in other regions.
The vulnerable Arctic environment represents an important example
of the need for new approaches to environmental uncertainty, since
the complex relationships between the economy, the environment,
and cultural values are strong and well-documented (ACIA 2005;
AHDR 2004; AMAP 2004). International and national policies in
the Arctic region focus strongly on climate change, its detrimental
impacts and potential beneficial impacts on accessibility and extraction
of natural resources.

Given the substantial environmental uncertainty, the irreplacebility
of the Arctic landscapes, and the complex ethical issues involved, we
argue that economic valuation should be supplemented with other
methods, such as focus on the processes for assessing uncertainty,
through interdisciplinary approaches and explicit incorporation of
stakeholders' values, interests, and knowledge. We consider it highly
important to approach valuation of nature in terms of sustainability,
resilience, and environmental responsibility.

In particular, valuation of nature needs to be addressed in terms
of multiple uses of the Arctic landscapes of frozen sea, glaciers, tundra,
grasslands, and forests. The valuation should reflect the different
options for subsistence production, biodiversity protection, and

[1]Financial support from the Norwegian Ministry of Foreign Affairs is gratefully
acknowledged. The authors also thank Anne Skoglund for excellent technical
assistance, word processing, and editing.

ecosystem services. The Arctic Human Development Report (AHDR 2004) emphasizes that the Arctic is homeland for diverse groups of indigenous people. The ecological values of the Arctic are compounded by their culture, and the indigenous and local knowledge is crucial for establishing the information basis for sustainable development.

The Arctic nature provides subsistence livelihood for indigenous and local people and resources for the market economy. The intertwined nature of the subsistence and market economies gives the Arctic societies their dual characteristics (Glomsrød and Aslaksen 2006). Climate change impacts and other environmental problems can dramatically affect the conditions for subsistence activities and the well-being of the indigenous and local people. Knowledge about these changes is crucial for identifying the conditions and policy measures to ensure economic, environmental, and cultural sustainability in the Arctic, within the framework of the global economy.

Climatic and other environmental impacts have dramatically altered the pre-conditions of life for indigenous peoples, and on-going economic and social impacts may substantially change their opportunities (Ford et al. 2006). The most recent IPCC (2007) report stated that:

In the Polar Regions, the main projected biophysical effects are reductions in thickness and extent of glaciers and ice sheets, and changes in natural ecosystems with detrimental effects on many organisms including migratory birds, mammals and higher predators. In the Arctic, additional impacts include reductions in the extent of sea ice and permafrost, increased coastal erosion, and an increase in the depth of permafrost thawing. For Arctic human communities, impacts, particularly resulting from changing snow and ice conditions, are projected to be mixed. Detrimental impacts would include those on infrastructure and traditional indigenous ways of life. Beneficial impacts would include reduced heating costs and more navigable northern sea routes. In both polar regions, specific ecosystems and habitats are projected to be vulnerable, as climate barriers to species' invasions are lowered. Arctic human communities are already adapting to climate change, but both external and internal stressors challenge their adaptive capacities. Despite the resilience shown historically by Arctic indigenous communities, some traditional ways of life are being threatened and substantial investments are needed to adapt or re-locate physical structures and communities (IPCC 2007).

Precautionary perspectives are required to balance the economic, environmental, and ethical values of the economic activities in the Arctic, to integrate diverging interests and to protect biological and cultural diversity. A key concept in precautionary strategies is resilience, understood as the capacity to recover after disturbance, absorb stress, internalize it, and transcend it (Berkes et al. 2000; Holling 1973; Holling et al. 1995; Gunderson 2000). Resilience refers to both ecological and cultural resilience—of individuals, of ecosystems, and of local communities. An important pre-condition for resilience is to involve local and traditional knowledge and practice.

Climate change is already having a strong impact on nature and livelihood in the Arctic. Although a comprehensive precautionary perspective necessarily would have addressed values and policies in the past, the on-going climate change process demands a continuous effort to learn from the 'late lessons' that may be drawn from earlier experience and to develop 'early warnings' for future impacts. We suggest that environmental uncertainty in the Arctic is addressed in terms of the framework in the EEA report 'Late Lessons from Early Warnings: The Precautionary Principle 1896–2000' (EEA 2001). The report describes environmental and health costs of not responding to credible scientific 'early warnings', summarizes some 'late lessons' that may be drawn from these experiences, and suggests important elements in precautionary approaches (see also Aslaksen et al. 2006). While a comprehensive empirical application of the framework suggested by EEA (2001) is beyond the scope of this chapter, some points can be outlined for future empirical application. We consider stakeholder involvement as crucial in identifying 'early warnings' as well as in elaboration of mitigation and adaptation strategies to cope with environmental and social change.

UNCERTAINTY, VALUATION, AND PRECAUTION

The Arctic ecosystems and social systems are unique and represent a valuable part of our common ecological and cultural heritage. The dual characteristics of the Arctic economies, with strong and complex relationships and barriers between subsistence activities and markets, represent considerable challenges for evaluating the conditions for sustainability and developing precautionary strategies for environmental uncertainty. The economic, social, and cultural well-being of the indigenous people living in remote areas are shaped under conditions that deviate from standard assumptions in economic theory and models for well-developed markets that do not take into account the barriers and transactions costs associated with their traditional basis for living.

To take into account this complexity, we apply the distinction between 'practical' and 'technical' problems as outlined by Ravetz (1971) and applied for environmental uncertainty by Cañellas-Bolta et al. (2005). 'Practical' problems are defined as problems for which the solution consists in the achievement of a human purpose, such as welfare, health, or the natural environment in a good state. In the context of the Arctic economy, the 'practical' problem may refer to the challenge of achieving balance between economic profitability and sustainable development. 'Technical' problems are defined in terms of a function to be performed, and their solutions consist in finding a technical specification that performs the function. In the context of the Arctic economy, the 'technical' problem may refer to the policy means to ensure sustainability. Despite their intertwined nature, the market economy and subsistence economy represent different spheres with different approaches to values. The challenge is to integrate the two approaches, to ensure that the 'practical' problems are explicitly addressed, to discuss how sustainable development in the Arctic can be achieved, while recognizing that the 'technical' problems and the instrumental approaches specific to each discipline do not necessarily capture the whole picture. Even problems that are considered as 'technical' have 'practical' aspects, in that their solution requires an explicit analysis of the human purpose that should be achieved (Ravetz 1971: 319).

Political approaches to environmental risk and quality, in particular at the local and regional levels, almost exclusively focus on technical solutions, neglecting the questions related to the practical targets: What type of nature conservation do we want? What is the authentic quality of this particular type of nature? Which results of development in nature should be preserved; which glaciers, boreal forests, and fishing communities? What is it like to be human without these places (Latour 2004)? Who are the stakeholders representing the sea ice and the polar bear? Raising these questions has implications for how to employ economic valuation and risk governance, and represents a dimension different from optimism or pessimism, different from being 'for or against' a particular economic or technological development, by demanding perspectives about need and goals at a more conceptual level.

Taking into account potential harm to a wide range of stakeholders implies a larger context than the application of cost–benefit analysis.

The 'post-normal science' focuses on uncertainties in valuation and complexities in ethics from a new perspective: When science no longer is imagined as delivering 'truth' irrespective of context, science should follow a new organizing principle, that of quality (Funtowicz and Ravetz 1991, 1994). A central concept in this approach is procedural rationality, a scientific principle with stronger focus on the process of knowledge-generation and the implicit values involved. Such procedural rationality could imply an extension of the peer-review community to people from other disciplines and to people affected by the particular environmental issue. It involves recognition of the importance of context and the possibility for more egalitarian access to knowledge and to the knowledge-generating processes. This may be facilitated by an extension of the peer-review community for accumulation of knowledge, encompassing the perspectives of multiple stakeholders (Kinzig and Starrett 2003). Examples include the processes involved in the work of IPCC, and also the Arctic Council, where cooperation between indigenous people across the Arctic builds an institutional framework for multiple voices. New institutions for participatory processes are needed to strengthen dialogue between stakeholders and to secure the role of less powerful stakeholders.

Uncertainty about valuation of nature can be understood not only as a lack of scientific knowledge, but also as the lack of coherence between competing scientific disciplines, each with their traditions, approaches, and models (Sarewitz 2004). The value orientation and normative assumptions held in different scientific disciplines can represent contrasting scientific views of nature, of human nature, of the relation between nature and humanity, and of the extent of the ethical responsibility of the individual, the scientist, and the politician. What Sarewitz (2004) denotes 'excess of objectivity' refers to the observation that available scientific knowledge can be interpreted in different ways to yield competing views of the 'practical' and 'technical' problems and how society responds. From this perspective, demand for 'more research' is not sufficient to reduce scientific uncertainty and infer the value of nature and the conditions for sustainability. In fact, the incapacity of science to provide a unified picture of the natural environment contributes to the lack of coherence about its valuation. What is needed is an explicit discussion of the plural values and scientific approaches involved in a particular environmental controversy, thereby obtaining a distinction between the 'practical' and 'technical' problems involved, and to manage the uncertainties that are characteristic of each field so that information of the highest possible quality can be obtained (Funtowicz and Ravetz 1990, 1994). Central to uncertainty management and environmental valuation is the recognition that the scientific, economic, and social contexts are intertwined (Myhr 2002). The challenge is to enhance communication between the various perspectives and implicit values in science. Only by acknowledging the importance of environmental responsibility can a comprehensive perspective on the relationship between environmental uncertainty and sustainability be developed (O'Neill 1993, 1996; Vatn 2005). Considering environmental responsibility for future generations, Jonas (1984) suggests that responsibility is a more basic ethical principle than reciprocity since there is no reciprocity between future generations and us. Taking responsibility into account, the distinction between 'is' and 'ought' is not relevant anymore. Environmental responsibility relates to human existence in the future, and suggests that the Earth should not be left in a worse state than when the present generations received it.

Economic valuation methods that rely only on quantitative valuations without taking into account the particular environmental qualities and uncertainties can appear as 'blind' to natural and cultural values that are difficult to measure. This apparent 'blindness' may induce a criticism from other disciplines that questions the relevance of economic trade-off for valuation of environmental qualities (Aslaksen and Myhr 2007).

Valuation without context refers to the practice of considering nature values as similar to the value of other goods, without taking into account the ecological processes and cultural context that these nature values are embedded within. As suggested in Figure 12.1, the bridge across this duality is to emphasize that multi-dimensional evaluation—not only one-dimensional monetary valuation—of environmental qualities, uncertainties, and impacts should take place in processes that recognize the ecological and social context of economic evaluation. More comprehensive and contextual evaluation methods could include multi-criteria analysis and participatory methods such as stakeholder participation and deliberative processes for assessing

Economic valuation	and	Evaluation in ecological and social context
Valuation without context		Neglecting economic trade-off

Figure 12.1:   Valuation and Evaluation in Social Context

uncertainty, for accommodation of scientific disagreements, and for integration of stakeholder interests and perspectives (Vatn 2005).

TRADITIONAL ECOLOGICAL KNOWLEDGE

To lift the veil and better see the appropriate context for economic valuation of environmental uncertainty, traditional ecological knowledge may be crucial, as for instance in the process of identifying the climate change impacts in the Arctic. Traditional ecological knowledge is defined as the knowledge, practice, and beliefs about the dynamic relationships of living beings and the environment, a knowledge that has evolved by adaptive processes and been handed down from generation to generation (Berkes 2008; Ingold 2000; AHDR 2004). For example, traditional ecological knowledge of animal migrations, ice patterns, vegetation, and weather is important in order to supplement and enrich scientific data on climate change impacts. Climate change impacts on the texture of snow and ice are important determinants of the access of reindeer to food. This makes the local inhabitants unique observers of how changing winter weather patterns are altering the grazing possibilities for reindeer. In reindeer herding, 'reading' nature is the process of observing and evaluating grazing pastures and weather conditions, the texture of snow and ice, wind directions, and the sequence of changes in nature, which determine access to nature and the behaviour of the reindeer (Heikkilä 2006; Berkes 2008).

Combining traditional and scientific knowledge about ecology is considered an important part of understanding the resilience capacity of ecological and social systems and identifying factors that can enhance it (Berkes 2008; Berkes et al. 2000; Berkes et al. 2003; Gadgil, Olsson, Berkes and Folke 2003). Although the informal character of traditional ecological knowledge makes it difficult to be recorded in scientific frames, many scientists contribute to integrating traditional ecological knowledge and western scientific knowledge (ACIA 2005). Traditional ecological knowledge is often embodied in practices and stories (narratives) that provide a systematic outline of the information relevant to particular habitats, ecosystems, and landscapes (Helander and Mustonen 2004). The stories about the landscape and their detailed and systematic description of changes in the environment can be brought forward in the process of analysing scenarios of climate change impacts. To ensure sustainable resource management, it is crucial to integrate the scientific knowledge with indigenous and local knowledge about weather patterns, seasonal changes, migration of animals, growth of plants, and traditional use of landscapes and natural resources.

Taking traditional ecological knowledge into account reminds us that there are multiple ways of knowing about the world and that effective resource management requires an understanding of this diversity. Awareness of traditional ecological knowledge also encourages participatory, community-based resource management systems that allow diverse approaches to knowledge, practices, and beliefs to become visible. This also makes the 'blind spot' of implicit normative assumptions in scientific approaches visible. Traditional ecological knowledge emphasizes the importance of the relationship between the human being and nature, a viewpoint that is also recognized in ecological economics.

As suggested in Figure 12.2, the bridge between the human-oriented perspective of mainstream economics and the nature-oriented perspective of ecological economics necessitates that a narrow anthropocentric view is avoided, and likewise, that disregard of human material needs is avoided. The relation between human being and nature needs to be recognized on many levels, in our own perception of our humanity and in the different scientific approaches, leading to interdisciplinary perspectives on environmental responsibility and the value of nature. Use of traditional ecological knowledge can contribute to strengthening the information basis for the complex relationships between the economic, environmental, and social conditions in the Artic.

Human needs	and	Relation between human being and nature
Anthropocentric		Disregard human needs

Figure 12.2:   Relation between Human Being and Nature

PRECAUTIONARY PERSPECTIVES: 'LATE LESSONS FROM EARLY WARNINGS'

The large uncertainty about climate change impacts requires precautionary approaches to economic and political decision making, in particular, that resilience capacity is taken into account and traditional ecological knowledge is recognized. Improved dialogue between stakeholders can give a better understanding of the social and scientific contexts where data are created and, hence, contribute to improving the empirical basis for policy advice on how to deal with environmental risk and protect environmental qualities. Precautionary perspectives should be developed within a specific context and evaluated case-by-case (UNESCO 2005). The climate change process in the Arctic demands a continued effort to learn from the 'late lessons' that may be drawn from earlier experience and to develop 'early warnings' for future impacts. We suggest that the climate change impacts and other environmental uncertainties in the Arctic are addressed in terms of the framework from the EEA (2001) report 'Late Lessons from Early Warnings'. The report suggests 12 precautionary strategies to address environmental uncertainty. Providing cases and examples to illustrate the 12 late lessons is the topic of our on-going research and a comprehensive discussion is beyond the scope of the present chapter, and here we will outline some points for future empirical application.

A key element in precautionary approaches is the recognition that not all future outcomes are well defined at the time of risk assessment. What is referred to as uncertainty can hide the distinction between uncertainty, risk, and ignorance, where the concept of ignorance refers to situations where the definition of a complete set of outcomes is problematic (see Funtowicz and Ravetz 1990; Wynne 1992; Stirling 1999). The usefulness of the concept of ignorance lies in its reminder that unexpected events are easily overlooked in risk assessment. Hazards not yet identified will not be analysed, unless the risk assessment explicitly searches for 'early warnings' of unexpected events. In the Arctic, ignorance about outcomes is particularly important to consider when outcomes are irreversible, such as climate change impacts and loss of ecosystem resilience. Systematically looking for 'early warnings' may be facilitated by investigation of resilience capacity in Arctic ecosystems and livelihoods, recognition of the traditional ecological knowledge of the indigenous and local people, and development of indicators for sustainable development.

Changes need to be monitored over time in order to establish indicators for 'early warnings'. Traditional ecological knowledge is crucial for obtaining information on how climate and ecosystems develop over time. Environmental and health parameters that need to be monitored include climate change impacts, for example, thawing permafrost, with detrimental effects on forests, roads, other

Box 12.1: 'Late Lessons from Early Warnings'

1. Acknowledge and respond to ignorance, as well as uncertainty and risk, in technology appraisal and public policy-making
2. Provide adequate long-term environmental and health monitoring and research into early warnings
3. Identify and work to reduce 'blind spots' and gaps in scientific knowledge
4. Identify and reduce interdisciplinary obstacles to learning
5. Ensure that real world conditions are adequately accounted for in regulatory appraisal
6. Systematically scrutinize the claimed justifications and benefits alongside the potential risks
7. Evaluate a range of alternative options for meeting needs alongside the option under appraisal, and promote more robust, diverse, and adaptable technologies so as to minimize the costs of surprises and maximize the benefits of innovation
8. Ensure use of 'lay' and local knowledge as well as relevant specialist expertise in the appraisal
9. Take full account of the assumptions and values of different social groups
10. Maintain the regulatory independence of interested parties while retaining an inclusive approach to information and opinion gathering
11. Identify and reduce institutional obstacles to learning and action
12. Avoid 'paralysis by analysis' by acting to reduce potential harm when there are reasonable grounds for concern.

Source: EEA (2001).

transportation infrastructure, and buildings (Ford et al. 2006). Moreover, there is need for monitoring long-range transported pollution of environmental toxins, harming life and subsistence living in the Arctic (WWF 2006). Information about the disproportionately high accumulation of persistent organic pollutants (POPs) in the Arctic and their impact on human health played a role in the successful effort to negotiate the 2001 Stockholm Convention to curb the production, uncontrolled use, and release of POPs (Downie and Fenge 2003). Large-scale resource extraction has considerable impact on the natural environment and human health. Examples are toxic discharges from gold and nickel mining, causing problems that have yet to be solved (AHDR 2004). Effects on the natural environment, human health, and social conditions are manifold and often poorly documented (AMAP 2004). Deposition of mercury in the Arctic is influenced by the scale of coal use and energy technology in other regions of the world, and thus influenced by climate policies and the costs of cleaner coal technologies.

Based on IPCC (2007) information, scenarios of how climate change impacts will influence Arctic economy and subsistence livelihood should be developed, for example, on how snow and ice conditions for reindeer grazing affect the Sami population, how reduction in sea-ice and worse conditions for hunting affect the Greenland population, and how thawing permafrost impact dwellings and transportation in the affected regions. To develop precautionary strategies for sustainable development in the Arctic, interdisciplinary approaches are needed, involving natural sciences, philosophy of science, anthropology, and economics, including approaches based on ecological economics (Norgaard 1994; Vatn 2005).

A precautionary approach may provide rationale to restrain certain industries and enhance others. Tourism in the Arctic is an important example of an economic activity with a high potential to flourish based on the natural and cultural qualities of the Arctic. The option value of preserving nature for tourism is high, but the value of sustainable tourism is not as widely recognized as other commercial interests. The conflict of interests between traditional and modern lifestyles is exemplified by a case from Finnmark in North Norway. In the 1980s, when a road project to a remote village was considered, one of the elders expressed: 'We have all what we need— and more than what we need. But if the road is built, we will be invaded by people who never get enough' (Nergård 2006: 109). This illustrates that the limits for sustainable use of nature, as embedded in the nature-related cultural and spiritual values of the Sami nature management, were not only based on knowledge about harvesting, but on insight into the forces that pull the human being away from traditions based on a long-term perspective. Arctic indigenous worldviews are characterized by their holistic nature, which means that they cannot be easily split into religious, cultural, economic, social, or other components.

The complex environmental problems of the Arctic require stakeholder participation. For example, fisheries represent an area of conflicting interests between small-scale coastal fisheries and large-scale industrial fisheries. Mineral extraction leads to conflicting interests between indigenous people and other Arctic residents (Duhaime et al. 1998). More systematic knowledge of the relationships and barriers between the subsistence and market economies will contribute to a better understanding of the resource basis of the indigenous and local communities, their production technology, and their values and preferences. Considering living conditions along these dimensions reveals a more complex picture than how economic inequality usually is perceived, as people in the Arctic have unequal access to the different bases for their livelihood. Rights to land and to natural resources have been and remain the essential challenge in Arctic governance systems. A main trend in both international and national law is the enhanced recognition and protection of the rights of indigenous people of the Arctic, within international human rights—the United Nations Declaration on the Rights of Indigenous People, and the International Labour Organization (ILO) Convention 169 on indigenous and tribal people.

A new approach to stakeholder involvement is, for instance, methods such as multi-criteria evaluation that can be used to map and investigate social choices and perspectives (Munda 2004). Multi-criteria methods can be used to supply a framework for policy analysis in a very effective way since it accomplishes the goals of being interdisciplinary (with respect to research team), participatory (with respect to stakeholders), and transparent (since all criteria are presented in their original form without any transformations in money or other measurement rods). To obtain this goal, it is crucial to develop a stakeholder approach: identify stakeholder groups and identify areas for stakeholder processes. For example, as part of strategies for corporate social responsibility, there is a necessity to develop dialogue between economic interests, authorities, and local communities.

PRECAUTIONARY RESPONSES: MITIGATION AND ADAPTATION STRATEGIES

Designing mitigation and adaptation strategies with explicit focus on stakeholder involvement is important for obtaining a comprehensive knowledge basis for environmental and social change and for understanding the diverging interests regarding these changes. While the Arctic is experiencing large effects of climate change more rapidly than expected, the feasible options for mitigating climate change through reduced GHG emissions are crucially dependent on actions taken by people living in more southern latitudes. The Arctic Climate Impact Assessment (ACIA 2005) report, therefore, has its main emphasis on adaptation strategies. However, as pointed out by IPCC (2007), there is a need to consider both mitigation and adaptation in the Arctic regions, given the trends in resource extraction and modernization taking place in these regions. The Arctic is also a powerful source of global warming. The Arctic regions are rich in fossil energy. Currently, they supply about 10 and 25 per cent, respectively, of the global oil and gas production (Lindholt 2006). Any measures of climate change mitigation will be strongly felt in the petroleum producing Arctic regions. Decisions on scale of petroleum production and exploration and emissions of CO_2 are beyond the influence of the indigenous people in the Arctic, yet they are recipients of the full impact of climate change impacts on environment and communities.

An important task for future assessments of impacts and strategies for mitigation and adaptation is to conduct vulnerability studies of Arctic communities, evaluating both environmental and social change. In order to obtain adaptive strategies, the perspectives, knowledge, and concern of indigenous people and other local Arctic residents will be essential (ACIA 2005: 1020). Studies of climate change impacts need to be conducted in the framework of stakeholder involvement, with dialogue between local residents, industry, and government. As some will gain and some will lose from climate change impacts and changing economic opportunities, stakeholder involvement is necessary to represent the diverging interests. Changes in public policy for Arctic regions, new strategies in resource management, extended petroleum exploration, industrial development, growth in tourism, and new means of transportation exemplify the need for stakeholder participation in order to evaluate how the development processes contribute to adaptation to climate change impacts. For example, increased ship traffic in the Northwest Passage will increase the risks and potential damage from oil and other chemical spills and change the social and economic conditions of the region (ACIA 2005: 1013).

The ACIA (2005) report presents examples of studies of adaptation to climate change impacts from Greenland and Sachs Harbour, Canada, pointing out that increased participation in the market economy and industries such as tourism raise new questions about sustainability and vulnerability of the socio-ecological system (ACIA 2005: 963). The involvement of indigenous people as key stakeholders is a crucial part of improving this framework for assessment of vulnerability, sustainability, and adaptation strategies. The ACIA

(2005) report also presents an in-depth study of adaptation to climate change for Sami reindeer herding in Finnmark, Norway. The report points out that the reindeer herding is not only affected by climate change, but also by the political and socio-economic environment in which it exists (ACIA 2005: 971). The flexibility to move reindeer herds between summer and winter pastures represents an important part of the traditional adaptive strategy, which may be challenged by climate change and difficult ice and snow conditions (ACIA 2005: 981). To enhance the adaptive capacity of reindeer herding, as well as of the traditional hunting, fishing, and herding activities in other Arctic regions, stakeholder participation of indigenous people is crucial because of their reliance of the changing environment and because their adaptive capacity has sustained their livelihood in the Arctic environment. For example, indigenous people observe weather patterns and animal movements and contribute to the understanding of climate change (ACIA 2005: 992). Involvement of indigenous and other local people will contribute to an adaptive and precautionary perspective by expressing qualities, values, and uncertainties that are easily overlooked in risk assessments, and hence, helping to obtain a more complete understanding of the interrelations between livelihood, climate change, economic development, and public policy.

CONCLUDING REMARKS

The large uncertainty about environmental impacts in the Arctic requires precautionary approaches to economic and political decision making under uncertainty, in particular that environmental responsibility, multiple value concepts, and resilience capacity are taken into account and traditional knowledge is recognized. Improved dialogue between stakeholders can give a better understanding of the conflicting interests, the values at stake, and the social and scientific contexts where environmental knowledge is created and, hence, contribute to improving the empirical basis for precautionary strategies to deal with environmental risk and protect environmental qualities. The conceptual and empirical challenges for developing precautionary approaches involve processes for stakeholder participation, multi-criteria approaches to the valuation of nature, and integrated knowledge bases for evaluating the sustainability of the unique values of the Arctic.

REFERENCES

ACIA, (2005), *Arctic Climate Impact Assessment*, Cambridge: Cambridge University Press.

AHDR, (2004), *Arctic Human Development Report*, Akureyri: Stefansson Arctic Intitute.

AMAP, (2004), 'Persistent Organic Pollutants in the Arctic', Oslo: Arctic Monitoring and Assessment Programme.

Aslaksen, I., B. Natvig, and I. Nordal, (2006), 'Environmental Risk and the Precautionary Principle: "Late Lessons from Early Warnings" applied to Genetically Modified Plants', *Journal of Risk Research*, Vol. 9, pp. 205–24.

Aslaksen, I. and A.I. Myhr, (2007), '"The Worth of a Wildflower": Precautionary Perspectives on the Environmental Risk of GMOs', *Ecological Economics*, Vol. 60, pp. 489–97.

Berkes, F., (2008), *Sacred Ecology*, New York: Routledge.

Berkes, F., J. Colding, and C. Folke, (2000), 'Rediscovery of Traditional Ecological Knowledge as Adaptive Management', *Ecological Applications*, Vol. 10, pp. 1251–62.

_____, (2003), *Navigating Social-Ecological Systems*, Cambridge: Cambridge University Press.

Cañellas-Bolta, S., R. Strand, and B. Killie, (2005), 'Management of Environmental Uncertainty in Maintenance Dredging of Polluted Harbours in Norway', *Water Science and Technology*, Vol. 52, pp. 93–8.

Downie, D. and T. Fenge (eds), (2003), *Northern Lights Against POPs: Combating Toxic Threats in the Arctic*, Montreal: McGill—Queen's University Press.

Duhaime, G., R.O. Rasmussen and R. Comtois (eds), (1998), *Sustainable Development in the North*, Québec: Gétic, Laval University.

EEA, (2001), 'Late Lessons from Early Warnings: The Precautionary Principle, 1896–2000', Environmental Issue Report No. 22, Copenhagen: European Environmental Agency (EEA).

Ford, J.D., B. Smit, and J. Wandel, (2006), 'Vulnerability to Climate Change in the Arctic: A Case Study from Arctic Bay, Canada', *Global Environmental Change*, Vol. 16, No. 2, pp. 145–60.

Funtowicz, S.O. and J.R. Ravetz, (1990), *Uncertainty and Quality in Knowledge for Policy*, Dordrecht: Kluwer Academic Publisher.

_____, (1991), 'A New Scientific Methodology for Global Environment Issues', in R. Constanza (ed.), *Ecological Economics: The Science and Management of Sustainability*, New York: Columbia University Press.

_____, (1994), 'The Worth of a Songbird: Ecological Economics as a Post-normal Science', *Ecological Economics*, Vol. 10, pp. 197–207.

Gadgil, M., F. Berkes, and C. Folke, (1993), 'Indigenous Knowledge for Biodiversity Conservation', *Ambio*, Vol. 22, pp. 151–6.

Gadgil, M., P. Olsson, F. Berkes, and C. Folke, (2003), 'Exploring the Role of Local Ecological Knowledge in Ecosystem Management: Three Case Studies', in Berkes, F., J. Colding and C. Folke (eds), *Navigating Social-Ecological Systems*, Cambridge: Cambridge University Press, pp. 189–209.

Glomsrød, S. and I. Aslaksen (eds), (2006), *The Economy of the North*, Statistics Norway, Oslo.

Gunderson, L.H., (2000), 'Ecological Resilience: In the Theory and Application', *Annual Review of Ecology and Systematics*, Vol. 31, pp. 425–39.

Heikkilä, L., (2006), 'The Comparison in Indigenous and Scientific Perceptions of Reindeer Management', in B.C. Forbes, M Bölter, L. Müller-Wille, J. Hukkinen, F. Müller, N. Gunslay, Konstatinov and Y. and (eds), *Reindeer Management in Northernmost Europe*, Heidelberg: Springer-Verlag, pp. 73–93.

Helander, E. and T. Mustonen (eds), (2004), *Snowscapes, Dreamscapes: Snowchange Book on Community Voices of Change*, Tampere: Tampereen ammattikokeakoulu.

Holling, C.S., (1973), 'Resilience and Stability of Ecological Systems', *Annual Review of Ecology and Systematics,* Vol. 4, pp. 1–23.

Holling, C.S., D.W. Schindler, B.H. Walker, and J. Roughgarden, (1995), 'Biodiversity in the Functioning of Ecosystems: An Ecological Synthesis', in C.A. Perrings, G.-K. Mäler, and C. Folke (eds), *Biodiversity Loss: Economic and Ecological Issues*, Cambridge: Cambridge University Press.

Ingold, T., (2000), *The Perception of the Environment: Essays on Livelihood, Dwelling and Skills*, London: Routledge.

IPCC, (2007), *Impacts, Vulnerability and Adaptation: Contribution of Working Group II to the Fourth Assessment Report of the Intergovernmental Panel on Climate Change*, Cambridge: Cambridge University Press.

Jonas, H., (1984), *The Imperative of Responsibility*, Chicago: University of Chicago Press.

Kinzig, A. and D. Starrett et al., (2003), 'Coping with Uncertainty: A Call for a New Science-Policy Forum', *Ambio*, Vol. 32, pp. 330–35.

Latour, B., (2004), *Politics of Nature: How to Bring the Sciences into Democracy*, Cambridge, MA: Harvard University Press.

Lindholt, L., (2006), 'Arctic Natural Resources in a Global Perspective', in S. Glomsrød and I. Aslaksen (eds), *The Economy of the North*, Statistics Norway, Oslo, pp. 27–39.

Munda, G., (2004), 'Social Multi-criteria Evaluation: Methodological Foundations and Operational Consequences', *European Journal of Operational Research*, Vol. 158, pp. 662–77.

Myhr, A.I., (2002), 'Precaution, Context and Sustainability: A Study of How Ethical Values May Be Involved in Risk Governance of GMOs (Genetically Modified Organisms)', Ph. D thesis, University of Tromsø.

Nergård, J.-I., (2006), *Den levende erfaring: En studie i samisk kunnskapstradisjon* ('The Living Experience: A Study in Sami Traditional Knowledge'), Cappelen, Oslo.

Norgaard, R.B., (1994), *Development Betrayed: The End of Progress and a Coevolutionary Revisioning of the Future*, New York: Routledge.

O'Neill, J., (1993), *Ecology, Policy and Politics: Human Well-being and the Natural World*, London: Routledge.

———, (1996), 'Cost-Benefit Analysis, Rationality and the Plurality of Values', *The Ecologist*, Vol. 26, No. 3, pp. 98–103.

Ravetz, J.R., (1971), *Scientific Knowledge and its Social Problems*, London: Transaction Publishers.

Sarewitz, D., (2004), 'How Science makes Environmental Controversies Worse', *Environmental Science and Policy*, Vol. 7, pp. 385–403.

Stirling, A., (1999), 'On Science and Precaution in the Management of Technological Risk, Volume I: A Synthesis Report of Case Studies', European Science and Technology Observatory Joint Research Centre (JRC) of the European Commission, available at *http://www.jrc.es*.

UNESCO, (2005), *The Precautionary Principle*, Paris: UNESCO World Commission on the Ethics of Scientific Knowledge and Technology.

Vatn, A., (2005), *Institutions and the Environment*, Cheltenham: Edward Elgar.

WWF, (2006), 'Killing Them Softly', Report on Environmental Toxins in Marine Mammals.

Wynne, B., (1992), 'Uncertainty and Environmental Learning: Reconceiving Science and Policy in the Preventive Paradigm', *Global Environmental Change*, Vol. 2, pp. 111–27.

PART 4

Science in Energy Policy

13

Radioactivity Within Without

MARTIN O'CONNOR

He has gone to the very root, he says, of existence. He has deciphered the secrets. .... At his hands, the molecules change, and changed and changing they enter his skin, hide in what he eats, secrete themselves in his tissue, alter the molecular structure of his body. He goes inside the heart of life, he says. He takes apart the form of matter itself, he strips energy from mass, he splits what is whole, he takes this force for his own, he says. But what he has split does not stop coming apart. Fractures live in the air, invisible fractures come into his body, split his chromosomes, unravel the secrets of life in him. (Griffin 1978: 134)

This Chapter begins by evoking the pathos of waste production as the unintended side-effect of our technological prowess. Next, it addresses the paradigmatic case of radioactive contamination of our natural environment and of ourselves. By considering in sociological and existential terms our long-term collective participation in the production and stewardship of radioactive wastes, sustainability is characterized as a complex problématique of human and ecological degradation and renewal—or in other words, a systems science and political epistemology enquiry into contemporary forms of domination and (self-) denigration, disaster, and repair.

PROLEGOMENON: DEGRADATION WITHOUT WITHIN

Man makes history, Karl Marx once said, but not always quite the history that he had in mind. And, as Engels (in his *Dialectics of Nature*) elegantly pointed out, it is nature as much as society which escapes the best made plans (Engels 1883):[1]

[1]The passage cited (in English translation by the author) is found on p. 160 in the French numerical edition prepared by Jean-Marie Tremblay, which is based on

We should not flatter ourselves too much on our victories over nature. She gets her revenge for each one of them. To be sure, each victory brings, in the first instance, the consequences counted on; but in second and third instance it brings effects that are very different, unanticipated, and which only too often spell ruin of the primary outcomes.

The history of the modern economic order can be read, suggests Jean Baudrillard (1990: 105), as a history of the liberation of energy— the physical energy of natural resources, and the creative energies of humanity. But, our sacrosanct liberty curve-balls around into confusion and catastrophe.

Energy is a sort of fantastic projection which feeds all the technological and industrial dreams of modernity, and equally it is energy which inflects the conception of man in the sense of a dynamic of intention. However we know, through analyses of phenomena of turbulence, chaos, and catastrophe in contemporary physical science, that any flux, any linear process, when one augments it, takes on a strange curvature which spells catastrophe.

Our liberty metaphysics thus are just as much a history of dissipation and degradation. As development theorist Gourlay writes in *World of Waste* (1992: 19):

The more we consider the industrialised world of today, and the Third World of tomorrow, the more we realise that we live in a world dominated by waste, a World of Waste, most of it undesirable, and that unless we do something about it, humanity may disappear under its own detritus, and the world we know with it.

And, clearly, this is degradation of people as well as of energy. What we have liberated comes back to re-make our day: laying to waste the environment without and our integrity within.

North American sociologist William Catton (1989) recounts the fate of the small town of Times Beach, Missouri, in the midwest of the United States (US), which was irrepairably contaminated with dioxin and finally evacuated through a mass buy-out of the community by the US. Environmental Protection Agency (EPA). The dioxin had accumulated in factory sludge as a by-product of the manufacture of the antiseptic hexachlorophene. When the manufacturing plant was closed early in the 1970s, the task of cleaning out the factory was given to a local odd jobs contractor, and a vat of sludge was combined with waste oil and sprayed as a dust-settling mixture on

---

the French language edition of Friedrich Engels (1883), *Dialectique de la Nature*, published by Editions Sociales, Paris, 1968.

the unsealed streets of Times Beach. Health complaints over ensuing years led eventually to EPA identification of the dioxin; and then a winter flood spread the contaminated dust/silt through the flood-plain homes. Access to the ghost-town is now barred by fences and armed guards, with huge warning signs stating 'Hazardous Waste Site'. Entry is possible only after signing a 'General Release of Liability' by which all risks and perils are assumed by the visiting individual.

Catton concludes that, metaphorically, we are all living in a global Times Beach. By our sovereign consumption choices we have collectively signed a 'General Release' on behalf of all generations to come. To which we should add, as evoked by Susan Griffin (1978), the intimate tragedy of a sort of contamination within.

Barely seen, soundlessly surrounding him, with hardly a breath of evidence, all he has burned, all he has mined from the ground, all he cast into the waters, all he has torn apart, comes back to him. He is haunted. Carbon monoxide, sulfur dioxide, beryllium, arsenic, peroxyacetylnitrate, formaldehyde, do not desert him. Dioxin, DDT, will not let him forget. Lead, mercury, live in his dreams. Strontium sticks in his bones. The equation for oxygen stays in his mind but he cannot breathe what he used to call air. The equation for water stays in his mind, but there is nothing he can drink that will not poison him....

LIVING WITH(IN) THE RADIOACTIVITY LIFE CYCLE

Notwithstanding natural radioactivity, we have greatly augmented, in recent decades, the prospects—sometimes called 'risks'—of exposure of present and future human beings to an unhealthy dose of radioactivity. In this context, legitimate authorities have comprehensive information about stocks and stockages of radioactivity of various sorts (high and low levels; long and short half-lives; solid, liquid, and gaseous phases; and so on). Most of this is referred to as wastes, some of it as contaminated sites. It is a long-term hazard; mankind has made itself a collective problem of having to live with its radioactive wastes.

Contaminated site stewardship decisions involve complex judgments about how we will live with, or cope with, or get along with, inconveniences and risks that have their origins in the past. Management of long-term radiological liabilities is associated with scientific uncertainties and with moral, political, and economic dilemmas. What principles should be applied for distribution of the costs, inconveniences, and on-going risks that are the 'downstream' legacy of benefits gained? In cases of major misfortunes or accidents, the people most directly concerned, or their descendants, will live with memories, scars, and the pain of things lost, and must confront the uncertainties of building a new life. Public policy in such situations must contribute to repairing, revitalizing, and rebuilding communities.

These challenges of partnership building and rebuilding are important even when—as with the majority of mining and industrial exploitation activities—site stewardship is not associated with past accidents or trauma. There are unique requirements of memory and purposefulness associated with monitoring and eventual intervention for different sorts of contaminated sites and unstable situations whose 'risks' extend decades (or, in some cases, many centuries) into the future. This is partly an economic resources problem, but it is also a cultural, social, and political problem of purposes and meanings.

What would be the basis, material as well as symbolic, of (re)building trust, hope, and joy while living with the radioactive wastes? Can we deduce from inventories, medical knowledge, and scenario speculations about the present and possible future levels of exposure to man-mediated radioactivity, what 'should' and should not be done? The short answer is no. The significance to an individual, to members of a community, to a society of exposure (or a danger of exposure) to a dose depends very much on how, by whom, and why the dose has been produced. By the same token, there are many different ways that our societies, and future societies, might seek to appraise the risks and might set about to watch over and live in relation with the wastes. Site stewardship and waste management strategies may differ considerably as regards the relationships (in social, economic, cultural, and symbolic terms) that they establish between the people—individuals, classes, interest groups, succeeding generations, whole nations—implicated in the situations of production, storage, and monitoring of the wastes. This social dimension cannot be deduced purely from technology and the medical and bio/physical information set.[2]

[2]Although the emphasis here is on societal and symbolic dimensions, this is not an argument to say that science and technology have no place. Scientific knowledge and engineering know-how are irreducible parts of any societal solution. Radioactivity of wastes is a material phenomenon and, even if a solution were merely agreed by all members of society that neglected technical concerns, there would nonetheless remain, in the words of the Argentinian writer Jorge Luis Borges, 'the problem of the material of some objects' (Jorge Luis Borges, 1970,'Tlön, Uqbar, Orbis Tertius', in D.A. Yates and J.E. Irby (ed.) *Labryinths: Selected stories and other writings*, English translation edited by Penguin Books, Harmondsworth, pp. 22–43).

Put across another way, radioactive waste storage sites, like accidentally contaminated sites, are socially constructed risk situations. As in the case of most socially mediated risks, the significance—and hence the acceptability or not—to an individual, to members of a community, to a society of exposure (or a danger of exposure) to a dose depends on how, by whom, and why the dose has been produced. Correspondingly, in order to assess to what extent or on what basis the members of a society will judge acceptable (or not) a given strategy for management of high-level long-lived radioactive wastes, it is necessary also to consider the meanings and relationships (in social, economic, cultural, and symbolic terms) that alternative remediation and stewardship strategies might establish between the people—individuals, classes, interest groups, succeeding generations, whole nations—implicated in the site stewardship process. In the rest of this chapter, some practical ways that this might be done are proposed.

LESSONS FROM THE PORT HOPE (CANADA) EXPERIENCE

One more case of accidental site of contamination is presented here. The OECD Nuclear Energy Agency's 'Forum on Stakeholder Confidence' Workshop held in Ottawa, Canada in October 2002, highlighted the experience of the communities of Port Hope, on the shores of Lake Ontario (Canada), whose townships have been contaminated with (mostly low level) long-lived radioactive wastes due to past factory activities of radium and uranium refining. More than 50 years on from the factory activities, the Port Hope (and neighbouring) communities have now, collectively and purposefully, set about to (re)build a social—and societal—relationship with their wastes. Working its way through 20 years of discussions and suggestions, the Port Hope community now insists on its 'ownership' of the local contamination problem, accepting, indeed affirming, it as a historical liability that the community adopts as a part of its identity. The community's favoured stewardship solution concept, formalized in terms of the Port Hope Area Initiative, is to accommodate the radioactive wastes as modern-day middens or burial mounds. The radioactive wastes, piled together and suitably 'capped', will become landscape features integrated into the everyday life of the community. The managed wastes thus become features in a kind of theme park, this becomes (it is hoped) a tourist draw card rather than a reason to shy away.[3]

[3]On the NEA's Forum on Stakeholder Confidence and the programme of workshops since 2000, see the website *http://www.nea.fr/html/civil/welcome.html*. This discussion of the Port Hope experience is adapted from O'Connor (2003).

There are several striking features of this example. First, the host community has consciously and deliberately refused alternative solutions for long-term waste management, such as deep underground disposal, that would—in the community's view—depend on expertise and knowledge that they feel is not sufficiently accessible to them. Rather than a solution that would place the problem 'out of their hands' (and out of their control), they prefer a solution that they can see and understand (and, hence, that remains within their control).

Second and related, the adopted solution has a strong social as well as technical specificity. Undoubtedly this solution for Port Hope has been facilitated by the fact that the radioactive wastes in question are due to factory activities (radium and uranium refining) that engaged many of the past generations of the town's inhabitants and, thus, that contributed fundamentally to the building of the local economy and community. This means that, even if the 'theme park' concept might work for Port Hope, it is not necessarily an appropriate solution concept for other contaminated sites or for the long-run management of large quantities of high-level radioactive reactor wastes. The point is that, whatever the details of the site contamination or wastes, relationships of stakeholders in society will and must be built and maintained.

Third, and generalizing from this example, we see that our civilization is now knowingly constructing the 'sites' that not only will be under permanent observation from now on, but also will be observed and assessed by later civilizations, as the durable traces of our current way of life. In a sort of post-modern irony, we are creating relics for later generations of archaeologists. Are the Port Hope storage/disposal sites appropriately to be considered as analogous to ancient burial mounds? Or as a new form of trash mound?[4]

---

[4]Archaeologists use the term 'barrow' to designate a variety of forms of burial mound that are features of sites of prehistoric civilizations (*http://www.henge.org.uk/general/glossary.html*),and identify two main sub-types: the long barrow and the round barrow. The long barrow is an elongated, roughly rectangular structure and may contain many burial chambers. Many long barrows appear to have been in constant use, with burials being added over a period of centuries, the old bones being moved around to accommodate the new interment. Round barrows, more common than long barrows, typically contain only a single burial or two or three individuals. The 'midden', by contrast, is the term used for soil incorporating decomposed food waste (including shell and animal bone), ash, charcoal and other organic debris, and tools and other living debris, built up at places where people have lived or worked (*http://www.statemuseum.arizona.edu/azsite/featerms.shtml*).

In the process of trying to satisfy regulatory requirements, and to put at rest some of the public mistrust, many thousands of millions of dollars have been spent on scientific investigations, technical experiments, and a variety of deep and surface storage feasibility studies. Simulation models and quantitative risk assessments project hundreds and thousands of years into the future. The chemical, thermal, and physical properties of minute fissures in geological formations are studied with great assiduity, in the hope of proving (or disproving) a containment prospect. It has to be wondered whether an object, and a disposal process that engages such an extensive, costly, and meticulous scientific attention, which has become the focus of deep societal controversy for more than 50 years, and which is expected to remain the object of permanent surveillance for hundreds or even thousands of years, can be considered to be just a 'waste'. Clearly, the nuclear wastes that most people have never seen, have become folkloric in the deepest sense of the term. The class 'nuclear waste' is already an icon, a symbol of the great adventure (and the uncertain destiny) of our technological civilization. This is a historical liability not just for us but also for entire future societies (and not just future generations of our forms of society) which will inherit the requirement for watching over our wastes, as a part of the cultural (and not just material) legacy of our times.

This suggests, from a societal point of view, the identification of three interdependent components for a viable solution to a radioactive waste management or site stewardship problem. These are:

(i) *Technical and scientific expertise*: The development, application, and maintenance of scientific knowledge and technical competency to measure and to control the present and eventual exposure of living beings to radioactivity;

(ii) *Building social/societal relationships with the site*: The envisaging and invention, in social and symbolic terms, of how the relevant community (or communities) will relate to and interact with the sites, risks, wastes, records, etc.;

(iii) *Political/economic partnership*: Permitting to mobilize the relevant knowledge and resources for the implementation of an agreed societal strategy for stewardship.

The societal challenges—that is, the second and third of these components—underlie all operational considerations for site stewardship, and will deeply bear on the effectiveness of technical and scientific expertise. Political and economic partnerships depend on the relationships that the different stakeholders develop and maintain amongst themselves and with the site. Without these on-going partnerships, the relevant knowledge for stewardship will not be mobilized or renewed, and the motivation for long-term engagement will be fragile. The same is true, in a deeper and more diffuse way, for living with anthropogenic radioactive pollution of the habitable Earth.

SOCIETAL CRITERIA FOR STEWARDSHIP STRATEGIES

Attention to partnership building (the third component as identified above) has emerged all over the world since the 1980s as a pragmatic response by public authorities (and, sometimes, by nuclear industry actors themselves).[5] Attention to the question of the nature of the relationships to be established and maintained by society with the sites and the radioactive materials (the second component as identified above) is much less in evidence. One reason for this is that the issue has indeed been treated, but more implicitly than explicitly.

In effect, a specific answer to the type of 'relationship' envisaged has dominated in the technical and regulatory literature, without really being made the subject of focused discussion. Since the 1950s, the prevailing solution concept for anthropogenic radioactive waste disposal has been the operation of a suitably designed and situated 'Modern-model rubbish dump' (O'Connor 2003). The prevailing concepts here are 'containment' and the (provisional and permanent) 'disposal' of wastes through the competent action of an authority, based on a principle that we can summarize as 'Out of the public's sight, therefore out of the public's mind'.[6] The comfort and safety

[5]In many of those countries directly concerned by an obligation of radioactive waste management associated with nuclear energy production, there is an incontestable 'deficit' of stakeholder confidence concerning the decisions proposed by the established expert and government bodies for the 'long term disposal' of radioactive wastes. For example, in each of the UK, France, Germany, and Canada, public outcry and dispute has forced the abandonment of envisaged programmes and/or a major reconstruction of the institutional and policy framework. Confronted by public disquiet about the risks, and the very long time frames involved in monitoring wastes, the authorities have turned to various forms of stakeholder consultation.

[6]This cursory description dovetails with a well known industrial model of public order and public health, in which comfort and safety of the public are assured by technological means implemented by a delegated authority, through the control of delinquency and the collection and then expulsion of noxious elements outside the society. As long as the members of society follow the rules (about 'putting out the rubbish for collection'), they do not have to think about what happens next.

of the public are to be assured by technological means, implemented by a competent authority, to achieve the segregation of the noxious elements outside the main society.

Since the waste or contaminated site was placed 'off limits', implementation of the solution did not directly involve the public. So it was perhaps not realized that, here as elsewhere, the social dimension and the scientific/technical dimension of societal problem solving are complementary but distinct. And indeed, current controversy about radioactive waste disposal and site stewardship arises out of the fact that this solution concept—based on the principle of containment and segregation, 'out of public sight, out of the public's mind'—does not have widespread social acceptance. The historical record of controversies since the 1970s show that many people are not willing to trust the waste to stay put (for thousands and thousands of years); and, many people are not willing to trust the experts when they say that, suitably contained, the wastes will stay put.

This lack of confidence undoubtedly arises from many factors. One relevant factor may be the accumulation of experience with nuclear energy, radiation, and spent nuclear fuel, revealing the meticulous and costly character of achieving long term and secure containment. Another factor may be the growing general awareness about the problems of waste management in modern societies (far beyond radioactive wastes alone) and about the spectrum of side-effects, often unpredictable and sometimes long-lasting, of contemporary technological inventions. Another, certainly, is the heritage of suspicion about official cover-ups of accidents and risks and hence perceptions of the unreliability in risk management matters of government administration.

This does not mean that people are irrational about radioactivity. Rather, it suggests that certain features of the model 'out of the public's sight, out of the public's mind' are felt to be inappropriate—and hence unacceptable—for some classes of waste management or contaminated site problems.[7] The challenge, therefore, is not to seek

---

[7]Nor should this be taken as saying that the solution concept 'out of the public's sight, out of the public's mind', when formulated (from the 1950s) for radioactive waste disposal, was necessarily a wrong one. The point is that, whatever the expert and societal situation 50 years ago, the public today does not have much confidence in this model when applied to long-lived high activity radioactive wastes. As such, it may be that this mistrust of both nature (the material wastes) and human nature (the possible failings of the experts) has contributed to the push to introduce the concept of 'reversibility' (including retrievability), into the formulation and evaluation

to 'restore confidence' by communication strategies highlighting the reliability of containment and segregation. Rather it is to explore and characterize different solution concepts and to identify and assess with an open mind the factors that might affect this or that solution's acceptability.[8]

The Port Hope example has shown a situation where (i) there is consensus that the enduring presence of hazardous wastes is bothersome and requires a societal response, and also (ii) there is a feeling that, precisely because this lurking 'risk' is not easily forgotten, a solution that inspires confidence must engage a permanent vigil in which concerned stakeholders are directly involved. This may involve stewardship procedures whereby an economically active community, in partnership with overall regulatory authorities, is living close to (or even within) and maintaining a watch over the site.

Generalizing from this example, the following set of questions can be proposed to identify broad social criteria for acceptability, or not, of stewardship strategies proposed for a given site. In the list given below, these questions are first formulated in descriptive language (that is, what is the case or features of the proposed solution). Then, in italics, the questions are reframed with normative or prescriptive language (that is, to function as criteria of acceptability, as a function of circumstance, and stakeholder's point of view).

- Q.1. Is there official recognition of a waste, residual risk, or contamination problem at the site? (*Should there be official recognition of a waste, residual risk, or contamination problem?*)

---

of waste management options. A mistrust that an unobserved waste might not 'stay put' is probably more significant in the public mind than any economic/technical considerations of possible benefits from retrieval at a future date. People strongly insist—as in the example of Port Hope for low-level wastes and perhaps also in public outcry over UK deep disposal proposals—that the wastes should in some way remain 'visible' or 'accessible to the society' and that the communities or society in question should be able to maintain an active relationship with the site(s).

[8]It was perhaps not realised (or was forgotten) by the nuclear scientists and technical experts doing their jobs since the 1950s, that (i) changing political realities and societal concerns can require reappraisal—sometimes quite radical reappraisal—of originally envisaged technical solutions and (ii) in such circumstances, dialogue and discussion with the public might be desirable, even necessary, in order to assure the identification of a robust and appropriate solution concept. What this chapter is affirming is that, whatever the lapses of the past, such dialogue and discussion—an open societal deliberation—are now overdue. Fifty years of not realising may seem a long time. But, we should not be too harsh; a lapse of attention by one or two generations is nothing at all compared with the typical average lifetimes of radioactive wastes.

- Q.2. If yes, is there, or is there planned to be, active stewardship of the site? *(Should there be active stewardship of the site?)*
- Q.3. Is there, or is there planned to be, an on-going public interaction with the site as a dimension of the stewardship process? *(Should there be an on-going public interaction with the site?)*
- Q.4. If yes, is the 'historical liability' made a feature of the site's new public identity or use? *(Should the historical liability be made into a feature of the site's new identity and use?)*
- Q.5. If yes, what sorts of activity are mainly associated with the contamination or waste features, for example, public good activities such as education, training, and research; or private benefit activities such as recreation and tourism? *(What sorts of activities should be associated with the contamination or waste features?)*
- Q.6. What sort of socio-economic status and prestige is accorded to the stewardship process? *(What sort of socio-economic profile, prestige, or importance should be associated with the stewardship process?)*

Box 13.1 (adapted from O'Connor 2006 in Falck 2006), gives examples of societal stewardship concepts that can emerge from different sequences or combinations of answers YES/NO to the above questions.

The purpose of this typology process is not to pretend an exhaustive enquiry, but rather to highlight the very wide qualitative range of different models that can be, and have been, envisaged for stewardship of toxic waste or contaminated sites.

Each category of solution has its appropriate analogies and metaphors and, thus, privileges different aspects of social life, different types of prestige and status, different communities, different relationships, and so on. Specific technical, financial, management, record-keeping, monitoring, and communication procedures would have to be framed with recognition of these qualitative societal and institutional choices.

Suppose, for example, that there are jobs attached to the long-term site stewardship activity, and salaries to be paid. In what terms will the jobs of site warden be advertised? Who will be recruited (job opportunities for the locals?)? What will be the sorts of skills required? What skin colour? What salary scale? What will be the relation of the site wardens to others in the local community (if there is a local community), and the perception of their role by the rest of the society?

In the context of high-level radioactive waste disposal, variations of the shrine/temple concept have been offered by many different

Box 13.1: Maintaining a Vigil—What Societal Model?

- The response to *Q.1* might be–*No*, but with an on-going controversy about whether or not there is a significant danger associated with a site.

- The sequence [*Q.1 YES, Q.2 NO*] would imply identification of an 'orphan' site (haunted house, ghost town, etc.) and, therefore, to the question of the acceptability of this orphan status.

- The sequence [*Q.1 YES Q.2 YES Q.3 NO*] would lead to concepts of a segregated or isolated site, with restricted access. Appropriate analogies might be a dangerous natural site, a rubbish dump, a warehouse for storing dangerous goods, a mausoleum, and, on a different plane, a hospital or nursing home. Answers to Q.6 would then permit a characterization of the socio-economic status of the stewardship activity for the site.

- The sequence [*Q.1 YES Q.2 YES Q.3 YES Q.4 NO*] leads to suggestions for 'ordinary' uses of the site, for example, industrial or forestry production, or recreational activities (such as a golf course) which do not in any way rely on (or 'exploit' the stewardship status of the site). These activities will, however, be under a regulatory shadow, and answers to Q.5 and Q.6 would highlight whether or not a negative stigma is associated with the site.

- The sequence [*Q.1 YES Q.2 YES Q.3 YES Q.4 YES*] leads, by contrast, to suggestions for uses of the site that specifically rely on or 'exploit' the historical liability as a distinctive feature of the site. This could include 'ordinary' commercial uses of the site such as tourist and recreational activities, but which specifically play on the identity of the site (for example, an advertising gimmick of a golf course with grass that glows in the dark...), or installations such as a shrine or temple, museums, and educational facilities that draw substantively on the heritage of the site.

commentators. The concept has appeal partly because it evokes the 'eternal' character of the guardianship task. It might also have appeal because, by the establishment of a prestigious guardian task, the stewardship roles could offer prospects for unemployed graduates from schools for nuclear engineers. One could imagine generation after generation of monks roaming the corridors in solemn contemplation, each generation handing down, by algorithm, ceremony, and song, a unique competence to those that follow, maintaining an eternal vigil.[9]

The contrasting nursing home concept brings quite a different set of connotations: patience, compassion, meticulous care, weariness, maybe even mourning, anger, and sadness with the pain of a long condemnation to watch over the aging residents of the rest home.

The theme park option already illustrated by the Port Hope (Ontario) planning, brings once again a distinct set of job profiles and social relations.

The typical profile of nightwatchmen and rest home nursing staff is not, on the average, the same as would be expected for technicians/engineers in a temple, or for the animators of a theme park. Choosing the 'model' also means introducing considerations and consequences for sex roles, gender specificity (or prejudices), perhaps colour of skin, ethnicity, social status, and economic class. Each 'model' for watching over (or neglecting) the wastes privileges different aspects of social life, different types of prestige and status, different communities, and different relationships.

ETHICS AND POLITICAL EPISTEMOLOGY

Stakeholder participation can, it is widely argued, contribute to all aspects of radioactivity stewardship activities (Falck 2006). We focus here on the idea of stakeholders as partners with regulatory agencies and technical experts, through looking at stakeholder deliberation as a component in decisions about stewardship strategies.

In the modern world, it is conventional to seek a 'rational' (or, at least, reasoned) justification for a choice through a comparison between options. However, it is well known that, as soon as the span of choices involves or will have consequences for more than one person, judgements typically differ as to what is preferable. Each option for site management will produce distinct types and differing distributions of benefits, costs, and risks that will be looked at differently by each of the individuals or sectors of society concerned. Not only will the

---

[9]The monks and acolytes watching the computer screens for a signal of alarm or a flicker of untoward movement would perhaps be reminiscent of the soldiers in the 1976 film *Il Deserto dei Tartari* (*The Desert of the Tartars*) by Italian director Valerio Zurlini, who gazed at the horizon waiting eternally for an eventual invasion by nomad Tartars.

different protagonists concerned have divergent views about what is their interest, their right, or their due; they may also propose quite different principles for resolving this problem of social choice. The particular difficulties of radioactivity stewardship can be summarized in the following four points about environmental complexity and dilemmas of choice (cf, Gallopin et al. 2001; Faucheux and O'Connor 2000):

- The choices relate to complex entities, processes, or outcomes (the geological systems, biology, and social systems), each option being characterized by a range of attributes. Comparison of stewardship options means comparing a vector of attributes with a wide variety of concepts, units of measure, and criteria. It is not always easy to pass from a multiple criteria appraisal to a ranking of alternatives along a single scale.

- The consequences of decisions are distributed in time and, often, different aspects of outcomes (good and bad, as perceived by different constituencies) will have distinctive time profiles, for example, vegetation cover; diffusion or dilution of dangerous substances in water, rock, and soil; financial costs of monitoring; financial benefit streams, including stewardship salaries and eventual site use.

- There are various degrees of uncertainty due partly to natural system complexity and partly to social indeterminacies such as decisions not yet made or whose consequences are not yet known, or future interest in the site, and so on.

- A great variety of different reasons or principles can be put forward as justifications for the acceptability, or not, of different outcomes (including perceived uncertainties and risks, distribution of benefits and costs across different constituencies within society, or across generations through time. It may not be possible to respect all principles simultaneously (this may be the case for the judgments offered by a single person, or for the judgements offered by a range of sectors). Because the principles may be 'irreducible' (that is, incomparable, in the sense of being grounded in qualitatively different considerations), choice can be characterized by dilemmas and the need to make sacrifices of principle, rather than mere trade-offs on quantitative terms.

Stakeholder dialogues cannot eliminate these complexities and uncertainties. But they can be used to help build up a clear picture about the merits and demerits of site stewardship alternatives that present themselves to the relevant authorities and stakeholders in the society. Broadly speaking, three points must be addressed in order to build a structured stakeholder dialogue process:

- First, there must be an explicit identification of the relevant stakeholders, and the establishment of an institutional framework within which exchange of information and opinions can take place.
- Second, there must be a clear picture of the relevant site management options. For example, remediation and long-term site stewardship issues and options can be explored in terms of a small number of scenarios, each of which expresses distinct technological, economic, and governance features. Sometimes, stakeholders can be solicited to contribute to the framing of these scenarios.
- Third, there must be a clear expression of the criteria for selection of the stewardship strategies, with the variety of different criteria reflecting the full diversity of societal concerns.

If these conditions are met, then stakeholder dialogue can be organized as an evaluation of the different stewardship solutions or 'scenarios', within a multiple criteria framework that covers a full range of governance issues. The distinct stakeholder perspectives become visible through the contrasting judgments made in relation to each option or scenario. As systems analyst Rittel (1982) has remarked, a policy maker or analyst in this sort of situation becomes like a 'midwife of problems'. Decision making is understood as an argumentative or deliberative process, 'one of raising questions and issues towards which you can assume different positions, and with the evidence gathered and arguments built for and against these different positions'. In this perspective, well structured participatory processes can help with:

- Identification and development of elements of common problem definition and common language for all the parties concerned;
- Understanding of the assumptions underlying expert solution proposals and evaluation techniques, of the terms in which these techniques can contribute to reasoned decisions, and limitations to their application;
- Sharing of the reasons and justifications brought by the different social groups to the process;
- Status and respect given to participation by both professionals and lay people in the deliberative processes.

Commitment to a stewardship role, or to cooperating with site stewards, can emerge alongside and partly through misunderstandings, disputes, and conflicts. Processes of information sharing and debate can be powerful for building goodwill, respect, and trust. A constructive stakeholder interaction can sometimes permit the emergence of novel solution ideas, including compromises between different performance criteria.

In this deliberative perspective, the idea is that radioactivity stewardship strategies, presented as 'scenarios', are identified to be assessed in a comparative way by people bringing a variety of preoccupations, expertises, and points of view (see Box 13.1).[10] For example, in the terms developed, above, we could focus on a range of different social models for a vigil concerning radioactivity wastes, such as the rubbish dump, temple/shrine, haunted burial site, and nursing home. We have seen that solution concepts may be qualitatively different, not just in the ways that they distribute the radioactivity dose (or risks of a dose), but in the ways that they build the symbolic meanings and social relations around the distribution of the (possible) dose.

The 'ethical' dimension of stewardship consists, in simple terms, of the articulation of the different principles that may underlie operational criteria. We can thus consider the spectrum of stewardship strategies as being, from one perspective or another, candidates for ethically principled actions, meaning that, they satisfy or respond to particular criteria of good or sound practice that are suggested by members of the community (cf. Fleming 2003). Box 13.2 provides a compilation of 'ethical bottom lines' typically suggested for the contemporary radioactivity stewardship domain.

Concluding Remarks

This chapter addresses features of some of the very great challenges of our times. It does not pretend to resolve them, rather simply points to the importance of human competence and capacity along planes of emotional intelligence and care, as much as technological expertise. This goes deeper than stakeholder dialogue as usually construed.

[10]No attempt has been made here to define categories of stakeholders in radioactivity stewardship. Obviously, they cover all of 'us and them' for a long time; but any operational framing depends on the specific situation. Nor, in this short chapter, is any space given to the problem of 'representation' in any real deliberation process (meaning, in what sense the persons participating in a process are taken to speak for the interests and concerns of others). Nor do we do any more than evoke in a partly implicit way, the evident problem of asymmetries in power, speech, influence, and communication capacities, and so on. All these considerations (that, among other things, justify and account for our use of the term 'political epistemology', here borrowed from Salleh 1984) can be explored reflexively within a deliberation process; which does not mean they will be resolved to the full satisfaction of all concerned.

Box 13.2: Radioactivity Stewardship: Ethical Bottom Lines

- PR.1 Have the responsibilities of existing parties been appropriately assigned? For example:
  - Application of a principle of national autonomy/responsibility ('take care of your own wastes' at national scale);
  - Application of the principle that 'the polluter pays';
  - Clear expression of, and respect for, local, national, and international regulatory conditions.
- PR.2 Have responsibilities 'towards other parties' in the short term been adequately addressed? For example:
  - Health security to workers and the public on or close to the site;
  - Security against attack in the face of external or internal sources of aggression.
- PR.3 Have responsibilities 'towards other parties' in the longer term been adequately addressed? For example:
  - A 'sustainability' principle of inter-generational responsibility (don't pass on problems to others that you cannot cope with yourself);
  - A thorough characterization of risks/uncertainties/future contingencies (with reference to: the dangerous substances, the engineering works, the living environment, and future societal evolutions);
  - An application of some version of the principle of precaution;
  - Is there likely long term stability of the necessary knowledge base (for example, transmission of records, specialised know-how, local knowledge) for competent stewardship?
- PR.4 Has available technical knowhow and systems science been mobilised? For example:
  - Rigorous profiling (in technical, medical, and sociological terms) of the exposure risks;
  - Standards of best practice (technical reliability, simplicity, ...);
  - Monitoring procedures attentive to the full spectrum of identified risks/uncertainties/future contingencies.
- PR.5 Is the solution economically viable? For example:
  - Are the immediate costs of stewardship affordable with the available resources?
  - Clear picture of the trade-offs and relationship between clean-up and stewardship;
  - Are the solutions cost-effective for the identified risk reduction results?
  - Are there major financial costs shifted into the future?

- Reasonable prospects of mobilizing resources for the forecast stewardship costs in the longer term?
- PR.6 Does the solution enhance the prestige of the host communities and other stakeholder groups closely associated with the residual/waste site?
  - Viable partnership between local and national stakeholders (for example, agreed distribution of responsibilities; legal mandate for stewardship activity; agreement on bases for financing of different cost components; etc.)
  - Site specificities clearly in evidence?
  - Local competencies clearly in evidence?
  - Well-defined framework for on-going involvement of stakeholders in stewardship oversight and review;
  - Links to educational and training activities at local and wider scales.

Sources: The initial 'Ethical Bottom Lines' checklist concept was developed in O'Connor (2003); the full 'checklist' as it appears here was presented in a conference paper by Chamaret and O'Connor (2005); a slightly abridged version of the checklist is also found in Falck (2006: 48–9).

In formal terms, it is proposed above that a comparative evaluation of radioactivity stewardship options can be undertaken from a variety of different points of view corresponding to distinct stakeholder preoccupations. Each stakeholder group will express different criteria of adequacy or quality in relation to each of the governance issues. Tensions, conflicts of interests, uncertainties, and dissent (amongst scientists as well as decision makers, administrators, and stakeholders from different walks of commercial activity and civil society) can be explored by comparison of the judgements made about the good and less good features of each solution concept or implementation strategy.

The hope here is that the multi-stakeholder deliberation can be an opportunity for a compassionate investigation into the social meanings as well as the scientific/technical quality of the different decision options and policy choices. There are many points that might be developed from this. The main one, for present purposes, is to insist that this 'deliberation' is not only a reasoning and listening process, but also has agnostic and existential dimensions.

The chapter has tried to evoke, through the example of anthropogenic radioactivity, the sense in which human economy and habitat are built up through relations of intimacy and mutual compatibility, and also incompatibility. As writers such as Susan Griffin (1978) and Ariel Salleh (1984) have suggested, our knowing is partly obtained in the fracturings of material reality: knowledge of self and of others, the touches, ecstasies and agonies, and dramas that life unfolds; the loves, the hates, dislocations, and impossibilities of being in this world. If we wish to build a base for addressing challenges of human health and ecosystem health in our current times, then we need to ask what it is like, not just to use and take (our well-being or happiness level according to certain strands of utilitarian philosophy and instrumental reason), but also, empathically, what it is like to be used up, contaminated, corrupted, transformed, loved, caressed, bulldozed, transmuted, erased, degraded, and dissolved? Our site stewardship strategies (extending, at the end of the day, to the whole planet) may fail not because they are technically deficient but because they do not mobilize human hope, compassion, and renewal capacity. Respect for multiple and sometimes divergent criteria of quality do not make the painfulness of dilemmas about living with radioactivity disappear. It does not mean the dissolving of all differences and conflicts. But it can help with willingness to accept limits, to accept vulnerability and sadness, to give weight to deeply felt considerations of identity and community, of dignity, honour, status, or prestige, and to make thoughtful compromises based on the hope of shared benefits to come.

References

Baudrillard, J., (1990), *La Transparence du Mal*, Paris: Galilée.

Catton, William R. Jr., (1989), 'Cargoism and Technology and the Relationship of these Concepts to Important Issues such as Toxic Waste Disposal Siting', in Dennis L. Peck (ed.), *Psychosocial Effects of Hazardous Toxic Waste Disposal on Communities*, Springfield, Illinois: Charles C. Thomas, pp. 99–117.

Chamaret, A. and M. O'Connor, (2005), 'Risk, Legitimacy and Governance: CSR, Stakeholder Dialogue, and Indicator Systems through the Life Cycle of Uranium', Paper for the International Conference URANIUM 2005 held at the International Atomic Engergy Agency, Vienna, June 2005. Available in *Uranium Production and Raw Materials for the Nuclear Fuel Cycle: Supply and Demand, Economics, the Environment and Energy Security*, IAEA Proceedings Series, International Atomic Energy Agency, Vienna, May 2006, pp. 84–95.

Chamaret, A., M. O'Connor, and G. Récoché, (2007), 'Top-Down/Bottom-Up Approach for Developing Sustainable Development Indicators for Mining: Application to the Arlit Uranium Mines (Niger)', *International Journal of Sustainable Development*, Vol. 10: pp. 161–74.

Engels, F., 1883, *Dialectique de la Nature*. Translated from German by Emile Bottigelli (1968, Paris: Editions Sociales.)

Falck, W.E. (ed.), (2006), *Management of Long Term Radiological Liabilities: Stewardship Challenges*, IAEA Technical Report No. 450, Vienna: International Atomic Energy Agency, Vienna, October.

Faucheux S. and C. Hue, (2001), 'From Irreversibility to Participation: Towards a Participatory Foresight for the Governance of Collective Environmental Risks', *Journal of Hazardous Materials*, Vol. 86, pp. 223–43.

Faucheux, S. and M. O'Connor, (2000), 'Technosphère versus écosphère. Quel arbitrage? Choix technologiques et menaces environnementales: signaux faibles, controverses et décision', *Futuribles*, No. 251.

Fleming P.A., (2003), 'Stakeholder Confidence: Observations from the Viewpoint of Ethics', in *Public Confidence in the Management of Radioactive Waste: The Canadian Context*, NEA Forum on Stakeholder Confidence, Workshop Proceedings, Ottawa, Canada, 14–18 October 2002, Paris: OECD, pp. 169–76.

Gallopín, G., S. Funtowicz, M. O'Connor, and J. Ravetz, (2001), 'Science for the 21st Century: From Social Contract to the Scientific Core', *International Journal of Social Science*, Vol. 168, pp. 209–29.

Gourlay, K.A., (1992), *World of Waste: Dilemmas of Industrial Development*, London: Zed Books.

Griffin, S., (1978), *Woman and Nature: The Roaring Inside Her*, London: The Women's Press.

O'Connor, M., (1994), 'Liberazione dell'energia, degrado della vita', *Capitalismo Natura Socialismo*, Vol. 11, pp. 38–52.

——, (1994), *Is Capitalism Sustainable? Political Economy and the Politics of Ecology*, New York: Guilford Publications.

——, (1999), 'Dialogue and Debate in a Post-Normal Practice of Science: A Reflection', *Futures*, Vol. 31, pp. 671–87.

——, (2003), 'Building Relationships with the Waste', in *Public Confidence in the Management of Radioactive Waste: The Canadian Context*, NEA Forum on Stakeholder Confidence, Workshop Proceedings, Ottawa, Canada, 14–18 October 2002, Paris: OECD, pp. 177–90.

——, O'Connor, M. (2006), 'Societal Challenges', in W.E. Falck (ed.), Management of Long Term Radiological Liabilities: Stwardship Challenges, IAEA Technical Report No. 450, International Atomic Energy Agency, Vienna, October.

O'Connor, M. and S. van den Hove, (2001), 'Prospects for Concertation on Nuclear Risks and Technological Options: Innovations in Governance Practices for Sustainable Development in the European Union', *Journal of Hazardous Materials*, Vol. 86, pp. 77–99.

Rittel, H., (1982), 'Systems Analysis of the "First and Second Generations"', in P. Laconte, J. Gibson, and A. Rapoport (eds), *Human and Energy Factors in Urban Planning*, NATO Advanced Study Institutes Series, The Hague: Martinus Nijhoff, pp. 35–63.

Salleh, A., (1984), Contribution to the Critique of Political Epistemology', *Thesis Eleven*, Vol. 8, No. 1, pp. 23–43.

14

Ignoring the Costs
Energy Planning and the Dismal Economics of Nuclear Power in India

M.V. RAMANA AND J.Y. SUCHITRA

> Gatsby believed in the green light, the orgiastic future that year by year recedes before us. It eluded us then, but that's no matter—tomorrow we will run faster, stretch out our arms further.... And one fine morning—So we beat on, boats against the current, borne back ceaselessly into the past.
>
> F. Scott Fitzgerald, *The Great Gatsby*

It is no secret that India has a problem with meeting the demand for electricity. Power cuts are common and many of those who can afford them resort to the use of diesel generators, battery inverters, or other forms of private electricity supply. This problem is not new. The National Electricity Plan of 2004 put out by the Central Electricity Authority, a key agency responsible for electricity sector planning, was explicit:

In spite of this massive addition in generation, transmission and distribution capacity over the last fifty-seven years, growth in demand for power has always exceeded the generation capacity augmentation. The country faced energy shortage of 7.1 per cent and peaking shortage of 11.2 per cent during 2003–4. Although the country has achieved capacity addition of about 1,00,000 MW over the last five decades, the capacity achieved is far below the target set during various plans. During the 8th and 9th plans the achievement was only about 50 per cent of the target. The capacity addition shortfall in various plans has resulted in increased power shortages in the country. (CEA 2005: 3.1)

The recent Expert Committee on Integrated Energy Policy set up by the Planning Commission opines, 'The energy policies that we have adopted since independence ... have encouraged and sustained many inefficiencies in the use and production of energy. We pay one of the highest prices for energy in purchasing power parity terms... The challenge is to ensure adequate supply of energy at the least possible cost' (Planning Commission 2006).

This scenario would lead one to expect that decisions on budgetary allocations would be based on sound analyses of the economics of different energy sources. This expectation is belied by the continued and ample financial support offered to atomic energy by the government.

The DAE offers two arguments for why India should expand nuclear power. The first argument starts with the idea that to increase electricity supply and ensure energy security, India should tap all available sources of energy. Then, all other sources are described as limited in availability or otherwise unsuitable (for example, wind energy is intermittent, solar power is expensive, coal is polluting). Atomic energy is then posited as the only option for meeting future power needs because the DAE's plans of using the so-called closed cycle and breeder reactors that generate more fissile material than they consume allow it to claim that it is a virtually limitless source of electricity (Bhabha and Prasad 1958; Bhoje 2001; Ramanna 1985; Shah 2002). Towards this end, the DAE has routinely drawn up ambitious plans, none of which have been fulfilled.

The second argument is that nuclear energy is cheaper than alternative sources, primarily coal. This chapter examines this latter argument in some detail. We look, in particular, at the economics of breeder reactors, which are the basis for the DAE's ambitious plans. We then discuss some ways in which the DAE has managed to garner support for its activities despite continued abysmal performance.

HISTORY OF THE NUCLEAR PROGRAMME IN INDIA

The nuclear programme was established in August 1948. That it started barely a year after independence is evidence of the importance accorded to the atomic quest. The main personalities involved in determining its contours were Jawaharlal Nehru, the first Prime Minister of India and Homi Bhabha, a charismatic physicist and the first head of the DAE. For various reasons of biography, interests, and outlook, Nehru unstintingly supported Bhabha's grandiose plans for nuclear energy in India (Abraham 1997; Anderson 1975).

Dream Sequences

The DAE's plans for nuclear energy in the country are centred on a three-stage programme (Bhabha and Prasad 1958; Chidambaram and Ganguly 1996). These plans were first announced in 1954, and the DAE offers regular and frequent expressions of commitment to this goal. The first stage of the three-phase strategy involves the use of uranium fuel in heavy water reactors (HWRs), followed by reprocessing of the irradiated spent fuel to extract plutonium.[1] In the second stage, the plutonium thus obtained is used to fuel breeder reactors. The third stage involves breeder reactors using thorium.

All of India's 17 existing reactors are part of the first phase. So are five of the six facilities under construction. One experimental breeder, the Fast Breeder Test Reactor (FBTR), constitutes the only operational part of the second phase. Its performance does not inspire confidence and has been marked by construction delays, numerous accidents, and frequent shutdowns (CAG 1993; Prasad 2001; Suresh Kumar et al. 2002). In October 2004, after 20 years of planning and repeated postponements, the DAE finally began building the first industrial-scale Prototype Fast Breeder Reactor (PFBR). Even by the nuclear establishment's optimistic timetable, thorium-based breeders will not start operating until the middle of this century (Grover and Chandra 2006), decades behind schedule.

Great Expectations

On the basis of this three-stage programme, Bhabha announced that there would be 8000 MW of nuclear power in the country by 1980 (Hart 1983: 61). As the years progressed, these predictions increased: the figure offered in 1962 was 20,000 MW to 25,000 MW by 1987 and that given in 1971 was 43,500 MW by 2000. All this was before a single unit of nuclear electricity was produced in the country.

---

[1] In heavy water reactors, heavy water is used to remove the heat produced and to slow down the neutrons produced by nuclear fission. The irradiated fuel (spent fuel) has to be stored under water for a few years to remove the heat and allow the most radioactive elements to decay. In the closed fuel cycle, the spent fuel is then reprocessed. Reprocessing involves the separation of the different categories of wastes in the spent fuel, and as a by-product generates plutonium, which is further treated and used as fuel in breeder reactors. Breeder reactors are typically fuelled by a mixture of uranium and plutonium and have a surrounding blanket made of uranium or thorium. When neutrons escaping from the reactor are absorbed by these blankets, they produce plutonium or uranium-233.

The reality was quite different. Installed capacity in 1979–80 was about 600 MW, about 950 MW in 1987, and 2720 MW in 2000. As of September 2007, nuclear power amounts to just 4120 MW, less than 3 per cent of the country's total electricity generation capacity. Six reactors with a combined capacity of 3160 MW are currently being constructed.

The only explanation that the DAE has offered for its failures has been to blame the cessation of foreign cooperation following the 1974 nuclear weapons test. While the sanctions did slow down the growth of nuclear power in India, they also provided the DAE with an opportunity: each development, no matter how small or routine, could be portrayed as a heroic success, achieved in the face of staunch opposition by other countries and impossible odds, while any failures could be explained away as a result of other countries' attempts to block India's technological advancements.

Despite this less than modest history, the DAE has continued to make extravagant predictions. The current projections are for 20,000 MW by the year 2020 and for 275,000 MW by the year 2052 (Grover and Chandra 2006). The likelihood of these goals being met is slim at best despite the hype surrounding the Indo-US nuclear deal. But even if they are met, nuclear power would still contribute only about 8–10 per cent of the projected electricity capacity in 2020, and about 20 per cent in 2052. There is, thus, little chance of nuclear electricity becoming a significant source of power for India anytime over the next several decades.

ECONOMICS OF THE INDIAN NUCLEAR ENERGY PROGRAMME

The promise offered by the DAE is not only that nuclear power would form an important component of India's electricity supply, but also that it would be cheap.

Shifting Targets

Since nuclear reactors were clearly much more expensive than the staple source of electricity in India, namely coal-based thermal power, the DAE's strategy was to compare nuclear costs with thermal plants that were situated far away from coal mines, thereby increasing the transport cost of coal and thus the fuelling costs of thermal power. To put the following figures in perspective, we note that one-third of India's coal plants are located close to a mine pithead, and another quarter or more are within 500 kilometres of a pithead.

As early as 1958, Homi Bhabha stated, 'during the *next 10 to 15 years*...the costs of [nuclear] power [will] compare *very favourably* with the cost of power from conventional sources in many areas' (emphases added) (Bhabha and Prasad 1958).[2] The 'many areas' referred to regions that were remote from coalfields. In the 1980s, the DAE stated that the cost of nuclear power 'compares quite favourably with coal fired stations located 800 km away from the pithead and in the 1990s would be even cheaper than coal fired stations at pithead' (Srinivasan 1985). But even at the end of the 1990s, the DAE could only offer: the 'cost of nuclear electricity generation in India remains competitive with thermal [electricity] for plants located about 1,200 km away from coal pit head, when full credit is given to long term operating cost especially in respect of fuel prices'. (Nema 1999).

Comparative Cost of Electricity Generation

In actual fact, even the 1,200 km claim does not hold up to scrutiny. The costs of generating electricity at the Kaiga atomic power station and the Raichur Thermal Power Station (RTPS) VII—both plants of similar size and vintage—have been compared using the standard discounted cash flow methodology (Ramana et al. 2005). The coal for RTPS VII was assumed to come from mines that were 1,400 km away. The comparison showed that nuclear power is significantly more expensive for a wide range of realistic parameters. These results are summarized in Figure 14.1.

One particularly key variable is the discount rate, a measure of the value of capital. Nuclear power, because of its capital-intensive nature, is competitive only for low discount rates. In a country where there are multiple demands on capital for infrastructural projects, including in the electricity sector, such low discount rates are not realistic. At market rates of return on investment, nuclear power could be 50 per cent more expensive. This comparison also does not include the significant expenses involved in dealing with irradiated spent fuel (Ramana and Suchitra 2007).

---

[2]Bhabha's claims about the economics of nuclear power were soundly rebutted elsewhere, but such work does not seem to have been widely known in India. Rosenstein-Rodan (1959) is particularly trenchant on Bhabha's idea that because of the shortage of electricity in India, the nation should embark on an ambitious and expensive nuclear programme saying 'When a man is hungry he may pay a high price for a meal, but he should not proceed to buy a restaurant'.

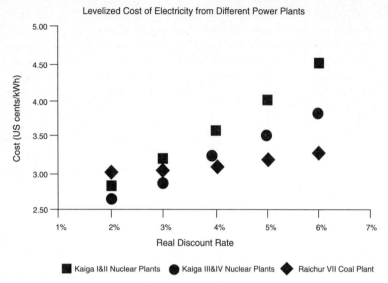

Figure 14.1:   Levelized Cost (the bare generation cost, which does not include other components of electricity tariff like transmission and distribution charges) of Kaiga I&II (operating nuclear reactors), Kaiga III&IV (nuclear reactors under construction; projected costs), and the Raichur VII (operating coal fueled thermal plant) as a Function of Real Discount Rate (a measure of the value of capital after taking out the effects of inflation) at 80 per cent Capacity Factor

These are the results of the most recent debate on the cost of nuclear power. Over the decades, other independent researchers, outside of the DAE, had established the same conclusion using cost values of those times (Bose 1981; Reddy 1990). Important among these was Amulya Reddy, a physical chemist who turned his attention to energy and rural development issues. In the 1980s, he pointed out several problems with the way the DAE was calculating the costs. Reddy went on to present his comparison of the costs of electricity from Indian heavy water nuclear power plants and coal plants at a National Workshop on Nuclear Power organized at the Indian Institute of Science (IISc), Bangalore in December 1988, which involved DAE officials and members of civil society (Reddy 1988). The meeting was part of a debate about whether a reactor should be constructed in Kaiga but Reddy's convincing demonstration that the Kaiga reactor would be expensive made no difference: the construction of the reactor continued.

A Costly Breed

The current projections of the DAE for the rapid expansion of nuclear energy are based primarily on the expansion of breeder reactors—in 2052, they constitute 260,000 MW of the projected 275,000 MW. Essential for this programme is the reprocessing of spent fuel from nuclear reactors to extract plutonium and fabricate fuel for breeder reactors.

There are no official cost estimates of reprocessing in India. Nevertheless, the DAE justifies reprocessing as both a waste management (of spent fuel) technique and as a means to generate plutonium. Based on government expenditures on the most recent reprocessing plant in the country, the Kalpakkam Reprocessing Plant (KARP), reprocessing each kilogramme of spent fuel is estimated to cost around Rs 26,000 ($590) (Ramana and Suchitra 2007). Currently, the tariff for electricity from nuclear reactors does not include this expense; the DAE bears it entirely (Thakur and Chaurasia 2005). In the DAE's analysis of the economics of Pressurized Heavy Water Reactors (PHWRs), 'the cost of waste disposal has been assumed to have trade off with the amount of reprocessed fuel generated for next stage of nuclear power programme (*sic*)' (Nema 1999). In other words, 'the economic viability of the first generation of nuclear power reactors is premised upon the viability of the second' (Muralidharan 1985).

One would expect that to follow consistent accounting, the DAE would include the production cost of plutonium in its cost estimates of electricity from breeder reactors. This is not the case either. The DAE maintains that the plutonium is available at 'zero cost' because breeder reactors allow for the production of more plutonium than they consume (Govindarajan 2003). But this argument is financially unsound because the plutonium generated will be available only after the reactor has stopped generating electricity and is decommissioned. The economically sound way of taking this future value of plutonium into account is by adding the cost of plutonium for fuelling the reactor and deducting the present value of the expected sale amount from that. This would only make a minor difference (Suchitra and Ramana forthcoming).

This 'cost-free plutonium' argument allows the DAE to posit that electricity from breeder reactors will be cheaper than thermal power (Jagannathan 2003). But the cost of the plutonium required for the initial fuelling of the PFBR core amounts to nearly half the projected construction cost of the reactor. Other major cost

Table 14.1: Difference in Cost of Electricity from Breeder and Heavy Water Reactors

Real Discount Rate (per cent)	Capacity Factor of PFBR (per cent)	Levelized Cost difference (cents per kWh)
5	80	1.62 (43 per cent higher)
6	80	2.01 (49 per cent higher)
6	50	4.05 (98 per cent higher)

Note: Preliminary figures.

components of breeder reactors include the fuel fabrication and reprocessing costs. Including these, our preliminary assessment of the cost of generating electricity at the PFBR (see Table 14.1) is that it will be significantly more expensive compared to electricity from the DAE's own HWRs (Suchitra and Ramana, forthcoming).

The DAE's argument that the 'primary objective of the PFBR is to demonstrate techno-economic viability of fast breeder reactors on an industrial scale' (Chetal et al. 2006) is thus invalid. Our results show that the PFBR will not be viable, even assuming the DAE's own optimistic projections of costs. If the time and cost overruns that are typical of the DAE do occur with the PFBR too, then its economic viability will be further reduced.

Games People Play

The DAE's claims about the economics of nuclear power are based on estimated costs rather than actual costs. Some components of the cost, for instance, the Operations and Maintenance (O&M) cost, are merely pegged at a specific percentage of the capital cost, with no basis to arrive at this. The DAE does not even keep track of certain cost components, such as the cost of radioactive waste management. It merely assigns an arbitrary figure (typically Rs 0.05 per unit) as the cost. Similarly, the figures taken for capital costs of nuclear reactors do not reflect the cost and time overruns that all DAE-built reactors have experienced.

The costing methodology adopted by the DAE is also flawed. For example, as already described, the DAE makes an invalid assumption about plutonium being free in the case of breeder reactors. Similarly, rather than including the cost of heavy water as a capital expense, it is assumed to be leased from the DAE (Muralidharan 1988). In addition to this implicit subsidy, the DAE only charges less than half the actual production cost of heavy water (Ramana 2007).

The DAE's claim that nuclear power is cheap is, therefore, based on notional cost figures and the use of unsound economic methodology. DAE officials have, nevertheless, popularized this claim extensively, presumably in the hope that it will become an accepted norm.

Challenging this claim is not easy and the DAE has thwarted independent analyses in various ways. A key roadblock that a serious researcher faces is with respect to data. Even standard sources of data, such as expenditure budgets of the central government, and performance budgets and annual reports of the DAE, tend to confound the researcher in many ways. Data are found to be not consistent across the years, heads of demand and expenditure are left unexplained, data on some facilities are simply not provided at all, some line items appear and disappear over the years, and data get aggregated in ways that hide the specific expenditures. In the case of most nuclear facilities (the exception is reactors because their electricity generation is publicly known), the level of performance (production figures, throughputs) is never revealed.

The 2005 Right to Information Act has not helped either. A series of petitions were sent by the authors to various units of the DAE requesting economic information pertaining to the PFBR. Practically all these requests were denied on the grounds that the disclosure of such information would 'prejudicially affect the sovereignty and integrity of India, the security, strategic, scientific or economic interests of the State, relation with foreign States or lead to incitement of an offence'. The authors' arguments that the denial of economic information constituted misuse of the relevant section of the Act have been in vain.

All of this implies that the DAE is unwilling to share its data in the public domain. Despite claims about nuclear power being cheap, the DAE does not maintain good data and is not really serious about economic considerations. The latter proposition is illustrated by Bhabha's dictum: 'no power is as expensive as no power'. To this we may add an anecdote reflecting the DAE's view of economic costs in general. During the tea break that followed Reddy's lecture at the 1988 workshop at IISc mentioned earlier, a senior DAE official was overheard exclaiming, 'what does nuclear power have to do with discount rates?'

Unfortunately, there is no forum where the DAE can be held accountable for poor data, faulty methodology, flawed analyses, or secretive behaviour.

Denial in the Nuclear Environment

So far we have focused on how nuclear energy policy has largely ignored economic considerations. In this milieu it should be no surprise that environmental and other societal considerations have played no part in decision making either. This is true of energy planning in general.[3] An illustration of such neglect is the Planning Commission's recent *Integrated Energy Policy*, a document that is intended to develop a long-term strategy to meet India's energy needs given the country's burgeoning economic growth. Of the 13 chapters in the document, only the last chapter deals with energy-environment linkages. And climate change, among the most important of environmental concerns today and offered as a motivation for a large-scale expansion of nuclear power, is literally the last sub-section.

While the general trend is to ignore environmental considerations, the nuclear establishment goes even further in simply denying any impact. For example, in response to several studies showing an increased incidence of congenital deformities amongst the largely indigenous inhabitants of the areas surrounding the uranium mines in Jaduguda (Gadekar et al., forthcoming), the chairman and managing director of the Uranium Corporation of India Limited (UCIL) simply stated: 'There is no health hazard in and around Jaduguda caused by our uranium mines' (Biswas 1999). His only rationale was that radiation levels are 'well within the stipulations' laid down by the International Commission on Radiological Protection. Contrary to scientific evidence that any amount of radiation, no matter how low, is harmful, the nuclear establishment, like its counterparts elsewhere, hides behind the notion of an 'acceptable level' of radiation. It should be no wonder that A.N. Mullick, who served as UCIL's chief medical officer for 25 years, claimed: 'I have not come across any radiation-related ailments during my entire career' (Tiwari 1999). This focus on radiation also ignores another environmental consequence of uranium mining: the presence of heavy metals and chemicals used during processing in the effluents. These also have public health impacts.

---

[3]The absence of systematic thought and effort towards making India's energy system sustainable has been soundly criticized by a leading ecological economist: 'Sustainable practices are becoming post-modern, ornamental experiments, kindly regarded as harmless by the economic and political powers. You do a little water harvesting while I build a very big dam. You build a breeder reactor while I build some biogas and solar energy capacity in rural areas' (Martinez-Alier 2006).

In addition to routine environmental releases, nuclear energy also comes with the risk of catastrophic accidents. The DAE has typically denied this possibility. For example, following the Tokaimura accident in Japan, the head of the DAE claimed that there was no possibility of any such nuclear accident in India because the DAE had a track record of '150 reactor years of safe operation' (Datta 1999).

One major concern the world over about nuclear power has been the production of radioactive wastes; it has been an important factor in the decision by some European countries to phase out nuclear power.[4] The DAE, on the other hand, has not even acknowledged that this could be a problem. Its standard response when the question is raised is that they do not consider spent fuel as waste but 'a resource to extract plutonium from' (Chidambaram 1996). Given this attitude, the long-lived nature of radioactive wastes and the likely impact on future generations have not informed either the DAE's policies or decision making regarding energy in the country.

POLITICS

The above sections show that the DAE's claims on the projected growth of nuclear energy and its cost competitiveness do not stand up to scrutiny and analyses. Yet it continues to receive unstinted financial and political support from the government. This is reflected in the extravagant budgets of the DAE. For example, in the late 1950s, the DAE cornered over a quarter of all resources devoted to science and technology development in the country (Abraham 1993: 177). The only period when the DAE did not get all that they asked for and, therefore, considered 'a period of total dryness and stagnation' was the early 1990s, a period marked by cutbacks on government spending as part of economic liberalization (Iype 2000). But this trend was reversed with the 1998 nuclear weapons tests: since then the DAE's budget has increased from Rs 18.4 billion in 1997–8 to Rs 50.3 billion in 2006–7, that is, more than doubled even in real terms. In comparison, the 2006–7 budget of the

[4]The German Federal Environment Ministry, for example, says, 'A problem yet to be solved, however, is the management of the radioactive wastes from nuclear power plants. Such wastes remain radioactive for millions of years—a dangerous legacy for future generations. For this reason the Federal Government decided to completely phase out the production of electricity from nuclear power' (GFEM 2007).

Renewable Energy Ministry, responsible for 10.4 GW of installed electrical capacity, was about Rs 3.87 billion.[5]

Some possible explanations for the DAE's ability to circumvent accountability and continue garnering resources are suggested below.

In High Places

The institutional structure under which the atomic establishment operates allows it to evade parliamentary checks and balances. Unlike most policy matters where the Cabinet has the ultimate authority, the DAE was set up in 1954 under the direct charge of the Prime Minister. This structure makes it difficult for most politicians or bureaucrats, let alone commoners, to challenge the DAE's policies or practices.[6]

In addition, many official decision-making bodies that set policies that impinge on nuclear matters are constrained to include members of the nuclear establishment. For example, one always finds DAE officials on various energy-related committees of the Planning Commission or the Central Electric Authority or the Confederation of Indian Industry. It has been observed that since the 1960s, 'the Planning Commission has tended to accept the DAE's recommendations because (i) the latter body is said to be technically qualified to pass judgement; (ii) there is a desire to avoid internal disputes amongst government offices' (Hart 1983: 35).

[5]The contribution of renewable energy sources to actual electricity generation would be smaller because these are intermittent sources of power. But these often have much lower maintenance costs. Further, exploitation of most of these sources started in earnest only relatively recently and there is ample scope for improvement.

[6]As a well known politician, Jayanthi Natarajan, was to despair publicly, 'I have been a Member of the Parliamentary Consultative Committee for Defence and Atomic Energy, and have tried time and again to raise issues relating to public safety, both at Parliamentary Committee hearings, and in the Rajya Sabha, and have achieved precious little for my pains. Since I was an MP (Member of Parliament) at the time, and a pretty aggressive one, I had to be dealt with. But they simply drowned me with totally obscure and incomprehensible scientific terms and explanations, which sounded impressive, and meant nothing. The rest was simply not forthcoming because they claimed it was "classified". I have repeatedly raised the issue of the hazards of radiation leaks, safety procedures, and environmental contamination, that might flow from the atomic power station at Kalpakkam, but have always received the bland and meaningless reply that the radiation was "within acceptable limits"' (Natarajan 2003).

The DAE also tries hard to maintain its position as the sole repository of nuclear expertise.[7] The 1962 Atomic Energy Act vests the power 'to produce, develop, use and dispose of atomic energy and carry out research into any matters connected' with the DAE. Few academic institutions offer courses in nuclear engineering, and even their graduates necessarily have to seek employment with the DAE. Therefore, even the government feels compelled to seek the DAE's advice on all nuclear matters.

Being on the inside helps. For instance, the recent Expert Committee on Integrated Energy Policy of the Planning Commission recommended that 'India has to succeed in realising the three-stage development process...and thereby tap its vast thorium resource to become truly energy independent beyond 2050. Continuing support to the three-stage development of India's nuclear potential is essential' (Planning Commission 2006), paying no heed to cost considerations. Similarly, the Central Electric Authority's Expert Committee on Fuels for Power Generation opined that 'nuclear energy has the potential of providing long-term energy security to the country and all research and development efforts must be pursued to realize this objective' but with the explicit admission that 'the cost of generation of nuclear projects have not been calculated (*sic*)' (CEA 2004: vi).

The institutional structure in which the DAE operates allows it to effectively stonewall external appraisal. Even the Comptroller and Auditor General (CAG), whose function is to enhance accountability of various public sector organizations and departments to the Parliament and State Legislatures, has been unsuccessful in doing so. The CAG, trying to estimate the cost of heavy water production at the DAE's facilities, came up with a figure about three times the cost estimated by the DAE. When questioned about this discrepancy, the DAE was unable to provide any calculations to substantiate its figure, justifying this by stating that 'Heavy Water being strategic material, it is not advisable to divulge information relating to its production and cost to functionaries at all levels'. Ultimately, the CAG could not obtain figures needed to credibly estimate heavy water costs.

[7]One arena where the DAE has actually tried to exclude outside expertise is at public hearings to discuss environmental impact assessments of nuclear projects. At a public hearing in June 2007 to discuss the impact of the Koodankulam nuclear reactors, the DAE denied one of the authors access to the project report on the grounds that even to look at it required a degree in nuclear engineering.

The DAE similarly explains away cost overruns. For example, in the case of the Manuguru Heavy Water Plant, the CAG found that the cost of the facility had increased by 133 per cent (CAG 1994). When questioned about the cost escalation, the DAE stated that 'the grounds for sanction of this project [were] strategic and not commercial'.

Technically speaking, there is nothing more strategic—that is, having military value—about heavy water than, say, coal. The only way by which heavy water production figures could be seen as providing any information with strategic implications is if the reactors in the country involved in plutonium production for military purposes were facing a shortage of heavy water and, therefore, could not either be commissioned or function efficiently. The argument about strategic significance often does not have any basis in fact. But this still enjoys credence among a large section of policy makers and the elite.

Mass Production, Consumption, and Destruction

Playing the strategic card does make ample sense from the DAE's perspective because it is the only entity that can both generate electricity and make nuclear weapons. In other words, it can promise the wherewithal for mass production and mass consumption, and for mass destruction. This unique combination of abilities is the key and most valued source of the DAE's institutional power.

This dual ability of the nuclear enterprise was clear to Nehru even at the inception of the programme in 1948. While he desired to 'develop [atomic energy] for peaceful purposes', he went on to qualify it: 'if we are compelled as a nation to use it for other purposes, possibly no pious sentiments will stop the nation from using it that way'. Barely two years after the destruction of Hiroshima and Nagasaki, the 'other purposes' were obvious (Mian 1998).

Prior to the 1998 nuclear tests, while not admitting openly to any weapons-related activities, the DAE did make sure that its ability to make the bomb was clear to everybody. For example, in October 1964, Bhabha declared that India could explode an atom bomb within 18 months of a decision to do so (Perkovich 1999: 65). The DAE also ensured that its ability to make nuclear weapons was maintained through appropriate technological choices and ensuring that India did not sign any international agreements that could bind its weapons activities.

The DAE's dual ability is also a source of elite support since much of the Indian upper and middle classes subscribe to a vision that calls for both these ingredients. Their vision of India becoming a superpower requires, in their view, both the possession of nuclear weapons and rapid economic growth, for which, in turn, they posit large increases of electricity generation capacity. The latter is very much part of a 'conventional approach to energy planning' in which 'energy is treated as an end in itself and the focus is on increasing energy consumption' (Reddy 1990).

Within this dominant paradigm, energy security is tantamount to mindlessly installing larger and larger quantities of centralized electricity capacity. Nuclear power, by positioning itself as a virtually inexhaustible source of energy, especially through the much advertised three-stage programme, has managed to capture the fancy of energy planners and the elite. The pursuit of this ever receding chimera of a nuclear powered future deflects attention from mundane measures, like reducing transmission and distribution losses or more efficient end-use of electricity, that are more realizable in the short run.

Modern Times

Nuclear power offered more than just a way to address electricity needs; it came with an image of being modern and highly sophisticated. Witness Nehru's speech in 1948: 'Consider the past few hundred years of human history: the world developed a new source of power, that is steam—the steam engine and the like—and the industrial age began. India, with all its many virtues, did not develop that source of power. *It became a backward country because of that.* The steam age and the industrial age were followed by the electrical age which gradually crept in, and most of us were hardly aware of the change. But enormous new power came in. Now we are facing the atomic age; we are on the verge of it. And this is something infinitely more powerful than either steam or electricity' (our emphasis) (Abraham 1998). Not opting for nuclear power was, therefore, seen as anti-developmental and going against the times. To this day, the nuclear establishment promotes this outdated notion of atomic energy being modern technology.

Nehru's speech is notable on another count: it avoids any discussion of the appropriateness of choosing nuclear energy as the path to India's development given the country's largely rural and scattered population. Trying to provide electricity for such a country through centralized and capital-intensive technologies makes no economic or technical sense. But nuclear power has failed even as a way of catering to urban and industrial electricity demand.

CONCLUDING REMARKS

The relationship between knowledge and policy-making is typically non-linear. Nuclear energy in India is an extreme example of how politics and power can deflect technical critique and allow decision making to not take it into account.

The history of nuclear energy in India is illustrative of larger problems concerning energy policy in the country. It has resulted in inability to meet targets, cost overruns, and failure to ensure equity. And yet, for the reasons described in this chapter, the nuclear establishment is also distinctive. It continues to corner disproportionately large shares of budgets, operate with little accountability, and confidently make unrealizable projections.

What we have described here has parallels in other countries too. Nuclear power around the world has proven uneconomical. Expectations that there would be technological learning or economies of scale have not been realized. Yet, similar institutional factors have allowed nuclear establishments in many countries to survive and even grow. What is special about the Indian case is that the same organization develops both nuclear energy and weapons. The DAE has been twin-faced like the mythical Janus—to those interested in development, it offers the promise (even if never realized) of large quantities of cheap electricity; to those who question this, it offers another unrealizable dream, of military security.

REFERENCES

Abraham, I., (1993), 'Security, Technology and Ideology: "Strategic Enclaves" in Brazil and India, 1945–1989', Ph.D. dissertation; University of Illinois.

———, (1997), 'Science and Secrecy in Making of Postcolonial State', *Economic and Political Weekly*, Vol. 32, pp. 2136–46.

———, (1998), *The Making of the Indian Atomic Bomb: Science, Secrecy and the Postcolonial State*, New York: Zed Books.

Anderson, R., (1975), *Building Scientific Institutions in India: Bhabha and Saha*, Montreal: Center for Developing Area Studies.

Bhabha, H.J. and N.B. Prasad, (1958), 'A Study of the Contribution of Atomic Energy to a Power Programme in India', in Second United

Nations International Conference on the Peaceful Uses of Atomic Energy, Geneva.

Bhoje, S.B., (2001), 'Atomic Energy Obvious Choice for India', Interview with S.B. Bhoje, Director, IGCAR', *Frontline*, 30 March, pp. 84–85.

Biswas, Soutik, (1999), 'Nuclear Fallout', *Asia Week*, 20 June.

Bose, D.K., (1981), 'Accounting of Nuclear Power', *Economic and Political Weekly*, Vol. 16, No. 32, pp. 1313–18.

CAG, (1993),'Report by the Comptroller and Auditor General of India', New Delhi: Comptroller and Auditor General of India (CAG).

____, (1994), 'Report by the Comptroller and Auditor General of India', New Delhi: Comptroller and Auditor General of India.

CEA, (2004), 'Report of the Expert Committee on Fuels for Power Generation', New Delhi: Central Electric Authority (CEA), Planning Wing.

____, (2005), 'National Electricy Plan—2004', New Delhi: Central Electric Authority.

Chetal, S.C., V. Balasubramaniyan, P. Chellapandi, P. Mohanakrishnan, P. Puthiyavinayagam, C.P. Pillai, S. Raghupathy, T.K. Shanmugham and C. Sivathanu Pillai, (2006), 'The Design of the Prototype Fast Breeder Reactor', *Nuclear Engineering and Design*, Vol. 236, pp. 852–60.

Chidambaram, R., (1996), 'India is not Isolated', Interview with AEC chief R. Chidambaram, *Frontline*, 29 November, pp.86–89.

Chidambaram, R. and C. Ganguly, (1996), 'Plutonium and Thorium in the Indian Nuclear Programme', *Current Science*, Bangalore, Vol. 70, No. 1, pp. 21–35.

Datta, Pradip, (1999), 'Safety in Indian Nuclear Plants: Assurance is Not Enough', *Ananda Bazar Patrika*, 2 November.

Gadekar, Surendra, Shreekumar, and Sanghamitra Gadekar, 'Health Impacts of Uranium Mining in Jaduguda, India', forthcoming.

German Federal Environment Ministry (GFEM), (2007), 'General Information: Nuclear Safety', available at *http://www.bmu.de/english/nuclear_safety/information/doc/4300.php*, Accessed on 21 September.

Govindarajan, S., (2003), 'Economics of FBR Fuel Cycle', in Nuclear Fuel Cycle Technologies: Closing the Fuel Cycle, Indian Nuclear Society Annual Conference (INSAC), 2003, Indian Nuclear Society, Kalpakkam.

Grover, R.B. and S. Chandra, (2006), 'Scenario for Growth of Electricity in India', *Energy Policy*, Vol. 34, No. 17, pp. 2834–47.

Hart, D., (1983), *Nuclear Power in India: A Comparative Analysis*, London: George Allen and Unwin.

Iype, G., (2000), 'I do Not Think Nuclear Plants are Polluting and a Threat to People's Health', *Interview with V.K. Chaturvedi*, *www.rediff.com/news/2000/nov/25nukec.htm*, 25 November.

Jagannathan, V., (2003), 'Powerful Leap: IGCAR Press Release', *http://www.igcar.ernet.in/press_releases/press6a.htm*, Accessed on 8 August.

Martinez-Alier, J., (2006) 'Energy, Economy, and Poverty: The Past and Present Debate', in J. Byrne, N. Toly, and L. Glover (eds), *Transforming Power: Energy, Environment, and Society in Conflict*, New Brunswick: Transaction Publishers,

Mian, Z., (1998), 'Homi Bhabha Killed a Crow', in Z . Mian and A. Nandy, (eds), *The Nuclear Debate: Ironies and Immoralities*, Colombo: Regional Centre for Strategic Studies.

Muralidharan, S., (1985), 'Compounding an Error? The Fast Breeder Reactor', *Business India*, 2–15 December, pp. 107–8.

———, (1988), 'Birth of Nuclear Power Corporation', *Economic and Political Weekly*, Vol. 23, No. 5, pp. 190–2.

Natarajan, J., (2003), 'Classified Dangerous', *New Sunday Express*, 29 July.

Nema, A.K., (1999), 'Nuclear Generation Cost in India', *Nu-Power*, Vol. 13, No. 1.

Perkovich, G., (1999), *India's Nuclear Bomb: The Impact on Global Proliferation*, Berkeley: University of California Press.

Planning Commission, (2006), 'Integrated Energy Policy: Report of the Expert Committee', New Delhi: Planning Commission, Government of India.

Prasad, R., (2001), 'India: FBTR passes 53-day Continuous Operation Test', *The Hindu*, 22 March.

Ramana, M.V., (2007), 'Heavy Subsidies in Heavy Water: Economics of Nuclear Power in India', *Economic and Political Weekly*, Vol. 42, No. 34, pp. 3483–90.

Ramana, M.V., A. D'Sa, and A.K.N. Reddy, (2005), 'Economics of Nuclear Power from Heavy Water Reactors', *Economic and Political Weekly*, Vol. 40, No. 17, pp. 1763–73.

Ramana, M.V. and J.Y. Suchitra, (2007), 'Costing Plutonium: Economics of Reprocessing in India', *International Journal of Global Energy Issues*, Vol. 27, No. 4, pp. 454–71.

Ramanna, R., (1985), 'Can Nuclear Energy Claim to be the only Source of Power in the Future?', Bombay: Department of Atomic Energy.

Reddy, A.K.N., (1988), 'Is Power from Nuclear Plants Necessary? Is it Economical?' in National Workshop on Nuclear Power Plants with Specific Reference to Kaiga, Bangalore, 10–11 December.

———, (1990), 'Nuclear Power: Is it Necessary or Economical?' *Seminar*, Vol. 370, pp. 18–26.

Rosenstein-Rodan, P.N., (1959), 'Contribution of Atomic Energy to a Power Program in India', C/59–15, Cambridge, MA: Center for International Studies, Massachusetts Institute of Technology.

Shah, A., (2002), 'North South East West: 10, 9, 8...Relaunch of Nuclear Power', *Indian Express*, 1 December.

Srinivasan, M.R., (1985), 'The Indian Nuclear Power Programme', in Indo-

French Seminar on Nuclear Energy, Bombay: Department of Atomic Energy.

Suchitra, J.Y. and M.V. Ramana, (forthcoming), 'The Costs of Power: Plutonium and the Economics of India's Prototype Fast Breeder Reactor'.

Suresh Kumar, K.V., R.P. Kapoor, P.V. Ramalingam, B. Rajendran, G. Srinivasan, and K.V. Kasiviswanathan, (2002), 'Fast Breeder Test Reactor: 15 Years of Operating Experience', in Technical Meeting on Operational and Decommissioning Experience with Fast Reactors, Cadarache, 11–15 March.

Tiwari, Manish, (1999), 'A Deformed Existence', Down to Earth, 15 June.

Thakur, S. and B.P. Chaurasia, (2005), 'Cost Effectiveness of Electricity Generating Technologies', Mumbai: Nuclear Power Corporation.

15

Re-negotiating the Role of External Cost Calculations in the Belgian Nuclear and Sustainable Energy Debate

Matthieu Craye, Erik Laes, and Jeroen P. van der Sluijs

In Belgium, as in most industrialized countries, debate about the place of nuclear power production in a sustainable energy mix has resulted in enduring and intractable conflict between actors holding antagonistic positions. External cost calculations can be seen as part of attempts to provide an 'objective' input in order to rationalize decision making regarding sustainable energy. In this respect, the most thorough body of work took place within the European Commission (EC) supported ExternE project.

However, in the Belgian nuclear debate, external cost data only played a very limited role, generally not extending beyond citing the ExternE results (by those in favour of nuclear power), with critics retorting by pointing out uncertainties (for example, costs of radioactive waste management for future generations) and/or unincluded externalities [for example, limited liabilities for owners of Nuclear Power Plants (NPPs)].

The controversial character of external cost data and their, until now, their limited use in policy-making processes can be linked to a number of interrelated factors: the complexity of the policy issue and the plural positions, values, and stakes that are into play; the proposed role for external cost data in decision making; and the value-laden character of the approach itself.

To explore if, and how, external cost data can contribute in a more effective way to policy-making, the Belgian Nuclear Research

Centre (SCK-CEN) organized a workshop in collaboration with the EC's Joint Research Centre and Utrecht University. Crucial assumptions and choices made in the calculation chain were discussed and qualified in a structured way, using the concept of 'pedigree of knowledge'. Participants in the workshop included policy-makers, stakeholders, and experts from various disciplines. The focus of the discussion was on assumptions related to the scenario used for evaluating the impacts of a severe nuclear accident, to the estimation of the related health impacts, and to their economic and monetary valuation. Special attention was paid to the value-laden character of these assumptions.

This chapter starts with a concise description of the Belgian nuclear debate and the problems with external cost approaches in policy debates, as covered by the scientific literature. Subsequently, we present the reasoning behind the structuring of the mentioned workshop around a discussion on assumptions and choices in the external cost calculation chain. Based on the workshop experience, lessons are drawn for enchancing the role of economic valuation studies in energy policy. These elements are not limited to what is generally referred to as better communication of science but entail a true re-negotiation of the role that such science can play in policy processes.

BELGIUM'S NUCLEAR HISTORY: FROM SOCIAL PACT TO PHASE-OUT

Today, about 55 per cent of Belgium's electricity demand is covered by its seven NPPs. They were all put into operation during 1975–85, as a result of a post-war social pact between the important socio-economic actors and the State. This pact aimed at a growing economic output in order to maximise welfare. In view of this goal, the crucial importance of the security of energy supply at a reasonable, competitive price was recognized. The deal included the decision to invest in nuclear power generation and encouraged direct state intervention in the energy sector.

Notwithstanding the existence of such a pact, the Belgian nuclear sector has also been subject to ever increasing disagreements. Starting from a siting conflict in the early 1970s, over the years, as in many other countries, a nuclear controversy developed. More actors were drawn into the controversy and the scope of the arguments expanded towards a more general debate about the desirability of economic growth 'at all costs' and general principles of democratic decision making. This resulted, starting from the late 1980s, in a stalemate regarding most high-profile nuclear issues, such as the decision on an eighth nuclear reactor and the siting of a low-level waste repository.

From 1990 onwards, the policy-making context changed, mainly by the combined forces of an increasing prominence of environmental issues on the political agenda (for example, climate change) and the liberalization of European energy markets. While these developments mostly took place in the context of supranational institutions and international negotiations, at the national level, the Belgian government decided in 2003 on a nuclear phase-out scenario. The phase-out scenario implies that the Belgian NPPs will be taken out of service in the period 2015–25 (after 40 years of operation). However, criticism of this phase-out law never disappeared, and it is doubtful whether it will ever be implemented as foreseen.

A major argument of opponents of the phase-out law is of an economic nature. They have found support in a recent study (Energy 2030, 2007) that indicates that nuclear energy is indispensible to keep acceptable the economic cost of respecting Belgium's engagements to reduce GHG emissions. To this type of argument, opponents of nuclear energy traditionally reply that the market price of nuclear energy has never reflected its true cost to society.

However, proponents of the nuclear sector point to the calculations of the external costs of several energy sources, showing that the nuclear option is, by and large, the most optimal economic choice.

EXTERNAL COST CALCULATIONS: COMMUNICATED PRECISION CONTESTED

The concept of 'externalities' is central both to markets and economics. Externalities of a traded product are defined as impacts borne by agents (human agents, the environment) other than those involved in the trade interaction. External costs are the calculated costs of those impacts. They are not included in the market price of the traded good or not compensated by its producers and/or traders.

While throughout the 1970s and early 1980s, the dominant analytical approach to the environmental appraisal of electricity supply options was provided by comparative risk assessment (Stirling

1997), the end of the 1980s saw the rise of neo-classical environmental economics research on the external costs of electricity provision, with major studies being commissioned by influential bodies such as the EC, the US Department of Energy (USDOE), the German electricity industry, and numerous other industry, state, national, and non-governmental bodies (US OTA 1994).

In response to the general theoretical difficulties experienced in attempting to quantify the external costs of electricity production (see below), the EC, together with the USDOE, launched a joint research project to identify the appropriate methodology for this type of work in 1991. After the first phase of the project, which established an operational accounting framework for the assessment of external costs of energy production (named 'ExternE' in Europe; see the project website *www.externe.info*, EC 1995, EC 1999), the EC continued an independent programme of follow-up activities.

The ExternE network is still actively engaged in updating the methodology, applying the accounting framework to previously unincluded types of externalities (for example, energy security), extending the network to new EU member states, and broadening ExternE's scope of application (cost–benefit analysis of European environmental policy measures, green national accounting, etc.). All in all, it is fair to say that ExternE represents the largest and most thorough body of work in the field of energy/environment economics, and as such has become a recognized brand in policy-making circles.

Application of the ExternE methodology to the Belgian energy system resulted in the following general findings (Torfs et al. 2005):

- Both wind and nuclear power show very limited external costs (< 1 Euro/MWhe); however, public perception for both technologies (visual impacts for wind, risk perception for nuclear) was not taken into account;
- Photovoltaic power has a low external cost (< 5 Euro/MWhe);
- Gas technologies have an intermediate external cost 10–30 Euro/MWhe);
- Oil and coal technologies fall within the high range of external costs (30–150 Euro/MWhe).

While the communicated precision of these results suggests that the determination and application of external cost calculations is clear and unproblematic, it has proven to be not too difficult for specialized stakeholders and energy systems experts to criticize these results. As such, it has been argued that there were unincluded externalities (for example, limited liabilities for owners of NPPs). Critics also pointed to major uncertainties in relation to the estimation of costs of the impacts of a severe nuclear accident and of radioactive waste management for future generations.

Confronted by a debate in which such external cost data are used in a snapshot way, creating confusion about their 'status' and meaning, SCK-CEN, through its programme for integrating social aspects in nuclear research (PISA), became interested in studying why these data were controversial in the first place, as well as the conditions under which such approaches could play a more relevant role in the discussions and decision making on energy policy.

A Technical Debate on External Costs as a Substitute for Socio-Political Debate

Based on more academically oriented criticism of the external cost approach, on an empirical reconstruction of positions taken in the nuclear debate, and on analyses of how policy-related science often intensifies controversies, a number of inter-related factors can be discerned to explain the problems with external cost data in the policy context:
- the complexity of the policy issue of sustainable energy;
- the plural positions, values, and stakes that are into play;
- the proposed role for external cost data in decision making, suggesting an unmediated relation between a scientific assessment of external costs and price-correcting measures.

From a constructivist point of view, robust scientific results, in conditions of complexity, can only be arrived at, through processes of reduction and simplification of the issue, involving negotiation about the issue's essential characteristics. Callon (1998) describes how the existence and magnitude of externalities necessarily depends on a particular framing of the interaction under consideration. Stirling (1997) clearly shows how 'framing' and 'bracketing' is performed in practice in the case of externalities of energy systems. While it is already often difficult to obtain consensus about the particular details of such 'bracketing' (system boundaries, externalities to include or not, etc.), another more fundamental problem arises as the external approach as such is itself only one of several possible ways to approach the complex issue of sustainable energy. In contrast to its presentation as objective and 'neutral', it is far from that as it imposes certain interactions and the way to approach them as the 'normal' ones.

Indeed, in the early 1990s, the relevance of recognizing, assessing, and internalizing external costs was quickly enlisted in the emerging political discourse on sustainability as a means to transform the 'fuzzy' concept of sustainability into an objectively measurable quantity (Stirling 1999). One of the key elements of this programme was 'to get the prices right' and to ensure that environmental externalities were accounted for in market mechanisms. As such, the sudden surge of public authorities' support for research into external costs was in line with the rise of 'ecological modernization' as a policy paradigm in rich industrialized countries, which can be understood as an attempt to reform capitalism in an ecological direction, without undermining the basic axioms of the system (Hajer 1995).

However, this way of promoting external costs as the key approach to support energy policy-making completely discards (elements of) some of the competing argumentation frames in the debate on sustainable energy, and the place of nuclear energy in this respect.

Based on interviews with representatives of key stakeholder organizations, Laes et al. (2004) made an ideal-typical reconstruction of the major argumentations schemes in the Belgian nuclear debate at the time when the phase-out 'scenario' was not yet translated into law (in the fall of 2002). The three perspectives were labelled the 'management', 'controllist' and 'reformist' perspectives, and are based on structural dimensions, that is, their communicated images of self and others, valid forms of communication, main problem focus, and main principal references.

From the description of the frames, it is clear that the external cost framework shares its basic values with the management perspective, that is, an outspoken belief in market mechanisms. It can also be meaningful within the controllist perspective, which seeks to reconcile several social goals and aims for more transparency and open debate, including about costs. Its relationship with the reformist perspective is, however, problematic. The latter sees the current energy system and the importance of nuclear energy production, not as the result of an economically sound process that now should be corrected for some 'forgotten' environmental impacts, but as the result of social processes dominated by political and economic power, leading to valid technology options (for example, renewable energy options) and 'rational' behaviour (for example, energy saving) being discouraged.

To summarize, while the complexity and plurality of perspectives make it difficult to arrive at one consensual framing, the proposed role for external cost results expresses a strong preference for one particular value-laden approach to the problem of sustainability. But as other competing frames are not taken seriously, the conflict about values, positions, stakes, and interests does not disappear but tends to enter the scientific-technical debate (Craye 2006). All the more, because of the suggested direct link between scientific input and policy measures. Very schematically, while managers and controllists will cite external cost results, reformists will be inclined to contest them. The conditions are there for disputes on the scientific facts (the external costs) serving as a substitute for policy disputes (Sarewitz 2004): the policy-related scientific assessments have become a *de facto* locus for socio-political contestation.

ROLE OF EXTERNAL COSTS IN GOVERNANCE PROCESSES FOR SUSTAINABLE ENERGY

To explore the question of whether there could be a more effective role for external cost data in the debate on a sustainable energy system and on the place of the nuclear in this, SCK-CEN organized a workshop, in collaboration with the EC's Joint Research Centre and Utrecht University (Laes 2007). While largely confirming the above analysis of the underlying reasons for the controversial character of external cost results, the process and the results of the workshop suggest that their role could be enhanced through a re-negotiation of the relation between external cost calculations and the governance context. Essential in opening the space for such re-negotiation appeared to be:

- organizing and structuring discussions between experts, stakeholders, and policy-makers as a reasoned debate;
- discussing explicitly the particular framing of the issue of sustainable energy through the approach of external costs;
- assessing and qualifying the potential value-ladenness of key assumptions in external cost calculations and their importance as sources of uncertainty and disagreement.

Conditions for a Reasoned Debate Between Experts, Stakeholders, and Policy Makers

Whereas traditional communication of policy-relevant science largely occurs through a one-way presentation and delivery of research reports, in its turn often provoking one-way critical reactions, the workshop showed the potential of direct and interactive discussion between experts, stakeholders, and policy makers.

Until then, in the context of the Belgian nuclear debate, use of external cost data had been limited to defending ExternE results (by those in favour of nuclear power), with critics retorting by pointing out uncertainties, flaws, and arbitrariness in the calculations. Participants in the workshop were positively surprised by the possibilities created to go beyond this black/white treatment of external cost results as 'hard evidence' or as 'bad science'.

Space was opened up to express and assess with nuance the merits, deficiencies, and limits of the approach as such and of the choices made in the calculation chain. Specific workshop preparations helped to assure such reasoned exchange of arguments. Workshop participants were selected with the particular concern of taking into account the plurality of scientific and socio-political perspectives on the problem. The workshop protocol planned that, for each discussion, an introduction was provided by at least two experts—a first one defending the external cost approach and/or particular assumptions made in it and a second one who was a 'critical judge'. Then, the discussion was explicitly extended to the views and reactions of the stakeholders and policy-makers in the panel.

The workshop moderator and a number of researchers, specifically trained in deliberative procedures and/or uncertainty assessment, had to guarantee that an informed and fair debate took place. To this end, the moderator presented some guidelines (included in the protocol). He also had at his disposal a catalogue of possible questions in order to (re)focus the discussion if necessary. These model questions were based on insights on the structure of argumentations (Toulmin 1958), the content of actors' frames of meaning (Grin 1997), and the different types of scientific debate and controversy when uncertainty is salient (von Schomberg 1997). They were intended to make the process more reflexive (Craye et al. 2005), both in terms of content, that is, opening up the problem definition and the scope of argumentation, and in terms of process, that is, placing the participants in new roles and rules of interaction. In this particular setting, the traditional and often institutionalized division between the scientist as a provider of facts versus policy makers and the public as defenders of values was challenged.

To provide a solid structure for the discussion, a so-called pedigree scheme (van der Sluijs 2005, see paragraph below) was used.

ASSESSING THE SALIENT SOURCES OF UNCERTAINTIES IN EXTERNAL COST CALCULATIONS: DISAGREEMENTS ON CHOICES AND ASSUMPTIONS

Confronted with open divergence of views on the robustness of external cost data, it is increasingly considered necessary to take the communication of related uncertainties seriously. All too often, such communication of uncertainties is limited to downstream results of the calculations which are commented upon through technical–quantitative means (Craye 2006).

However, the above description of the problems with the use of external cost data in the policy context made clear that the uncertainty to focus on was not the type that could be described by ranges of error and probability distributions. Neither is it the uncertainty, which can be seen as a provisional deficiency of external cost calculations which can best be solved through an increased research effort, separate from the policy context.

The workshop followed the logic that the relevant uncertainties to consider in relation to external costs, as expressed through the existence of different scientific opinions and/or divergent interpretations and use of results in the socio-political debate, are those that find their source in different value-laden choices, assumptions, and framings entering into the (long) chain of calculations leading to an estimation of externalities.

The resulting uncertainty is of a deeper nature and is related to what has been described in the literature as ignorance ['not only we have no basis to estimate probabilities, but we don't know what can be the impacts' (Funtowicz and Ravetz 1990)], indeterminacy ['causal chains are open and influenced by non-predictable behavioural systems', but also 'all knowledge is to a certain degree conditional and contingent upon framings, choices and assumptions' (Wynne 1992)], and ambiguity ['precise meanings of the issue are not agreed, or unclear' (Wynne 2001)].

A procedure was developed to select key assumptions in a process involving all workshop participants. During the workshop, these assumptions were discussed and qualified using a scheme based on the concept of pedigree of knowledge. As a pilot, it was decided to focus specifically on the externalities of a potential large-scale nuclear accident in a Belgian NPP.

After going through the ExternE research reports and gathering information on points of disagreement and controversy, preparatory interviews with ExternE experts and stakeholders were held, allowing to list in a structured way the main steps in the calculation chain, as well as the crucial assumptions in each of these steps. In this way, a list of 30 assumptions was arrived at and, through an internet survey, held weeks before the workshop and involving all workshop participants, a final list of six assumptions was selected.

As a result, the focus of the discussions was on assumptions related to the scenario used for evaluating the impacts of a severe nuclear accident, to the estimation of the related health impacts, and to their economic and monetary valuation. Special attention was paid to the value-laden character of these assumptions. See Box 15.1.

Box 15.1: Assumptions Assessed and Qualified Through a Set of Pedigree Criteria during the Workshop Organized by the Belgian Nuclear Research Centre (SCK-CEN)

1. External costs of a potential large-scale accident in a Belgian NPP can be determined on the basis of a calculation for a hypothetical NPP located in the middle of Western Europe.
2. In a large-scale accident scenario for a Belgian NPP, all radionuclide dispersion routes other than the atmospheric release route are negligible.
3. A linear correlation exists between exposure to ionizing radiation and health effects, even for very small radiation doses.
4. All health impacts other than the radiological ones caused by exposure to ionizing radiation can be neglected when assessing the consequences of a large-scale nuclear accident in a Belgian NPP.
5. The 'risk-aversion factor' for accidents of the 'low probability/high consequences' type cannot be determined in a reliable way and, therefore, does not have to be reported.
6. The cost indicators adopted in the ExternE methodology (cost of countermeasures, direct economic damage, short- and long-term health impacts) are sufficiently representative for the total costs of a potential large-scale nuclear accident in a Belgian NPP.

To evaluate and qualify these assumptions a scheme was used (see Table 15.1), developed by Van der Sluijs and Kloprogge (Kloprogge et al. 2005). Based on a literature study, and on the concept of pedigree, as introduced by Funtowicz and Ravetz (1990), they discerned a set of criteria to discuss and qualify the potential value-ladenness and the influence of assumptions on the end results of an assessment. Value-laden here is not to be exclusively understood as politically and/or ethically controversial. It refers to the fact that making an assumption involves going through a choice process.

The criteria used to discuss the assumptions were:

- Influence of situational limitations: The degree to which the choice for the assumption can be influenced by situational limitations, such as limited availability of data, money, time, software, tools, hardware, and human resources.
- Plausibility: The degree, mostly based on an (intuitive) assessment, through which the approximation created by the assumption is in accordance with 'reality'.
- Choice space: The degree to which alternatives were available to choose from when making the assumption.
- Agreement among peers: The degree to which the choice of peers is likely to coincide with the analyst's choice.
- Agreement among stakeholders: The degree to which the choice of stakeholders is likely to coincide with the analyst's choice.
- Sensitivity to the view and interests of the analyst: The degree to which the choice for the assumption may be influenced, consciously or unconsciously, by the view and interests of the analyst making the assumption.
- Influence on results: In order to be able to pinpoint important value-laden assumptions in a calculation chain, it is not only important to assess the potential value-ladenness of the assumptions, but also to analyse the influence on outcomes of interest of the assessment.

The qualitative discussion of each assumption was closed by giving a score for the assumption for each of the criteria, as indicated by the pedigree matrix. The scoring was organized as an inter-subjective process of negotiation that enables one to summarize the main points of discussion for each criterion, to explain why different participants suggested different scores, and to clarify any ambiguity in the descriptions of the criteria. The pedigree process allowed one to qualify the robustness of the assumptions, as assessed by the participants, as well as to discern options for possibly making

Table 15.1: Pedigree Scheme Used to Assess Assumptions during the Workshop Organized by the Belgian Nuclear Research Centre (SCK-CEN)

Score	Influence of situational limitations	Plausibility	Choice space	Agreement among peers	Agreement among stakeholders	Sensitivity to views and interests of analyst	Influence on results
4	No such limitations	Very plausible	No alternatives available	Complete agreement	Complete agreement	Not sensitive	Little or no influence
3	Hardly influenced	Plausible	Very limited number of alternatives	High degree of agreement	High degree of agreement	Hardly sensitive	Local impact in the calculations
2	Moderately influenced	Acceptable	Small number of alternatives	Competing schools	Competing perspectives	Moderately sensitive	Important impact in a major step in the calculation
1	Importantly influenced	Hardly plausible	Average number of alternatives	Low degree (embryonic stage)	Low degree of agreement	Highly sensitive	Moderate impact on end result
0	Completely influenced	Fictive or speculative	Very ample choice of alternatives	Low degree (controversial)	Controversial	Very highly sensitive	Important impact on end result

alternative assumptions to improve the external cost calculation or make them more meaningful.

Overall, the scores given were low, reflecting the stakeholder and expert panel's scepticism about the assumptions made: generally these were considered to be not very plausible, subject to disagreement, and to a large extent inspired by contextual factors. The only real exception to this was the assumption that there exists a linear correlation between exposure to ionizing radiation and health effects, even for very small radiation doses. This was the least contested assumption of the workshop. Three experts agreed that the so-called 'linear no-threshold hypothesis' (LNT) constitutes the best scientific basis to regulate the risks of ionizing radiation and that the LNT assumption could be qualified as a precautionary approach to managing radiation risks. This statement was qualified to some extent as a result of the discussion with stakeholders. There was a suggestion, however, that perhaps different dose-effect curves should be used for different fractions of the population.

Clear suggestions for improvements in the external cost calculations were made in relation to the assumptions regarding the NPP location which was used as basis for the calculation, and regarding the neglect of other than atmospheric release routes for the dispersion of radionuclides in case of an accident.

The main criticism of the first assumption was that, because of the specific location of the Belgian NPPs—near major cities with important industrial activities—the results obtained by using a hypothetical location in the middle of Western Europe would (seriously) underestimate the externalities of a potential accident for the Belgian context. Therefore, the critics among the stakeholder group argued that a study of the potential consequences of a severe accident (a 'Probabilistic Safety Assessment (PSA)—Level 3') for the specific case of a Belgian NPP would likely bring much more insight into the nature and extent of the resulting externalities. The ExternE experts present at the workshop agreed in principle to this objection.

In relation to the second assumption, a PSA expert present at the workshop explained that contamination of ground and river water by radionuclides in case of a severe nuclear reactor accident cannot be entirely excluded. Such contamination could be caused by a failure of the NPP's pressure vessel and a possible melting of the reactor core through the bottom of the reactor building, resulting in steam explosions. This accident sequence is considered to be highly improbable, but would nevertheless result in a long-term ecosystem pollution, which is not included as an externality in the ExternE approach (only impacts on human health count). This view was not really challenged in the discussion.

A second category of assumptions was formed by those who were heavily criticized and for which, only to a certain extent, proposals were made for how external cost calculations could be improved to overcome this criticism. The assumption that the used cost indicators (cost of countermeasures, direct economic damage, short- and long-term health impacts) are representative of the total costs of a potential large-scale nuclear accident in a Belgian NPP, has to be mentioned here.

Mainly, representatives of environmental NGOs pointed out that an entire catalogue of economic impacts was not included in the ExternE methodology: direct and indirect costs of lost production in industries adjacent to the NPP, forward ripple effects in the entire European economy (for example, caused by an evacuation of the Antwerp harbour), costs of 'stigmatization' of a region contaminated by nuclear fallout, economic impacts on the nuclear sector worldwide (for example, costs of cancelling new nuclear programmes, enhanced safety measures in existing plants, etc.), and so on. The discussion on this assumption led to most of the participants seeing a continued great potential for public contestation of it.

Some assumptions were clearly seen as problematic although it was not clear how to overcome the related problems through other ways of calculation. This category of assumptions included the neglect of all health impacts, other than the radiological ones, caused by exposure to ionizing radiation when assessing the consequences of a large-scale nuclear accident in a Belgian NPP. This was criticized by a radiation protection expert on the basis of the experience after the Chernobyl reactor accident in 1986. Follow-up studies show a significant increase in the population suffering from post-traumatic stress symptoms, anxiety, estrangement, dislocation, etc. However, according to this expert, it is difficult (if not impossible) to relate these psychological impacts unequivocally to a nuclear accident as such or rather to the risk management interventions of (Soviet) authorities. Therefore, he concluded that non-radiological (psychosomatic) health impacts of a potential reactor accident could prove to be a major—albeit hardly quantifiable—factor.

The overall average pedigree score attributed by the workshop participants to this assumption shows that this expert qualification was largely shared.

Also belonging to this category of assumptions is the acceptability of not reporting a 'risk-aversion factor' for accidents of the 'low probability/high consequences' type. The ExternE experts present at the workshop admitted that within the ExternE network, a better conceptualization of the 'risk aversion factor' for potential severe nuclear accidents was not considered to be a priority issue. Within the ExternE network, the prevailing opinion was that since risk aversion is a highly contextual factor which varies enormously from individual to individual, no robust theoretical framework could be advanced to determine the exact extent of the externality resulting from risk aversive attitudes. Participants in the workshop found this to be one of the weakest links in the calculation chain since it is not up to researchers to implicitly decide that individuals or segments of society should not have different degrees of aversion for different categories of risk.

Implicit 'Framing' Imposed by External Costs

The reasoned exchange of arguments and the expression of a lot of nuance during the detailed discussion of the assumptions was helped immensely by the fact that, preceding the pedigree assessment, the implicit framing imposed by the overall aproach of valuation and monetarization had already been debated. In this way, a forum was given to the more fundamental critique of the external cost approach.

This critique, that is, that reasoning in terms of external costs establishes particular meanings of the issue of sustainable energy, was confirmed in the workshop discussions. Through a presentation by ExternE researchers, it was made explicit that the project fits in a policy framework that attaches crucial if not exclusive importance to market-based instruments to achieve sustainable growth. Based on cost–benefit type of assessments and correct prices, optimal allocation of resources can be achieved. In this framework, it is believed that external cost results can play a determining role by providing the basis for the adequate taxation of certain energy sources. This view is one of 'weak' sustainability, that is, in which material welfare can be exchanged against taking risk with the environment and *vice versa*.

Critics wanted to see it explicitly recognized that the external cost approach:

- only partially deals with the issue of sustainable energy as, even if it aims for price corrections, it leaves untouched other fundamental mechanisms of importance for sustainability such as the role of growth in economy and society;
- reduces citizenship, also with its socio-political dimensions, to consumer behaviour (expression of individual preferences through the willingness-to-pay approach);
- reduces the nature of public goods to consumer goods, thereby overlooking the ethical concerns with nature conservation;
- takes a decisionist position towards time, neglecting the historical context which led to current possibly unsustainable patterns as well as valuing future impacts according to today's preferences.

The workshop showed that, to play a more relevant role, the presentation of external cost data should openly refer to its basic values in which it finds its foundation and not be communicated as if it was the normal, neutral, and naturally privileged approach. On top of this, it should be made clear that other equally valid views of sustainable energy exist, and that this should be recognized through providing the policy debate with insights obtained through other approaches.

Critical aspects that are not considered or neglected by the ExternE approach but which should be addressed in policy-relevant research and in policy debates include:

- concerns of distributional justice;
- institutional factors influencing the relation between the organization of an economy and its ecological performance;
- assessment of visions of sustainable energy systems as well as different political visions of future organization of society, as external costs implicitly promote a status quo (through the willingness-to-pay approach which is very much dependent on current income structures and distribution);
- collective decisions for which there is co-responsibility in society, are not simply the sum of individual preferences;
- uncertainty about societal values in the future, as external costs implies that these remain stable;
- sustainability criteria for innovative technologies.

Finally, it was seen to be of utmost importance that together with the results of external cost studies, the limitations are communicated.

The inherent problem of 'demarcation' in all external cost studies makes the results critically conditional on system boundaries set. But all too often, a view is conveyed as if external cost results allow to make manageable all the complexities and uncertainties of the sustainable energy issue. It is presented as if one can unequivocally define what the optimal choices are to ensure sustainable development—and thus to be sure of what sustainable development is.

CONCLUDING REMARKS

Based on an analysis of the underlying reasons for the limited role of external cost studies in the Belgian debate and decision making on sustainable energy options, and of the nuclear option in particular, it can be argued that traditional patterns of one-way communication in the science–policy interface should be at least complemented, if not abandoned.

Through a workshop, conditions were explored that could enhance the relevance of external cost results in governance processes dealing with the sustainable energy issue. The underlying fundamental critique of the approach can only be dealt with adequately through a re-negotiation of the place and role of external cost data in the sustainable energy debate. The assumed 'ideal' relation between external cost results and policy measures has to be openly discussed and debated, allowing the implicit meanings and value-laden assumptions behind the uncritical presentation of such a direct link to surface. Possibilities for such re-negotiation can be created through direct interaction between involved stakeholders, relevant experts, and policy-makers in a setting which allows experimentation with the socio-institutional roles 'normally' taken up in the science–policy–society interface. In this respect, the workshop showed the potential of the approach of pedigree assessment, to assess assumptions made in external cost studies. By using pedigree assesment, the following results can be achieved:
- qualifying assumptions when they are communicated to the policy sphere;
- evaluating how assumptions relate to different perspectives and frameworks, as held by involved actors;
- generating suggestions for improvements in the calculation chain to deal with disagreements and divergence over assumptions as well as suggestions for communicating this type of policy-relevant science;
- conveying a more adequate image of policy-relevant science.

References

Callon, M., (1998), 'An Essay on Framing and Overflowing: Economic Externalities Revisited by Sociology' in M. Callon (ed.),' *The Laws of the Markets*, Oxford: Blackwell Publishers.

Commission Energy 2030 (2007), Final Report, 'Belgium's Energy Challenges towards 2030', available at *www. ce230be.*

Craye, M., S. Funtowicz, and J. van der Sluijs, (2005), 'A Reflexive Approach to Dealing with Uncertainties in Environmental Health Risk Science and Policy', *International Journal of Risk Assessment and Management*, Vol. 5, Nos. 2–4, pp. 216–36.

Craye, M., (2006), 'Reflexively Dealing with Uncertainty and Complexity in Policy Related Knowledge: What Can It Mean?', in A. Pereira, and S. Guedes Vaz, (ed.), *Interfaces between Science and Society*, Sheffield: Greenleaf.

European Commission (EC), (1995), *ExternE: Externalities of Energy, Vol. 1–6*, Project Report EUR 16520–16525, Luxembourg: Office for the Official Publications of the European Communities.

———, (1999), *ExternE: Externalities of Energy, Vol. 7–10*, Project Report EUR 19083–19086, Luxembourg: Office for the Official Publications of the European Communities.

Funtowicz, S. and J. Ravetz, (1990), *Uncertainty and Quality in Science for Policy*, Dordrecht: Kluwer.

Grin J., H. van der Graaf, and R. Hoppe, (1997), *Technology Assessment through Interaction: A Guide*, Den Haag: Rathenau Instituut.

Hajer, M., (1995), *The Politics of Environmental Discourse: Ecological Modernization and the Policy Process*, Oxford: Oxford University Press.

Kloprogge, P., J. van der Sluijs, and A. Petersen, (2005), *A Method for the Analysis of Assumptions in Assessments*, Bilthoven: Netherlands Environmental Assessment Agency (MNP).

Laes, E., G. Meskens, W. D'haeseleer, and R. Weiler, (2004), 'Trust as a Central Paradigm for Advisory Science: The Case of the Belgian Nuclear Phase Out', *International Journal of Sustainable Development*, Vol. 7, No. 1, pp. 1–26.

Laes, E., Meskens, G., (2007), Externe kosten van een potentieel grootschalig kernongeval in een Belgische kerncentrale—Verslag van een workshop (26 oktober 2006), SCK-CEN, Mol.

Sarewitz, D., (2004), 'How Science Makes Environmental Controversies Worse', *Environmental Science and Policy*, Vol. 7, pp. 385–403.

Stirling, A., (1997), 'Limits to the Value of External Costs', *Energy Policy*, Vol. 25, No. 5, pp. 517–40.

———, (1999), 'The Appraisal of Sustainability: Some Problems and Possible Responses', *Local Environment*, Vol. 4, No. 2, pp. 111–35.

Torfs, R., L. De Nocker, K. Aernouts, L. Schrooten, and I. en Liekens,

(2005), *Internalisatie van externe kosten voor de productie en verdeling van elektriciteit in Vlaanderen*, Brussels: MIRA.

Toulmin, S.E., (1958), *The Uses of Argument*, Cambridge: Cambridge University Press.

US Congress Office of Technology Assessment (OTA), (1994), *Studies of the Environmental Costs of Electricity*, Washington, DC: OTA.

Van der Sluijs, J., M. Craye, S. Funtowicz, P. Kloprogge, J. Ravetz and J. Risbey, (2005), 'Combining Quantitative and Qualitative Measures of Uncertainty in Model-based Environmental Assessment', *Risk Analysis*, Vol. 25, No. 2, pp. 481–92.

Schomberg, Von, R., (1997), *Argumentatie in de context van een wetenschappelijke controverse*, Universiteit Twente WMW-publicatie 27, Delft: Eburon.

Wynne, B., (1992), 'Uncertainty and Environmental Learning: Re-conceiving Science and Policy in the Preventative Paradigm', *Global Environmental Change*, Vol. 2, No. 2, pp. 111–27.

———, (2001), 'Managing Scientific Uncertainty in Public Policy', Paper presented at the Conference on 'Biotechnology and Global Governance: Crisis and Opportunity', Cambridge, MA.

PART 5

Science for Sustainable Development Policy

16

Impact Assessment and Quantitative Modelling in European Policy Development

ANDREAS THIEL[1]

A recent strand of European research projects contracted under the sixth research framework programme[2] of the European Commission is to develop quantitative *ex ante* assessment tools that feed into the policy development cycle, or more specifically, IA practices in the European Commission (CEC 2002a, 2005). Hence, these research projects are to provide scientifically grounded tools that produce arguments for deciding between various options of policy-making and for achieving pre-defined policy ends. This article assumes that, to be useful for policy-making, these modelling tools and the processes by which they are designed should be aware of the features of the policy-making process into which they are to be embedded. Modelling tools themselves prescribe an attitude to policy-making that has elsewhere been described as 'decisionism' (Majone 1989), in which the sphere of scientific analysis and its political judgement were assumed to be separable. The overall task of analysing policies is viewed as a process in which the benefits of a limited number of policy alternatives to reach pre-defined objectives were compared and the most effective policy was singled out as the preferred policy option. Highly pre-structured quantitative policy assessment tools are necessarily functioning that way. However, in line with the work underlying this article, Majone (1989: 23) describes overall policy

---

[1]This chapter is based on research work that has been undertaken as part of the 'Institutonal Analysis' of the 'SENSOR' project which has been funded by the sixth Framework Programme of the European Union.

[2]See also: *http://ec.europa.eu/research/fp6/index_en.cfm*, accessed on10 July 2007

analysis as the 'ability to provide acceptable reasons for one's choices and actions'. Policy and its administration (or detailed implementation) are inseparable as many legislative mandates are vague, ambiguous, or contradictory. Furthermore, as Ravetz put it: 'The previous belief that scientists should and could provide certain, objective factual information for decision-makers is now being increasingly recognised as simplistic and immature' (1999a: 648). Rather, science is recognized to be part of the policy process. In issue-driven science, stakes are high, values in dispute, and decisions urgent, which require what Ravetz called 'post-normal science' (1999a), which is directly associated with policy-making. The challenge of post-normal science is to achieve high quality of the process in which its results are produced as well as high quality of its outcome.

Having overcome the era of decisionism, that is, the 1950s and 1960s, nowadays it is clear that models at best, and only 'if developed and used with care,...provide evidence which, together with other sources of information, may be used in arguments supporting a certain conclusion or argumentation' (Majone 1989: 51; also Robinson 1992: 161). This was the primary objective of the development of the modelling tool that the work presented in this article contributed to: to be used in European policy development. This chapter is concerned with one element of post-normal science—to make quantitative assessment tools relevant for policy and decision making. Therefore, it addresses the questions of 'what determines if an *ex-ante* quantitative assessment tool is selected for use in the European Commission' and 'what should be its features'. It presents a short description of the way modelling tools are used and, at the end, it briefly reflects on the quality of the process into which it is embedded.

The next section provides some background on the conceptual and methodological approach. Subsequently, the current setting in which *ex-ante* quantitative assessment tools are used in European policy development is presented. The chapter concludes by making a link between the question and the data presented.

Conceptualization of the Problem Setting and Method

This chapter cannot be predominantly concerned with establishing scientific truth about what determines if, and what, modelling tools are used for policy assessment. The research necessarily had to extrapolate trends from past policy development and assessment practices in order to come to conclusions useful for a quantitative modelling tool which will only be available in the future and which is confronted with a policy development setting in the European Commission that is in constant flux. This situates the research underlying this chapter in the realm of post-normal science, which in this case provides for reasons for policy assessment tool design rather than truths about how tools have to be designed.

Institutional Analysis and the Use of Modelling Tools

The application of a quantitative *ex-ante* policy assessment tool that is largely software and hardware based substantially pre-structures the way an assessment is undertaken. It predetermines which data is used for the assessment, which assumptions are made while relating data sets to each other, and it computes impacts regarding a pre-defined set of dimensions. This way of assessing policy options has to be embedded into existing ways of assessing policy options. Nonetheless, the successful introduction of a modelling tool into existing policy development procedures changes existing practices of policy assessment. Therefore, the underlying assumption is that, for being useful for policy-making, quantitative *ex-ante* policy tool development needs to take account of the (institutionalized) practices and constraints under which policy analysts in the European Commission assess different policy options.

Before moving forward, the paper structures the setting in which quantitative assessment tools are used, using Ostrom's Institutional Analysis and Development Framework (IAD) (Ostrom 1998, 2005). The setting in which quantitative *ex-ante* policy assessment tools are used is conceptualized as an action situation in which European desk officers, on behalf of the European Commission, take the decision on whether a tool is to be used and which one is used. In this context, it is of interest to see how the preferences of Commission officials emerge. Insights on the way preferences are formed provide information on the scope for influencing decision-making over alternative tools. This in turn may be relevant for the way quantitative *ex ante* policy assessment tools are introduced into the institutional context in the European Commission. In conceptual terms, the research referred to either the logic of appropriateness, in which actors adapt their behaviour to the rules that govern a community and which can be actively changed, or the logic of consequentiality, where actions are chosen in order to reach a specific predefined outcome that suits the decision-makers' preferences. Institutions structure the setting in which the decision about policy assessment tool use is taken. Institutions are conceptualized as regularized patterns of social interaction that may be formalized in written form and which establish acknowledged or unacknowledged guidelines to people's behaviour (see also Peters 1999). The setting is established by the actors that participate in policy development. Their specific characteristics and those of the overall community have to be grasped[3] as well as the institutions that govern the setting in relation to the *ex-ante* policy assessment procedure.[4]

The Modelling Tool Use Setting in European Policy Development

The setting for assessment tool choice is shaped by several categories of factors: (i) the characteristics of the policy options that are assessed (salience, interests at stake and the political resources of their representatives, certainty of its effects, their possibility to be quantified, the type of rules they affect, and if they are targeted or not); (ii) the features of the input data (source, reliability, comprehensiveness); (iii) by specific features of the assessment tool (assumptions, transparency of tool creation, ownership, reputation, track record, focus, etc.); (iv) by the way the output is presented; and (v) the context of the decision is the policy development cycle, which, with regard to tool selection, is the IA procedure within the European Commission. The paper presents its conclusions referring to this conceptualization

[3]The IAD framework describes collective and individual actors (participants in an action arena) with recourse to their preferences for potential outcomes, the way they acquire, process, retain, and use knowledge and information; their selection criteria to decide upon a particular course of action; and the resources that an actor brings to a situation. It describes the community of actors through the generally accepted norms of behaviour, level of common understanding about action arenas, extent to which preferences are homogeneous, and the distribution of the resources among the community.

[4]The IAD singles out position rules, which specify positions of actors and the number of participants that hold each position; authority rules, which specify the set of actions associated with each position; aggregation rules, which specify the transformation function that map actions into intermediate or final outcomes; scope rules, which specify the set of outcomes that may be affected, information rules which specify the level of information available at a certain position; and payoff rules, which specify the costs and benefits associated with certain actions and outcomes. Furthermore, it matters how often this situation will be repeated. However, many policy assessment exercises are so unique that we can assume they are one-off decisions.

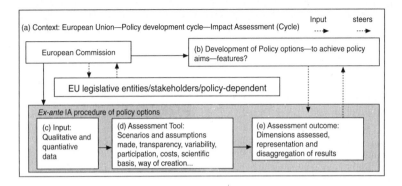

Figure 16.1:   Conceptualization of Modelling Tool in EU-Policy Development

of the research setting, which is visualized in Figure 16.1. The choice of the modelling tool is based on the assumption that what is at stake is (i) if a policy is adopted and (ii) what features this policy option has if the specific tool used has a direct influence on the policy-making outcome. In what follows, the context of policy assessment tool choices is described, and the features of the community of actors, and the criteria for action selection is discussed. This description of the setting for tool selection is subsequently rounded off by a description of the way *ex-ante* policy assessment tools were used in policy development in the European Commission so far. The conclusions present the factors that shape the way modelling tools are selected, and a brief reflection of their relation to post-normal science.

Notes on Methodology

The empirical basis of the work were 26 interviews with European Commission officials and stakeholders involved in activities which were considered relevant for modelling tool design for IA at least in some respect: policy development practices in general, IA as the European Commission's procedure to assess the impacts of new policies and major policy revisions, and modelling tool use. For reasons of confidentiality, the statements of desk officers could not be quoted or referenced in detail. The empirical work was complemented by drawing on existing literature on the way the European Commission functions and how desk officers operate within.

CONTEXT: EUROPEAN IMPACT ASSESSMENT PRACTICES FOR POLICY DEVELOPMENT

Policy development in the European Commission is structured by the so-called policy development cycle. Since the introduction of IA in 2002, issues that are dealt with in the European Commission's annual policy strategy have to be accompanied by a roadmap, which lays out the contents, schedule, and participating Directorate Generals (DGs) throughout IA. Before the introduction of IA, various procedures already existed in European policy-making to assess policy processes (see also Radaelli 2007). However, those can be classified as insignificant disparate initiatives. IA, on the other hand, was 'intended to integrate, reinforce, streamline and replace all the existing separate IA mechanisms for Commission proposals' (CEC 2002a: 3). Its objective was to 'improve the quality and coherence of the policy development process' (CEC 2002a: 5). Furthermore, policies that had little chance of passing the legislative process are to be detected and halted early on, to avoid wastage of resources of the Commission, and of desk officers' time. IA assesses the economic, social, and environmental impact dimensions of policies. They are detailed in a number of tables, promoting 'thinking out of the box' in terms of the impact dimensions of European policies that are assessed.

The material on which the article is based showed that Commission officials associate the introduction of IA with a culture change in the context of the European Commission's initiative on good governance. Aspects of this culture change are the increasing importance of structured cross-sectoral consultation and participation throughout policy development, the increased transparency of the overall policy development process, and the increasing importance of evaluating European policies in terms of their costs and benefits and cost effectiveness, an aspect which is said to have strengthened the role of economists in policy development. As a consequence of the introduction of IA, policy preparation is said to have become much slicker and more time consuming. After initial opposition, desk officers seem to increasingly recognize that 'better' policies are the outcome of such a lengthier policy development process. Similarly, the European Parliament and the European Council are asked to undertake IAs of changes they propose to policies (Council of the European Union 2003).

Within the Commission, IAs are undertaken by the desk officer in charge of a specific policy proposal and under consultation with further desk officers representing other units and DGs which are relevant for the proposal. Every IA is different, as desk officers stress. Majone makes a useful distinction between 'contributing' IAs that discover aspects of policies and 'legitimizing' IAs that justify a policy choice *ex post* (Majone 1989). The empirical material confirmed this distinction and even some desk officers make this distinction. 'Legitimizing' IAs do not influence the final policy-making outcome in terms of the policy that the European Commission proposes. Their purpose is rather to confirm the policy option that has been agreed upon in advance. The reasons for this may be that the policy is subject to a more intergovernmental negotiation style (as in regional policy) or that it has something to do with budget-spending, or that timing simply does not allow for a meaningful consideration of various policy alternatives. 'Contributing' IAs, on the other hand, actually have an influence on the policy that is adopted. Ideally, their result is open and they help to select a more effective and efficient policy option to reach a pre-formulated policy goal. However, desk officers confirm that in reality the process is more iterative and policy goals may be altered as assessment advances. 'Contributing' IAs are considered to be equivalent to the policy development process. The roadmap and the final report of the IA illustrate the various steps undertaken at certain stages throughout the policy development process such as the various consultation, participation, and assessment steps and the conclusions that the Commission drew up for further assessment and the final policy. Participation and assessment exercises throughout the IA are to be subject to the 'principle of proportionate analysis', which stipulates that '[t]he more significant an action is likely to be, the greater the effort of quantification and monetisation that will generally be expected. Furthermore, it depends on the political and legal nature of the proposal under preparation, its sectoral particularities and the point in the policy making process at which the IA is undertaken...' (CEC 2005: 8). Torritti (2005) wrote that so far the use of quantification was minimum. Currently, several research projects commissioned by the European Commission under the 6th Framework Programme[5] have the objective of improving the modelling capacity with regard to specific impacts that the European Commission is interested in. The aim of the material presented in this paper is to contribute to these efforts.

[5]Sensor, Seamless, Eforwood, Spicosa.

ACTION ARENA: THE PARTICIPANTS AND COMMUNITY OF EUROPEAN POLICY ASSESSMENT IN THE EUROPEAN COMMISSION

Participants, in what Ostrom (1998, 2005) would call the quantitative *ex-ante* policy assessment tool selection 'action arena', are those actors that influence whether a tool is used throughout policy assessment procedures, and which one is used. Participants are desk officers in the European Commission and the hierarchy that legitimizes their decisions. Furthermore, the European Parliament and the Council are participants in adopting a legislation. Stakeholders are indirect participants consulted throughout the preparation of a legislation whose interests are impinged upon by the legislation. Furthermore, consultants and/or experts who may be asked to provide input to an IA are described.

The overarching norms of behaviour of the community of participants in IA are determined by the actors that directly participate in European law-making. However, these rules need to be acceptable to stakeholders and those legitimizing the Commission and the Council. It can be assumed that the preferences of these actors with regard to the substantive policy outcome vary significantly. Similarly, the resources of the various members of this community to influence policy development vary. The Commission has significant influence as it has the right of initiative in European policy-making and guides the policy development cycle and the associated IA. On the other hand, desk officers lament that an important constraint on the Commission's policy development capacity are its limited human resources and time available, which lead to considerable outsourcing and the need to employ consultants. Depending on the type of legislation that is to be adopted, the European Council and the Parliament only have varying possibilities to express themselves on the proposal, adopting or rejecting it or sending it back to the Commission for alterations.[6]

---

[6]No less than 32 legal bases fall under the co-decision procedure. They require a qualified majority in the Council with the exception of the common agricultural policy, commercial policy, and fiscal policy where policies have to be adopted unanimously. The procedure gives a significant role to the Parliament in the legislative process. However, among others it does not apply to the financial perspective, regional funds, or fiscal matters. The cooperation procedure is limited to certain decisions relating to economic and monetary union. Therefore, it is not relevant for policies that develop a direct impact on land use. The assent procedure applies to legislations relating to the structural funds. Parliament can only approve a draft. It has become

The detailed properties of the actors vary significantly. Research showed that the task of Commission staff shifted increasingly from policy formulation to a 'catalytic research activity' and the use of policy analysis as a means of persuasion, while always seeking to extend the scope of the Commission's role (Cram 1997: 37). The empirical material underlying this article showed that desk officers usually do not have a substantial programmatic preference with regard to policy-making. For career purposes, gains in wage and prestige, their objective must be to have policy proposals that they are working on adopted by the various levels of the hierarchy of the Commission and subsequently by the European Council and/or the Parliament (Hooghe 2001: 21). This can be called a procedural motivation as opposed to a substantive motivation, which would aim at including very specific aspects into the final policy. The latter seems to be subordinated to creating adoptable policies.

Substantive preferences of desk officers seem to be shaped by their membership in a specific DG and by their previous education and experience, which vary considerably (see also Hooghe 2001: 199). It can be assumed that, for contributing IAs, substantive preferences are shaped by the ongoing IA and policy development. The interviews showed that desk officers have best access to the technical information on a policy proposal and on the ways to assess it. Some of them even have longstanding experience in a policy field. In other cases, they only develop their knowledge of a policy field as policy development and IA unfold. In such cases, substantive preferences are shaped by the process. On the other hand, desk officers hardly have the time to do extensive assessments themselves. They state that, as certain questions are raised throughout the steps of policy development, consultation, and lobbying, they learn about the policy, its implications, and the interests they impinge upon and then develop answers to them. Providing answers to the questions that emerge throughout policy development is about assessing the impacts of a policy. Choices

---

the practice to previously involve Parliament informally. The Financial Framework (the multi-annual spending plan of the Union) on which regional fund and agriculture policy funds depend is decided on the basis of a proposal from the Commission, which is then unanimously agreed by the European Council as a basis for negotiations between the Parliament, Council, and Commission. The council, therefore, has the key role in its adoption. When the three institutions have reached a decision on the framework, the negotiations on the sectoral proposals are developed (see also: *http://www.europarl.europa.eu/facts/default_en.htm#*, accessed on 29 June 2007).

about what impacts are being assessed, and how, can be assumed to have an impact on the policy outcome and its adoption. For this reason, it is widely recognized to be a matter of debate and political relevance. Desk officers guide policy development and assessment. It can be assumed that this gives them considerable influence over the content of a policy and the way it is developed. On the other hand, desk officers have relatively less control over the policy-making outcome as it has to be approved by many levels of the hierarchy and several entities (Commissioners, Council, and Parliament).

Senior officials are more aware of the political implications of a proposal (Stevens and Stevens 2001: 178). Hooghe writes: '[s]enior Commission officials have always been conscious of their vulnerable position at the intersection of politics and expertise' (Hooghe 2001: 8). 'Yet, as unelected officials [are] appointed for their expertise, they are presumed to be above the political fray. If they do not handle these tensions well, they may weaken their legitimacy' (Hooghe 2001: 12). It can be assumed, therefore, that objectives of more senior officials shaping policy proposals and assessments are similarly procedural, impregnated by the values and positions the specific DG in question represents and their education and previous experience. '[T]op Officials work in an environment where competition for attention from principals, agenda setting, resources, prestige, influence, and promotion is harsh. To be ignored or by-passed by their principals may publicly taint an ambitious official' (Hooghe 2001: 21). They have greater control of the outcome of policy-making given their greater authority. Also, they may interfere with the selection of a specific policy assessment tool. However, senior officials' interest and influence on technical details varies with the different personalities involved (Cini 1996: 152).

Other participants, such as stakeholders, consultants, and experts have no direct influence either on policy development, adoption, or IA. The Committee of the Regions specifically pressed for a role of the regions in IA (AEBR et al. 2003). However, regions and their European representations are only interfering where a policy has specific impacts on a region (Thielemann 2003; Keating and Hooghe 1996: 219). The Commission itself has to deal with the competent national authority to address issues in a specific region. Stakeholders are consulted by, or lobby officers in the various sectoral DGs, in the Council or the European Parliament (Beyers 2002). Therefore, they may exercise considerable indirect influence over the way assessments are undertaken and the content of policies. Some stakeholders have very clear preferences with regard to the outcome of policy-making. The empirical work showed that they may even provide additional assessments to inform or confront the policy development process when significant stakes are at play (for the case of REACH, see for example Jacob and Volkery 2006). Resources of stakeholders vary widely. It is well known that environmental NGOs are often underfunded while some private sector interests have significant resources at their disposal. Resource availability also determines the information processing and acquisition abilities of stakeholders.

Consultants and experts contribute in a very limited remit. It can be assumed that, to some extent, experts are bound by their expertise on specific issues, while consultants are bound by contractual arrangements that ask them to undertake certain analytical steps in order to receive a remuneration. They are not supposed to have their substantive preferences impinge on their work. For consultants, experts, and stakeholders it is assumed that information availability and processing capacities are concentrated on substantive, technical issues, rather than on political issues.

Selection Criteria for Quantitative *Ex-ante* Policy Assessment Tools

Desk officers as well as the hierarchy controlling their actions have limited information and processing capacities with regard to the implications of the choices they make throughout an assessment and its impact on the final policy. In order to guide that choice, they apply what Ostrom called a heuristic of (selection) criteria throughout an assessment process. Some of these criteria are codified in the IA guidelines. Others are based on experience and institutionalized throughout more informal processes. Research is concentrated on uncovering these selection criteria to determine what type of quantitative assessment tools are useful for European policy-making.

The use of quantitative assessment tools follows the principle of proportionate analysis. This means that specifically those policies are to be assessed that are new or imply significant changes and whose assessment is salient therefore. Furthermore, it was described above that the way policies are adopted on the EU level has an influence. Where the European Parliament has a significant role in policy adoption, as it is the case of the co-decision procedure, the IA seems to become an arena for preliminary influence on policy-making.

Therefore, choices of assessment may develop a considerable contribution for the content of the policy which is presented by the Commission. Finally, the time that is awarded to policy development has a crucial implication for the way an assessment is developed. The latest version of the IA guidelines details the impacts that should be assessed, in a non-conclusive table which formulates specific questions with regard to social, environmental, and social impact dimensions of European policy-making (CEC 2005: 29–32). Impacts have to touch upon important stakes with regard to the dimensions that are modelled and translate into the criterion that a modelling tool has to answer a question that must have been raised by an important stakeholder throughout the policy development process. However, a Commission source explained the relatively scarce use of modelling tools: 'there are a very large number of various types of modelling tools available while, on the other hand, their applicability to the questions relevant for evaluations of public policies is limited' (CEC 2002b). Throughout the fieldwork, desk officers representing various sectoral DGs confirmed that the most prominent are the macro-economic and sectoral economic impacts of different policy options. Issues other than those that the policy focuses upon and on which the policy still has an impact may also be looked at. Desk officers maintain that unintended impacts and issues over which the Commission does not have any competence are of specific relevance. However, where a policy's impact on a specific dimension depends on a member state's subsidiary implementation competency, many desk officers would advise not to undertake modelling (for example, in the case of land use impacts). In European policy-making, the fieldwork often showed that semantics matter with regard to the dimensions that are modelled. The way issues are formulated in assessments has to be legitimized in European policy-making, for example, competitiveness and growth as opposed to multifunctionality of land use.[7] The impacts of salient new regulations on dimensions that are recognised as European competencies and priority (such as economic growth) are most likely to be assessed through modelling. European competencies and issues of relevance for assessment at the European level are determined by the institutional set-up of the Union laid down in the treaty, on-going European policy-making and agenda setting.

[7]Multifunctionality of land use describes the fact that land use produces various overlapping services to people. It can be perceived as a descriptive as well as a normative category.

The empirical material showed that officials appreciate further features of European modelling tools for IA. The results of modelling tools have to be plausible, which means that they have to make intuitive sense rather than being extraordinarily innovative. Tools should be user-friendly, so that, at best, desk officers need to be able to use tools themselves after a brief training. Alternatively, they have to be able to explain how modelling tool results were produced, which means that the lid is taken off the 'modelling black box'. The principal stakeholders should also be invited to such training and information workshops. The Commission has to be able to make explicit the way in which results of modelling tool use were produced. Assumptions, restrictions, risks, weaknesses, and data sources of the use of the tool have to be made explicit. The tool has to have a good scientific track record. Similarly, once the Commission has gathered positive experiences with the use of a modelling tool, it would rely on the same tool for further assessments. Legitimacy and adequacy to European policy-making needs are important for tool use by the Commission. Tools that have been created with input from the Commission, member states, and relevant stakeholders are preferred as their legitimization is based on a broader footing.

Desk officers confirmed that a significant constraint to further modelling tool use in the Commission is the lack of official data on many relevant issues. Data used in modelling should come from official sources such as Eurostat or Espon. Some regularly even doubt their legitimacy (Sverdrup 2005: 26). Data that is gathered by consultants or even provided by stakeholders should be treated with great caution. The way in which the outcome of modelling is presented depends principally on the nature of the data. The Commission is free to choose the way it presents the outcomes. Maps are generally seen as very effective ways of communicating data to the public (see also Robinson 1992; Funtowicz and Ravetz 1990). The use of maps is not an issue throughout the stage of assessment exercises. Nonetheless, where policies are instrumental to policy-making or even the distribution of funds, they are strongly disputed. DGs, such as, for example, Regio would, therefore, only rely on descriptive maps.

QUANTITATIVE *EX-ANTE* POLICY ASSESSMENT TOOL USE AND IMPACT ASSESSMENT

Enquiry into the way the European Commission uses *ex-ante* quantitative policy assessment tools has shown the following. In

IAs whose outcome is not pre-determined, the tool, the data, and the scenarios that are used would be extensively discussed within the Commission (see also Sverdrup 2005). Scenarios may be approved within a directorate before use. The outcome may be checked with experts from the Member States (MSs) with regard to its plausibility. Desk officers have to be able to explain the way a model produced its outcomes as assumptions are regularly the object of extensive scrutiny and discussion. For this purpose, the Commission would hold meetings among the services involved, with participation of the consultants that did the modelling and, sometimes, stakeholders. Consultancies and the Commission may be asked at this occasion to 'open up the black box'. In discussions with other services and stakeholders, the Commission aims to 'close issues' by adopting a final position on the best way of modelling or how the results of modelling should be viewed. For critical points it may also agree with stakeholders on how to study unresolved issues in a more in-depth manner.

For specifically salient policies, modelling tools and their results may be discussed with representatives of the MSs or the parliament within the legislative process. Tool use is never unquestioned where policies involve significant stakes. Where modelling tools are used, desk officers recognize that they refocus the debate on the issues at hand in modelling (for example, assumptions made, data used, upscaling and downscaling of data). Desk officers describe this as 'rationalizing the debate'. Jacob and Volkery (2005), on the other hand, wonder if such a refocusing of the debate on modelling details instead of actual policy implications actually contributes to better policy making. Also,

[c]ompared with textual information, figures are particularly effective in reducing complexities and enabling comparisons.... Numerical value also seems to affect the value and trust attached to the information...[on the other hand i]n the EU the lack of a common language makes textual information even more difficult and costly...but numerical information creates a form of communicating across fairly heterogeneous member states (Sverdrup 2005: 5).

Desk officers and employees of the European Parliament explained that the role modelling tools play in political debate depends on the attitudes of the people involved. Some political representatives such as Members of the European Parliament instrumentalize modelling tools. Others are reluctant to take their results on board altogether and separate analysis and assessment of policies from their debate in the political arena. Attitudes depend not least on the technical understanding policy-makers are able to develop. The latter may argue that decisions, once they reach the political level, should be made on a political basis rather than on the basis of quantitative evaluations.

CONCLUDING REMARKS

The chapter described the setting of quantitative *ex-ante* modelling tool selection as part of European IA practices. The setting was conceptualized using Ostrom's IAD framework. The basic questions were: 'what determines if an *ex-ante* quantitative assessment tool is used', and 'what should an *ex-ante* quantitative assessment tool look like to be useful for European policy making' and 'how it is used'. In order to answer these questions, the research tried to address conceptualised modelling tool use as determined by the features of the policy that is assessed, the characteristics of the data that go into tool use, the features of the tool and the way it was designed, and the way in which a tool presents its outcomes (see also Figure 16.1).

With regard to the characteristics of the policy that is assessed, the principle of proportionate analysis states that quantitative assessment tools are used where significant impacts are expected from a new policy or a substantial amendment. The empirical work showed that it has to impinge on the interests of a significant stakeholder and an impact dimension that is considered to be of European interest, such as those where the EU has a mandate. In-depth discussion and assessment of policies including modelling seems to be more likely for policies that are subject to the co-decision procedure and where sufficient time for the assessment is available. Overall and sectoral economic impacts are the dimensions that are most frequently assessed. The input data used for assessments should be accepted by member states and stakeholders, so that, principally, data from official sources qualifies.

In principle, the use of *ex ante* quantitative assessment tools has to answer a significant question/issue that emerged in the course of an IA. Desk officers who steer the IA have, what has been referred to above as a procedural motivation to have policies adopted. Therefore, they are interested in finding answers to the questions that are raised throughout the IA. The IA community regarding a specific policy, therefore, has some scope to mould the assessment preferences of desk officers. Alternatively, conflicting issues could be raised *vis-à-vis* the hierarchy, the parliament, or the council later on, hindering adoption of the policy at a later stage. The hierarchy and other sectoral administrations within the Commission, the Council, and the Parliament are the object of often resourceful lobbying activities which at times express significantly diverging substantive preferences of the various participants of policy development. Given their procedural preferences, desk officers as well as the hierarchy approving their work are interested in 'closing' issues among participants of IA as early as possible. This means finishing off discussion and justifying the adopted stance in order to prepare for opposition at a later stage.

Desk officers apply a number of criteria for selecting a quantitative assessment tool. These can be translated into features that a modelling tool should have. It has to produce plausible results rather than being innovative. It should be user-friendly and desk officers have to be introduced to its workings so that they are able to explain the way results are produced themselves. Assumptions, data used, and weaknesses, therefore, have to be made explicit, and the tool should have a good scientific track record. Tools with which the Commission has previously had good experiences are preferred. The output of tool use should be communicated effectively, using maps or graphs as appropriate. The technical details of the tool and the outcome of its use would be discussed in depth. Modelling tool use is perceived by desk officers to rationalize the debate with stakeholders, other DGs, and European bodies.

The findings presented in this chapter concur with the findings of different studies on the effectiveness of assessment exercises to shape policy-making. Eckley (2001) found that what she named 'saliency', 'credibility', and 'legitimacy' of an assessment contribute to its effect on policy-making. These categories are further detailed by Farrel (2006) and Jäger and Farrel (2006). Following them ensures that assessment exercises are effective for policy-making, which is assumed to be equivalent to their fruitful use. In relation to the introduction of this chapter, the question remains open as to how *ex-ante* quantitative assessment tool use performs in relation to what Funtowicz and Ravetz described as post-normal science.

Post-normal science implies science which contributes to (political) decision-making. It requires that the outputs as well as the process which produces these outputs are of high quality to cope with decision making situations where uncertainties may be high or where significant stakes are involved (Ravetz 1999a; Funtowicz and Ravetz 1992). For many cases, this adequately describes the way *ex-ante* quantitative modelling tools are used in IA. For this reason, in concluding the chapter, brief reflections on modelling tool use in IA are presented in the context of post-normal science. In his contribution, Ravetz extensively discusses the problems of modelling tool use in guiding decisions. The quality of their output can only be judged in hindsight. Therefore, the quality of the process is the only available criterion to judge the outcome of *ex ante* modelling tool use by the time they produce their outcome. Ravetz advocates principles of 'professional consultancy' to guide those leading the process. They comprise craft skills of judgement and moral qualities of decisiveness and integrity (Ravetz 1999b: 259). Ravetz pleads for an 'uncertainty and quality' audit on scientific information. The key is to enable users to make their own reasoned judgements of the strengths of an instrument for particular purposes. He proposes a societal process for these purposes where 'the "hardware" is a tool for guiding discussions' (Ravetz 1999a: 261). Within the IA community of participating desk officers, there is a general agreement that modelling tools help to structure the policy development discussion. In specifically disputed cases, the modelling tool itself is discussed in depth. However, in the case of REACH, for example, Jacob and Volkery (2005) lament that such a discussion focuses on technicalities of a modelling tool while failing to discuss the impacts of envisaged policies. According to Ravetz (1999a), steps within a policy development process that evaluates the use of a modelling tool has to be characterized by four principles: knowledge, congruence (internal coherence of ideas, plans, and realities), resources, and trust. The outcome would provide a 'Pedigree' with regard to the quantitative results in which a 'class is assigned and inherent limits are displayed' with regard to the tool.

When modeling tool use in IA is evaluated with regard to these process criteria based on the empirical work presented in this article as well as on other studies (see for example EEAC 2006), the way in which the quality of quantitative *ex-ante* policy modeling is appraised in European policy development appears to be deficient. The use of quantitative assessment tools in EU policy-making seems to be biased towards economic dimensions (IEEP 2004). The resources of stakeholders representing private sector economic interests seem to largely outweigh those of other interest groups. However, Commission officials argue that the IA process itself provides sufficient quality assurance, as representatives of various interests obtain the opportunity to express themselves on the IA. However, in reality, some stakeholders seem to have a privileged position in accompanying assessments (not least due to the unequal resource distribution) and no independent, reliable process exists by which the quality of an overall IA can be reviewed in a transparent way. Therefore, the criteria of 'trust', 'knowledge', and 'resources' proposed by Ravetz seem to be insufficiently complied with. In other words, the use of *ex-ante* quantitative assessment tools throughout IA in the European Commission does not yet fully reach the standards of 'professional consultancy'. Therefore, following Ravetz, scope for improvement remains if IA is to meet the challenges of great uncertainty and high stakes in decision making in an era of post-normal science.

REFERENCES

AEBR, CEMR, CPMR, EUROCITIES, (2003), 'Joint Response to the Commission Working Paper "Ongoing and Systematic Policy Dialogue with Local Government Associations", available at *http://ec.europa.eu/regional_policy/consultation/territorial/reponse_jointe__lettre.pdf*, accesseed on 2 February 2006.

Beyers, J., (2002), 'Voice and Access: Political Practices of Diffuse and Specific Interest Associations in European Policy Making', Mimeo, Oslo: Arena Working Papers, WP 02/39.

CEC, (2002a), Communication from the Commission on Impact Assessment, COM (2002, 276 final).

_____, (2002b), Expert Meeting on 'Modelling Tools for the Ex Post Evaluation of the CAP', Meeting held in Brussels, 1 July 2002.

_____, (2005), 'Impact Assessment Guidelines', SEC (2005) 791.

Cini M., (1996), *The European Commission*, Manchester: Manchester University Press.

Cram, L., (1997), *Policy-making in the EU*, London: Routledge.

Council of the European Union, (2003), 'Interinstitutional Agreement on Better Law-making', Brussels, 23 September.

Eckley, N., (2001), 'Designing Effective Assessments: The Role of Participation, Science and Governance, and Focus', mimeo, Report of a workshop co-organised by the European Environment Agency and the Global Environmental Assessment Project, Copenhagen, Denmark, 1–3 March.

EEAC, (2006), 'Impact Assessment of European Commission Policies: Achievements and Prospects', mimeo, available at *www.eeac-net.org*, accessed on 23 March 2007.

Farrel, A.E. and J. Jäger, (2006), *Assessments of Regional and Global Environmental Risks*, Washington D.C.: Resources for the Future Press.

Farrel, A.E., J. Jäger, and S.D. VanDeveer, (2006), 'Overview: Understanding Design Choices', in A.E. Farrel and J. Jäger (eds), *Assessments of Regional and Global Environmental Risks*, Washington D.C.: Resources for the Future Press.

Funtowicz, S.O. and J.R. Ravetz, (1992), "Three Types of Risk Assessment and the Emergence of Post-normal Science', in S. Krimsky and D. Golding (eds), *Social Theories of Risk*, Greenwood: Westport CT.

____, (1990), *Uncertainty and Quality in Science for Policy*, Kluwer: Dordrecht,

L. Hooghe, (2001), *The European Commission and the Integration of Europe*, Cambridge: Cambridge University Press.

IEEP, (2004), 'Sustainable Development in the European Commission's Integrated Impact Assessments for 2003: Final Report', mimeo, London: IEEP.

Jacob, K. and A. Volkery, (2006), 'Europäische Rechtsetzung: Die Auseinandersetzung zur Europäischen Chemikalienpolitik Reach und die Rolle nationaler Regierungen und Akteure im Policy Prozess', *Technikfolgenabschaetzung: Theorie und Praxis*, Vol. 4, No. 1, pp. 69–77.

Keating, M. and L. Hooghe, (1996), 'By-passing the Nation-state? Regions and the EU Policy Process', in J.J. Richardson, *European Union*, London and New York: Routledge.

Majone, G., (1989), *Evidence, Argument and Persuasion in the Policy Process*, New Haven and London: Yale University Press.

Ostrom, E., (1998), 'The Institutional Analysis and Development Approach', in E. Tusak Loehman and D.M. Kilgour (eds), *Designing Institutions for Environmental and Resource Management*, Cheltenham: Edward Elgar.

____, (2005), *Understanding Institutional Diversity*, Princeton, N.J. and Woodstock: Princeton University Press.

Peters, B.G., (1999), *Institutional Theory in Political Science: The 'New Institutionalism'*, London: Pinter.

Radaelli, C., (2007), 'Whither better Regulation for the Lisbon Agenda', *Journal of European Public Policy*, Vol. 14, No. 2, pp. 190–207.

Ravetz, J.R., (1999a), 'What is Post-normal Science', *Futures*, Vol. 31, pp. 647–53.

____, (1999b), 'Developing Principles of Good Practice in Integrated Environmental Assessment', *International Journal of Environment and Pollution*, Vol. 11, No. 3, pp. 243–65.

Robinson, J.B., (1992), 'Of Maps and Territories', *Technological Forecasting and Social Change*, Vol. 42, pp. 147–64.

Stevens, A. and H. Stevens, (2001), *Brussels Bureaucrats?*, Houndmills: Palgrave.

Sverdrup, U., (2005), 'Administering Information: Eurostat and Statistical Integration', mimeo, ARENA Working Paper Series, 27/2005, Oslo.

Thielemann, E.R., (2000), 'Europeanization and Institutional Compatibility: Implementing European Regional Policy in Germany', mimeo, Queen's Papers on Europeanization, No. 4/2000, Belfast.

Torriti, J., (2005), 'Functional Dimension of the European Commission's IAs: Openness, Transparency and the Extent of Quantification'. mimeo, Draft paper presented at EcoEasy Conference, Manchester, 15–17 June.

17

Innovation for Eco-friendly Development
Towards Institutional Reform in Scientific Research and Policy-making

RAJESWARI S. RAINA

SCIENCE AND TECHNOLOGY AND THE HIGH STAKES OF POVERTY REDUCTION

Science for eco-friendly development often conveys images of highly sophisticated scientific endeavours and technologies that encounter high stakes in reversing current trajectories of industrial development, cause retrenchment of workers in polluting industries, and problematic relocation of industries. The decision stakes, risks and uncertainties, and information constraints, it may appear, are relatively low when it comes to the conduct and application of S&T for increased employment and rural/agricultural development, which can positively affect millions of poor people. But empirical evidence of continuing poverty in the face of resources (though inadequate) spent on S&T and government schemes devoted to S&T for rural development points to very high stakes. There is a major risk of social disruption and ecological degradation worsening with poverty and inequality, and the potential S&T applications that can positively change these trends, co-existing in a context of deeply entrenched institutional rigidities; a fear of or unwillingness to learn and change. This chapter addresses the need to reform or change these institutions that maintain the 'business as usual' or routine mode of conducting S&T and making policies for implementing S&T-based interventions for eco-friendly development.

Rural poverty and the poverty–employment–energy–environmental degradation nexus is characteristic of South Asian countries.[1] A large proportion of the South Asian population is still engaged in primary production (agriculture, mining, gathering, etc.) and value addition activities (FAO 2006). Any application of knowledge in this context of poverty, largely generated by un- and under-employment of otherwise productive hands in the economy, has to address how these hands can be selectively withdrawn and converted into productive forces in other sectors in the economy, without adversely affecting the production levels, environmental quality, and human health/well-being in the primary sector (Sen 1967; Lewis 1954; Schultz 1964). The capacity to create additional employment opportunities without adding to environmental degradation and global warming, and reclaiming lost environmental quality and services even if in a marginal or incremental manner, will determine the future of economic development and social and environmental systems in South Asia (MEA 2006). With the South Asian states, especially countries like India embarking on rapid globalization and economic liberalization processes, the relatively disadvantaged rural population already facing degrading environmental quality will be increasingly marginalized and slip further into poverty if policies to create environment-friendly employment and income opportunities are not aggressively pursued.

A major and singularly uncontested assumption is that scientifically validated eco-friendly technologies enable employment, income generation, and sustainable development. This chapter argues that when the complex social contexts and deep-seated decision stakes are taken into account, S&T for sustainable rural development is akin to post-normal science that is characterized by high stakes, global dimensions, and uncertainty. The decision processes that underpin S&T application for sustainable development are governed by the norms of technological determinism and linear knowledge hierarchies of normal problem-solving science. This chapter contends that these norms impede environment-friendly development by foreclosing the

[1]While the population living below the poverty line or at the edge of poverty is increasing steadily in sub-Saharan Africa, the poverty-afflicted population in South Asia is by far the greatest problem in the developing world—in terms of sheer numbers (living on less than US$1 per day) (World Bank 2003). There is a strong likelihood of at least another 500 million joining the former (currently living on US$1–2 per day) by the end of 2010.

opportunities for science and policy to learn from social contexts. The chapter uses empirical evidence from some schemes of the Government of India to make the case for alternative non-linear, non-hierarchical, and socially embedded norms for governing S&T and policy-making to enable eco-friendly development. The application of S&T to address the problems of poverty and environmentally sustainable development demands a paradigm shift. Too much has gone on for too long in the normal ways of working of mainstream science, effecting too little change in the lives and livelihoods of millions of the poor in the world.

In highly complex contexts, high uncertainty, strong and deeply entrenched decision stakes and multiple stakeholders, limited and unclear information, etc., it is best to make decisions in S&T based on consultations with a wide range of peers, with different stakes, information, and skills. These ideas and recommendations for policy-making in a post-normal era of scientific research decisions, marked by contexts of high uncertainty or wide and high decision stakes have been around for a few decades now (Funtowicz and Ravetz 1990, 1993). Mainly, post-normal science points to the need for science and S&T policy-making to communicate pro-actively with a wide range of stakeholders to ensure that their agenda or contents are relevant and will lead to socially and economically productive outcomes. Innovation systems analysts also demand that science and S&T policy-making actors cultivate appropriate interactions and learning with a range of other actors who are equally important sources of knowledge, information, and skills necessary for innovation (Lundvall 1992; Hall et al. 2004). Innovation, defined as the processes of change that occur when knowledge (including technological) is generated, accessed, and used in socially progressive and economically productive ways, is increasingly attracting policy attention. But the acceptance and application of these frameworks, be it the innovation systems framework or post-normal science for S&T policy-making, is constrained by severe institutional inertia. This inertia can be broken either by active learning within policy circles or by radical changes in social organization.

The objective here is to understand how science—natural sciences and social sciences—can contribute to better policy-making for pro-poor environment-friendly development through more effective and well-informed S&T policies. In planned economies like India, even during the post-liberalization phase, the government maintains a major commitment to promoting eco-friendly technologies for rural development. This chapter analyses the rules/institutions that govern S&T, research policy-making, and schematization within the government. The purpose is to explain how these institutions enable or constrain the utilization of knowledge for development. Institutions, or the rules, norms, and ways of working, evident most explicitly as the habits, routines, and practices in an organization or an individual, define the way an organization or individual functions. In conclusion, the chapter addresses the changes in policy research and the interactive learning processes between policy, science, and stakeholders in society that are essential to address the twin goals of economic development and ecological sustainability.

S&T-BASED GOVERNMENT SCHEMES

Increasingly, policy makers and decision makers in S&T establishments are concerned about the lackadaisical performance of government schemes that use science and technology for eco-friendly development. An analysis in response to this concern raised by a Rural Innovation Policy Working Group (RIPWiG), conducted by a research team, reveals a policy vacuum in understanding and planning for the institutional aspects of knowledge generation and utilization.[2] Several cases of rural innovation analysed by this research team reveal a number of mutually linked actors involved in each innovation, continuously learning and changing their ways of working, skills, and capacities. The cases also highlight the ways in which technological change and institutional change always go hand in hand to enable innovation.

The team used the innovation systems framework to analyse some government schemes that use technological knowledge for development. The analysis was to ascertain whether the ideal features of an innovation system—a system of interlinked actors working to achieve knowledge generation and utilization in socially progressive and economically productive ways—were evident in the structure and functioning of these schemes. The team chose schemes from different

---

[2]See Hall (2005). The RIPWiG is an expert advisory group established by UNU-MERIT and its partners in India as part of a UNU-MERIT/CRISP project 'New Insights into Promoting Rural Innovation: Learning from Civil Society Organizations'. The mandate of RIPWiG is to facilitate dialogue between the project team and decision makers from government and civil society organizations with the responsibility for planning and implementation of science- and technology-based rural development initiatives.

ministries with different mandates. The discussion below presents two of these schemes that were specifically targeting environmental goals through the creation of employment and income for rural populations using eco-friendly technologies.

The schemes here are:
(i) the Science and Technology Applications for Rural Development (STARD) Scheme of the Department of Science and Technology (DST);
(ii) the Scheme for Promotion of Integrated Pest Management (IPM) of the Department of Agriculture and Co-operation (DA&C).

These schemes focus on development (rather than research); the important role of civil society and NGOs; and emphasize support for technology transfer, and training/demonstration. Yet the two schemes approach this in very different ways.

The STARD Scheme provides core funding to support NGOs for building innovation capacity. It facilitates the development of civil society groups/organizations with a proven record of or active involvement in S&T-based rural development. The Core Support programme of the STARD Scheme identifies and supports civil society organizations (with adequate scientific expertise) over the long term, to nurture them to become Centres of Excellence for Rural Development. The support is for 'activities connected with the generation, demonstration and application of rural technologies on an integrated and continual basis'. Many of these are eco-friendly, income-generating technologies that can and have led to the establishment of rural enterprises/industries. Two specific cases are those of fuel-efficient stoves and dryers [core support given to Technology Informatics Design Endeavour (TIDE), a small NGO in Bangalore] and animal carcass utilization and eco-friendly tanning technologies [core support given to Centre for Technology and Development (CTD), an NGO in Delhi]. Both TIDE and CTD have had positive impacts on thousands of poor families and their livelihoods and have made important contributions to reducing firewood use, pollution, and natural resources degradation.

The guidelines of the STARD Scheme specify that a local context analysis be conducted and presented by the NGO that receives core support. It also demands a listing and acknowledgement of various actors or organizations involved in the programme, their roles and capacities, and encourages public sector scientists to participate in the Core Group activities. The Programme Committee (subject matter specialists are decided based on each project's or Core Group's needs and commitments), monitoring mechanisms, and routine decision-making processes in this scheme are project-specific, and flexible. The members of the Programme Committee differ for each specific Core Group supported, depending on the expertise, local knowledge, social capital, etc. of the members. The Scheme is designed to facilitate sustained support over a long period, starting with a five-year grant but extended up to 10 or 15 years, to enable NGOs to build scientific and technological capacities. No specific technologies are specified, but processes are built in to ensure that the Core Group gains capacities (to build relationships and credibility with local/target populations, experts, other knowledge like market or process skills, etc.).

The IPM Scheme does recognize the complexity and evolutionary nature of its goal as evidenced from the interviews with scheme leaders in the DA&C, scientists involved, and the NGOs. But it is designed in a fairly linear manner, with IPM technologies (scientifically selected for selected crops in given regions) identified from public sector agricultural S&T organizations, transferred to extension workers in Agricultural Departments/NGOs or others wishing to apply IPM technologies. The guidelines (for NGOs applying for training or for establishment of the bio-control labs) do not demand a write-up on the local social and economic contexts. IPM technical experts are decided at the DA&C and are to advise all projects. The experts are mostly within public sector S&T and training institutes (Directorate of Plant Protection). The steps for implementation of IPM are given, IPM packages (about 20) developed are also listed in the scheme (from which the NGO has to select the crop and package it intends to implement), and the funding (as well as allocation for construction of the lab and equipment in the lab) pattern under the scheme is specified. Monitoring and implementation mechanisms are fixed.

Overall, the IPM scheme (i) is exclusively 'IPM technology focused', (ii) involves a typical linear hierarchy of research–extension–adoption, (iii) has participation of NGOs limited to implementation of IPM packages developed, (iv) makes no mention of other stakeholders or their processes of involvement, and (v) has prescribed, well defined, and clear roles specified for the Indian Council of Agricultural Research (ICAR) and the State Agriculture Universities (SAUs), the Extension Departments, NGOs, farmers, etc. which conform to their technology generation, demonstration/dissemination, and adoption mandates. Though targets set (for establishment of bio-control labs by NGOs, number of training programmes conducted) are being achieved, the scheme does not seem to generate adequate capacity at the local levels (involving a range of actors/organizations) to promote a locally adapted and owned IPM innovation system. Processes or institutional arrangements are not acknowledged. The questions related to lessons learnt by the DA&C and the future of the scheme are not even being asked!

The STARD and the IPM schemes use S&T for eco-friendly rural development, but embody two very different approaches. The STARD Scheme seems to take the view that it is not technology *per se* that is important; it is designed to make sure that NGOs are linked into the sources of scientific expertise and other local knowledge systems that they can then use in the design and implementation of technology-based rural development initiatives. The ways of actually doing this are not specified too rigidly and this has allowed different sorts of linkages and interactions to emerge.

The IPM Scheme seems to take the view that once specific pest management technologies have been validated by science for use in specific crops, these can be transferred for use in different locations. The scheme is very tightly controlled so that these specifications are adhered to at all times in all locations/crops.

The STARD Scheme promotes rural innovation not just by transfer of technology, but by also building the relationships needed to link that technology and associated knowledge and expertise and several other market information, local caste or political information, etc. The scheme helps NGOs make these linkages and develop new ways of working; the NGOs are in turn intermediaries with poor people who utilize these technologies in rural areas. This knitting together of these different organizations is helping build capacity to use science and technology more effectively. The IPM Scheme is not helping to put these relationships in place. While it might help deliver some IPM technology, it will not build the relationships needed to sustain innovation.

The innovation systems diagnosis of what ails S&T-based government schemes reveals the need for scientific research organizations and policy-making bodies to be aware that (i) S&T is only one part of the solution to problems and (ii) S&T has to find ways of working with and learning from other actors in society. The STARD scheme offers a lesson on how to link scientific organizations into the network of actors involved in rural development. The IPM shceme shows how certain institutions (for instance, a norm that selects one Programme Advisory Committee for all the IPM projects) constrain innovation.

The fact that the two schemes, one actively encouraging institutional change and the other focused exclusively on technological change, co-exist within the portfolio of Central Government schemes that use S&T for eco-friendly rural development reveals how little learning takes place within public policy and planning organizations and within scientific research organizations. How can governments, and policy and scientific research organizations within the public sector become conscious of, seek, and encourage institutional change? Even DST, the official sponsor of the STARD Scheme, does not seem to acknowledge and appreciate the Scheme for its institutional reforms or new ways of working.

TECHNOLOGIES, GOVERNMENT SCHEMES, AND LESSONS

While it is acknowledged that scientific knowledge and technologies generated by scientific research can play a major role in generating more environment-friendly employment opportunities, there is much disappointment in the fact that there are thousands of technologies that have not found any place in society beyond research publications and the shelves of research organizations. This is despite the fact that there are several models of and approaches to technology dissemination, and incentives for adoption of environment-friendly technologies. S&T organizations cannot afford to hand down a technology to be schematized by the government, just as policy-making cannot afford to formulate an S&T-based scheme and let it run its course as a mere technological intervention. A major lesson from the schemes analysed in the project on pro-poor rural innovation is that both S&T and policy-making actors need to pay attention to and be involved in accompanying institutional changes.

In developing countries, government schemes are an important vehicle in the 'normal' cycle of generation and dissemination of technologies for development. The schemes are designed as part of a 'normal' problem-solving endeavour, controlled and conducted exclusively within the public sector, with other actors such as NGOs inducted as tail-end support/dissemination organizations.[3] Many of these government schemes which use technologies for development

---

[3]The idea of NGOs being equal partners with the government is still alien to many government agencies (Brinkerhoff 2002). NGOs are not seen as actors who offer substantial local context lessons and trust/relationship building advantages among communities (Hall et al. 2005). Partnerships that change the inter-organizational relationships and intra-organizational ways of working are few in India.

have a specific focus (marginal or wastelands, tribal areas, small farmers, rural youth, rural women, etc.), and specific choice of technologies (solar energy equipment, land reclamation chemicals, erosion control structures, integrated pest management technologies and practices, fuel efficient devices) depending on the compartmentalized mandate of the respective ministry or department that implements the scheme.

The structure of almost all the schemes involves three main components: the Central Ministry and Department within it that hosts, sponsors, and controls (sets the rules or norms of) the scheme, the State Departments, research institutes, universities, or any agency that implements the schemes, and a third, and often relatively new, entrant, the NGO or civil society actors who are the tail-end implementers designated to achieve the targets set by the State/Central Departments or the sponsors. S&T or the research organizations are no longer part of the scheme once the technology has been schematized.[4] Adoption of the technology by the ultimate beneficiary is often the target set, though the target of number of beneficiaries trained is a safer bet to meet. In terms of function, most schemes follow a pre-determined pattern of allocation of funds (Centre: State costs or commitments being 75:25, 50:50, etc.). Once a scheme is planned and implementation sanctioned, it can run indefinitely irrespective of the livelihoods/ecological issues it addresses.[5] It is also often the case that schemes work at cross purposes. One with a mandate to reclaim sodic lands, create infrastructure, and social

---

[4]There is, for instance, no scope in the IPM scheme for research in the scheme's field sites to generate new knowledge or apply new knowledge on variations in pest incidence, pest behaviour, etc. in different ecological zones.

[5]The example of the Central Scheme for Reclamation of Alkali Soils, which offers a subsidy on gypsum (the chemical used for treatment of alkali soils) to farmers, implemented by the state governments, often with an additional subsidy being sanctioned by the state, is a good illustration. This central scheme and its subsidy (implemented since 1973) still continue in the states of Haryana and Punjab, despite the fact that more land has been reclaimed (using the amount of gypsum supplied under the scheme) than exists in all of Haryana and Punjab. In the light of these statistics, the request from the Central Ministry to assess the need for the scheme and the subsidy to continue (Ministry of Agriculture 1994) was answered affirmatively. The scheme and subsidy continue till date—the only difference being that the Central Government subsidy on gypsum has been reduced from 50 per cent to 25 per cent since 2004. The role of science in legitimizing the continuation of the scheme and subsidy programme was based on both science and policy accusing farmers of not following the specific technologies and practices recommended by science (Raina and Sangar 2002).

capital investments to sustain reclaimed land, and another with a mandate to provide irrigation, digs tubewells for individual farmers in the same villages, destroying the land reclamation investment and the collective water use and land management practices initiated by the former in the villages (World Bank 2004).[6]

Evaluation of government schemes, even ones that use S&T for development, is reduced to a box-ticking exercise, where the only questions are whether targets set in terms of disbursements and activities—number of demonstration plots, trainings conducted, women beneficiaries trained, etc.—have been achieved. When there are stunningly successful cases of application of S&T to bring about eco-friendly rural development, a few analyses are conducted and some academic publications produced. Several new programmes or variants of the success are attempted as part of the scaling-up or replication exercise launched. But there is no attempt to learn from the positive—to ensure that the positive deviants who made a difference are acknowledged (Biggs 2007). At best, the technologies they promoted are 'scaled-up' further; their processes or ways of working are not studied or emulated in other systems. Neither policy-makers nor research managers get the opportunity to learn anything from these schemes. Deep-seated institutional ennui is a formidably silent and omnipresent obstacle in the application of S&T for development. There are opportunities, however, to learn from positive cases wherever given institutional arrangements have been altered and technological as well as institutional change promoted to achieve innovation (Biggs 2007). But it must be remembered that:

While learning from the positive is a simple idea, it is always challenging to implement as it inevitably questions the histories, past explanations and perceptions of some scientists and development planners, especially those who promote a mainstream, formulaic approach to the design and implementation of best policies and best practices, and a simplistic, non-political/cultural approach to the transfer and scaling out and up of technology and institutional models. (Biggs 2007)

Existing institutions or ways of working pose very high stakes. The assumption that the application of S&T can solve rural

[6]See Box 3 on lack of co-ordination between various Government Departments— on how the Minor Irrigation Department had jeopardized the sustainability of the resource reclamation investment made by the UPBSN (World Bank 2004: Box 3).

development and environmental problems lives on. Mainstream government schemes continue in the same institutional mode.

LEARNING CAPACITIES AND INSTITUTIONAL CHANGE

Two important streams of literature analyse the application of S&T to solve social problems—especially rural poverty and development issues—the science, technology, society (STS) literature and the innovation systems literature. Both these streams of literature have repeatedly pointed out (i) the evolutionary nature of technological change and economic growth and (ii) the systems relationships, interactions, learning processes, and new rules/norms that mark an evolving system of innovation or scientific/technological/disciplinary change. Yet, technological determinism and linear hierarchical norms govern the generation of knowledge/technologies, and their utilization in society promoted through public sector schemes designed for the purpose.

The linear design and technocentric functioning of S&T-based schemes, for instance, the IPM Scheme, come in the wake of several studies on agricultural and environmental innovation, which prove that:
   (i)   there are multiple sources of knowledge and information that farmers access and use to make decisions in their farm, about the crop, market, cultivation practice, input/chemical use, etc.;
   (ii) innovation involves several actors (organizations and individuals) working together in a coalition and, therefore, demands the capacity of these actors to build relationships/linkages with other actors;
   (iii) every case of successful generation and utilization of knowledge reveals technological and institutional innovation;
   (iv) the capacity for learning and evolving new rules/norms to face changing contexts seems to be crucial for innovation. (see, Biggs 1990; Roling and Wagemakers 1998; Hall et al. 2004; Lundvall 1992).

Compared to the fast-track institutional changes evident in the private sector or public–private collaborations and technology utilization in industry (especially in information technology, bio-technology, etc.), where the erstwhile contours and compartments of knowledge generation and utilization have blurred to a rapid and iterative learning and change mode (called Mode II; see Gibbons et al. 1994), the application of S&T to agriculture, health, environment, small and medium enterprises, etc., mainly through public sector agencies, are untouched by institutional reform. In countries like India, S&T is now located in a vast enterprise that has bifurcated into two estates that almost have nothing to do with each other. One, a rapidly growing and evolving (Mode II) estate involving the livelihoods and impressive economic opportunities for a few million urban educated, and the other, a rigid and indifferent conventional estate that continues in an archaic Mode I involving the livelihoods and increasingly indigent economies and degrading eco-systems for hundreds of millions of rural people. Strangely though, the survival of the latter—the compartmentalized, linear Mode I estate—is legitimized by the very poverty and vulnerability of the rural poor. Our analysis of government schemes (the STARD Scheme) shows that there are options to design Schemes differently, to involve wider peer groups/stakeholders, enable interaction and learning, and to improve the innovation capacities of a range of actors.

There is evidence that policy-makers and bureaucracies do learn to enable institutional change—especially institutional change that allows increased participation of other stakeholders in their decision-making processes (Thompson 1995). But these trainings for participatory approaches and the institutional change they facilitate seem to solve only a part of the larger problem of capacities to learn and evolve (Thompson 1995). Moreover, the capacity of S&T to learn and enable learning among policy-making organizations is highly limited. Several research organizations made a formal shift to participatory research modes, with specific programmes for Farmer Participatory Research (FPR) and Participatory Technology Development (PTD). Participatory methods (like transect walks and participatory resource mapping) were added to the bag of research methods and facilities created for field visits as organizational changes enabling FPR and PTD. But these did not alter the hierarchy or professional norms of research organizations. But research organizations, and scientists/research managers within, did not learn about the nuances of rural poverty and the differences among groups even within the village/community because of the new participatory approaches they had adopted (Guijt and Shah 1998; Green 1998). The need to change existing ways of working in mainstream science is now an absolute necessity (Chambers 2005).

The need for institutional reform in scientific research and policy-making organizations has been a much discussed topic in the literature (including management, STS, capacity building, innovation systems, and public administration). But compared to the wealth of new frameworks, methodologies, and guidelines/manuals designed for institutional reform, little has been achieved, especially in terms of institutional reform in public sector organizations mandated to use S&T for development. In India, as in much of South Asia, public sector organizations seem more or less impervious to institutional reform that can enable pro-poor and eco-friendly innovation. The case of repeated recommendations for institutional changes in agricultural research in India provides interesting empirical evidence of public sector science being shielded from institutional changes by the hype of food security and provision of public goods for the small farmer (see Raina 2003).

CONCLUDING REMARKS: THE POLICY RESEARCH VOID

Why does the application of S&T for eco-friendly development continue in the mainstream mode of linear schemes that hand down technologies to the farmers or beneficiaries (as they are called in policy terminology)? To go further down the road, why does S&T continue to produce these technologies which may at best end up in one such scheme, bereft of any of the accompanying actors, linkages, or institutional ferment that can enable its utilization in society? What is it that prevents S&T from learning from the way these technologies are disseminated routinely and from positive cases that enable its utilization in society? What is it that can shake the existing comfortable, complacent line of communication between S&T and policy, where other stakeholders or wider peer groups are either non-existent or fade into tail-end implementers of programmes/projects within these schemes? Let us recall that in the 1950s and 1960s, a fear of the likelihood of a red revolution led to a global-scale change in the application of S&T to agriculture, bringing the green revolution to Asia.

The chapter began by pointing out the axiomatic assumption that S&T applications can enable eco-friendly development. The cases of government schemes that use S&T for eco-friendly development point out the well documented and well established need to move from technology-focused schemes to ones that enable both technological and institutional change. Following this, questions were asked why policy-making organizations and mainstream science are unable to or not compelled to learn about different ways of putting knowledge and technology to use in society. There are no easy answers. But a major concern and some questions emerge from this issue of inability or indifference of policy-making and scientific research to learn. The concern is about the role of the social sciences in this conundrum.

While it remains a fact that STS and innovation systems analyses have to a great extent contributed to our awareness of non-linear, complex, and post-normal ways of working in science and society and, therefore, the need for institutional reform in the scientific research and policy-making arenas, these findings seem to have little impact on the ways of working in policy research. Policy research continues to be conducted in the same linear, top-down, hierarchical, and prescriptive mode. Policy-makers, especially in the S&T policy arena, seem to be increasingly interested in the more visible and dynamic Mode II knowledge systems. Perhaps, unlike the policy-makers of the 1960s, the policy-making community today is less perceptive of the risks of ignoring the persistent poverty and accompanying ecological degradation in South Asia. The agricultural and rural technologies enshrined in government schemes seem to be unable to address the livelihoods demands of a massive section of the population in the South Asian countries. Even with findings from positive cases about how partnerships are built and how pro-poor innovation takes place, there is little that has changed in mainstream S&T and policy-making organizations and the policy research that informs them. There is a critical need for interactive policy research in place of current prescriptive and closed policy-making models, and for institutional reform in S&T as well as public sector policy-making organizations.

REFERENCES

Biggs, S.D., (1990), 'A Multiple Source of Innovation Model of Agricultural Research and Technology Promotion', *World Development*, Vol. 18, No. 11, pp. 1481–99.

Biggs, S., (2007), 'Building on the Positive: An Actor Innovation Systems Approach to Finding and Promoting Pro-poor Natural Resources Institutional and Technical Innovations', *International Journal of Agricultural Resources, Governance and Ecology*, Vol. 6, No. 2, pp. 144–64.

Brinkerhoff, J.M., (2002), 'Government–Nonprofit Partnership: A Defining Framework', *Public Administration and Development*, Vol. 22, No. 1, pp. 19–30.

Chambers, R., (2005), *Ideas for Development*, London: Earthscan.

FAO, (2006), *The State of Food and Agriculture in Asia and the Pacific*, Bangkok: Food and Agriculture Organization, Regional Office for Asia and the Pacific.

Funtowicz, S. and J. Ravetz, (1993), 'Science for the Post-Normal Age', *Futures*, Vol. 25, No. 7, pp. 735–55.

——, (1990), *Uncertainty and Quality in Science for Policy*, The Netherlands: Kluwer.

Gibbons, M., C. Limoges, H. Nowotny, S. Schwartzman, P. Scott, and M. Trow, (1994), *The New Production of Knowledge: The Dynamics of Science and Research in Contemporary Societies*, London and New Delhi: Sage.

Guijit, I. and M.K. Shah (eds), (1998), *The Myth of Community*, London: Intermediate Technology Publications.

Green, R.H., (1998), 'Problematics and Pointers about Participatory Research and Gender', in I. Guijit and M.K. Shah (eds), *The Myth of Community*, London: Intermediate Technology Publications, pp. 71–7.

Hall, A.J., B. Yoganand, R.V. Sulaiman, R.S. Raina, C.S. Prasad, C.G. Naik, and N.G. Clark, (2004), *Innovations in Innovation: Reflections on Partnership, Institutions and Learning*, Patancheru and New Delhi: CPHP, South Asia, ICRISAT, and NCAP

Hall, Andy, R. Raina, R. Sulaiman, N. Clark, S. Prasad, and G. Naik, (2005), 'Institutional Learning and Change: A Review of Concepts and Principles,' Policy Brief No. 21, National Centre for Agricultural Economics and Policy Research, New Dehi: NCAP(ICAR), May.

Hall, A. (ed.), (2005), *RIPWiG Reporter No. 1*, UNU-INTECH Project, Hyderabad: CRISP, UNU-INTECH.

Lewis, W.A., (1954), *Economic Development with Unlimited Supplies of Labour*, Manchester School of Economics and Social Studies, No. 22, pp. 139–91.

Lundvall, B.A., (1992), *National Systems of Innovation: Towards a Theory of Innovation and Interactive Learning*, London: Pinter.

MEA, (2005), *Ecosystems and Human Well-Being: Synthesis*, Washington, D.C.: Island Press.

Ministry of Agriculture, Government of India, (1994), Letter No. 11-3/93-SWC-I dated 19 January 1994, from Joint Commissioner, Soil and Water Conservation Division, to the Managing Director, HLRDC, Chandigarh. New Delhi: Ministry of Agriculture.

Raina, Rajeswari S. and S. Sangar, (2002), 'Water Quality, Agricultural Policy and Science', *Knowledge, Technology and Policy*, Vol. 14, No. 4, pp. 109–25.

Raina, R.S., (2003), 'Institutions and Organizations: Enabling Reforms in Indian Agricultural Research and Policy', *International Journal of Technology Management and Sustainable Development*, Vol. 2, No. 2, pp. 97–116.

Roling, N. and A. Wagemakers (eds), (1998), *Facilitating Sustainable Agriculture*, Cambridge: Cambridge University Press.

Schultz, T.W., (1964), *Transforming Traditional Agriculture*, New Haven: Yale University Press.

Sen, A.K., (1967), 'Surplus Labour in India: A Critique of Schultz's Statistical Test', *The Economic Journal*, Vol. 77, No. 1, pp.154–60.

Thompson, J., (1995), 'Participatory Approaches in Government Bureaucracies: Facilitating the Process of Institutional Change', *World Development*, Vol. 23, No. 9, pp. 1521–54.

World Bank, (2003), *World Development Indicators*, Washington, D.C.: The World Bank.

_____, (2004), 'Project Performance Assessment Report–India: Uttar Pradesh', Sodic Lands Reclamation Project, Washington, DC: The World Bank.

18

Quality Tales in Sustainable Water Governance Cases

ÂNGELA GUIMARÃES PEREIRA

INSPIRATION: QUALITY ASSURANCE OF RIVER BASIN GOVERNANCE PROCESSES

In this chapter, it is suggested that governance of river basins may be framed as a quality assurance process, where evaluation procedures ensure that outcomes are technically and scientifically reliable, as well as socially robust. To attain the latter, a special type of quality assurance process is required—an extended quality assurance process (Funtowicz and Ravetz 1992)—that is, the governance of river basins should be inclusive of all those concerned, embedded in the social context in which the governance of the basin takes place, from framing through implementation. In other words, we are arguing that river basin governance is well-suited for the extended model of science and policy (Funtowicz 2006); see also Introduction by Guimarães Pereira and Funtowicz in this volume.

Five past cases of river basin governance in Europe are the basis of the study of quality 'expression' around four vertices: context, information used and produced, assessment, and participation processes, adopted in the context of an European Commission funded project[1] (Guimarães Pereira and Corral Quintana 2009). Insights into justifications to adopt certain practices were sought, namely on the importance of institutional, knowledge, methodological,

[1]ADVISOR project–Integrated Evaluation for Sustainable River Basin Governance, a Shared Cost Action under the 5th Framework Programme of Research. CONTRACT EVK1-CT-2000-00074.

and societal contexts. Patterns found among the cases suggested that their quality was in many cases rather poor, namely, in relation to original objectives, to societal expectations, to regulation, and to knowledge deployed and produced during the process.

The review of the cases suggested that regardless of the evaluation methods and decision tools that may be used in river basin planning or governance, the issue remains essentially a process of 'concertation' of framings and assessment procedures.

In this chapter, four principles (three pillars and one beam) that may set quality of evaluation of river basin planning and governance processes are proposed: inclusive governance, transparent assessment, socially robust knowledge,[2] and extended peer review (Funtowicz and Ravetz 1992); Guimarães Pereira and Corral Quintana 2007. They all invoke the need to extend the processes of evaluation to recognize that there might exist different framings, perspectives, values, divergent interests, different types of uncertainty, and ways to deal with these and as such, those involved in processes of river basin governance are determining the very nature and culture with which those processes develop. They also remind of, in one way or the other, the principles of 'good' governance as established in CEC (2001b): openness, effectiveness, accountability, participation, and coherence.

River basin governance qualifies as a complex context in which many legitimate dimensions of institutional, social, economical, political, ethical, cultural, and environmental nature concur. All these are often bound by intrinsic (different types of) uncertainties and unknowns, hence their articulation in an evaluation process may determine the quality of the process and its outcomes through deliberate and accidental omissions, ambiguities, arbitrarinesses, unchecked assumptions, etc. that are often 'usefully' explored by specific social actors in order to produce a suitable analysis that legitimate *a priori* decisions taken based on motivations of a lesser transparent kind.

A term of reference is necessary to facilitate the exploration and assessment of the characteristics of the governance processes. In this sense, the concept of quality, initially suggested by Funtowicz and Ravetz (1990, 1992, 1993) is adopted here.

---

[2]This expression was first used by Gibbons (1999), when he and his colleagues developed the concept of Mode 2 science production.

Patterns and Linkages from the Review of Five Case Studies of River Basin Governance

A revision of five cases of European river basin governance was conducted based on a tetrahedron structure (see Videira et al. 2007), that is, in terms of context (Kallis and Coccossis 2003), information (Guimarães Pereira 2003); and two evaluation processes, that is, assessment (Hill et al. 2003) and participation (Videira et al. 2003). This review took into consideration five case studies (see Table A18.1 for a short summary) which addressed different aspects of water governance, the majority being engineering projects, grounded on a hydraulic paradigm: the Alqueva dam (Videira et al. 2002), the Evinos reservoir (Hatzilacou et al. 2002), and the Ebro water transfer as part of the Spanish National Hydrologic Plan (Del Moral et al. 2002) and gravel extraction in the Maaswreck river (Van Leeuwen et al. 2002). The latter and the river Ythan and estuary as a Nitrate Vulnerable Zone in the UK (Hill et al. 2002) case study addressed issues of water quality. The review of the cases along the vertices of the tetrahedron brought some insight into patterns on evaluation practices in Europe, as well as opportunity to seek for preliminary justifications (linkages between information, context, assessment, and participation), taking into account contextual and framing issues.

Context Dependency Issues

Analysis of context (Kallis and Coccossis 2003) took into consideration the institutions involved and the main social actors in the evaluation processes. Context seems to reflect in the patterns found for all vertices, being understood as socio-political framing, institutional arrangements, and regulatory provisions. In particular, the following was looked at:

- How political systems organization and water management historical–cultural practices shapes water governance activities;
- What, and how, lobbying activity of strong vested interests belonging to sectors such as engineering, agriculture, construction companies, utilities (electricity, etc.), and hydraulic bodies operate and influence water governance;
- How the regulatory setting and funding resources, in particular that imposed by the European Commission, pull a set of evaluation demands, shapes the types of assessments carried out, and determine the role they play in the whole appraisal process.

So, what was the context influence in knowledge flows? In this section we look at how context influenced knowledge flows during the evaluation process, namely on the framing, assessment, and public involvement activities of the cases taken.

The review of the 'information vertex' done in Guimarães Pereira (2003) provides an analysis of the quality of knowledge based on flows of knowledge (data, tools, assessments made, communications to the public, etc.) during the several steps of the evaluation process: framing, assessment, and public participation. These were reviewed on grounds of quality categories adapted from Corral Quintana (2000)(see also Chapter 3 in this volume).

Two different flows can be identified, knowledge that is deployed in the various evaluation phases and knowledge that is produced as outcome of those processes that aim at 'informing' societal and policy spheres. The socio-institutional contexts in which evaluation has taken place has determined in all cases the quality of information used and the outcomes of assessment and participatory procedures. Also, the very same context defines quality, that is, what 'knowledge' is fit, relevant, and legitimate at each step of the evaluation phase, and establishes when completeness and accuracy is acceptable from the viewpoint of the policy/decision makers. The following aspects are commonly found among the ADVISOR case studies:

• There seems to be no provision in the national legislations to reflect upon quality of information, in any phase of the evaluation processes; at best this is an issue that is left to those who perform the assessment, while deciding on data sets and sources or analytical/processing methods. The precautionary principle or extended consultation can, in some cases, be interpreted as a political attempt to deal with uncertain or poor quality information.

• Since there is not, in the majority of the cases, involvement of an extended community at a strategic level of the evaluation process, no normative or explicit recommendations for quality checking (for example, regarding compliance to wider concerns of relevant societal sectors) is performed on issue framing, scope of the assessment, information or methods deployed, etc. Moreover, in none of the cases is there any institutional requirement for advice on framing or scoping by relevant wider sectors of the society, something that is usually discouraged by hierarchical, centralized socio-political structures.

• Decisions are taken in contexts of uncertainty, arguable assumptions, or poor justifications, for at least four of the case studies.

332 SCIENCE FOR POLICY

Knowledge in Framing and Assessment

> We continue considering scenarios of old times agriculture, without taking into account the evolution of the markets, the distribution of products (Alqueva Dam Project: Environmental Consultant Interview, 2003—Wrong Framing for Alqueva?)

To describe the patterns found, the structure proposed in Hill et al. (2003), is partially borrowed, the knowledge being limited here to data, tools, and methods deployed in the assessment phases of the project. Throughout the studies, assessments are done on the basis of the problems framed on economic or political objectives, including compliance with regulation; framing determines knowledge requirements and affects its quality by establishing (explicitly or implicitly) required accuracy, social robustness (contextualization), legitimacy, etc, which, in turn, determine the quality of the whole evaluation process.

- In four of the cases, Environmental Impact Assessment (EIA) type of studies were carried out in the assessment phase; although they are inherently multi-disciplinary, the outcomes are far from reflecting 'integrated perspectives'. The quality of such studies is strongly dependent on the quality of accessible information, as well as on the problem framing and on the scoping of the assessment. These, in all cases, were set by political opportunity or lobbying and not surprisingly, compliant with not too demanding regulation.
- Assessment tools selection in the case studies is quite arbitrary. It has different forms, like poor justification of its choice, poor fitness for purpose, and non-contextualization of tools serving just as legitimacy devices of decisions taken ahead. In the Spanish case study, the authors of the technical studies were deliberately not known, hence a peer review of the study was not possible.
- Uncertainty is either not dealt with, masked by usage of formal mathematical methods, or in a cautious perspective claiming for further studies or data collection, which is the closest to a sort of uncertainty management.

The relation quality of the water-ground was an important problem. The [dam authority] was worried and decided to consult other technical opinions. The technical–scientific advisory panel's diverged from the technical board, but there were no concrete studies to sustain such opinions. Hence, the impact was described as unknown and it was proposed to be studied in a research project, which was never done (Alqueva Dam Project: Environmental Consultant Interview, 2003—Uncertainty Management?).

- In three of the cases, the most important outcome of the assessment activities are the mitigation measures; in the Alqueva project, for example, the number of mitigation measures in the study is almost as large as the assessment section itself. That suggests that a negative impact statement would have probably been ignored and that there was no *a priori* intention to stop the project if the assessment would have recommended so.

Knowledge in Public Participation

This section addresses knowledge provided for the participatory activities and knowledge gathered through these activities. As public involvement in the water governance processes seemed in all cases to be a mere act of compliance with existing regulation, it is in a sense 'controlled' at the decision level and prone to lobbying; unfortunately it might not give anything else than a sense of consensual 'harmony'.

- The EIA processes require a 'non technical document' to be accessible to all the public, the full EIA being also available for consultation in specific places. These documents were generally available and accessible but, in some of the cases, were loaded with jargon, with little care for communication aspects.
- Accessibility to the projects' documentation by the public reflected the quality of the studies, and because the relevance of the assessment was often not compliant with the concerns of societal sectors, it is not surprising that the information available was limited and often irrelevant for the participatory activities;
- This probably also explains why involvement (understood here as spaces for exchange and co-production of knowledge) is poor, being a one-way flow of information to (often) unprepared participants to engage in a debate: a sort of public understanding exercise of the projects and not a genuine act of engagement; consequently, irrelevant for those who promote the participatory action; this is a perverse mechanism to deny the possible benefits of extended participation in processes of this type, since it does not recognize that the pitfall is on the organization of the participatory activity and not on the inability of social actors to respond and actively engage in a participatory initiative;
- Also, what is missing in most of the cases is the recognition that participatory outcomes could be useful for the whole process in terms of knowledge brought, beyond a mere justification or

(pseudo) conflict resolution means. With few exceptions (namely the Dutch case study) the participatory mechanisms did not inform the evaluation activities effectively.

THE CONTEXTS OF EVALUATION: IN PURSUIT OF JUSTIFICATIONS

This section gives some insight, based on the analysis and diagnosis provided earlier, into the possible justifications underlying past evaluation of river basin projects; tales of rather poor quality of dubious sustainable river basin acivities. This insight is based on what is identified as contexts of evaluation: institutional, knowledge, societal, and methodological. These four contexts set out, in a sense, possible types of justifications that determine the quality of the evaluation processes. Although they are analysed in separate sections, they overlap and are intertwined.

Institutional Context

Historical Legacy

The time gap (chronologically speaking) in which the older projects developed (Evinos reservoir, Alqueva dam, and Ebro interbasin transfer) plays an essential role in the characteristics of the evaluation process. In some of the case studies developed under autocratic regimes, where dialogue was restricted, there were heavy hierarchical institutional structures, and water management and project assessments were bound by technocratic values and approaches. Moreover, historical analysis provides insight into the changes of framing, respondent to changing national and international economical and political strategies. Because these projects were long-standing political promises, and there was no political courage to abandon them or make major reformulations in view of different societal or political contexts, what is reformulated is the types of justifications to have the project going ahead.

Hence, wordings like integrated perspectives, inclusionary governance, extended framing and scoping, acknowledgment of uncertainties, quality of information, plurality of framing, etc. were not part of the inspiration context of planners and decision makers.

Institutional Arrangements

Three of the evaluation processes of river basin management instances in ADVISOR have operated under governance styles that are now arguable. First, as we have seen, centralized structures make it difficult to actually frame the governance issues adequately, the proposals for action often being far from desirable integrated development of river basins and its communities, and mostly responding to nationwide political objectives (for example, the case of Alqueva and Ebro).

Lack of specific competence to deal with public involvement jeopardizes the usefulness of the process, including timely organization of the event, purposeful creation of spaces of exchange of 'knowledges', and incorporation of outcomes in the assessment phases.

Institutions in Europe are in transition, to accommodate new perspectives on governance. After a number of trust crises, there is some process where those in charge of planning try to tentatively collect inputs in the field, mostly for political reasons, seeking legitimacy, and seeking conflict resolution. In one way or the other, there seems to be a tendency to have more inclusive forms of governance than in the past, as the Dutch and UK cases demonstrate.

Regulation and Guidance

At present, there is a great deal of legislation in Europe that regulates and guides environmental evaluation including water issues (Environmental Impact Assessment Directive: CEC 1985, CEC 1997, and CEC 2001c; Water Framework Directive (WFD): CEC 2000; public participation in environmental assessment: CEC 2003). In relation to public participation, for instance, provisions do exist in principle, but they are in many cases quite ambiguous as to its implementation, leaving space for smart arbitrary implementations in terms of timing and methods of involvement, as well as information exchanged and impact on the evaluation process. Hence, lack of operational guidance may be nullifying the institutional endeavour to accommodate participatory procedures in their practice, and make the results useful for the various stages of the evaluation process.

Water Function

Until quite recently, water was considered only as a highly politicized production factor, from which stems the hydraulic and engineering paradigms in order to manage it. In recent years, its social, environmental, and cultural functions are recognized (for instance, in the Dutch case, the water function is considered), and that inevitably leads to changes in the evaluation processes and its governance.

Societal Context

In recent years, the rhetoric of governance requires dialogue as a key feature, in an attempt to make wider sectors of the society accountable in decisions about complex situations, where relevant knowledge may be limited, inadequate, or uncertain. In these cases, it is seen that when involvement is effective, it is essentially linked to vested interests, lobbies, or attempts to resolve potential or idenfied conflicts.

It is obvious that those who participate, determine outcomes; institutions will tend to maintain status quo so that decisions taken are not contested (Kallis and Coccossis 2003). Added to this, as we have seen before, institutional arrangements are naturally resistant to change, rigid, and more willing to conform to installed practice. The timing of the participatory steps within the whole assessment process could change this. Except for emergency planning situations, river basin governance and planning should not be constrained by tight timings; in the five cases when they existed they seemed to have been related to political affairs, including government programmes or funding opportunities.

The absence of a purposeful institutional infrastructure that is specifically in charge of organizing societal involvement is one of the key reasons for the lack of articulation and poor results of participation exercises. This is not exclusive of water governance issues. Participation is an organized event, deploying specific methodologies, very much like any other evaluation task, and should be practised just like any other step of the evaluation process. It is not merely enough to have regulation allowing the 'publics' to participate, and it cannot be left to societal initiative and self-organization. That is a naive assumption; in cases where self-organization occurred (mobilization), it arose from serious conflict and anger in interested parties, leading to disruption of dialogue and concertation, taking the forms of serious dissent.

In fact, apart from poor correspondence with normative and legislation drivers of new governance styles (especially in European directives, white papers, etc.), the styles of governance in which the evaluation processes operated were exclusionary, creating situations of intense conflict and crisis of societal trust, in some cases culminating in total disruption (this was the case of the Spanish Water Plan).

Methodological Context

The types of tools deployed in the studies are bound, on the one hand, by the types of vested interests associated with the projects and on the other hand, by the regulatory framework. The studies associated with river basin management are typically technical and economical—CBA studies and EIA studies—the latter being the most 'integrated' of all. In general, the assessments performed were poor, incomplete, arbitrary, based on inadequate scopes, and resulting in unattended effects.

Uncertainty management has reflected (until recently) a typical approach in political and also scientific spheres, which consisted of either minimizing or ignoring the uncertainly, instead of acknowledging and stating it and acting in precaution. The legitimacy with which science and science practitioners have been operating in the past is also held by the professional consultancy which develops the assessment activities. The technocratic and reductionist methodologies and methods deployed are those shared among professionals and policy circles. They tend to ignore the societal context in which they are applied and to emphasize economic aspects in pursuit of sound justifications for rubber stamp policy options. Probably, some guidance about tools and methods could improve the assessment contexts.

Most methodological problems of the evaluation processes can be easily resolved, methodologically speaking. In view of more integrated assessments, there are a number of formal and 'informal' methods that have specific roles on dealing with complex, multiple perspectives and values, through which alternative projects can be assessed and compared. In other *problematiques*, such as climate change—where systemic relations are complex, facts are uncertain, and stakes high—integrated assessments have proved useful at least in having a systemic view and promoting an informed debate about options for action. That is the most important benefit from assessment tools, to allow for organization (and not amalgamation) of available relevant knowledge in order to promote focused debates and knowledgeable choices that can eventually lead to decisions.

Knowledge Context

Knowledge deployed in many of the cases was unfit for the purpose, non-contextualized, prone to different types of uncertainty, controversial, or unavailable. Apart from expected gaps in scientific and technical knowledge, this might have to do with unavailability of historical data, inconclusive research, inadequate formats (aggregation, scale, etc.), and other types of problems arising, for instance, property rights, poor articulation (including lack of regulation) of those who perform assessments with the providers of information. In addition, the quality of knowledge also suffers from reliability and legitimacy of sources as well as problems of peer acceptance of processing tools and methods.

On the other hand, as already discussed above, if there are no mechanisms that ensure the articulation of knowledge coming from different sources into the assessment phases (framing, assessment activities, communication), the knowledge context cannot be expected to be plural, holding multiple perspectives and being socially robust as vented in inclusive governance.

A FRAMEWORK TO OPERATIONALIZE QUALITY ASSURANCE OF RIVER BASIN GOVERNANCE PROCESSES: 3 PILLARS AND 1 BEAM

In the analysis in the previous sections, the focus was on 'quality', as the thread that guides the development of river basin evaluation procedures. River basin governance and planning is essentially a contested terrain, characterized by complex situations (many conflicts worldwide are due to water governance issues), values in dispute, high stakes, and different types of uncertainty. These are features of what Funtowicz and Ravetz (1990) described as post-normal situations, which require a different type of framing which they called post-normal science (see introduction in this volume).

Hence, it is argued here that in order to achieve good quality river basin evaluations, a number of principles should be respected. These are formulated as 3 pillars and 1 beam, as the basis to enhance the quality of evaluation of river basin governance (Guimarães Pereira and Corral Quintana 2009). The 3 pillars are:
• Socially robust knowledge
• Inclusive governance
• Transparent assessment procedures;
and the beam (crossing all pillars):
• Extended peer review.

Extended Peer Review

In environmental and health problems, the maintenance of quality depends on an open dialogue among all those affected. This is what Funtowicz and Ravetz call an extended peer community, consisting not merely of persons with some sort of institutional accreditation, but rather of all those with a desire and commitment to participate in the resolution of the relevant issue (Funtowicz and Ravetz 1992; Funtowicz 2001). Their contribution is not merely a matter of broader democratic participation, but to relevant knowledge. The procedure for assessing the quality of such policy processes is an extended peer review, performed by an extended peer community.

Hence, extending decision processes entails:

- the creation of conditions to identify, involve, and engage the relevant community, which imply methodological and institutional aspects;
- the creation of mechanisms of reflection of participatory outcomes in the evaluation process, which imply methodological and institutional aspects; and
- encouraging of society to access and to take stock of these attempts to change democratic rights, which imply societal and institutional aspects.

This is the realm of participatory activities.

As discussed above, participation as an organized process entails, first of all, the creation of spaces whereby social actors interact with process which have to be accommodated in institutional practice; institutional bodies should know what format is best in order to have useful, meaningful, effective dialogues, to develop ownership of the issues, and competence development, since that requires the knowledge of the context in which the exercise takes place. However, it is not up to the institutions to decide who participates. But it is up to the institutions to organize the context in which the participation takes place and ensure that relevant parties can participate. Secondly, institutions have to create 'ears', that is, mechanisms by which relevant outcomes are incorporated into the evaluation process. The realization that societal involvement is relevant and effectively contributes to producing robust knowledge that feeds an evaluation process is also an issue of trust, essential to further societal involvement.

Little time for involvement means little time to cope with gaps, late justifications, pretence extended review, and questionable incorporation of consultation outcomes into the review process and final decisions. This is acknowledged by the provisions of WFD's Article 14 (CEC 2000).

Inclusive Governance

Recent years have seen a growing institutional interest in governance issues that can affect or be affected by a relevant extended community. Partly stemming from an agenda generated by the 1992 United Nations

Conference on Environment and Development, accountable, inclusive processes have been progressively encouraged over the last decade. In its White Paper on European governance (CEC 2001b), the European Commission emphasizes the need for a revised relationship between existing institutional arrangements and civil society. Recent cases related to health and safety are part of the justification for the urgency of reform, but discussion on the need for change in institutional arrangements and relationships has been on-going for some time. Specifically, commentators have identified a need for constructing new processes of decision making, including new structures and new modes of thinking, communication, and interaction between parties. As a result, there has been a very significant increase in opportunities for citizens' involvement in decision making. EU legislation is beginning to reflect this conceptual re-definition of governance relationships by modifying regulations to shift the form of entitlement from a right to be informed, to a right to participate (De Marchi et al. 2001). This is what is referred to here as more inclusive governance, one of the pillars of good quality evaluation of river basin governance.

Socially Robust Knowledge

Socially robust knowledge, that is, knowledge which fits the purpose and is contextualized (Gibbons 1999), cannot be circumscribed to scientific quality but to the actual fitness to context and relevancy to the social actors concerned. Socially robust knowledge is another pillar for the quality of river basin evaluation.

In order to produce socially robust knowledge, extended peer review, that is, involvement of all those concerned in the quality assessment process (Funtowicz and Ravetz 1990; Funtowicz 2001), is needed in several phases:

- Extended scoping: it became obvious from the studies that governance of river basin is dependent on the type of information produced during assessment activities and its relevance, adequacy, intelligibility, and legitimacy for the actors concerned. Extended scoping aims at genuine coverage of issues, so that assessment is not just a means of meeting prior commitments.
- Extended review: this corresponds to current consultation processes. Their effectiveness entails issues such as information accessibility, intelligibility, and legitimacy; timely mechanisms of public and other social actors' involvement; and formal mechanisms of processing the involvement outcomes into the

assessment processes, yet another aspect of creating interfaces between society and policy.

A knowledge assessment protocol is desirable as part of the formal requirements of the evaluation process used in normative (guidance) and descriptive fashions. This is a protocol to assess the quality of information used and methods; it should be applied to all phases of the process, namely framing, assessment, and public involvement activities. The protocol should specifically address the pedigree of the information used, along the same methodological lines deployed in Guimarães Pereira (2003) (see also Guimarães Pereira and Corral Quintana 2009).

Information used for public and other social actors' involvement has to correspond to other dimensions of quality, namely it has to be suitable for the potential audiences. Therefore, non-technical summaries as they are currently produced are not enough. There is a need for specific establishment of procedures for delivering scientific and technical knowledge to non-expert audiences.

Last but not least, guaranteeing quality of information and methods deployed in river basin assessment activities is the condition *sine qua non* for effective and respectful dialogue among all the actors of a basin. Otherwise, the danger is that the debate will shift from governance issues to quality of the assessments done.

Transparent Assessment

Transparency is one of the pillars of more inclusive styles of governance, and this should be visible throughout all processes related to policy implementation and decision making. Transparent assessments entail explicit assessment procedures, supported by good quality information. Transparency is an essential condition to create trust, and as with information quality, assessment outcomes are to be the focus of debates about river governance, and not be questionable about their legitimacy.

The desirable tools and methods to improve the quality of assessment activities are those that can capture the characteristics of river basin governance, namely their complexity, multiple values and perspectives, different vested interests, uncertainties of different types, etc. These tools have to address different knowledge representations, different languages or articulation of arguments, systemic and transdisciplinary integration, and essentially they should allow the necessary dialogues on options for river basin planning and governance. Many of these tools were tested promisingly in the ADVISOR work.

CONCLUDING REMARKS

Past Quality Tales of Sustainable River Basin Governance

The quality tales of the five past European river basin governance processes on the grounds of context, participation, information, and assessment activities covered types of unwanted outcomes, and provided insights into justifications of adoption of certain procedures, linkages across all the vertices addressed by the ADVISOR project. Timing seems to cross all steps of evaluation, being particularly relevant for assessment and participatory activities, as well as for collecting and integrating appropriate knowledge. Some patterns could be found, such as the bad quality of knowledge: observations mostly dealt with a great deal of uncertainties and, most of all, there was incomplete knowledge about relevant issues. In addition, there was little space to include knowledge, other than technical and scientific, in the assessment procedures; linked to the poor quality of information used there was a standing problem with poor, incomplete, and arbitrary assessments, limited scopes, leading to reported unattended effects. In addition, conflict is a common pattern arising from exclusionary governance processes or late involvement of those concerned in the processes. Finally, very often, there was a poor correspondence of the governance processes with normative and legislation drivers of new governance styles encouraged in Europe through regulation.

New Tales of Quality Assurance of Sustainable River Basin Governance

The 3 beams and 1 pillar framework constitute a starting basis to assure the quality of river basin evaluation processes, also through the categories and criteria suggested in this chapter. The WFD (CEC 2000) does not have an implicit request for quality control, but its Article 14, refers in point 1 that 'Member states shall encourage the active involvement of all interested parties in the implementation of this Directive, in particular in the production, review and updating of the river basin management plans'. The text of this Article does not explicitly recommend that consultation is made for the purposes of framing or scoping: it only refers to '(a) a timetable and work programme for the production of the plan, including a statement of the consultation measures to be taken' whereas in the subsequent points emphasis is clearly laid on the review of the plan, that is, *ex-post* knowledge reviews instead of *ex-ante* knowledge co-production

(Jasanoff 1996). This could be interpreted as a way to seek 'external' (extended) legitimacy and accountability of public policies in the area of river basin governance. Framing the evaluation processes as a quality assurance process, in which an extended community intervenes at each level in order to ensure that the outcomes are fit for use is not an unreasonable proposal. Again, a serious issue is the articulation of quality checks with installed institutional practice and their impact on the planning and governance processes.

REFERENCES

Council of the European Communitie (CEC), (1985), 'Council Directive 85/337/EEC of the 27th June 1985 on the Assessment of the Effects of Certain Public and Private Projects on the Environment', *Official Journal of the European Communities*, C175, pp. 40–9.

——, (1997), 'Council Directive 97/11/EC of the 3rd March 1997 Amending Directive 85/337/EEC on the Assessment of the Effects of Certain Public and Private Projects on the Environment'. *Official Journal of the European Communities*. L 73, pp. 5–15.

——, (2000), 'Directive 2000/60/EC of the European Parliament and of the Council Establishing a Framework for the Community Action in the Field of Water Policy', *Official Journal of the European Communities*, L 327, 22 December.

——, (2001a), 'Democratising Expertise and Establishing Scientific Reference Systems'. Document of 2 July 2001, available at: *http://europa.eu.int/comm/governance/areas/index_en.htm*, accessed on 15 July 2007.

——, (2001b), 'European Governance: A White Paper'; COM(2001) 428, Brussels, 25 July 2001, available at: *http://europa.eu.int/comm/governance/white_paper/index_en.htm*, accessed on 15 July 2007.

——, (2001c), 'Council Directive 2001/42/EC of the European Parliament and of the Council on the Assessment of the Effects of Certain Plans and Programmes on the Environment'. *Official Journal of the European Communities*, L 197, p. 30.

——, (2003), 'Council Directive 2003/35/EC of the European Parliament and of the Council Providing for Public Participation in Respect of the Drawing up of Certain Plans and Programmes Relating to the Environment', *Official Journal of the European Communities*, L 156, pp. 17–24.

Corral Quintana, Serafín, (2000), *'Una Metodología Integrada de Exploración de los Procesos de Elaboración de Políticas Públicas'*, Tenerife, España: Universidade de La Laguna.

Corral Quintana, S. and Â Guimarães Pereira, (2004), 'Protocol for Qualiy Assurance on Information Used in the Participatory Activities on Baixo

Guadiana Planning Activities', Report for Work Package 3 of Project ADVISOR, Ispra.

Crosby, P.B., (1979), *Quality is Free*, New York: McGraw-Hill.

De Marchi B., S. Funtowicz, and Â Guimarães Pereira, (2001), 'From the Right to Be Informed to the Right to Participate: Responding to the Evolution of the European Legislation with ICT', *International Journal of Environment and Pollution*, Vol. 15, No. 1, pp. 1–21.

Del Moral, L., B. Pedregal, M. Calvo, and P. Paneque, (2002), 'River Ebro Interbasin Water Transfer', Report for Work Package 1 of Project ADVISOR, Sevilla: Universidad de Sevilla.

——, (2006), 'Why Knowledge Assessment?' in Â. Guimarães Pereira, S. Guedes Vaz, and S. Tognetti (eds), *Interfaces between Science and Society*, Sheffield: Greenleaf Publishing, pp. 138–45.

Funtowicz, S. and J. Ravetz, (1990), *Uncertainty and Quality in Science for Policy*, Dordrecht: Kluwer Academic Press.

——, (1992), 'The Role of Science in Risk Assessment', in S. Krimsky and D. Golding (eds), *Social Theories of Risk*, Westport: Praeger, pp. 59–88.

——, (1993), 'Science for the Post-Normal Age', *Futures*, Vol. 25, No. 7, pp. 739–55.

Funtowicz, S., (2001), 'Peer Review and Quality Control', in N.J. Smelser and P.B. Baltes (eds), *International Encyclopedia of the Social & Behavioral Sciences*, Oxford: Pergamon, pp. 11179–83.

Guimarães Pereira, Â, (2003), 'Quality of Information in River Basin Governance Review of Case Studies: Information Vertex', Report for Work Package 2 of Project ADVISOR, Ispra: European Commission, Joint Research Centre.

Guimarães Pereira, Â., J. Blasques, S. Corral Quintana, and S. Funtowicz, (2003), 'TIDDD—Tools to Inform Debates, Dialogues and Deliberations: The GOUVERNe Project at the JRC', EUR 21189 EN. ISBN, Ispra: European Commission, Joint Research Centre.

Guimarães Pereira and S. Corral Quintana, (2009), '3 Pillars and 1 Beam: Quality of River Basin Governance', *Ecological Economics*, Vol. 68, pp. 940–954.

Gibbons, M., (1999), 'Science's New Social Contract with Society', *Nature*, Vol. 402, pp. C81–C84.

Hatzilacou, D., G. Kallis, and H. Coccossis, (2002), 'The River Evinos Reservoir', Report for Work Package 1 of Project ADVISOR, Athens: University of the Aegean.

Hill, G., K. Urama, C. Spash, and G. Wynn, (2002), 'The Designation of the River Ythan and Estuary as a Nitrate Vulnerable Zone', Report for Work Package 1 of Project ADVISOR, Aberdeen: The Macaulay Institute.

Hill, G., L. Del Moral, P. Paneque, B. Pedregal, C. Spash, and K. Uram, (2003), 'Evaluation Practices in Water Project Decision Making Processes: Comparative Analysis of Alqueva Dam (Portugal), Evinos

Reservoir (Greece), Ythan NVZ (UK), The Grensmaas (The Netherlands) and Ebro River Transfer (Spain)', Report for Work Package 2 of Project ADVISOR, Aberdeen: University of Seville and Macaulay Institute and University of Aberdeen.

Jasanoff, S., (1996), 'Beyond Epistemology: Relativism and Engagement in the Politics of Science', *Social Stud. Sci.*, Vol. 26, No. 2, pp. 393–418.

Kallis, G. and H. Coccossis, (2003), 'Comparison of the Institutional Context of the 5 Case Studies', Report for Work Package 2 of Project ADVISOR, Athens: University of the Aegean.

Ravetz, J., (1996), *Scientific Knowledge and its Social Problems*, New Brunswick, NJ, and London: Transaction Publishers.

Van Leeuwen, E., J. Dalhuisen, R. Vreeker, and P. Nijkamp, (2002), 'The Grensmaas Project', Report for Work Package 1 of Project ADVISOR, Amsterdam: Vrije Universiteit Amsterdam.

Videira, N., G. Lobo, P. Antunes, R. Santos, and Â. Guimarães Pereira, (2002), 'Alqueva Multipurpose Project'. Report for Work Package 1 of Project ADVISOR, Lisbon: New University of Lisbon.

Videira, N., G. Lobo, P. Antunes, and R. Santos, (2003), 'Public Participation in Integrated River Basin Governance', Report for Work Package 2 of Project ADVISOR, Lisbon: New University of Lisbon.

Videria, N., G. Kallis, P. Antunes, and R. Santos (eds), (2007), *Integrated Evaluation for Sustainable River Basin Governance*, London: IWA Publishing.

Appendix 18.1

Table A18.1:   Summary of Main Characteristics of Past European River Basin Governance Processes Reviewed in the ADVISOR Project

UK case study: River Ythan and Estuary as a Nitrate Vulnerable Zone	• Observations of the water quality of the River Ythan and estuary have shown clear evidence of a steady increase in nitrate concentrations; nitrate levels have exceeded the EC standard on occasions. • Problem framing done by an environmental agency as a problem related to agricultural nitrate pollution. • Not widely shared scientific evidence used to frame the problem. • Stakeholders are environmentalists, farmers, Central governments, EC.
Spanish case study: River Ebro Interbasin Water Transfer	• For over a century, hydraulic policy has prevailed in Spain. Project for geographical transformation of the country: regeneration of an adverse landscape, characterized by aridity and barrenness and consequences of under-development and lack of growth. Irrigation became a national enterprise playing a decisive part in the solving of agricultural, economic, and social problems. The 1993 PHN Draft is a formalization of this. • Framing of issues has been done mainly by the government, ignoring many variables such as drought conditions, underground water, climate change, and uncertainties; assumptions and conceptual basis pertain to old paradigms of water governance, ignoring largely the changing context. • Information used was not up to date (River basin Plans' data collected in the 1980s); controversies on the use of demand driven approaches: Projection of demand/supply highly criticized. • Consultation was controversial.
The Netherlands case study: The Grensmaas project, Maaswreck river	• Coping with great quantities of water from rivers and seas has played a predominant role in Dutch history; the floods of 1993 and 1995 destroyed faith in dykes and other man-made safeguarding measures. • Problem framed on the basis of observed natural disasters (floods) and awareness of undesirable landscape changes. • Problem framing shared between local authorities (province of Limburg), Dutch government, and inhabitants of the region. • Problem perception shared across society; public participation very important.

Portuguese case study: The Alqueva Multi-purpose project	• Framing done mainly by the government but supported by people from Alentejo, a semi-arid region, socio-economically depressed and the scarcity of water is perhaps one of the most important factors. • Generations of people in Alentejo were awaiting the development for developing agriculture into irrigated agriculture. Alqueva Project regarded as the main solution for the development of the Alentejo region, supported through decades and through different central administration mandates; it became a mythical project, the 'Project that would save Alentejo'. • Luso–Spanish agreements were determinants for the options considered. • Assumptions and conceptual basis pertain to old paradigms of water governance, ignoring largely the changing context: namely the Common Agricultural Policy, European accession countries' role in agriculture, market globalization, etc.
Greek case study: The River Evinos Reservoir	• Athens is a city which experienced fast urbanization and economic growth. In the early 1960s, in view of possible shortage, the government approved the construction of a reservoir and aqueduct. • In view of an imminent drinking water supply shortage, a series of emergency measures were taken from May 1990 to 1993, also including a call for proposals for a supplementary reservoir. Evinos was an option. • Problem framed on the basis of observed deficient water supply created by prolonged dry years and also mismanagement of existing infrastructure and fears of future inadequate potable water supply to the city of Athens. Formulation largely shared by population.

Contributors

IULIE ASLAKSEN is a researcher at the Statistics Norway, Oslo, Norway.

PAUL BAER is the Research Director of EcoEquity, Salt Lake City, UT, USA.

ROSA BINIMELIS is a PhD student at the Institute of Environmental Science and Technology (ICTA), Autonomous University of Barcelona, Spain.

LIM LI CHING is with the Third World Network, Malaysia.

MATTHIEU CRAYE is a researcher at the European Commission, Joint Research Centre, Institute for the Protection and Security of the Citizen (IPSC), Knowledge Assessment Methodologies Group Ispra (VA), Italy.

JEAN-MARC DOUGUET is a researcher at UMR C3ED (IRD-UVSQ), Centre for Economics and Ethics for Environment and Development, Université de Versailles Saint-Quentin-en-Yvelines, France.

SILVIO FUNTOWICZ is a researcher at the European Commission, Joint Research Centre, Institute for the Protection and Security of the Citizen (IPSC), Knowledge Assessment Methodologies Group, Ispra (VA), Italy.

MARIO GIAMPIETRO is professor at the Institute of Environmental Science and Technology (ICTA) at the Universitat Autònoma de Barcelona, Barcelona, Spain.

SOLVEIG GLOMSRØD is a researcher at the Statistics Norway, Oslo, Norway.

PETER H.M. JANSSEN is with Netherlands Environmental Assessment Agency (PBL), Netherlands.

Sheila Jasanoff is a Pforzheimer professor at the John F. Kennedy School of Government, University of Harvard, Cambridge, MA, USA.

Erik Laes is a researcher at the SCK-CEN (Belgian Nuclear Research Centre) PISA project—Program of Integration of Social Aspects into Nuclear Research, Belgium.

Lim Li Lin is with the Third World Network, Malaysia.

Laura Maxim is a PhD student at UMR C3ED (IRD-UVSQ), Centre for Economics and Ethics for Environment and Development, Université de Versailles Saint-Quentin-en-Yvelines, France.

Anne Ingeborg Myhr is with the Norwegian Institute of Gene Ecology, Tromsø, Norway.

Alejandro Nadal is professor at the Science, Technology and Development Program, El Colegio de México, Camino al Ajusco 20, México.

Martin O'Connor is professor at UMR C3ED n 063 (IRD-UVSQ), Centre for Economics and Ethics for Environment and Development, University of Versailles Saint-Quentin-en-Yvelines, France.

Tiago De Sousa Pedrosa is a researcher at the European Commission, Joint Research Centre, Institute for the Protection and Security of the Citizen (IPSC), Knowledge Assessment Methodologies Group, Ispra (VA), Italy.

Ângela Guimarães Pereira is a researcher at the European Commission, Joint Research Centre, Institute for the Protection and Security of the Citizen (IPSC), Knowledge Assessment Methodologies Group, Ispra (VA), Italy.

Arthur Petersen is Director of the Methodology and Modelling Programme of the Netherlands Environmental Assessment Agency, (Plan-bureau voor de Leefomgeving—PBL), Netherlands.

Rajeswari S. Raina is a researcher at the Centre for Policy Research, New Delhi, India.

M.V. Ramana is a Senior Fellow at the Centre for Interdisciplinary Studies in Environment and Development, Institute for Social and Economic Change (ISEC), Bangalore, India.

Jeroen P. van der Sluijs is professor at the Copernicus Institute for Sustainable Development and Innovation, Department of Science, Technology and Society, Utrecht University, The Netherlands.

CLIVE L. SPASH is professor at CSIRO, Sustainable Ecosystems Division, Canberra, Australia.

ROGER STRAND is professor at the Centre for the Study of the Sciences and the Humanities, University of Bergen, Norway.

J.Y. SUCHITRA is a researcher at the Institute for Social and Economic Change (ISEC), Bangalore, India.

SAMARTHIA THANKAPPAN is a researcher at the Centre for Business Relationships Accountability Sustainability & Society (BRASS), Cardiff University, Cardiff, United Kingdom.

ANDREAS THIEL is a researcher at the Humboldt Universität zu Berlin, Department of Agricultural Economics, Germany.

SERAFIN CORRAL QUINTANA is professor at the Department Economics of Institutions, Applied Statistics and Econometrics, University of La Laguna, La Laguna, Spain.

Index

digital data miners xii
Dioxin contamination 234–5
DNA data banks xii
Doha Round 103

Ebro water transfer and Spanish
National Hydrologic Plan 330
Eckley, N. 308
eco-friendly technologies 313–16;
for rural development 314–15,
319
Ecological economics xxi
Ecology, Traditional Knowledge on
220–1
*Economic Development and Food
Consumption* 90–1
Economic Mechanism to Sideline
Farmers 89
Economic valuation methods 219–20
economic weight 76
electricity, demand for 253;
Generation Comparative Cost of
257
energy 8; related committees 264
Engels, F. on nature 233
Environmental Council 122
Environmental Protection Agency
(EPA) 234–5
environmental risk, political
approaches to 217
Equity and Distribution 179;
weighting of benefits of mitigation
179–81
Error Propagation Equations 25
ethics and political epistemology
245–8
European Commission 120;
Conference on Risk Perception
152; funded project 328
European energy markets,
liberalization of 274
European Environment Agency
(EEA) ix, 123; report 'Late Lessons
from Early Warnings' 216, 222–3

European Food Safety Authority
(EFSA) 6, 123, 153
European River Basin Governance
Processes Reviewed in ADVISOR
Project 346–7
European Union (EU) 103; biosafety
laws 146; General Food Law 155;
policy-making for economic
dimensions 309
European, GMO controversy 120;
Impact Assessment Practices for
Policy Development 298–300;
modelling tools for IA 305;
Policy Assessment in European
Commission 300–3; policy-
making 304
Eurostat or Espon 305
Evaluation for Justifications,
contexts of 334–8
Evinos reservoir 330
Expert Elicitation 25, 29
extended participation model 5, 10
extended peer communities 18; and
Judgements about Pertinence of
Indicators 34–8
Extended Peer Review (review by
stakeholders) 25, 28
Extended Quality Assurance
Framework For 53–5; features of
processes 48; problem-solving
process 49; socio-environmental
planning processes 48
ExternE, experts 286; methodology
285; network 275; project and
European Commission (EC) 272;
research 281; researchers 286
extreme and catastrophic impacts
169, 178–9, 186

Farmer Participatory Research
(FPR) 323
Fast Breeder Test Reactor (FBTR)
255
First Assessment Report (FAR) 201